PUBLISH THIS BOOK

THE UNBELIEVABLE[1] TRUE[2] STORY OF HOW I WROTE, SOLD, AND PUBLISHED THIS VERY BOOK[3]

[1] *UNFORGETTABLE, HEARTWRENCHING, INEXPLICABLY PROFANE*
[2] *FOR THE MOST PART*
[3] *THAT YOU ARE ABOUT TO READ*

STEPHEN MARKLEY

sourcebooks

Published by Sourcebooks, Inc.
P.O. Box 4410, Naperville, Illinois 60567-4410
(630) 961-3900
Fax: (630) 961-2168
www.sourcebooks.com

Library of Congress Cataloging-in-Publication Data

Markley, Stephen.
   Publish this book : the unbelievable true story of how I wrote, sold, and published this very book / by Stephen Markley.
      p. cm.
   Includes bibliographical references and index.
   1. Authorship—Humor. I. Title.
PN6231.A77M37 2009
070.502'07—dc22

                           2009036474

          Printed and bound in the United States of America.
              VP 10 9 8 7 6 5 4 3 2 1

For Sarah
They're pretty much all for you
But especially this first one

Contents

The Gist

I had two ways to start this book. In the first, I would tell a completely irrelevant and unnecessary anecdote that would nevertheless say something about what kind of book this would be. Something like:

> *One day in college I was sitting in my room, when my roommate Scott burst out of the bathroom, half of his face still covered in shaving cream, and declared, as if he had just figured out time travel, "You know what they need to invent? A machine that lets you shave and take a shit at the same time."*
>
> *I stared at him for a moment, my mind racing as I envisioned all kinds of complicated gizmos (my composite notion included some type of suctioning tubing and a robotic razor arm), before I realized that what he was describing could be "invented" quite easily by building a sink and mirror facing a toilet. Despite being two members of Miami University's elite honors department, this was the typical level of intellectual discourse in our apartment. Whenever I hear politicians say something trite about how our young people are the future, I think of Scott.*

So that was one option. My second choice would be something stark, bold, and declarative like:

"My name is Stephen Markley, and I'm a writer."

Obviously, I had trouble deciding which way to go, so here we are nearly half a page later already feeling like this is the beginning of some epic disaster—the Iraq war of book openings.[1] Let me try one last time:

My name is Stephen Markley, and I call myself many things—son, brother, friend, Cavs fan, erudite,[2] liberal, incompetent, Buckeye, OSU fan, emotionally distant, Blazers fan, sexually adequate well over 40 percent of the time—but first and foremost, I call myself a writer.

I guess that designation depends on how you define a "writer." Hell, plenty of people write—maybe in a daily journal or a blog or perhaps they fiddle with poetry or simply jot down notes and amusing anecdotes. Basically everyone occasionally records something for posterity.[3]

Most people, however, do not consider a person who simply writes to be a "writer." No, I am a writer in the sense that I want someone to pay me for my unrelenting genius. I want some poor bastard to plop down between seven and fifteen dollars for my sentences because I've demonstrated the mesmerizing ability to match nouns with verbs and, occasionally, adjectives. If you're reading this, then that poor bastard is likely you, so I thank you for spending money on my humble insights, my analysis of the human condition.[4]

I need you to pay for my writing because I have no other way to

---

1 Too soon? That was probably too soon.

2 I didn't actually know what that word meant when I wrote it. Thank you, Microsoft Word thesaurus tool...

3 I don't want to get too philosophical here, but once you commit a thought to paper it takes on a separate life from the organism it was while living inside your head. While in your head, this thought is like a high school dropout taking bong rips in his parents' basement. Once committed to paper, however, this thought becomes a college graduate with a degree in marketing, a thought who has even begun to date a respectable girl. In other words, this thought now has a future.

4 I apologize in advance for the profanity, violence, pornographic digressions, and for calling you a poor bastard just then. That was definitely out of line.

support myself. Other than writing, I've never had any discernable talent. Sure, I'm kind of smart and always did well in school. I'm not bad at basketball, as long as I'm playing against mid-sized rural and suburban white kids who, like myself, never advanced beyond the high school level. And I like to think I'm okay in bed, although I'll often undergo a crisis of confidence and entertain the paranoid notion that every girl I've ever dated was lying when she assured me I was a good lay, and that these girls will frequently get together for lunch dates where they share in vivid, snickering detail stories about my incompetence (I picture them saying, "Teaching him about the clitoris was like giving a lesson on quantum physics to a Labrador retriever.").

So unfortunately I am stuck with writing for better or worse.

This, as the kids say, sucks. Writing is hard. Not the actual writing part, which varies. It can be like eating cotton candy through a straw or off a stick, depending. The making-money-from-writing part— that's a bitch.

The problem is that being a successful writer is somewhat akin to being a professional athlete: you see these assholes all the time, so you just assume that it can't be that hard a field to crack. As it turns out, however, these fields are incredibly crowded, difficult, and frustrating. I remember taking creative writing classes in college, and out of twenty kids in the class, eighteen would think they'd have their first novel in print by their twenty-fifth birthdays. They harbored no special passion for what they were doing, however, and it showed. Now, out of the dozens and dozens of kids I know from those classes, I can't think of one of them who still writes regularly, who still aspires to publish, who still thinks of him or herself as a "writer."

I, however, due to the aforementioned lack of other discernable talents, plow valiantly forward. Naturally, there's a history to all this, a story, so to speak, of how I came to consider myself a writer and what steps along the way got me to where I am.[5] But we'll save all that for a later time, as my intention now is to tell you about this wicked cool idea I had.

Unlike most wicked cool ideas, this one came not from inspiration but desperation. And occasionally desperation can create the very best ideas. It's like in the movies when the hero and his comrades find themselves in some type of extremely dire situation, and suddenly he suggests doing something crazy that would probably kill them all under normal circumstances. Usually it has to do with "blowing" some kind of "hatch."

> *"We'll blow the hatch!" the hero will say.*
> And inevitably there will be a more prudent character who denounces this plan. *"That's crazy! We can't blow the hatch."*
> *"It's our only hope!"*
> *"You know what's on the other side of that hatch?"*
> *"We're dead if we don't do it!"*
> *"It's a flaming alligator with its claw on the detonator of a nuclear bomb. That's what's on the other side, you asshole."*
> *"I know. It's so crazy that it just might work."*
> *"And it has the Ebola virus. The goddamn alligator has the Ebola virus."*

Of course, blowing the hatch always works (minus a peripheral, usually non-Caucasian, character), and the hero never would have even thought to blow the hatch if he and his companions hadn't been so severely screwed in the first place. This just goes to show that sometimes desperation can work better than anything else.

Why am I desperate, you ask? Do I have a drug addiction? Cancer maybe?

---

5   ("The Steps Along the Way That Got Me to Where I Am"—that would make a good, hip title for a memoir if I get cancer or a drug addiction.)

Not as far as I know.[6]

I'm desperate because I've spent the better part of my career as a writer being told by nearly everyone that I am exceptionally talented. I'm not talking about family or friends here, but rather teachers, professors, contest judges, entire faculty departments, and strangers (and now you know it, too, because of that brilliant, brilliant shit I just said about the alligator with the Ebola virus). I took this praise as well as I could, trying to keep my head down and ego grounded. Still, I'm not without ambition. I want to start publishing, and I want to do it while I'm still young, while I have that wind of youthful optimism at my back.

For years, I've treaded the waters of the literary short story market, mailing my material, again and again. I pushed a novel that I spent three years of my life writing. I wrote nonfiction articles, ceaselessly researching, gathering quotes and perspectives, and shaping it all with consideration and zeal.

Other than a few very minor successes, all this work amounted to $250, hundreds of rejection letters, and the dreaded sensation of burnout creeping up on me before I'd even turned twenty-four.

Oh, I can hear you crying already: "Twenty-four? Nobody does anything at that age, especially not as a writer. You get by, you pay your dues. So-and-so didn't publish until he was thirty-five. Such-and-such piled up 239,000 rejection letters before she got her first story published. How can you whine about not having overwhelming success before you've even lived a quarter century?"

I know this speech almost as well as I know the "Steve-wake-up-you're-not-in-the-bathroom-dude" speech. I know it because I've

---

6 Although one time I thought I had testicular cancer because one of my balls was sore. I walked around for a week thinking I was going to die, carefully probing the offending teste every time I took a shower the way they showed us back in eighth grade health class. Of course, I had no idea what I was actually "probing" for—a lump, I guess—but as far as I could tell everything down there is some kind of lump, and I had no knowledge of what this new, foreign lump should feel like as I don't generally "probe" my testicles, except recreationally. Oh, and it turned out my nut was just sore.

heard that empty bullshit dressed up as wisdom more times than I've actually gotten rejected. And you know what? I don't care.

There. I said it. What every aspiring writer has ever wanted to say about *that* speech. I don't give a watery shit how many rejection letters F. Scott Fitzgerald got or how many John Grisham got or how many Kurt Vonnegut got. Those empty platitudes mean about as much to me as does a duck constructing a life-sized statue of William Howard Taft with nothing but Fruit Roll-ups.[7]

As far as I can tell, if you start believing that your life is only a few years away from beginning, that your train will be rolling 'round the bend shortly, that your hardest efforts will eventually bring your just rewards if only you can be patient… Isn't that essentially ceding precious days of this one existence that's already too short to begin with?

This is not to say that success arriving later in life has no worth. In fact, it has all the same worth, but this notion of "Just relax, no one under the age of thirty can complain about anything" chaps my ass. And, unfortunately, I read, so I know full well that there are writers getting published who are objectively less talented than certain species of animal that have yet to evolve emotive capabilities other than blinking.

My frustration with the publishing industry in general will have to wait for another chapter, but suffice it to say that my experiences with publishing had gotten me down, strung-out, defeated. I couldn't even bring myself to open the freshest pile of manila envelopes sporting my address in my own handwriting. I didn't want to even look at another form rejection letter.

The most recent one was the typical one-sixth sheet of paper with three typed sentences blandly stating that the editors were sorry, but my work did not fit their needs at this time—except that this one included a handwritten note in the corner. Eager for even the smallest indication of support or interest, I read it.

---

7   See? What the hell does that mean?

It said: "Apologies for the water damage."

I had no idea what this meant (An alternate title? Some sort of obscure literary reference? A clever comment on the inherent absurdity of the human condition?) until I removed the copy of my story and found that, indeed, the manuscript looked as if it had been dipped in a toilet bowl. I believe this was the literary equivalent of forgetting your umbrella during a thunderstorm and having a passing car douse you while standing on the curb.

It was with this latest defeat fresh in my mind that I lay in bed late that night and then into the early hours of the morning, wondering if I was going to spend the rest of my life telling people at cocktail parties that I was an insurance adjuster to avoid the shame of being a failed writer. It also didn't help that I was preparing to make a move to a major city in a few weeks without money, a place to live, or a job. This would surely make the cocktail party conversation even more strained if, that is, I even managed to secure an invitation to this theoretical party.

So, lying in bed, I said to myself, *One day, I swear, I'm going to write a book about just how much it sucks to publish a book.*

Ha, my Ego replied, *why not do it now? You'll never be more of an expert on the subject.*

That's a good one! I chuckled in response. *I'll just write an entire book about how hard it is to publish my novel.*

Why even bother with your novel? he guffawed. *That ain't going nowhere anytime soon.*

I hooted. *You can say that again! You'll sooner see a mainstream novel about hard-core male-on-male anal rape than my novel!*

Haha! That is what your novel's about, dummy!

Haha! No wonder!

Hahahahaha!

Hahahahaha!

Hey, I got it. What about this:

And suddenly, silence. My inner monologues all shut down—run off to go play hop-scotch and shove each other into the bushes or whatever the hell it is they do when I don't need them. In that moment I recognized an idea so profoundly dumb, so outlandish, so crazy...

I'd blow the hatch.

I would write a book about publishing a book.

But that book would be the book I was trying to publish.

Your mind could run around in circles on that for days, so let me try to explain the gist of it: there is no book. This is the book. The book I'm writing right now: that's the book. The entire aim of the book will be to publish the very book where I explain how I published the book.

Some of you reading may find this idea inane or idiotic, and to these people I gladly say s'long, thanks for the fifteen dollars. For the rest of you still collecting your skull fragments from the floor after I blew your damn mind, let me offer an explanation of how I think this will work. And I suppose since I'm a writer, I should give you an analogy.

Imagine a squirrel... No, that's stupid.

Okay, imagine a band sitting down in the studio to record an album. They don't have any music written, they don't have any lyrics, they don't have a producer. All they have are themselves and their instruments and a studio recording them for an hour. So instead of hearing just music, you hear them talking about what they're going to play, how they'll play it, what parts to sing, where the solos are, and so on. Maybe you hear them begin a song, maybe you hear them sing a little, but then they're talking again, and one of them is saying, "Dave, what the fuck are you doing with that riff? That sounded like shit." And Dave says back, "Maybe if you learned how to play the drums like you *didn't* get dropped on your head as a kid—" And then, "Well, maybe if you weren't such a coke fiend, you could make your fingers form a fucking A minor chord." And Dave says, "Yeah, well I fucked your girlfriend, you piece of shit. It was right after your mom died, too. Probably while you were at the funeral."

And then maybe they play some more music for a while.

Admittedly, taking that analogy alone, this idea sounds awful. And maybe it will be awful. But what it won't be is boring. Or dishonest. Look on the bookshelf at your average Borders, and what do you see? A lot of boring-ass books and a lot of books that are full of shit—emotionally dishonest or intellectually dishonest or both.

But not this book. No, not this one. This book is an awful idea. It's senseless, it's pointless, it's so profoundly self-indulgent you can barely wrap your head around it, and every time you do, you just want to grab me by the shoulders and shake shake shake me and scream, *"Steve, what are you doing? What is this? Grow up, man! You sound like an asshole! And what was that little footnote earlier about your balls being sore? What the hell are you talking about?"* I know I know I know!

But it's also so crazy that it just might work.

Where to Begin

So what I have is a book that won't be boring or dishonest. But outside of that, I don't have a whole lot in the way of ideas or narrative direction or words to follow my first six-page chapter.

Obviously, I strike out on this project the way I do any major undertaking in my life, by which I mean I do nothing.

Sure, I want to get cracking. That'd be just peaches. I wish that my life would turn into one of those montage scenes where a great amount of work or self-improvement occurs in the space of a minute or two. Unfortunately, this is just not who I am. So instead, I slip the idea beneath my pillow and sleep on it.

The problem is that right now my life is something of a catastrofuck. A grisly head-on train wreck, if you will. I spent the last year traveling the country, and after eight months on the road through twenty-nine states and one Canadian province, I'm broke, jobless, and kicking my liver's ass like I'm still in college. I detailed all of my many adventures in a tome called *A Land I Saw in My Dreams: One Hedonistic College Grad's Personal and Political Journey Across the Excoriated Landscape of the American Dream in the Last Years of the Reign of Bush,* which is yet another book for which I failed to attract interest from publishers or agents. This is a shame because I could have written off 12,000 miles of gasoline purchases on my taxes.[8]

Back home while I prepare to move to Chicago,[9] I spend this strange, detached interim floating along with a few old hometown buddies who also find themselves suspended in time. These are the kinds of friends everyone has: the ones who go by absurd nicknames like "Kdoe," "Shady Hill," "Rat," "Zolli," and "Phil." The kind of friends with whom the conversation deviates very little from sports, chicks, drinking, penises, and theoretical contraptions that can transport feces from one person's bowels to another's.[10] As you might imagine, I make little forward progress on getting my book published.

Home is a small, rural town in central Ohio where there ain't a whole lot going on, yet I always seem busy. This comes to a head during one memorable summer weekend that includes a job interview in Columbus, a friend's wedding, my five-year high school reunion, and another friend's baby shower. In one weekend, I knocked out five rites of passage to adulthood, and remained sober through almost two of them.

The wedding proved particularly problematic; I enjoy weddings way, way too much, and within the first two hours of the reception, I was already *that guy*, shouting profanities across the dance floor, stealing the garter from a real couple, hitting on a delicious pair of sisters, the first of whom turned out to have a boyfriend (not cool) and the second of whom turned out to be only nineteen (so cool). But the important part of the night was that during the

---

8 If you weren't aware, that was a joke. The joke being that I don't know how to pay taxes and only use the term "writing off" because I hear grown-ups use it from time to time.

9 Why Chicago? Because I was talking to a girl in a bar who was from Chicago, so being the farsighted genius that I am, I said to her, "Oh cool! I'm moving to Chicago," in case this geographical similarity would induce her to make out with me. Long story short, it didn't, but I figured I might as well stick to the plan.

10 Further evidence that young people are not the future: This is probably one of the more substantive conversations the six of us have ever had.

reception I got caught up in a conversation with my friend Jenna about my writing.

Here's the thing: I hate talking about writing with people who don't do it. That's not a snotty, oh-how-dumb-and-unread-can-they-be kind of thing, but about my extreme level of discomfort with talking about my work. For me, the process of writing—of being a writer—is intensely private. I don't like it when people read pieces I haven't finished. I never write with someone else in the same room. And I hate, hate, hate trying to explain to people why I'm still largely unpublished.

"So when are you going to write a book?" Jenna asked me.

I sighed. "That's not the problem. I've written a book. I have three of them sitting on my laptop. The hard part is getting someone to read them."

"I'd probably read anything you wrote."

"Then you should become a literary agent and we'll both be golden."

This is by no means the first time I've had this type of conversation. I hear this blather all the time: "So when's the first novel due?" "Steve, you should really write a book." "Hey, Markley, why don't you just write a book and get rich?"

I've begun to respond less and less good-naturedly. Imagine if you were a pre-med student and people were always grinning at you like a wanker and saying half-seriously, "Hey, why don't you invent a cure for cancer? Man, that would be great because it would make you famous *and* be good for humanity!"

This weekend of adult development behind me, and with a vague determination to one day be able to tell Jenna, "Yeah! The book's done, so shut up!" I begin to test the waters for my bizarre book idea, going to trusted sources of wisdom like the aforementioned Shady Hill, whose real name is Justin. At a cookout I pitch my prospective book to my friends, who receive the idea with a mixture of approbation, head-scratching, and disparagement.

"But what's it about?" Justin asks.

"It's about publishing the book. That's what I'm saying, it's not about anything but my struggle to publish the very book I'm writing."

"Okay, but what's in it?"

"This! This is in it. This is all the book is about. This conversation right now is in the book."

"That sounds boring as shit."

"But that's the point: it should be boring, but it won't be. It will be hilarious just because it's such a ridiculous concept."

Another friend asks, "Wait, so am I in your book?"

"Yes, although now I think I'll put all of you together as some type of anonymous composite character so as not to inflate your egos."

"Markley, this whole idea is completely retarded."

"Ah," I say wisely. "There are no retarded ideas. Only retarded people who come up with ideas."[11]

"I can't judge the idea," my friend Dave tells me, "because I have no idea what the finished product will look like. It's impossible to say if it's a good or bad idea because it all depends on what the book ends up being like."

"But you can't see it first," I explain. "That's the point. You just have to like it or not like it based on the concept."

"So what's in the actual book?" asks my friend Jeremy. "What goes between the goddamn covers?"

"This!" I exclaim for perhaps the fortieth time in a week. "This very conversation. These events. This is the book."

---

11 Let me stop this scintillating narrative right here to explain that I don't like taking notes or recording the people I interview or really even listening to what any of my idiot friends have to say, so just consider all dialogue in this book to be an approximate representation of what was actually stated—the gist—and I apologize profusely if I slander anyone by wildly misrepresenting what he or she said. For instance, if my friend Kdoe actually said to me, "Steve, I think your book idea is intriguing but a bit unwieldy," yet I quote him in my book as saying, "Steve, I hate Chinese people," I would certainly say I'm sorry, but that's the way the kitten bathes and shaves, so sue me (actually, I'm told by my lawyers that a lawsuit is a strong possibility, and by "lawyers" I mean, "this guy Phil, who's planning on going to law school").

"So if I were to do this…" He stands, turns around, and lowers his pants.

"Exactly," I say. "Now that dumb shit you just did is in the book."[12]

When I ask my ex-girlfriend, who remains my ongoing Love Interest, her opinion, she can only respond with, "Oooh! I want to be in your book."

"Fine. Done. But what do you think of the idea?"

She ponders this a moment. She and I are exes only in the sense that we no longer live in the same state. Besides that small inconvenience, most of our time together consists of endless, prattling conversation and raw, animal sex that would frighten any adolescent viewing his or her first act of human copulation. Because of these factors, I value her opinion.

"It's probably already been done," she says.

"Oh really? By who?"

"I don't know. Someone's probably thought of that, though."

"That's not fair. Anyone can *think* of an idea, but it takes balls, brains, and brass to actually execute it."

"Look," she says, "why don't you just relax and let me strip you naked, so I can shove your enormous, throbbing manlove inside of me until I orgasm so hard and loud that the neighbors call the police and make their children hide in the closet."[13]

Still, despite her best intentions, my Love Interest has awakened a fear in me that my idea may only be the effluvium of some other writer's better, sharper notion. I quickly make my way to Google, the greatest, creepiest search engine on the Internet: "book about publishing book." Nothing. I try several different approaches, including "self-referential publishing book." Nothing still. I move on to Amazon.com. Nothing. I scour the Internet, searching in every

---

12 Yeah, fuck you, Jeremy.

13 This may be an instance where I'm not quoting as faithfully as I should (see footnote, previous page). It's possible she said something more along the lines of, "Yeah, whatever."

way I know how for a single author of a single book anywhere in the world with this same idea, and after an exhausting twelve minutes of work, I come to the only logical conclusion.

I am a singular genius with an idea so unique it may very well melt readers' faces the way the Ark of the Covenant did to the Nazis in *Raiders of the Lost Ark*.

Just as I suspected.

• • •

My first true move on the book (i.e., seeking advice from professionals rather than the people I most frequently run into when drinking beer on a couch) is to email a college professor who was integral in developing my identity as a writer. The professor-student relationship is an interesting one. In college, your teachers are no longer the glorified jailers of your youth. They don't care if you chew gum or make you ask permission to take a piss. The worst of them are still more tolerable than most of the frighteningly clueless gasbags you had to endure for the first thirteen years of your education, and the best tend to stay with you, either through friendship or in your subconscious as inner voices.

Steven, with his bastardized, bizzarro-world version of my name, happened to teach the very first creative writing course I ever took at Miami University. I remember walking to class that first day during my sophomore year and wondering if this class—specifically, my professor, who I imagined as a statuesque, goateed patriarch with wire-rimmed spectacles, an aristocratic nose, and a breezy all-white outfit that would simultaneously call to mind Tom Wolfe and Jimmy Buffett—would jump-start my life as a writer. I remember dismissing that idea as naïve and childish. Now I can't believe how prescient it was.

Steven is fond of telling me how unimpressive he found me during the first two-thirds of that class. According to him, I sat with my mouth shut, arms crossed, and head down waiting for time to run out. He pegged me as another arrogant Miami frat boy, who likely used sneering homosexual slurs when describing the class to his friends.

In truth, I never said anything because I was wildly intimidated. The first day, when people from the class recited their one-page descriptive scenes, I remember thinking how artful and well imagined they all were. We did writing exercises that didn't make sense to me. We were told to keep a journal, a "daybook," in which we wrote down thoughts, vignettes, or dialogue. Toward the end of the semester when I realized I had only filled thirteen pages, I went a little mad trying to think up things to fill space. I even wrote the following paragraph, assuming my professor would never actually read every word of every kid's daybook:

> *Damn this daybook. Damn this goddamn daybook. What do I write in it? Everything that comes to mind? If people wrote down everything that popped into their heads the mental hospitals would be overflowing. We'd all be enemies of the goddamn state.*

So I sat in that class for the first two months with my arms crossed and my head down, never saying a word, mostly eyeing the pretty girls and wondering what clever combination of flirtatious parrying would lead one of them to fall in love with me. But then we had to turn in our stories. I still have the separate sheet of paper Steven typed and attached to my story, and even if I were to win the Pulitzer some day, I doubt it could ever mean as much as those two brief paragraphs.

> *I have to say that—in its length and amplitude, in the amount of time it covers, in its wisdom about relationships and human psychology— this is one of the most astounding stories I've ever received in a 226 class. On every page there are grace notes, details which resonate with the clarity of true observation, moments when the story stops and life in all its mystery and complexity blazes through…*

> *This is a piece of writing that—far from being good enough
> for a 226 class—could get you into an extremely well-rated MFA
> program in fiction writing. I actually find it hard to understand
> how you (if this is an indication of the depth of your interior life)
> could have remained so hidden from the class this semester.*

After this incident, and my subsequent graduation into the higher
ranks of Steven's fawning students, I became a regular in his office.
He read my stories, made suggestions and corrections, and told me
flatly when he thought what I had given him was crap. He asked me
about myself, told me a bit about his own life, his own experiences
with writing. We debated the merits of the various seasons of *24*, a
show we both adored.[14]

Before I even realized it, I had a mentor, something my solitary-
rogue self-image had never before considered. I had always thought
that my writing basically sat in some kind of vault that only I need
have access to. The thought of someone else trying to get a look
inside the vault was purely ridiculous. Slowly, however, I began to
realize that not only did my writing need that outside eye, but I
actually enjoyed hearing Steven talk about it. Somehow he always
seemed able to cut through my prose and find the root of what I was
trying to say. He'd yank that root out and suddenly I could see how
the whole God-almighty tree was dug into the ground.

Needless to say, before embarking on any major journey of words
and soul, I felt I should consult him, if not for advice than for the
equivalent of spiritual guidance. Therefore, I sent him the following email (you will have to excuse with the inclusion of the initial
anecdote, which was just too thrilling to leave out):

---

14 For the record, seasons one, two, and five were tits, season four middling, three
underwhelming, and season six a disaster.

From: s_____@yahoo.com
To: s_____@muohio.edu
Subject: questions, advice, etc.

Steven,

Okay, I have two things for you, one a meaningless anecdote
that very few people in my life would actually appreciate, and
the other a general query.

First off, I was eating brunch at an Irish bar in Wrigleyville
this past Sunday, nursing a hangover and generally not being
very good company for my friends, when who walks in?

If you guessed anyone other than Tony Almeida from *24*,
you would be wrong. Yes, Carlos Bernard is there in the bar
right before a Cubs game (remember his mug from every single
season?), and I couldn't think to do anything other than tap
his shoulder and tell him that I was a fan and thought it was
bullshit that they killed off his character. I will say he looked
pretty annoyed and pissed off before I even approached him,
but then again, he always looked kind of annoyed and pissed
off running around CTU trying to figure out if Stephen Saunders
was going to release a deadly virus in an L.A. subway, so
maybe that's just his default emotional state.

Annnnyway, I also wanted to get your feedback on this
project I've begun. While I've secured a freelance job for the
Tribune's free "hip" daily, continue to work with my fiction, and
pursue other literary avenues, I've also begun to write a book
with the working title of "Publish This Book."

The general idea is this: the entire book is about my
endeavor to publish the book. The book is not about anything.
It's about trying to publish the very book that I'm writing.
Subsequently, all correspondence (with agents, with publishers,
with editors, with anyone) will be included, including this email.

Of course, on a basic level, the book is a stupid idea, and it will revel in how stupid of an idea it really is. On another level, though, the book is of course an autobiographical look at a young writer's pursuit of his dream—the travails of taking that road less traveled, the pitfalls and angst of starting a writing career from scratch, brief autobiographical snippets of how that writer came to find himself in this situation in the first place (I've attached the unedited bit that includes you).

I'm not yet sure if this is serious or just a vanity project I dreamed up to keep my sanity while I slum for small change at some fairly nauseating publications (more on that later). What I wanted from you, however, is this: anything.

Any ideas, any tactics, any thoughts at all, but for now just your initial thoughts will be more than sufficient. In the end, I kind of picture the book as a cautionary guide to becoming a writer. How many twenty-year-old kids across the country are sitting in a creative writing or journalism class dreaming of how they can make a living, a name, and a life with their pen (or laptop for those born after the Hoover administration)? Call me crazy, but they call that an audience where I come from.

Hope all is well,
Steve

Steven's response remains pending for a while, during which time I mull over the providence of the Carlos Bernard encounter.[15]

---

15   In a completely unrelated celebrity anecdote, I once drank with Jared Padalecki—star of the television show *Supernatural* with roles in *Flight of the Phoenix* and the Elisha Cuthbert–Paris Hilton horror update *House of Wax*—in a Vancouver bar. It was during my aforementioned Epic Road Trip across the country and I had to scour the entire Canadian city to find a sports bar that would be showing the Ohio State–Texas game of 2006. I found myself drunk and ranting at some asshole Texas fans, who turned out to be Padalecki and his entourage. Padalecki was actually a fairly nice guy, which is unfortunate because I was a complete dick to him (this has something to do with college football, which I feel largely strips us of our social niceties).

I remember the very first day of class my sophomore year, Steven, this tall, lanky, white-haired man with a wry smile always playing at the corners of his lips, asked his motley assortment of hopeful writers what the best show on television was. I don't know why, but boldness overtook me, and the two-digit Kiefer Sutherland–vehicle just spilled out of my lips (it really was a pretty badass show). Those were the first words anyone in the class had uttered. Steven gave me a surprised, bemused look, and said, "Yes. That's exactly right."

I'm not one to believe in fate, but if I had known all that would spring forth from that first encounter, it would be hard to deny the tingling sensation of some otherworldly cosmic force. Then again, I suppose that is how all of life's truly important moments come and go: with all of us poor souls suddenly glancing up from a moment of boredom to realize Important Shit has just gone down. And who the hell can ever possibly warn you when those moments have arrived?

His response follows a few weeks later:

From: s_____@muohio.edu
To: s_____@yahoo.com
Subject: RE: questions, advice, etc.

Hey Steve,

Sorry for the delay... We're just back from the east where we looked at the new house and made a decision to get there as soon as possible. What this means I don't know yet.

Basically, throughout our conversation, he acted like the star-crossed writer on a journey of destiny and freewheeling soul, and I acted like a narcissistic C-list actor. After he bought me a shot and proposed a toast to college football, I clinked his glass and told him, "Fuck you. And fuck Texas." I proceeded to ridicule Texas football, call Vince Young a girl, and when he showed me a picture of his girlfriend, remark, "That chick gave me herpes." Our conversation ended with a threat to break his arm (even though he stood about six inches taller than me), at which point his entourage snatched him up and spirited him away. In conclusion, I can only offer my sincerest apologies to Jared Padalecki.

As for Carlos Bernard: he had a great run on *24* and he's sorely missed—any *24* fan is pining for the good old days. He's young, he's got plenty of cash (if he's not a gambler or idiot), he's good-looking and he has Cubs tickets. What does he have to be pissed off about? I assume he just sneered at you from his Olympian perch on a barstool and told thee to hie thyself back to the filthy rabble from wherest thou came.

I like the basic idea for PUBLISH THIS BOOK but think you need to be careful. Of course, it's very "high concept" (it's totally high concept) and of course, by definition it's completely self-conscious, which means it could become cute. Any book which calls attention to itself as a book, and in this case a book in the process of being written and shopped around, is going to get lumped with other po-mo screeds.

The success will depend on the voice, and on whether the reader (or editor) wants to spend time with that voice and feels a sense of sympathy/empathy for the writer. When you write "The book is not about anything," that, of course, brings back *Seinfeld*'s famous description of itself, and the episodes in which George and Jerry try to sell that concept to TV executives. But that's O.K.

My initial thoughts: Make this kaleidoscopic. Include your basketball career and your hopes/dreams of becoming a bball player (How far did those dreams go? What stopped them?), or your hopes/dreams of becoming a political insider or a catalyst for social change or a high-flying journalist. It seems to me that any straightforward narrative (I got good grades in English, my high school teachers told me I should be a writer, wretch, vomit) will be both a bore and an exercise in bathos. So you've got to jump around, stay lively, elude the criticism, maintain your irreverence. (On the other hand we don't need a book that recapitulates the ethos of www. everyonewhosanyone.com; one Gerald Jones is enough; check out the site—he's now included prizes and has decided to take on "creative writing.")

As a cautionary guide, your book has to be funny—and in order for it to be read it has to be published, which means it will have a happy ending, which will—grossly speaking—make it a comedy. So put in the highs as well as the lows, stay confident (and funny), and mostly try to remain as innocent as possible. By innocent I mean idealistic, trusting, hopeful. Irony, pessimism, and bitterness will kill this book.

As for the prose which includes me in it—I liked it a lot because it has that voice I was looking for, even though it does tend to crack wise (maybe a tiny bit too wise). I think the voice for this book needs a little bit of the gee-whiz-I-never-knew-there-were-so-many-stars-until-I-drove-through-Kansas twang. (I know you keep that voice in the vault along with all your writing, but maybe you can let it out just a little.) Even as you come to know that the old bromides ("the cream always rises to the top," "publishers are eager for new young voices," etc.) are so much happy horseshit, you have to continue to believe in them inside the book (I think). Your natural proclivities will keep you from ever going too far.

Anyway, I'm self-conscious as hell writing this to you and will try not to edit the life out of it (if it has any) in order to make it sound like I'm wiser or smarter than I am. Even the IDEA of publication is enough to make one crazy.

This has legs, I think, but you won't know for sure until you've gone with it for a while. (With the speed at which you write, that will mean another week or two.) Let me know.

Your mentor, wretch, vomit,
Steven

As usual, Steven's email gives me plenty of food for thought. I enjoy soaking in his initial impressions, and already I can begin to feel them shaping the tale I wish to tell. I also send roughly the same general query to another Miami professor named Margaret, who worked closely with me on my novel as well as several other longer writing projects. Her response arrives days after Steven's.

From: m_____@muohio.edu
To: s_____@yahoo.com
Subject: RE: catching up, ideas, stuff

Hi, Steve:

It's nice to hear from you, and I'm sorry for the slow response. I've been thinking a little bit about your project in the interim. I'm on leave now, thank goodness, so I have time to write and catch up on my reading and writing. London was fantastic; I can't wait to go back. I made a lot of notes for future stories (possibly), wrote one decent story, and wrote some god-awful crap that resulted from assignments that I gave to the class. This has me thinking about the nature of writing assignments, how something can be a good exercise and yet produce crappy writing nevertheless. Crappy in the sense that it's well written, but uninteresting. We can talk more about London exploits another time. We went to Paris, too, and I went to the Hay Festival, a literary festival in Wales. Bill Clinton famously described it as "the Woodstock of the mind."

I do have some big news: I just found out last week that LSU will publish my collection of short stories. It's not official yet (haven't seen the contract), but it should come out early next fall. I'm relieved, and resisting the urge to count up all the rejections the manuscript has earned. Some of the rejections are very special to me, including the one that refers to it as a novel. These are stories that I wrote and revised between 2000 and 2005. Most are Florida stories; only two are Ohio stories—just to give you some sense of elapsed time. I think six of the sixteen stories have been published in magazines, journals, or anthologies. I'm about one hundred pages into a new collection of stories, and of course it's in the back of my mind that this new one won't necessarily find a publishing house. I don't have an agent, and I'm not likely to get one unless I publish a story in the *New Yorker*.

Having said that, I almost think it's better for young writers not to know some of this process. Writing a good book and getting a book published are two separate activities that don't have anything much in common, as you've already noticed. The publishing end can be very gloomy, and even when success comes there's a renegotiation of what success means. Okay, the book will be published, but will it be marketed? Will anyone read it? Will it be reviewed? Will it get good, bad, or indifferent reviews? Etc.

Anyway, I like your book idea. It's an experiment, like most writing. You can't know what you'll end up with; you have to go through the process to find out if there's anything there.

I always thought it would be interesting to collect manuscript rejections from many writers, to see if there's a common language around the rejection. I've always suspected that agents and editors have polite and standard ways to reject without giving much information that's useful to a writer. They don't want to burn any bridges, just in case the writer turns into someone they want to work with later.

You might check the *New York Times* online for an essay called "No Thanks, Mr. Nabokov." Knopf has opened up its archive of rejection letters, and Nabokov was among the rejected (*Lolita*, of course) as were many other writers who went on to fame and critical acclaim.

I might put you in touch with one recent Miami grad (she was in the graduate program) who's had a novel published. I believe she said she sent the book to one hundred publishers before it was accepted. If you're interested, let me know, and I'll see if she's willing to chat with you.

That's all for now. I'd be happy to talk/write more about this. Looking forward to hearing about all that you're up to. Chicago sounds like a good place to be.

Best,
Margaret

• • •

Indeed, the arrival of word from the two most influential writers in my life sets me off thinking. This idea, it seems, is not completely insane, so I'm already way farther than I thought I'd get with it.

I tend to have sleepless nights. I've had them since I was a child: inexplicable but ferocious bouts of insomnia where I shift positions a thousand times, curse a thousand more, and fret over every wasted second ticking off my already too-short life. Not long after the arrival of these letters, I find myself awake at 3:23 a.m. with an alarm clock set for 7:20. I've only just moved to Chicago, and being awake at this hour in this new city has a strange feeling of slippery alien contact.

I used to despair at moments like these, but over time I've learned to accept them. I tend to think best in these late, desperate hours, the creative and critical juices getting shocked and fused and sometimes, I swear, I can almost visualize the currents sparking bright blue and white the way the trains do when they rumble along the tracks in the dark.

I have ideas. Some for my new freelance gig, another for a couple of articles I might be able to sell, a few for future columns on my website. What spring to mind primarily, however, are the letters from Steven and Margaret. I especially keep coming back to a phrase Margaret used: "...Even when success comes there's a renegotiation of what success means," she wrote.

When I first thought I wanted to be a writer, years and years ago, I imagined the lifestyle as not too dissimilar from that of a rock star. You got published, and once that happened people thought you were smart. They thought you had interesting things to say and an interesting way of saying them. Girls wanted to sleep with you. Young writers asked you fawning, obsequious questions. You never had to worry about money again. You skipped from city to city, book-signing to book-signing. You pounded away at the keys of your laptop by day and soaked in the riches you'd earned by night. I pictured writing as a glamorous gig, a lifestyle to bridge the gap between art and worldly desires. Writing was power and wealth and fame and most of all vindication—a sense of relief that the people who floated above you all your life were suddenly yanked back to earth when they heard of what you'd accomplished. Writing was triumph.

It took me years and years to understand that I was missing the whole point. No writer waltzes into a world like that, and if one does, it's more than likely that what's coming out of his or her pen is garbage. The life of a writer can be a lonely road to travel, and it's one you always have to travel by yourself. It doesn't matter how many other writers you befriend, doesn't matter how many "mentors, wretch, vomit" you enlist. In the end, it's just you and that writing utensil and some kind of fantastical fucked-up world pinballing around in your head.

That night it occurs to me that every writer had his or her tale: the winding path they took to whatever varied degree of success they had managed to achieve. How disheartening, how amazing, how fascinating would it be to simply tell that story? To hear from the mouth of success, just how hard-won that success had been. Or to listen to the voice of failure and discover the moment when a dream died its hard, dirty death in the shadow of mounting reality.

And suddenly, lying there in my new cramped room miles and miles from home, I am onto something. After having begun this book with only a good idea of what the first fifteen pages would look like, I had struck a rich, bloody vein and the ensuing geyser washed me into dreams.

THREE

Chicago-Based Freelance Writer

Lightning strikes across the canvas of a Chicago skyline the color of gunmetal. Rain, whipped into a fury by a warm, brisk wind, pelts my bare skin. Waves on Lake Michigan form whitecaps and sluice against the rusted metal barriers of the docks and their coats of algae. Normally, this route is packed with bikers and joggers, but today I am one of the only people out running during this mid-August thunderstorm, dashing along a path that winds around the cusp of Lincoln Park and down past North Avenue Beach. I wear no shirt, and the water has completely soaked my shorts, weighing me down even as it washes the sweat from my torso. In this warm rain, I feel as if I might be able to run for decades. The city is mystic in the violet summer air—a ghostly mixture of careening skyscrapers and nature's fickle inclinations. The sounds of rain and wind and my own rapid heartbeat all drum in my ears.

I pass another guy, about my age, who has removed his shirt and tucked it into the front of his shorts. We pass each other, our chests slick and glistening with a mixture of rain and perspiration; we exchange a look that says, *All those miserably hot days with people shoving and pushing for a spot on this trail—fighting the crowds, trudging up and down the shore.* All it takes is one look to the south or one glance across the dark, stewing body of water to be completely captivated, filled with wonder at this living mural of glass, brick, steel, and dark, pulsing precipitation. *Of all the days, how could anyone miss out on this?* I ask him with my look.

His glance says the same.

Well, either the "same" or:

Dude, would you mind if we didn't exchange a look while our chests are slick and glistening with a mixture of rain and perspiration? That'd be cool, thanks.

Then we are past, and I'm grinning madly.

Man, you have no idea, I think at him. *But I did it, my semi-naked friend. I moved to Chicago.*

• • •

Why did I move to Chicago?

The answer is as obscure as the sky overhead. Somewhere in my mind, if I can ferret it out, there is probably an explanation, but as when you tell a member of the opposite sex that you love him or her, there are a number of footnotes to the truth.[16]

What I told myself—and my parents and my friends—was that I wanted to move to a large media market with plenty of opportunities to write, and Chicago just happened to be the closest major city. I considered New York, but with no job, no money, no place to live, and all manner of illicit ways to get into trouble stacked up like cordwood, I thought I'd better hold off until I can actually afford a cocaine habit.[17]

As I've said, I spent a year driving around the country until I ran

---

16 Footnotes customarily exist more in life than they do in literature. With literature, it seems as if these days they are used primarily for snarky comments that would not otherwise fit the flow of the prose.

17 During a road trip to New York City that summer to visit my friend Ian, I single-handedly spawned one of the most epic, bizarre, disturbing stories my tightly knit friend group has yet had the pleasure of hearing. I cannot and will not repeat exactly what happened in these pages. However, I will say it involved a Brazilian woman with very recent breast augmentation surgery and a frantic solo cab ride out of SoHo at six in the morning.

out of money. Moving to the next step after that unbridled road lust was hard. Before my decision to move to Chicago, I told people I was moving to the following places: Iowa, Nevada, Ithaca, Brooklyn, New Hampshire, Columbus, and Boston. Each time, I felt as if what I was saying was more or less true, but the problem was finding a job that would have me.

I interviewed with the Public Interest Research Group. I sent applications to Democratic congressmen. I interviewed for teaching jobs in inner-city schools. I applied to Greenpeace. None of it felt right, but I was at a complete loss. I had all but locked down a job with PIRG, but I hesitated. Did I really want to canvass sixty hours a week in the heat of the summer, bound by a two-year commitment, broke, subsisting off Ramen noodles and slices of American cheese, and coming home too tired to write a single word? I began to doubt it.

I felt like none of this took me in the direction I needed to go. There are many routes to the same point, yet the path to becoming a writer seemed poorly lit, dense with fog, and wound around and around in a complex and ceaseless maze.

Yet there I was sitting at home in Ohio, twenty-four years old, a year out of college, and getting itchy again, feeling as if there was something out there for me to grab and call mine, if only I could figure out what it was and where to find it.

So I just went.

I called up a good friend of mine and asked him if he wanted to move to Chicago.

With the wind of youth, idealism, and, yes, stupidity at my back, Chicago would become my new home, and in August of 2007—a gritty, dangerous year if there ever was one—I packed my bags and headed west.[18]

Lightning flashes—a jagged tear in the sky just above the Hancock Building. I finally come to a stop by the overpass that

---

18 Well, more westish Midwest, at least.

crosses Lakeshore Drive and let the rain and the wind ripple all around me.

So was this a good idea? I ask my shirtless friend, who's probably on the other end of the city by now. *Out of all those endless, poorly lit, circuitous paths, is this one at least a contender?*

I knew this was a bad idea, I imagine him saying with that gaze of his. *Only the real creepy fuckers go out running when it's raining like this.*

• • •

Now that I've made the move to Chicago, though, it means trouble for the book.

As Steven and Margaret both told me, I need to run with this project for a while before I'll know if I have anything. In other words, I need more than an idea. I need actual words on paper. This is complicated because I now live in a small room in a house in central Lakeview with four young male roommates. If the idea for this project had come to me at any other juncture in my life, I might have had a routine, some normality, a stable system from which I could build on my pinwheeling thoughts and emotions. As it stands now, since I just moved to a new city, I'm planning to undertake this complex, bizarre book while I also need to locate and procure a job, furniture, money, health insurance, and reassurance in some shape or form that I am not going to end up homeless, a drug addict, or in sales.

I begin by interviewing for a freelance position at *RedEye*, the Tribune Company's free daily that serves young "hip" commuters and professionals. You can tell its audience is "hip" because the publication is light on such trifling matters as "news" and heavy on all things Spears-, Gyllenhaal-, and Bow Wow–related. An entire issue can be read cover-to-cover in a twenty-five-minute train ride, along with the Sudoku and crossword completed sans effort.[19]

---

19 "6 Down: This actor is married to Angelina Jolie, starred in the movie *Fight Club*, and goes by 'Brad' to his friends."

I take the train downtown to the Tribune building and wait in the lobby for one of the editors to come meet me. I'm usually not nervous during interviews because all one has to do in an interview is master one subject, and it always happens to be the subject I know best.[20] You get thirty minutes to talk about how great you are? Usually, I save that for the second date.

In this case, however, I've been wracked by nerves deciding what to wear. My friend who interned in the *RedEye* office told me the dress was extremely casual. "Should I wear a tie?" I asked.

"I don't know," she said. "I'm a girl. We just wear dresses."

As I prepared for the interview I put on the tie, took off the tie, put on the tie, took off the tie—maybe thirteen times. I eventually decided against the tie. Now, as the editor walks toward me with his hand outstretched, I see his gaze fall to my neck briefly, and even though he wears no tie himself, I cannot help but believe that he sees my open collar as a glaring faux pas, and in my world of neckties and no neckties, I am devastated on a scale usually reserved for characters in films like *Sophie's Choice*.

"You settling into Chicago all right?" the tall, moon-faced editor asks me on our way to the elevator.

"Yeah. Sure. I got a place and… stuff."

This is entirely true except for the part about "stuff."

"What are you doing for a day job?"

"Oh, I've got a whole slew of interviews in the next couple of days."

This is entirely true except for the part about a "slew of interviews."

He leads me to the conference room with the *RedEye*'s blood-red signature color lending the walls enough gravitas to make me wish I'd worn a tie. I can see my reflection in the glass of the window that looks out over the newsroom, and I'm dismayed to see that I have opted for the Ricky-Martin-without-the-sex-appeal look. I wonder to myself if poorly manicured chest hair spilling out the top of a shirt is considered "hip" these days.

---

20 Me.

A second editor joins us, younger and more female. The two of them look through a portfolio I've brought along. This includes one article I wrote for *Private Investigator's Magazine*, clippings from my college newspaper, and a conspicuous absence of any other material that would lend credence to my claim that I am a writer. Still, the two of them seem impressed enough.

"This *P.I.* article is well-written. A lot of good bullet points," says the female editor.

"Thanks!" I say brightly, as if noting the number of short sentences I placed beside bullet points on Microsoft Word was roughly equivalent to "You are a man of letters and your genius is surely unsurpassed in the realm of literature." It is not until this moment that I understand just how badly I want this job.

"Looks good. We can start you out with some more basic assignments," says the moon-faced editor. "We have a Chi-Tunes section where we feature Chicago bands. It's an interview and about five hundred words, usually with one specific hook. You a music fan?"

"Oh yeah. Of course."

"You ever hear of…" He proceeds to list off five to ten of what I think must be Chicago-based bands, but it's hard to tell because it's possible that some of the names are running together. He says something like: "Soul rebel neon gods three way to make run a hammock silent sirens escapade Sunday morning chameleon?" And I have no idea where to put the commas in that sentence. Needless to say, I've heard of none of these acts (although since none of them are Springsteen, Dylan, or 2Pac, this doesn't surprise me).

I nod thoughtfully. "Yeah, a lot of those sound really familiar," I say, like I'm trying to pull from the vast web of memory my experience with the band Silent Sirens Escapade (or Escapade Sunday… or Hammock Silent Sirens).

"And I saw your website," says the female editor. "You write columns?"

"Definitely," I say.

"Awesome. We have regularly rotating column slots for our

freelancers on Thursdays and for the weekend edition. If you're interested…"

"Definitely. Definitely interested," I say, wildly understating how excited she has just made me.

Here is what these two editors do not know: while fiction is my first love and passion, columns come hurtling in at a close second. During my undergraduate career at Miami University, I more or less lucked into a role as a columnist for *The Miami Student*, and then to the position of editorial editor. The story is a long and torrid one, too involved to tell here (see Chapter 13 "Autobiographical Digression #2: Confessions of a Campus Firebrand"), but suffice it to say that I developed a reputation on campus. There is no way to say it other than the most conceited way imaginable, so brace yourself: over the course of my junior and senior years I morphed into a kind of campus quasi-celebrity; not by face (the picture was a grainy little black-and-white smudge) but by name.

I was a political sex columnist, which is to say that politics and sex are just about one and the same: they both promise glory, entertainment, excitement, and salvation and ultimately deliver vague disappointment that can never quite be reconciled with all the passion that goes into the activity in the first place.

I loved writing that column so much that I built a website for the sole purpose of continuing it after I graduated. I find the experience of writing one of those brief rants cathartic in the same manner as masturbation, and that's not a joke at all. When you masturbate, you are inherently reaching for a lofty goal in a quick, sloppy, simplistic manner. There are no bells and whistles to what's going down,[21] but in the end, when the result is raining down on your stomach, you don't really care. For me, writing a column is similar in that you're reaching for epic scope in less than a thousand

---

21 I bet somewhere a really bizarre fetishist will read that sentence and think of something gross to do with a bell and a whistle.

words. It approximates writing something expansive and revela-tory the same way jacking off approximates sex. Of course, it ain't the same—not by a long shot—but sometimes you're not trying to write *Ulysses*.[22]

The thought of more than just my die-hard fans finally reading me in print again—hell, the thought of a good chunk of Chicago turning to my byline—gives me a vicious thrill as soon as she makes the suggestion.

As the male editor escorts me out of the building while we make small talk, my inner monologue begins, *Now don't get carried away, Markley. This doesn't mean*—

I'm famous, motherfuckers! my Id screams as it comes bursting out of the subconscious basement of my mind, tap dancing a jig and chugging a bottle of mouthwash. *Fuck this small-time website, freelance, paying-my-dues bullshit! This motherfucker's about to hit the jackpot! Every last one of you Chicago whores is going to be reading my shit and laughing your sorry asses off! Worship my shit! Worship my shit! Gravy train, I'm on my motherfuckin wa*—

"…Give them a call by Tuesday," finishes my editor as we reach the lobby of the Trib building.

I shove my Id back into the basement and come hurtling out of my daze. "Sorry, say that again?"

"Oh, just make sure you give Run a Hammock Silent a call by Tuesday, and we can get your first piece in the following week."

"Oh, sure. Cool."

• • •

With a writing job secured, I am feeling more confident. When I made the decision to move to Chicago, it was in part because I had seen *RedEye* and felt like if I could get a job there, it would make for

---

22 Although clearly this last paragraph will win me comparisons to Joyce, who often had the authorial courage to cover the aftereffects of masturbating in the prone position.

a nice logical step in a writing career. This lends me enough confidence to begin a sharp, jagged burst on *Publish This Book*. It is only appropriate that I describe the living situation in which much of this tome will be birthed—screaming, naked, and almost indistinguishable from its own afterbirth—into this world.

The house, just south of Wrigley Field, is an architectural disaster in the midst of a flourishing, picturesque, middle-class Northside neighborhood. Both the front and back stairs look as if they were built by fourth-grade boys who'd grown tired of constructing haphazard tree houses with signs that said "No Girlz Alowd!"

My room is the smallest in the house, and I manage to cram in a mattress (which I just lay directly on the floor), a small trunk, a shelf where I stack my clothes, and a hutch for a bookshelf. Alas, I have no desk because I can't afford one, and even if I could I'd have nowhere to put it unless I was willing to stack it on my floor mattress. Because I plan to write the masterpiece that is this book in this dismal little cave of a room, I procure a collapsible lawn chair I got for free in college when I opened an account with Fifth Third Bank. I nickname it my Throne of Genius.[23]

As I sit on my Throne of Genius and begin to craft this book, all I have are my numerous wall decorations. Although surely no one has any interest in the posters I've sticky-tacked to my walls, I believe that by listing them, I can give you a windfall of information about me, your humble narrator, that will offer you a great degree of insight into my intellect and disposition.[24]

There are the posters that have been resurrected from my college apartments, including Johnny Depp's twisted visage from *Fear and Loathing in Las Vegas*, an infantry helmet with a peace sign and the words "Born to Kill" from Kubrick's *Full Metal Jacket*, John Lennon with the lyrics to "Imagine," Cesar Chavez wearily carrying a shovel

---

23 Not to be confused with my floor mattress, which I nickname my Bed of "I'm Not Hooking Up With You on a Floor Mattress."

24 And also save me a whole fucking lot of exposition later.

through a field, and Tommie Smith and John Carlos bowing their heads and holding their black-gloved fists to the sky during the playing of the National Anthem at the 1968 Olympic games after winning a gold and bronze medal, respectively. There is a Portland Trail Blazers beach towel covering one wall and above it an enormous rainbow flag with the word "PACE," which I bought while studying in Italy.[25] There is a Far Side calendar and an entire slice of wall covered in Bruce Springsteen albums (including *Nebraska*, two versions of *Born in the U.S.A.*, *Darkness on the Edge of Town*, *The River*, and *The Wild, the Innocent, and the E Street Shuffle*; I stole them from my parents, who I deemed not cool enough to own Bruce Springsteen records). There is a cover from *Newsweek* with a picture of Barack Obama. There are small movie posters for *Into the Wild* and *In the Valley of Elah*. There is a small piece of pop art, which features Jesus in a white robe offering his hand and the words—cut and pasted from an advertisement for sexual aid video tapes for couples—"Needless to say, later that night we had the most phenomenal, mind-blowing sex EVER." There is the framed fake ID I used in college and a clipping from the Cleveland *Plain Dealer* with my grinning mug.[26]

See how much more you know about a person from what he or she chooses to display on the walls?

If it were just me staring at my Springsteen albums and working

---

25   "Pace" is Italian for "peace." These flags are very popular in Italy as protests against the invasion of Iraq, while in the United States they are very popular for having to explain to everyone that no, you don't have a gargantuan gay pride flag in your room.

26   Okay, a great story behind that: The clipping from the *Plain Dealer* is from the 2004 election when a group of friends and myself went to protest an appearance by Vice President Dick Cheney at a church in Parma. The girl who would become my Love Interest was there, and I was desperate to impress her with my wit. Therefore, on my protest sign, I wrote in enormous letters: "Dick, You're Such a Greedy Sleazebag I Couldn't Even Think of What to Put on This Sign." I'm not sure if it did impress her, but I know it impressed several burly members of the local police, who kept pointing to it and laughing before Cheney arrived. A *Plain Dealer* photographer captured the entire scene.

away on my Throne of Genius, I would probably have this book done in a month. Alas, I have distractions, and these distractions are called "roommates."

Although I'm trying to build a career as a serious writer (and yes, the term "serious" applies to this book, including anecdotes about fake IDs, amusing political protests, and Brazilian women with recent breast augmentation), I still have one foot firmly entrenched in the world of post-adolescent debauchery. Living with four other recent college graduates does not help me advance into my next phase of maturation, nor will it help me actually sit down and do the work necessary to tackle this book.

Now for the last couple of chapters, I've been claiming I'm this crazy awesome writer, so at this juncture it would be appropriate to use that writing prowess to craft a telling scene that would illuminate my roommates' individual personalities and transform each into a fully realized character…

Or I could give you an easily digestible list that you can refer back to in the likely event that their names come up again.

- **James:** An old traveling companion, who shall be referred to by a semi-fake name (more on that later) to protect his identity and shield him from the serious blowback that all the stories involving him will surely rain upon his already heavily-tarnished name.[27] Over the last three years James and I have navigated both Venetian canals and Teton Mountain paths. Having nothing better to do with his B.A. in history and complete lack of ambition, he was up for giving Chicago a stab. We spend most of our time discussing literature, chicks, the upcoming presidential

---

27   For example: He and I once worked in Grand Teton National Park and shared a small, cramped dorm room. One day after returning from a run, I opened the door to find him standing on my bed, wearing only a towel, holding a pair of my boxers to his nose, and pretending to masturbate. His eyes went wide, and he dropped the boxers. "Dude!" he exclaimed. "What are you doing back so soon?"

primaries, our inclinations toward Barack Obama, philosophy, history, doing shit with chicks, and the occasional scathing joke about the instability of the Kurdistan region of Iraq and Turkey. As James puts it, "Just two mediocre renaissance men. We don't do anything particularly well but at least we cover a lot."

- **Elliott:** Quiet, computer-savvy, video game expert, and a fucking awesome, rattle-your-fillings musician. Given Elliott's quiet, reserved nature, it's shocking to watch him play the guitar. He's so unassuming that it's hard to believe he's the same person when he picks up the instrument; his fingers strike and flow and dance across the strings with a precision and flare I could only dream of.[28] Elliott inexplicably uses the word "fuzzy" to describe situations he finds unfavorable. For instance: "Fuzzy, man, so my boss is having me work late." "Fuzzy these slow-ass trains." "Fuzzy, where are my keys?" It does not work quite like "fuck" (because you can't say, "Yeah, fuzzy me hard."). It can only be used as an interjection. I guess what I'm saying is that I do not understand the etymology of "fuzzy."

- **Liam:** Sardonic, loves cycling, *24,* and karaoke. I used to write for Liam at Miami's entertainment magazine when he was co-editor. No one can launch into a diatribe like Liam. One time Elliott simply asks him if he wants to order Thai food, and Liam replies, "Yeah, I could do that. Yeah, that makes perfect sense, spending fifteen dollars on shitty Thai food or—*or!*—and this is a wild idea—I could go into the kitchen and make a plate of delicious pasta that would cost me about 65 cents for the pasta, 25 cents for the sauce, and maybe another 10 or 12 cents for the cheese I'll grate over the top. But no, Thai,

---

28 My own set list on the guitar is punctuated by a bitching rendition of "Three Blind Mice."

that's a fantastic idea—" This honestly might have gone on for five more minutes if Elliott hadn't cut him off, "Fuzzy, Liam, I get it." In a completely unrelated but bizarre anecdote, Liam's favorite band of all time is Super-Drag, and when they reunite for a six-city tour in the fall, Liam spends all of his vacation days and several thousand dollars following them around the country. During this period, I wonder if this is why he did not want to order Thai food that one time.

- **Erik:** Capable, incisive, dependable, with an ordered mind that demonstrates a remarkable maturity for his age—these are all a bunch of words that don't remotely describe Erik. Erik is a sex-addicted Democratic political consultant who happily could not give a fuck what the world thinks of him. He sleeps on a round orange velvet bed under the watchful eye of a Barry White album cover, which along with an Obama yard sign make up the only decorations in his room. He will wear ankle-high socks, skimpy red sprinter's shorts, and a pink dress shirt without any hint of irony, and whenever he opens his mouth, he's just as likely to launch into a fevered debate about the viability of corn ethanol as he is to tell the story about the girl who tried to videotape him while they were having sex. The fact that such a tape may exist continues to haunt my dreams.

We all get along well and that's just fantastic, but I didn't move to Chicago to get along with people. Hell, I could've done that in Ohio. No, I'm here to become a writer, but in order to do that, I need to not starve to death, and *RedEye's* $75-per-column compensation is definitely a starving kinda gig. This means I need a regular job.

• • •

James and I enlist the services of a staffing agency to find work. I am essentially broke, and even if I wanted to move forward boldly on my book or other writing projects, I can't even afford the ink and paper for my printer.

I talk to a perky girl over the phone, who says that the agency has the perfect position for me: a trade publication that pays twelve dollars an hour for a three-month trial period, after which it becomes a real job with a $26,000 salary and full benefits. It sounds too good to be true (I know what you're thinking right now: *26K sounds "too good to be true"?* But sometimes even a dry bone looks good to a hungry dog).

And of course it *does* turn out to be too good to be true. Once it has us in its claws, the staffing agency just hires James and me internally to screen and schedule candidates for ten bucks an hour.[29]

Just for a while, I tell myself. *Just temporarily until you can find something better.*

We find ourselves taking the Brown Line to work each day, dressed business-appropriate in shirts and ties. We work in a skyscraper downtown in the Loop. *The Dark Knight* is filming outside our building, just before Heath Ledger went and made that movie permanently and morbidly iconic. We sit at desks and make lackadaisical evaluations of résumés. A week's paycheck comes to approximately $322, give or take a few bucks depending upon how much I've lied about my lunch breaks. Despite this being the most money I've ever earned in any job in my life, it feels like that scene in *The Simpsons* when the old lady hands Bart two quarters after he weeds her entire lawn.

"This job sucks," says James one day. "I should have been a Rap Mogul."

"Yeah, but you'd have to start out as an entry-level Rap Mogul," I explain.

---

29 And to top it all off, there is someone there with my old traveling buddy's first name, and he quickly receives an order from the higher-ups that he shall hence be referred to by his middle name, which is James. This seems like a particularly bizarre practice—that no one in the entire company can go by the same first name—but it only begins to scratch the surface.

He begins his impression of me. "Hi, this is Steve with the _____ Staffing Agency. I have your résumé here, and I see that you have a degree in psychology from Brown? Yes? Good. Well, right now we're actually working on an entry-level position..."

"You'll be doing some work with musicians, reconciling beefs, assassinating bitch-ass punks, tossing up fugazi motherfuckers..."

"Pistol-whipping snitches..."

"Gang-banging pussy of all different varieties..."

"And you'll present at the Source Awards."

But I grind by. I make my calls. I schedule my faceless résumé pawns for interviews that will likely lead nowhere.

The key to being a writer with an awful day job is finding time to surreptitiously craft that masterwork. In my case, I'm kicking around a few short stories, a new novel, and of course *This Book*, which I've brought with me by way of a notepad I keep in my desk. I craft much of the first two chapters during my lunch hour. Frequently, I find myself taking five-minute breaks between cold calls to jot notes to myself[30] while fervently wishing I had a better job. My existential dread usually goes away after I've had a few cups of coffee.

Besides free coffee, the job has two other perks:

1) The owner of the staffing agency, hereafter known as the "SoulSuck Agency," is a rock-solid feminist. By this, I mean he hires lots of women because a) he can pay them less and b)

---

30 Some of the notes from this period that for whatever reason will never make it into the book include:

"I'm from Ohio where Bob Evans is a food group and bestiality a competitive sport."

"Rupert Murdoch looks exactly like Emperor Palpatine from *Star Wars*. How has no one else noticed this?"

"I got this text from my friend: 'U r a lover sperm. i am a sexy donky... make me your whale!' What could that possibly mean?"

"The first time I heard about the concept of a blowjob, I thought to myself, 'Wait—then why do my parents make me wash my hands after I go to the bathroom?'"

"The film *Predator* is obviously an allegory for colonialism. The predator is basically a British aristocrat on vacation in Africa circa 1870."

they are nice to look at. Thus there are a large number of freshly minted college graduates with long legs and pretty faces who occupy most of my attention throughout the day.

2) Given perk #1, I quickly find I don't care about perk #2.

Perk #1 is a pretty good one. Twelve to fifteen times a day beautiful girls will streak by my desk, none of whom look to be more than two or three years out of college. With my Love Interest having moved to Boston, and both of us too poor to buy a plane ticket in the foreseeable future, I spend a lot of my time trying to match good-looking girls to names based on the list of phone extensions taped to my computer. This proves difficult because 75 percent of the names are female, and James and I have a hard time determining which girls we find attractive.

"You know, the one chick," he'll say. "With the dark hair. And the boobs."

"Dark complexion?"

"Yeah."

"Melissa?"

"No, Melissa's the old one that looks like Hulk Hogan."

"I thought that was Patti?"

"Patti has the freckles. The one that keeps calling you Brian."

"I thought she was talking to you."

"Why? My name's not Brian."

"Neither is mine."

"Do you think the chick with the boobs is hot or not?"

"Well, I'm not sure who you're talking about, but on general principle, I'd say yes."

In all seriousness, perk #2 is that at least I am employed, which is more than I can say for most of the people I spend my time with on the phone.

If you've led a mostly comfortable life and ever want to know what the sinking, nauseating sensation of economic desperation feels like, I suggest you join the staffing industry for a while. When I first began working, I thought to myself, *Okay, this is a somewhat noble calling. I'm helping people find work. Sure, it's not lobbying against polluters or teaching inner-city kids, but at least it's not evil.* Turns out, I am cured of that notion right-quick.

The more people I talk to, the more I hear the same stories again and again. While James works with customer service and office service applicants, I primarily talk to accountants, from non-degreed clerks to MBAs. Most of them tell me the same story: laid off due to downsizing or outsourcing. I talk to person after person whose position has been terminated and sent overseas (Brazil, India, South Korea) because someone there is willing to do it for a fraction of the salary.

"You better watch it," says one forlorn staff accountant. "As soon as they figure out how someone can do your job for two dollars a day, you'll be outta work, too."

I scoff at him. "No way. They would never figure out my filing system. I'm bulletproof."

My experiences with these people tend to reinforce my inherent mistrust of the unbridled globalized economy. All it takes is one look across my desk to where James sits to see that most of the jobs the SoulSuck Agency are trying to fill are customer service positions— jobs that a fourteen-year-old Chinese girl would have trouble doing from the Jilin province. It seems like eventually there will be only three types of jobs left in the U.S.: CEO, politician, and customer service representative.

My job is not to sympathize with the proletariat, however; it's to bring them in for an interview. At first, I learn how to white lie about the positions we're "working on" because my manager is constantly after me to schedule more and more people. This seems odd to a naïve, idealistic college grad like me because I'm constantly talking to people on the phone who say, "I just interviewed with the SoulSuck Agency. I came in because you guys told me you had a job and then I never heard from you again."

"Gosh golly jeezum pleezum, fellas! I don't get it," I say. "Why don't we just give this guy a job?"

I talk to a guy named Mike who says it best. After I give him my spiel about a senior accountant position we're working on in the western suburbs of Chicago, he stops me.

"So you guys are a staffing company?"

"A staffing and recruiting agency, yes."[31]

"So this is the thing where I come in, get interviewed by the twenty-two-year-old, and take the sixth-grade math test?"

This is exactly what will happen.

"Um…" I say in defeat.

"Right," says Mike. "I think I'll pass."

It doesn't occur to me until I've worked there for over a month, but the SoulSuck Agency and companies like it don't make money from the people looking for work; they make it from the companies who pay them to find employees. Thus the whole purpose of the interview process is fourfold: 1) to build a massive database of the unemployed to have at their disposal, 2) to find new employer contacts through the references interviewees are asked to bring in, 3) to find "leads," as in positions recently vacated by the schlubs they're interviewing, which they can fill and thereby make money, and 4) to place people in jobs they're overqualified for so that the companies employing them can pay those people less.

The SoulSuck Agency's interest in finding anyone anything other than temporary, benefits-free employment is equivalent to my interest in finding a magical talisman that keeps me safe from dinosaurs: sure, it would be nice to have, but I'm not about to break a sweat looking for one.

James frequently despairs at all this.

"It's okay, man," I tell him, holding up my notebook. "I'm

---

31 I add the "recruiting" and "agency" because they make the entire operation sound less like a snake oil sale.

surreptitiously crafting my masterwork when I should be making calls and scheduling interviews. I'm totally taking this place for at least twelve dollars a day."

"Dude, cool! I mostly read the *New York Times* online while I hold the phone to my ear and listen to the dial tone."

I scoff at this amateur-hour nonsense. "It's like Costanza in *Seinfeld*," I explain. "If the boss comes by, I just stare at my notebook real hard and look annoyed—like I have a lead on this awesome staff accountant but just can't rope her in. They love me here. Hell, I'll probably give up writing after they tap me to be VP of this motherfucker."

Eventually, I throw out my bag of tricks and white lies and just start telling people the truth, which is that if they're desperate and out of ideas, SoulSuck might be worth a try, but if not, don't waste the time.

Occasionally, after listening in on one of my calls and waiting for me to hang up, James will look to his right, look to his left, and then carefully place an imaginary conductor's cap on his head. He'll toot the imaginary train whistle and say, "Last call! All aboard! The Straight-Talk Express is now under way. Our conductor for the afternoon will be Steve Markley, and our first stop will be Telling-It-Like-It-Is-Ville. Population: You!"

His exuberant hilarity recedes only when he is tasked with recruiting people for an "Entry-Level Fundraising Position for a Nonprofit." While searching through the résumés of fresh grads—most of whom are young, idealistic, and looking for work in non-profit fundraising—James makes a call upstairs to the recruiters. He wants to find out a bit more about the position, so he has something to tell all these wonderful civic-minded kids who want to change the world. Only it turns out there is no such thing as an "Entry-Level Fundraising Position." The recruiters made up the job and posted it online to draw in smart, fresh grads for interviews.

"This is ridiculous," he says, lowering his head to his desk. "These people are so cool. This dude spent two years in the Peace Corps teaching illiterate kids to read in a third-world country and now I'm bringing him in to interview for a job that doesn't exist."

I shake my head. "You know, I thought it was strange. When I got the call from that girl saying she'd seen my résumé and would love to have me in for an interview, I thought to myself: 'Wow. I didn't think my résumé was that good. In fact, I thought it kinda made me look like an idiot, but this chick says she *loved* it. Said *everything looked great* and they *couldn't wait to meet me*.' I thought I must be something special and just didn't realize it."

I lean across my desk so that I can get good and close to James, who remains collapsed and defeated. "I guess I just never realized being full of shit was actually a marketable skill."

• • •

Regardless, I write.

I've completed the first two chapters of this book. I print them out, go through them line by line with a red pen like a cranky teacher; I eviscerate the prose. I chop and drag large blocks of text, drawing arrows, dipping into the margins, crowding in asterisked chunks of description or dialogue.

Yes, I may be a $10-per-hour temp by day, but by night I am Stephen Markley, Chicago-based freelance writer. This is what I put in my query letters as I shoot off short stories to literary journals and nonfiction pitches to magazines. This is what I put on my résumé in place of "ABCO Construction: Forklift and ZoomBoom operator."[32] And most importantly, this is what I tell girls in bars. I'm not sure if I fully believe those words yet myself—each time the phrase leaves my mouth, I have to shove it, kick it, and bite its little fingers so it will let go of the door jamb.

---

32 When it comes to that job, there are so many twisted remarks/bizarre anecdotes/ Marxist rants I could put into this footnote that I am completely paralyzed and thus will include none.

This is what I do, I tell myself. It's the truth: I write.

Writing falls somewhere between a chore and a narcotic. For as long as I can remember, I've tried to make a habit of sitting down at my computer for an hour a day, six days a week. There are days when I don't want to do it, naturally. I can hear my roommates playing video games or watching sports or drinking, and all I can think is how much better any of those activities would be. Yet I force myself. As Steven tells every one of his classes, the most important part of being a writer is "Apply Ass to Chair." There is no substitute.

Each night I start slowly, as I did when I began this paragraph. This is often how it works: you sit down to write something specific, but you can't get your head around it, so it frustrates you. It feels like you're trying to open a can of soup while wearing boxing gloves. I long ago learned that you have two choices: fight through it or try something else.

You can't always sit down and spew beautiful, insightful prose, but if you force yourself to write every day, eventually you'll stumble upon something worthwhile. And that feeling—I can't even describe it except to say that it's better than any drug I've ever taken.[33] No drug can duplicate that sensation of absolute mastery of another world. When I'm on one of those streaks, I can almost feel a physical power. Basketball players describe it as "being in the zone." Witness Michael Jordan's performance in Game One of the 1992 NBA finals against my beloved Portland Trail Blazers. He scored fifty-some points, draining threes like he was tossing in lay-ups. Or LeBron James in Game Five of the 2007 Eastern Conference finals when he scored Cleveland's final twenty-five points to beat the Detroit Pistons single-handedly in overtime.

---

33 And of course at this point some drug-addict friend of mine will inevitably claim this to be ridiculous and launch into a diatribe about how high you can get huffing the fumes of burned plastic shower liners. This is the problem with drug aficionados: They are all thoroughly obnoxious because each one thinks he is the first person to have figured out that damaging brain cells can be fun.

Now maybe I've never had a Michael Jordanesque zone while writing,[34] but I know what it feels like to get on a roll, to get to that point where I can't type fast enough to keep up with my thoughts. I've discovered my life revolves around chasing this wired sensation. Everything I do is based around the fact that I want to be a published, self-supporting writer so that I can spend all my days tracking this feeling like a bloodhound on the trail of an escaped convict.

Nothing has changed. I'm in Chicago now, but the only difference is that instead of writing at a desk, I write on a foldout lawn chair from Fifth Third Bank. I work steadily. I have short stories. I have columns. I have a new novel. I have my travel memoir from the previous year. And of course, I have this: *Publish This Book*—a project so vague, so unhinged, so cathartic that it consumes me even as it lends me a wicked, wild freedom.

The truth is I have no idea what I'm onto here other than a grasping, experimental thoughtfuck on every front.

---

34 What's the literary equivalent of that? A Baldwin zone? A Vonnegut zone? Why is it that sports analogies are inherently superior to all others in every facet of life?

FOUR

The Parts of This Book that Belong in the Toilet

By fall, the first two chapters of my book have come together nicely, and two chapters are all you need to submit a book to an agent. They feel more or less complete, which means I need two things: 1) a book contract and 2) a thick-necked bodyguard to keep the screaming, heaving-breasted, sleek-thighed, Jolie-lipped groupies from assaulting me at bookstore readings.

No, what I really need is a proposal to go along with my two chapters, but before that I will need some shred of a notion of a clue about what the rest of this book will have between the covers. Because in order to write any more of the book, I'm going to need to actually *get* an agent, so I can *publish* the book, because after all, *that* is the rest of the book. The next part of the book will *have* to be about me finding an agent or there will *never be* any book (emphasis added for *emphasis*).

However, even this is putting the job before the urine test. What I really need is an outside opinion; I need eyes on the first two chapters because of course I think they are entertaining and profound, but almost every writer thinks everything he or she writes is entertaining and profound. I need to see if anyone agrees.

I consider giving the first two chapters to James, who is something of a writer himself. Employing a writing style similar to a homeless man haranguing passers-by on a street corner, he mostly rails against the absurdity of organized religion. This is all well and good, but the problem is that James knows me, which would add all sorts of baggage to the feedback process.

I go in search of a writing group: like-minded individuals also trying to break through the surface into the daylight of authorship. This leads me to craigslist, which my roommate Elliott uses to procure more or less everything he owns, from free furniture, to vinyl records, to movie projectors, to hot tubs—everything except casual sex.[35]

"Fuzzy, man, craigslist is awesome," he tells me when I ask him about finding a writing group.

Sure enough, within days I stumble upon the Thousand Fibers writing group. I head north to meet them in a coffee shop in upper Lakeview on a chilly Wednesday night. This group is just coming together, so of course no one knows what anyone looks like, but pretty soon we begin to peg each other: the nervous-looking youths walking around with heavy bags and a degree of uncertainty that they should even exist let alone be in this coffee shop. We look uncomfortable in our skin even as we order coffee and worry that it's too late to be drinking caffeine. We are on the bottom rungs of the ladder for white, middle-class kids trying to make a go in the real world because we did not go into finance, and—as we slide into uncomfortable hard-back chairs at a table sticky with spilled latte residue—it is likely most of us have not had as much sex as we figured we would get to at this age.

Two girls sit together and appear to be looking around for more souls, so I approach them. "Suzanne?" I ask one with dark hair and hip glasses.

This is indeed Suzanne, along with Katie. We sit and begin to get acquainted. Slowly the other group members trickle in. A short girl with closely cropped brown hair that has a streak of gray running

---

35   The weirdest part of craigslist is that people now use it to have casual sex with strangers. This seems like a particularly poor idea, seeing as how it's kind of like sleeping with someone you meet at a garage sale by way of reasoning, "Well, she did come to this garage sale, too."

through the side introduces herself as Mary. Another girl enters, Bridget, with full lips and blonde hair.

Oh dear God, I think, as the group begins to discuss what kind of writing we do, our jobs, our schools, our pasts, our futures, *this is going to be an all-chick writing group, isn't it?*

Suzanne suggests we name the best book we've read recently. Most of the girls say something in the vein of Marilynne Robinson's *Gilead*.

"Robert Stone," I say when it's my turn. "*Dog Soldiers*."

None of them have heard of this book (which incidentally is fantastic and has a scene where the protagonist has his ear burned on a hot plate).

The meeting concludes, and we all agree to submit a short piece of our writing for the group to read and critique at the next meeting. As I trudge back to the El with my collar flipped up and bitter shrieks of wind stinging my bare ears, I wonder if I should return or send them a polite email saying I don't have time to be in the group. Maybe it makes me a chauvinist to think so, but I have doubts that this group of girls will "get" me. In case the first three chapters of this book haven't made it apparent, my writing is something of an acquired taste, and I worry that I will submit a story about the nature of violence and get back comments that say, *Is this violence really necessary?*

• • •

These fears are not unfounded and serve to remind me about both the promise and peril of the so-called "writer's workshop."

Generally, a workshop consists of a small group of writers who take turns sharing pieces of their work. The group reads it, and then muzzles the writer while they tell him or her what they liked about the piece and what needs work.

This sounds simple enough, but it can be a grueling, cutthroat little endeavor. A workshop can quite easily degenerate into a blood-soaked Christians versus the Lions in the Colosseum kind of deal: egos stabbing and slashing and spearing, egos mauling, shredding flesh, bleeding out in the dirt. It's shocking how easy it is to become annoyed when someone critiques your work and does not immediately recognize it as unadulterated genius that puts past chroniclers of the American Story like Hemingway, Cheever, and O'Conner to shame.

In school I took a class with a visiting professor who quite clearly did not care what the hell his students did, said, or advised. We met in this bunker of a room on the eastern edge of campus, and I felt like reaching for the armor and spear every time I went to class. The egos couldn't be refereed, and because the class was without rules or guidelines, often you'd find kids arguing how good their stories were, and why others were wrong. To say the least, it was an unproductive semester.

On the flipside, sometimes you end up in workshops with people like Ryan.

I met Ryan in a workshop with one of my favorite professors, Margaret, during my senior year. Ryan looked like a misanthrope, with stringy, unkempt black hair, a wiry frame, and a beard he grew in semi-regularly only to shave and cause himself to look about twelve years old.[36] Like most misanthropes, Ryan was pretty brilliant, but to his credit, he was also funny and interesting. I don't want to sound like I'm in love with the guy, but I knew I could check the "One Less Person in the World Who Makes Me Want to Bludgeon My Head Against the Wall" box after he critiqued my story.

The details aren't super-important, but let's just say I turned a story into Margaret's class that I was 85 percent happy with. There was something wrong with the main character, though: a father who had lost his son. I couldn't get a clear picture of him, and it was fucking up the story.

While commenting on the story and being overwhelmingly complimentary, Ryan—head lackadaisically lying against the wall behind his desk, teeth tormenting the cap of a pen, one hand tugging at

---

36   Actually, he looks a lot like the actor Jeremy Davies (*Saving Private Ryan*).

the gnarly strands of his beard—said, "Except we can't see the dad. That's a problem. But I picture him having a beard and being able to kick the shit out of most anyone."

My eyes must have bulged a bit. Ryan was not just right, but exactly, perfectly, 100 percent, eerily right. This character was a barrel-chested fifty-year-old who did look like he could kick the shit out of most anyone—like a Hell's Angel who went into academia instead of prison. Oh, and he sure as hell did have a beard.

And that's why writers go to workshops. After a point, you can't edit your own story anymore. You need those fresh eyes. You need your ego bruised, and you must keep yourself hungry by having people tell you that you're not as good as you think you are. And often the best of them can get inside your story and tell you things you should already know but haven't figured out yet.

It's not out of the question that this all-girl writers group can do that, so I suck it up and force myself to continue attending the meetings. As with most things in life, I soon realize I was quick to judge and entirely wrong about these girls.[37] Over the course of the next few months, as we get into each other's writing, I find each of them more interesting and our meetings become enjoyable diversions from life's day-to-day grind. Naturally these girls are not my ideal audience. The bulk of the stories and nonfiction pieces I've submitted are chock-full of violence, sex, and extremely foul language (who would've thought?), and as I predicted, the girls spend large swaths of our group time wondering aloud if I'm a sociopath and if my story's cocaine-addicted preacher really had to molest his grandmother with a spatula.[38] On the other hand, sometimes it's good

---

37 Other instances when I was quick to judge and entirely wrong: the inevitability of a John Kerry presidency, the superiority of Domino's Pizza, the physical attractiveness of Britney Spears, and the brilliance of the movie *Sphere* (this is not a complete list, but includes the worst offenses).

38 I promise that I have not written a story where a cocaine-addicted preacher molests his grandmother with a spatula. It's actually a novel.

to have a combative audience. It helps you ferret out what works and what doesn't, what truly has the power to touch, shock, offend, upend, or galvanize and what is simply extraneous nonsense.

I also come to respect each of them based on her own particular contribution to the group. Let's try another helpful, easy-to-reference list.

- **Suzanne:** Nominally the leader of the group—the ringmaster, if you will—Suzanne is a liberal arts major composite character. This is not to say she herself is a composite character, but as a human being, she pretty much hits all the bases: creative writer, intellectual-looking hipster glasses, applying for a masters from the University of Chicago in liberal studies or human studies or humanities studies or some degree where you just take a slew of English classes and reference Derrida as often as possible. Suzanne turns in stories that describe the biological functions of dragonflies and where the dead mother tells stories of magical dragonflies and then later the daughter wakes up in the middle of a forest with more dragonflies. Suzanne will likely be the most successful literary writer I know.

- **Katie:** Speaks slowly, as if every word coming from her mouth is its own new thought that is still in the process of occurring to her. Katie graduated from Ohio University with Suzanne, which I guess makes both of them my rivals (kids from the Mid-Atlantic Conference do not really care about rivalries). With long blonde hair and a boyfriend in a band, Katie casts herself against type by randomly saying irreverent yet fascinat-ing things. For instance, she once says, "I really like poetry… but only when I'm a little drunk." This is perhaps the smartest statement ever made about poetry. In addition to her fiction pur-suits, Katie is hard at work writing the biography of an elderly couple. The two seniors are scientists who felt their lives were interesting enough to merit a biography, which they hired Katie to write. This makes her the luckiest person I know because her job is to sit around all day in her pajamas and write.

- **Bridget:** Would look more at home at some kind of high-end sorority function, yet Bridget proves herself a very talented writer when she turns in a story about a high school boy with a growing crush on a classmate. Her crisp prose and economic manner of storytelling reminds me of how I would attack the same subject. When I write my comments on the story, I include a note that I think she should send the story out to literary magazines to see what kind of responses she can get. At the next meeting she says, "Yeah, I think I'll send it to *The Alaska Quarterly* and once they reject me, I have a list of three others." It heartens me that both Bridget's writing and attitude toward writing remind me of my own. An editor for a children's book publisher, she comments to me that she's having trouble seeing beyond the next year and her job. "People talk about having a five-year plan," she says. "I would settle for a 'next year' plan." I picture Bridget as a rather effective character in a sitcom, in that she's very funny but not in a loud way. She tells us about a date she went on with a guy who could not name either a book he had read recently or a "favorite" book—which, unless you're illiterate, is like not being able to name a favorite food item. "Just say something," says Bridget. "Anything. It doesn't matter."

- **Mary:** Works with nuns, was raised Catholic, and defends herself with heart when I tease her for having a repressed upbringing. We instantly bond over a shared affinity for *The Economist*, because we both read it, love it, and know that it is overbearingly self-important. Or as Mary puts it in a story she hands us: "*The Economist* is an asshole." Short and spunky with eyes that always seem as if they are on the verge of exiting her skull, they open so wide, Mary has a class clown streak as evident as the thin gray wisp running the length of her short, spiky hair. She does imitations of her dad that sometimes involve him yelling about Bill Walton on the UCLA Bruins. It would be an outright lie if I told you that Mary was not the one I was most afraid of accidentally making out with.

More than anything, the girls and I begin to fit together because we recognize each other as the same hopeless creatures. We want to be writers, and we hate that it's so goddamn hard, so frustrating, and that all of our friends who don't care to be writers simply cannot understand the urgency we live with. They turn in stories that ring true, that make this need evident and tangible in their eyes.

It's not that I decide these girls *must* read this book, but I need *someone* to read it, and over the course of a few months with each other, I've decided that if I don't exactly trust them, then what I feel is at least close to trust: maybe trust's first cousin who's chronically unemployed and high all the time. I send them the first two chapters of this book, and we set up a meeting to discuss.

At first, I was just going to write this as another scene, but I was again having trouble re-creating dialogue faithfully.[39] Also, there is the problem that Mary did not technically show up to the meeting in this scene and handed me her comments later. This creates all sorts of narrative problems, so rather than go through the scene faithfully as it occurred, I will use a composite of my notes to create a minimalist play.

---

39   An example: "Hey, Katie," says Bridget. "Do you want to forget these book chapters and just make out?"

"God, yes," Katie replies. "but first—if you had to hazard a guess—how breathtaking would Steve's penis be?"

"At least," adds Suzanne, "as long as my arm and as aesthetically pleasing as a daffodil."

Publish This Book: A Critique
A One-Act Play

By Stephen Markley

BRITISH NARRATOR

[Stands off to the side of dark stage, chewing on unlit pipe]

The setting is a middle-of-the-road Mexican restaurant in the Lincoln Park neighborhood of Chicago, Illinois, USA. The characters include the visible: the protagonist, Stephen, sits silently and eats cheese and bean nachos. Surrounding him are Suzanne, Katie, and Bridget. Not visible to the group is Mary, who sits stage-left shaving a dead rat. Invisible even to the already invisible Mary are Stephen's Ego, and of course, me, your narrator, who looks and sounds like a great British stage actor, probably Sir Ian McKellen. For now, suffice it to say, the group is unsure of this new unwieldy idea and how to critique such a bizarre piece. As the meeting begins, they are slow to comment. Mary shaves the rat and looks catatonically into the distance.

STEPHEN

[Sitting at table, stage light comes up illuminating others]

Don't everyone rush to heap the praise at once. Save something nice to say about the rest of literature.

SUZANNE

I like the idea. My question is where do you put this in the bookstore? In the writing section? What genre is this?

NARRATOR, PROBABLY SIR IAN MCKELLEN

Stephen does not keep his Ego locked in the basement where he keeps his Id. His Ego does attend anger management classes every once in a while, but these are not particularly effective.

STEPHEN'S EGO
[While dealing himself a hand of blackjack]
  Hold up—what's this bitch talking about?

KATIE
  I don't think it can go in the writing section.
[Flips pages, scans prose]
  It's not about how to get a book published. At least, that's
not what I saw it as.

BRIDGET
  Maybe pop culture? Have you read Dave Eggers? Or Chuck
Klosterman?

KATIE
  Or Tucker Max?

STEPHEN
  Nope.

NARRATOR, MAYBE SIR ANTHONY HOPKINS
[Sipping Earl Grey tea, looking discontentedly into distance]
  This is important, and we will get to these men later in
this epic tome. For now, we will trust that Stephen tells us
the truth, although his Ego stands nearby, having given up
his game of blackjack. He eyes the table with the bloodthirsty
hunger of a starving cannibal.

KATIE
  It's not about publishing. I mean, that's what it's about
on the surface, but really it's about you, your life. It's a
memoir, but "memoir" is kind of a poofy word. This is
not that kind of memoir.

SUZANNE

I just think—

[Pauses to flip through pages. Stephen's Ego stands poised invisibly by her side, swinging a golf club—a nine iron—in one hand like a pendulum]

I'm not sure who would be the audience for this. Some of the stuff in here is just so offensive.

STEPHEN'S EGO

[Swinging nine iron erratically through the air, flailing like he's trying to bust open an invisible piñata, shrieking]

Offensive? Offensive!

STEPHEN

[Aside, to his Ego]

It's cool, man. Be cool.

STEPHEN'S EGO

[Smacking golf club against ground until the head snaps off]

Fuck that! Fuck that shit! Next story I write's gonna be about throwing your daddy down a flight of stairs, honey.

BRIDGET

I agree. It's a lot of frat-boy humor, and I think that's kind of a crutch for you.

STEPHEN'S EGO

Frat boy? Aw bitch, I know you did not just call me—

NARRATOR, PERHAPS PETER O'TOOLE

[Eating a crumpet]

As his Ego lunges toward poor, sweet Bridget with the broken end of a nine iron aimed at her neck, Stephen quickly grabs his Ego and wrestles it to the ground, locking into a furious, high-stakes match of strength and stamina. The girls continue on unaware.

KATIE

Yeah, sure, but I think that makes it real. I think that's the world he lives in and this kind of thing is just more or less being real. He's a twentysomething guy and this is what being a twentysomething guy is about. It reflects a certain culture, and even if someone doesn't understand that culture that doesn't make it irrelevant.

BRIDGET

Right, okay, but is the only way for him to get that point about twentysomething guys across to make anal rape jokes?

STEPHEN'S EGO
[Struggling to scream as Stephen attempts to silence him with his palm]
I win, bitch! I win—

NARRATOR, POSSIBLY KENNETH BRANAGH
[In full costume from the film Hamlet]
Indeed, Stephen's Ego does win for making sweet, kind Bridget discuss anal intercourse humor in a serious literary setting.

KATIE

No, but that's not all that's here. I agree that parts of the first two chapters get repetitive, but I think once he finds what's driving this, what gives it forward motion, he's going to start putting himself out there. And honestly, how many twentysomething guys have you ever known who can put themselves out there like this? Even Eggers and Klosterman wrote what they did years after the fact. Not right while they were living it.

BRIDGET
[Quoting from the manuscript]
"I don't generally probe my testicles, except recreationally."

SUZANNE
I don't know. Is there enough here to really sustain a book?

BRIDGET
[Quoting from the manuscript]
"And Dave says, 'Yeah, well I fucked your girlfriend, you piece of shit. It was right after your mom died, too. Probably while you were at the funeral.'"

KATIE
I think there is enough. As long as he expands it. As long as he gets into his life. I think some of the most interesting passages are of him interacting with other people, and I feel like there will be more of that as the book progresses.

BRIDGET
But then why does it have to be about the crap he took in the morning?

KATIE
Well, I don't think that's all it's about. That's misdirection. But also the crap he took in the morning makes it real.

SUZANNE
But how can you sustain the concept?

KATIE
What I think is good about this idea—and I do want to read more of it as it comes along—is that it's completely transparent.

You talk about how glamorized the word "writer" is, but the truth of it is that being a writer is hard and it is lonely. To tell you the truth, I've started telling people I'm a glass-blower because I don't want all those associations anymore. This is what it is to be a writer and not have your face on a book jacket, to not even have a name you can find on Amazon.com. And that's where I think you'll find out what this book is about.

STEPHEN'S EGO
[Head popping up from Stephen's grip]
Fuck yeah, Katie, you smart-as-Einstein-on-crack mother-fucker! Finally we ain't just hearing gibberish! Finally one of these broads is talking some fuckslopping sense! Finally we got ourselves an actual goddamn—

NARRATOR, GREG KINNEAR DOING A BRITISH ACCENT
In a vicious move, Stephen grabs his Ego by the hair and forces his face into an imaginary bathtub of the mind where he proceeds to hold his Ego's face in the water even as he chokes and sputters, and finally just as his Ego's thrashing has begun to ebb, just as he's about to allow the bathwater to fill his lungs, Stephen throws him onto the tile floor where he coughs, chokes, and finally shuts up as he passes out. Stephen thanks the girls and collects their copies of his first chapters. Mary finishes shaving the rat, washes it with soap and water, and pats it dry with a towel.

THE END

At home with the girls' notes, I spread the four critiques on my lap. I read over the comments carefully. I note places where the voice grew too intense, too prickish, too utterly self-indulgent. Bridget has been the harshest, even listing a whole slew of what she calls "parts of this book that belong in the toilet," a phrase she took from the first chapter. I am surprised by how strongly she objected to some of it, and at one point in her notes, she wrote, "Stephen, you're better than this."

"Gee thanks, Mom," I say to the comment, knowing that in this particular case she is 100 percent For Sure right.

Still, these girls aren't getting away scot-free after forcing me to almost drown my Ego, and while I sit on my Throne of Genius with their comments, I know how I will get back at them by writing about this experience.[40]

But that's not the point.[41]

The point[42] is that this is all exactly what I needed.

Like Katie said, writing can be a lonesome, solitary endeavor. Even if I resented Bridget for not clasping her hands in prayer, wonder, and awe at the story about my sore testicle, her critique served a valuable purpose. I needed this grounding, this chiding of my most obvious excesses. With my Ego out of the way, staring at the pages now alone in my room, what I think of as Puritan badgering has helped me tap into something. I can feel the ideas percolating. I feel as if now I can get these chapters to more closely resemble what I want to express without Bridget's so-called crutch.[43]

---

40   And including dialogue where they speak glowingly of my penis.

41   Rarely do I say anything that is.

42   Oop, here we go!

43   And yes, the first and second chapters are a compromise between elements of the most vile, offensive content, some of the worst narcissism, and an acknowledgment that there is more to this search for validation. It's obviously not just about becoming a published author—how could it be? It's about a fire that simmers in you, a beast that eats you from the inside out. It's the reason distance runners slash years off their lives by training to run unreasonable lengths. It's the reason politicians lie, cheat, and steal to win elections, justifying each step as a necessary evil. It's the reason God made us in His image in the first place: It's because sometimes when you want something badly enough, it changes the way your soul works—sometimes for the worse, and sometimes for the better. And that, you see, is what I needed to hint at in those first two chapters. This was a difficult balance to strike, as I only have two settings: "Vile, Offensive, and Narcissistic" and "Off."

It took me a long time before I was comfortable calling myself a "writer." Until I was a sophomore in college, I never told anyone—friends, family, girlfriends—that I wanted to be a writer. I kept this secret guarded, not because I was ashamed but because I felt like if I let even one person in on my secret, the rest of the world would come streaming through the crack and drown it. This dream was small and fragile and I thought if I let anyone get a hold of it, surely it would wither and die the way a captured firefly will lose oxygen and suffocate if a child forgets to poke holes in the lid of the jar.

And you wonder why writers become so fucked up—why they drink and shoot heroin and abuse their families and walk into rivers with rocks in their clothes. You really can only spend so much time with your own thoughts. You reach a point where you wonder if anything you have written is of any value at all to anyone other than yourself. You need a community who understands this. You need people who are okay with making themselves vulnerable. Sure, you want validation and you want to have your ego stroked a bit, but you know that's not why you're there, why you hand your writing out only to have it marred by other people's pens. You need that honest assessment, not of the world you believe in but the one that exists on the page.

It's fairly simple math when you break it down, and this is true for anyone in the "arts" (and I do hate that vague, generalized word): you, the artist, want people to like your shit. Sure, it's cool if a few people don't like your shit. Such is the way of things. But you need at least *a few* people to like it. Even Michael Bay has people who like his shit. You need someone other than yourself to give your piece of art a once-over, kick the tires, check under the hood and say, "All right. This has value. This deserves to exist."

In fact, if this book were ever to be published, all the critical acclaim I'd need would be simple, and the publisher would put it on the back of the jacket in stark, bold lettering:

"Yeah, sure. This deserves to exist."
—Michiko Kakutani, *New York Times*

So Ms. Kakutani, I believe the ball is now in your court.

FIVE

Nick Hornby Must Be in This Book

As I revise those first two chapters, I simultaneously begin the third and fourth. This puts me and the book in a strange state of limbo—like two men trying to decipher interrelated treasure maps tattooed on each other's backs, spinning and spinning, following and following, neither man able to catch a sufficient glimpse. Furthermore, as I begin the third chapter—a description of my somewhat reckless move to Chicago—I have to decide what role my Love Interest will play, for in recent weeks the distance between us, and the fractured nature of our relationship, has knifed at me. I put her in the flow of the story, I take her out, I put her in, I take her out. I finally decide to leave her in.

On top of all this vacillating, I begin to think about my query letter and proposal as well as how to draft a chapter outline for a book that depends on unknown future events. I do most of this while sitting at my desk at the SoulSuck Agency, pretty girls streaking by every five minutes and demanding my attention. The thing is, I've written queries before: by-the-book, down-the-line professional queries as Steven taught in his classes at Miami. Yet I know for this book, the query must be… different. It cannot just be attention-grabbing; it must actively subvert the rules.

While I think of how to write that truly slam-bang query letter, a few minor successes manage to depress me. How can success depress you?

First, an article I wrote appears in the western journal *Weber Studies*. I spent the first leg of my Epic Road Trip working in the Tetons and researching an article on the tenth anniversary of the National Park Service's re-introduction of the gray wolf to Yellowstone. Since then, the wolf has continued to be a lightning rod in the American West, and I found the politics surrounding the animal fascinating. For three months, I interviewed wolf experts, park personnel, ranchers, and environmentalists while crafting the piece. After numerous rejections, I gave up, only to get a letter from *Weber Studies*, approximately six months after I'd sent them the article, saying they wanted to publish it. Roughly four months after that, it finally appears and I get my copy in the mail. It's satisfying at first: my moppy head in a picture taken at the peak of the Cascade trail in Wyoming next to large chunks of words I'd penned.

Around the same time, I land an assignment for a Texas newspaper called *The Populist Progressive*. I have this crazy notion that Barack Obama might upset Hillary Clinton in the Iowa caucuses based on a large youth vote that will overwhelmingly support him.[44] I talk to a slew of young Obama supporters, most of whom seem resigned to Clinton thrashing him. The piece appears on the paper's front page next to what might be one of the worst political cartoons of all time (it features Obama on a surfboard in swimming trunks riding a wave of cheering young people and appears to have been drawn in crayon; this next to the not-sanctioned-by-the-author headline "Obama Rides the Youth Tide").

These mild successes buoy me for about five seconds before undebatable realities kick in: a combined four months of work has netted me $250. *Weber's* is a respectable but obscure western journal, and the *Populist Progressive* appears to be under the editorial control of

---

44 I'm sure it helped that in the query I used my potent phrase "I'm a Chicago-based freelance writer," as if I had some kind of penetrating insight into the machinations of the Obama campaign simply because I called unemployed accounts payable clerks from the same city.

MoveOn.org's third grade classroom. I feel farther removed from my dream than ever. Frustrated, I begin to understand what Margaret meant in her email about success. So this is how it works, huh? You just keep redefining the word over and over again until you've chased it across the deserts and oceans and moons without ever really getting close.

My roommates and I throw a party in our house, during which a college friend picks up *Weber Studies* to read my article. "I like how even in your straightforward work," she says, "you can still tell Steve Markley wrote this." She begins quoting, "'In 1973, the wolf was finally given protected status thanks to the Endangered Species Act and its bleeding-heart, environmentalist champion, none other than Richard Nixon.' I love it."

"I think you're the first person besides my mom to read that far."

"That was on the first page."

"Oh, I know."

Meanwhile, my work at *RedEye* is not going much better. Before beginning, I envisioned pitching any number of ideas, my byline crawling across the pages with environmental, social, and politically active journalism. Immediately, I discover that the *RedEye* editors have almost no interest in most of my story pitches. In fact, when I approach my moon-faced editor to tell him that Bruce Springsteen is coming out with a new album and that I have more expertise on this subject than anyone on the planet except for possibly Bruce Springsteen,[45] he gives me a puzzled look.

"I'm not sure he's really in our age range," he says, as if I just suggested we do a cover story on the abacus ("Counting Just Got Crazy!").

"You sure?" I say. "I think lots of younger people dig Springsteen."

---

45 Quick, Bruce: Name the lyric that the song "Maria's Bed" from 2006's *Devils and Dust* shares with "Further On Up the Road" from 2002's *The Rising*... Can't recall? Nope? It makes you wonder which of us should really be the legendary rock icon, doesn't it?

He folds his hands behind his head and stares at me thoughtfully. "I'll think about it, sure... Hey, did you get in touch with the Texas Shine Globalism yet?"

Yes, writing for *RedEye* is like dating a jaw-droppingly sexy girl who talks exclusively about MTV reality programming and won't let you touch her private parts. In the aftermath of hiring me, *RedEye* runs cover stories on the following topics:

How it sucks to live in an apartment above a bar.

How yoga can cause injuries.

Why it's not socially acceptable to cry in public.

What it's like to be young and live with your mom.

I find myself ranting to James during our lunch break at SoulSuck as we negotiate how to get the cheapest, most filling meal for four bucks at Corner Bakery. "Keep in mind," I tell him, "these were not sidebars or blurbs. They ran on the cover. Now maybe these are topics people are interested in, but I refuse to accept that in a time of unprecedented government infringement on basic civil liberties, in a time of war, genocide, and radical religious terrorism, in a time of uncertainty and fear, in a time of deadened thought and bland conformity, in a time when pop culture roars with importance and the issues of the day are clouded by obfuscation, in a time when we as a country need information and debate and courage, what social, political, or economic relevance does any of this nonsense have? How can an editor of even a free daily justify this abject deadening of thought? You want crying in public? Every time I see the cover of *RedEye*, I'm close."

James looks up from the book he's reading while we stand in line, Joyce's *Portrait of the Artist as a Young Man*. He tilts his head and smiles. "Dude, you're so cute. Let's just kiss and see what happens."

Of course, I know I'm being unfair to *RedEye* and the opportunity it represents. It's the most widely circulated paper in Chicago, picked up by thousands of commuters on their way to work, so I disregard my qualms and turn in stories on Beyoncé falling down some stairs and the annual Chicago Air and Water show.[46]

Getting my first column into print is a hurdle as well. My young female editor cuts almost everything out of the first draft I send her. I think the only words left were "the," "at," and "Keynesian." Gone were all semi-lewd jokes, references to the instability in Pakistan, and my patented journalistic style of desperately asking people to like me for debasing myself in print.[47]

After going back and forth for several weeks, an innocuous version of what I sent her finally appears in the seldom-read weekend edition. In case you're interested, my female editor gave it the title of "Caught between antics and adulthood," and it went like this:

I'm too old to be fooling around with a woman while still wearing socks, but before I explain that, let me give you some background.

After graduating from college, I spent the better part of a year wandering: Wyoming, Vancouver, Oregon, L.A., Arizona, Texas, New Orleans. Eventually, when I ran out of money, I decided to move to Chicago—not for any particular reason, but simply because I felt that moving to Chicago was an adult thing to do. Previously, the most adult thing I had done was to cut the retort "That's what she said" out of my vocabulary (at least during first dates and funerals).

I felt like I needed to grow up, and I guess I thought living in a big city, taking the train to work every day, and wearing a tie would somehow act as a catalyst to adulthood. I would leapfrog over any growing pains and quickly find myself a true grown-up rather than an over-stimulated, foul-mouthed adolescent whose goals in life revolve entirely around alcohol and women.

---

46 I'm not a sell-out, although I'm sure a younger version of myself would think so. However, my younger self probably didn't realize that the term "selling out" is different from "getting actual money for writing," which I'm sure he would have thought was pretty cool—right up there with the feature film *Men in Black* and touching a boob.

47 I like to think of it as the literary equivalent of "Dance, monkey! Dance!"

In my short time as a freshly minted Chicagoan, however, I have not advanced one iota further into adulthood and have probably regressed a whole bunch.

This is partly because of my living situation, which involves five single guys crammed into a dumpy house in central Lakeview. This is the kind of house where instead of cleaning the mildew on the shower curtain, you simply give it a name and consider it a domesticated pet. It's the kind of house where you can walk downstairs at 4 a.m. and find a dude playing Guitar Hero in his underwear with an open beer and a bowl of cereal nearby.

This kind of adultolescence seems fairly typical of the young, urban college graduate suddenly thrust into the "real" world.

As a matter of fact, I bet there are a few of you who are familiar with the notion I carry that I am a complete phony playing dress-up in a world of people who know what they're doing.

Every weekday I find myself on the Brown Line trying to look professional while passing the time by ranking my fellow passengers in terms of do-ability and wondering what the hell a "portfolio" is and why it must be "diversified."

So how does one become an adult? From what I can determine, adulthood will occur sometime around the time when my gut becomes just big enough that I decide to marry the woman I'm seeing at the time, before she figures out that I'm about to completely let myself go. This, of course, will mean maturing more out of fear than genuine emotional and philosophical development.

The entire process of going from a hedonistic, sex-crazed adolescent to a serious, contemplative adult—who knows more about the stock market than 2Pac lyrics and no longer considers a bare mattress on the floor an appropriate place to take a lady for a date— remains a complete, gaping mystery to me, as it does many of us.

Which brings me to the socks. This is pretty much the only simple, one-step, surefire method to feeling more mature. When fooling around with the opposite (or same) sex, take your socks off. There is nothing that reeks more of furtive, unsatisfying college-age sexual activity than advancing past first base with your socks on.

This is the one facet of our lives over which we all have complete control. If, like me, you're still at the beginning of your journey to maturity and responsibility, you can take solace in the baby steps, in hard-won accomplishments, however minor they may be. There is a reward, even in something so small.

Which, I'm ashamed to say, is totally what she said.

Obviously, I'm proud enough of this column to include it here, but the process of getting it into print was so arduous that the victory feels slight. Consolation comes from an acquaintance who mentions that not only did he read the column and enjoy it but that he spotted a guy in his office who had cut it out, highlighted certain sections, and pinned it above his desk. I can only assume that the image of a dude playing Guitar Hero at four in the morning while eating cereal and drinking beer resonates with the members of my generation.

The topics of future columns include text-messaging ("It's so dumb!"), video games ("They're so cool!"), and meditation ("It's so weird!").

Maybe it's not what I envisioned, sure, but it's writing all the same. After all, there is my name in print. There is my byline and my picture. There are words that came straight from my mind and into the minds of at least a few thousand readers. I'm not *not* a writer, I reason. A not-a-writer certainly couldn't say, "Well, I publish columns and articles in a major Chicago paper, but I'm not a writer." That would be a bald-faced lie.

"Okay," I say to myself after seeing that first column below my name and gritty mug, "It's not *not* a start."

• • •

Then, out of the blue, my moon-faced editor asks me if I like the author Nick Hornby.

I hate it when people phrase questions about your opinions in this open-ended way. It always feels like a trap, like if you say the wrong answer, then a crowd of your best friends and the people you most admire, living and dead, will burst out of closets and manhole covers aghast, laughing and ridiculing you.[48]

"Yeah, he's... cool," I finish, wishing I'd hedged my bets a bit more.

"Would you want to interview him? He's coming to Chicago to promote his new book."

Suddenly, I fucking love Nick Hornby.

"Yes, yes, yesyesyesyes," I say. "He's my favorite. Aw, I love Nick Hornby! *High Fidelity*! Awesome! And that other one... that he wrote. Yeah. Love him. Huge fan."

Obviously, this is a lie. It's not that I don't like Nick Hornby, but I've definitely never read any of his books. I think I might have seen the movie version of *High Fidelity* when I was in high school, but if I recall, the DVD skipped at the end, and I didn't finish it. My entire life is based on specious premises like this.

Weeks earlier, however, I had decided on a new tactic that might help me sell my book: put famous people in it. If I interview famous authors, agents and editors might then look at this project and say, "Well, this kid kinda freaks my shit out, but maybe it would be cool to hear what Toni Morrison has to say about the craft of writing."[49]

Of course, I don't actually know any writers of any level of fame at all, but I viewed this as overwhelmingly inconsequential.

---

48 Once on a date, the TV show *The X-Files* came up, and the girl asked me if I had watched it, but she did so in such a way that I could tell my answer was important. I *had* watched the show religiously until David Duchovny left, but this felt like the wrong answer. I basically ended up saying both that I had watched the show yet never seen it and then hammered out a lame correction where I said I had probably seen *every other* episode, but not the series as a whole. After stumbling through this nineteen-minute explanation, my penis sighed and resigned itself to at least another week of inactivity.

49 Toni Morrison declined to be interviewed for this book. In fact, I think they would have taken away her Pulitzer if she had agreed to an interview for it.

Sure enough, here I am with an assignment to interview *New York Times* bestselling author Nick Hornby. I immediately decide that I have in hand that elusive Lucky Break everyone's always raving about. Nick Hornby, I reason, must at all costs be in my book.

I take the weeks following my twenty-fourth birthday to cram on Nick Hornby, so I don't sound like an asshole when I talk to him. I chug through *High Fidelity* and enjoy it quite a bit. Not so much with his nonfiction memoir, *Fever Pitch*, although I don't fault Hornby for this.[50] His new book is a breezy little young adult novel that I finish mere hours before I call him at his hotel in New York.

If you look at his picture on the inside cover of one of his books, Nick Hornby does not look like you'd expect Nick Hornby to look, which is to say like either John Cusack or Hugh Grant. He is completely bald and has rather large ears—in other words like a soccer (sorry, "football") hooligan, who became a writer. However, Nick Hornby pretty much sounds exactly like you'd expect Nick Hornby to sound, which is to say, delightfully British.

He is bright and cheery on the phone, and although I'm doing this interview for *RedEye*, supposedly about his new book and ties to Chicago, I quickly forget my questions and find myself grilling Hornby on Bruce Springsteen, who plays a bit part in some of his writing.

"So what do you think of Springsteen's new album?" I ask, referring to the recently released *Magic*.

In his charming British accent, which makes me think of the word "poppycock" uttered over a mouthful of biscuit, he replies, "I don't like the production. It feels like there's a gel smeared on it. You know, I'm always disappointed when every song on the album is right around

50 It's all about being a fanatic European soccer (sorry, "football") fan, and I am neither European nor a "football" fan. That soccer (sorry, "football") sucks is the one argument where Americans unequivocally have the rest of the international community dead to rights.

three-and-a-half minutes, sorta verse-chorus-verse-chorus. And I got sick of 'Radio Nowhere' pretty quick. What do you think?"

So much for the *RedEye* interview. As I said, this is a topic I could go on about at some length.

"Well, I think you gotta blame Brendan O'Brien, the producer. He did the same thing to *The Rising*. And I know what you mean by 'gel.' The whole thing just feels as if it's polished but not in a good way. On the other hand, I think it has three of his best songs from the second half of his career on it, too."

"And what would those be?"

"'Magic,' 'Livin' in the Future,' and 'Long Walk Home' are as good as anything he's done since the eighties."

"Hmm… I guess I can see those."

"Overall, I'll agree it was uneven. It still didn't stop me from spending $150 to go see him at the United Center."

"Good seats?" Hornby asks.

"Bleeders, but who gives a shit? I feel like one day he'll be dead and I'll have wished I had spent the money."

"Sure," he says, laughing. "But Dylan fans have been saying that same thing for thirty years."[51]

We talk about Springsteen for too long, and pretty soon I realize I'm going to have kept this poor jet-lagged author on the phone for the better part of his morning without either fulfilling my primary duty for *RedEye* or my own self-interested duty to surreptitiously interview him for my book.

I snatch up my notepad with all of my questions and begin hitting him rapid fire: "Whatmadeyouwanttowriteayoungadultnovel? Didyouapproachitanydifferentlythanyouradultfiction? Isthebookbeingmarketedanydifferentlythanyourotherfiction?"

---

51 I'm pretty sure he actually said "thirty sodding years" but I don't want to put foul language in his mouth if I can't remember. In fact, I'll probably forget a lot of those quaint little Brit-isms that he peppered throughout the soon-to-be-dialogue of my book.

He mentions that he's been visiting schools, talking about *Slam*, because the plot involves a teenage pregnancy. I find this idea amusing and ask, "Visiting schools for a book about teen pregnancy—is that like a 'Nick Hornby promotes abstinence' tour?"

He laughs hard at this, and suddenly my mind is a tornado siren: *oh shit, snap, I just made Nick Hornby laugh! The man that* TIME *magazine called "a true original… as fine an analyst as he is a funny man."*

"No," says Hornby, his laugh dying down to a chuckle. "I wouldn't think I would be a very good sell at that."

Nick-Fucking-Hornby just laughed at the words that came out of my mouth! I didn't even have to think of them earlier and write them down on a cue card like how I asked Ashley Gentille to Homecoming in the ninth grade. All I did was hear his answer and then say that funny, funny shit right back to him! And the motherfucker laughed!

"You still there, mate?" he asks.

I jot down his words even though I long ago stopped caring what we were just talking about or what it had to do with or what I even said that made him laugh in the first place.

I finish this segment of the interview with the typical how-do-you-relate-to-Chicago questions[52] and realize I've had him on the phone for over half an hour. I apologize.

"Most of what I'm asking won't even end up in the interview, but I have my own ulterior motives to satisfy here…"

"No, mate, go right ahead."

"So just to get ready for this interview, I was reading some of your other stuff, and in *Fever Pitch* there was this one line in

---

52 My favorite question in this regard was, "As a die-hard fan of Arsenal football, can you find sympathy for Cubs fans?" To which he replied, "Oh, absolutely. It must feel as if they're locked into an alternate universe. The whole thing is so incredible and inexplicable… But I guess it would be foolish to stop cheering now, am I right?" Anyone who has ever felt the gut-wrenching pain that comes with caring about sports way, way too much knows how absolutely right he is.

particular that really struck me. You talk about carrying around this feeling of inevitability, a certainty about your talents, that you must be destined for success. But then in the very next paragraph you seem to rule it out, saying this must be how every talented person feels. Yet ultimately, for you, this feeling of inevitability proved true. What's your take on this sense of inevitability that artists have?"

I know how much of a one-eighty this question is from asking him about jazz clubs he likes in Chicago, but after a slight pause, he dives into his answer.

"I think most people who work in the arts, whether it's writing or music or acting or art, they have to have that to a certain degree when maybe the thing to do is give up. That feeling of 'I've got something to say and you'd better listen'—that's not healthy at all. But then again, if you can't bring yourself to give up, maybe there's something in there. I'm saying: if you can give up, then maybe you're not a writer after all. But this can result in a pretty unhappy life."

I nod vigorously at this. "Yeah, sometimes I think there's nothing my parents would like better than for me to go to law school."

"Sure," he says, a smile in his voice. "But usually all of the most interesting people are the ones who don't go to law school."

"So is your success surreal to you? What I mean by that is it seems like so much of a writer's life is spent waiting—for success, for fame, for happiness. Now that you've achieved at least two of those, is it surreal?

When he answers, his voice is quieter, reflective. "All of this began happening for me about fifteen years ago," he says. "I was thirty-five when *Fever Pitch* came out, and a lot of people didn't think I had a second book in me. Certainly not a novel and certainly not *High Fidelity*. Sometimes I still feel like I'm living the life before all that, the one I didn't want to know. So the answer is yes." He hesitates, seems to want to say more, and then stops himself. "Definitely surreal," he finishes. It's this moment when it becomes very easy for me to see past Nick Hornby, Bestselling Author, whose name is used to sell movies with the phrase "from the author of." With stunning clarity, I hear a guy who is not that far removed from a small apartment, slothful, cretinous roommates, and a useless, meandering job that was taking him nowhere.

"Did you ever feel like giving up?" I ask. "Settling for a career with a steady paycheck?"

He sighs heavily. "Absolutely. A number of times. I figure forty is the cutoff. Like I said, I was thirty-five when *Fever Pitch* came out, so I was close, but if you still haven't done anything by the time you're forty, you'd better pack it in."

"Is that feeling of restlessness—staticness—is that what led you to write *High Fidelity*?"

"Oh, definitely."

"Well, when did it dawn on you that you were going to make it? That you weren't going to have to find a real job and that your 'before' life was over?"

"It was a gradual sensation I suppose."

"Give me a moment," I almost demand.

He takes a second to think about it. "The paperback of *High Fidelity* came out and it had sort of hovered up on the charts for a bit but was falling off. Then this radio DJ, this popular DJ in England, started talking about it. He picked up on the book and just started going on and on about it, asking listeners what page they were on. But once you've published, there's no reason not to do it again was what I figured."

I wind the interview to a close. We've been on the phone forty-five minutes for a piece that will be no longer than six hundred words. "No worries," he says. "It was fun."

I can feel a shameless plug for myself coming on. Before the words are even out of my mouth, I'm cringing at my awkward, pathetic young-writer shtick. I say, "But anyway if you're really bored sitting in an airport with a laptop or anything you can always check out my website www.stephenmarkley.com."[53]

"Okay then," he says. "Take care."

With a blend of amusement and disappointment, I think, *Ah, that's exactly what I would have said.* And that is the end of our conversation.

The interview appears the following week, a page of Hornby's face and my questions, buried in the back section of *RedEye*—the page you only see if you have to take the train all the way from Evanston to the Loop.

Still, it's a good story to tell. I felt like I'd had a more or less human conversation with a very accomplished author, which was better than my previous Top Celebrity Conversations, which included only my brief encounter with *24*'s Tony Almeida and *Supernatural*'s Jared Padalecki. So at least there's that.

On another level, though, it was good for me to hear Hornby talk about his life "before all that." It was reassuring to know that a successful author can sound recognizable, that he has no secret key but is subject to the constraints of earthly talents and luck like the rest of us. Most importantly, he could still easily recall the life "before." The life where nothing is certain and everything is equally up in the air and you feel like whether you smack a home run out of the park or watch the ball go zipping over the plate is basically a coin toss left to the Fates. The more I think about it, the more affirming my conversation with Nick Hornby becomes: that a guy whose books frequently become major motion pictures was once thirty-five years old and on the verge of calling it quits.

I figure there's hope for me yet.

---

53 This was so totally lame. It was the same feeling as when you're talking to a really attractive girl, and you realize you no longer control the words coming from your mouth: "Yeah, my doctor once prescribed me this medication so the rash on my thighs would dry up and flake off, but instead it just got really chapped and bled on all of my pants. That's why in middle school all the kids called me the Rag, because it looked like I was having a period, but really it was just my thigh rash getting really dry and chapped and then bleeding. What were you saying? You played the violin in high school?"

Forget This Book

Astonishingly, I land a real job.

Let me ask if this sounds familiar: you have an idea of how your life will go, how the narrative will progress, yet suddenly you find yourself diverging from that notion wildly. However, because it's impossible to have any perspective on your own life, it all seems perfectly normal—even if a few months earlier such a situation would have seemed outlandish.

That's how you wake up one morning and say to yourself, "I think I'll get on the Internet and see how all the different trim levels for the 2009 Honda Pilot stack up."

I say things like this to myself now that I've landed a job at a car blog called KickingTires, which is the editorial arm of the online classifieds website Cars.com, which, in turn, is the vehicles portion of Classified Ventures, which is an online company co-owned by several major media companies including the Tribune Company (which I also work for under the guise of *RedEye*, thus allowing them to own my soul in its entirety[54]).

Now I write about cars and automotive-related news and have my own desk, stapler, and this wonderful, handy-dandy service they refer to as "health insurance." Oh, *and* this other thing, which they call—I think this is right—"mun-ee."

---

54 They are overpaying.

The most glaring fallacy of the American Dream is social mobility. Despite the insistence of American mythology, we all pretty much stay tethered to the economic class we are born into. This is why at the heights of my fiduciary difficulties, I still considered myself safely embedded in the middle class simply by virtue of my birth.

Seriously, when the corporate recruiter tells me the starting salary, I accept without hesitation in case he suddenly realizes how much this is and changes his mind.

To get an idea why a low five-figure salary would thrill me so, here is a list of how much my labor has been worth in my previous careers:

Youth columnist for *The Mount Vernon News*: $0.12 per word
Mover (off the books): $6 per hour
Community pool maintenance: $6.75 per hour
Construction (off the books): $8 per hour
Library circulation desk: $5.15–$6.45 per hour
Editorial editor for *The Miami Student*: $5.45 per hour
Dock wrangler, Jackson Lake: $7.55 per hour
Buffalo Wild Wings short-order cook: $7.45 per hour
Pizza delivery, Pizza Hut: $6.45 per hour (plus tips)
Freelance writer for *RedEye*: $25–$75 per article
Temp, SoulSuck Agency: $10 per hour

Now mind you, half of these positions I had in high school and college when my parents were at least offering me meager financial assistance. However, beginning with my boat maintenance duties in the Grand Tetons, I have been more or less consistently broke. My nadir came in the spring of 2007 when I looked in my bank account and saw I had an exact balance of $40.02. Working for the SoulSuck Agency in Chicago and making less than $320 a week after taxes was also particularly trying, even with dirt cheap rent and utilities split among five guys. Despite this, I refused to consider myself poor.

Then I got my first paycheck from Cars.com, which had not two, not three, but *four* numbers before you even got to the decimal.

Wow! I thought. *Tonight's a Bud-fancy night!*

Aside from ordering a non-light domestic beer, this paycheck got me reflecting on some of my so-called "middle-class" behavior over the last two years: subsisting on a diet of ramen noodles, hot dogs, tuna, and PB&J almost exclusively; when working for Pizza Hut, quitting that diet and existing on free pizza and leftovers from the lunch buffet; selling my plasma for forty dollars cash; failing to buy a stitch of new clothing for two years, even as underwear disintegrated to an elastic band I pulled around my waist each morning; ransacking my parents' home for twenty dollars in loose change, which I lived on successfully for two days; paying the first set of utility bills in Chicago by borrowing money from three separate people, pooling it together, and now that I think about it, still having not paid any of them back.

My intention here is not to make myself out to be the Erin Brockovich of twentysomething men or to make you feel sorry for me[55] but to illustrate how jarring it is not to have to worry that the soup and sandwich you're buying for lunch is going to make you short on the rent. I only wish I could report something profound from my year of fixing outboard motors and hauling pizzas for what would amount to less than $10,000, but all I can say is that being poor sucked (which you probably could have guessed anyway) and that I'm lucky and grateful that once I set my sights on something, a liberal elitist college degree and a bit of natural talent I'd cultivated over the years saw me through.

• • •

How did I get this job? My roommate Elliott works for Apartments.com and recommended I apply for a position there. "Yeah, fuzzy man, I feel

---

55 There are plenty of other reasons for that. Have you ever heard of a scrotal goiter?

like there are three new people every day, and none of them are ever hot girls, so I bet you'll get the job."

I sent my résumé and landed an interview for an assistant editor's position on the car blog.

I sat in a small room off to the side of this sea of cubicles, wearing my snazziest shirt and tie (I definitely went with the tie on this one), while the editor-in-chief, Patrick, asked me the simplest question: "What about cars interests you?"

Ah, great, I thought. The first one's a softball… and already I have no answer. What am I supposed to say to this? Power steering? Torque? Is that a thing? Torque? Sounds like a thing. You should probably stop staring at him and say something.

"Umm… Nothing, I guess… Except for the eventual death of the internal combustion engine."

Ah, brilliant, Markley! "Son, why do you want this job selling this here soap?" "Well, because I hate soap and want it wiped off the face of the planet and replaced with mud! Did I get the gig, boss?"

The interview meandered along like this, and at last we got back into territory I know about, such as "Why do you consider yourself a talented writer?"

"I have a strong, unique voice and a drive to become knowledge-able on every subject I tackle," I told him.[56]

Then, at the end of the interview, Patrick asked me, "So why would you be the best person for this job?"

I thought about it. "Well, I'm not sure that I would be," I said, feeling as if candor was my best option, since I knew so little about torque.

A perplexed frown darkened Patrick's previously serene face. His pause lasted a little too long. "Let me give you an interview tip," he said. "When someone asks you a question like that, it's probably

---

56 This is a nice euphemism for: "A breathtaking combination of ego, drug experi-mentation, and a peculiar bleakness of soul."

better just to make up a reason. Hard-working, quick learner—that kinda bullshit."

"...Not sure that I would be," I continued, like the Kennedy administration ignoring Khrushchev's second letter and only responding to the first more moderate version during the Cuban Missile Crisis. "But I will be the best writer you'll have in here. Anyone can learn what they need to learn about cars, but someone who can write concisely and with a little flair is probably more valuable."

I got the job.

• • •

This has been a consistent pattern in my life: being clever enough to stumble into a situation I know nothing about and winging it until I catch on. Pretty soon I'm a cranky old cigar-chomping, car-blogging veteran, eviscerating the Chevrolet Malibu for its poorly executed grille.[57] I'm immensely relieved to no longer be hunched over a phone at the SoulSuck Agency, trying to con the unemployed into thinking jobs exist for them. The workload at KickingTires is quite light compared to most of the manual labor jobs I've done, so I find myself with a lot of downtime to surf the Internet, chat with friends online, follow sports scores, and ponder hypothetical questions like: Could a Lightsaber Cut Through Superman?[58]

James, my traveling companion and partner in misery at the SoulSuck Agency, is sorry to see me go, and after I've been in my new position for a week, I debrief him over sandwiches at our

57 This is just an example of something car-related I might write. I honestly have no idea about the design of the Malibu's grille and certainly don't intend to learn about it for the purposes of this footnote.

58 The answer: It depends. According to Gizmodo.com, a lightsaber might be able to cut through Superman if it were powered by a kryptonite crystal or if kryptonite was present, thus weakening Superman and making him more vulnerable to everyday forces like an unremitting sword-like beam of pure energy. On the other hand, a lightsaber cannot just cut through any material. While it could potentially pierce Superman, it might not actually be able to make a cut, the way the weapon cannot simply cut through a blast door in *Episode I: The Phantom Menace*.

favorite cheap food joint, Pane's on Sheffield and Wellington. Pane's is cheap tables, a single counter, and an enormous mural on the wall of ghostly apparitions baking a pizza. A sandwich and chips will set you back six bucks. The Oaxacan pork with red peppers may be one of the finest things I've ever put in my mouth.

"Cubicles, man. Gray cubicles and purple walls for an entire city block. A trip to the bathroom takes two minutes there, two minutes back."

"How are the people?" he asks.

I shake my head, chew, and swallow what can only be described as the flank of a pig nestled into a loaf of bread. "That's the thing; I really have no idea. The job doesn't require me to talk to anyone. I can make it a whole day without speaking to another person." I think of the sounds of the office: the soft ticking of fingers on keyboards and hushed mouse clicks interrupted by the occasional fleeting ends of a conversation that sound like cacophony in comparison. "It's the kind of place where everyone's emailing each other from four feet away."

"Nobody wants to talk about cool stuff?" he asks. "What about how Mitt Romney sucks? Doesn't anyone wanna stop working for half an hour to talk about how much Mitt Romney sucks?"

"No! I know, man. If it weren't for the money and the benefits and not feeling like there was a stain on my soul, I totally would be back at SoulSuck."

• • •

However, a benefit I failed to mention to James during our powwow is that the SoulSuck overseers can no longer look over my shoulder at the screen now, so rather than surreptitiously writing this book in bits and pieces on errant scraps of paper and a notepad in my desk, I can actually spend time at work typing prose on a computer screen like a big boy. In fact, I'm doing so right now. I literally am sitting at my desk ignoring a much-needed blog about the pricing for the 2009 Mazda6 in order to work on this chapter. (Sorry, Cars.com.)

As I sit at my desk one day, ignoring the blog post I'm tackling on the Mitsubishi Lancer headlight-shape controversy and pondering ways to get agents to pay attention to me and my book, an email suddenly explodes into my inbox. It is from a literary agent named J—.[59]

Upon arriving in Chicago I had sent my novel and nonfiction book to every agent in the city. Figuring this for just another rejection, I open the email and read the following:

From: j—@_____.com
To: s____@yahoo.com
Subject: Re: Query

Dear Stephen,

Thanks for sending me your proposal and sample writing for "A Land I Saw in My Dreams." I've read the materials you sent and have checked out some of your writing on your website. I'd like to share your proposal with my business partner, S—. Do you have this stuff available electronically? If so, if you could email it to me, that would be great. I really like what I've read so far and want to get S—'s opinion before making a decision.

Cheers,
J—

---

59 To clarify: This literary agent was not named "J-dash"—which would be a great name for a misogynistic rap star—but I have chosen not to include all the letters of his name because I did not ask his permission to use these emails and do not want to get sued before the sixth chapter of this book. For the record, however, it could only help this man's career if he changed his name to "J-dash."

Sitting in my cubicle at Cars.com, my first reaction is: *ah, fiddle-fuckin-sticks.*

You'd think I would be happy, but the truth is I never thought anyone would actually want to read a book with the unwieldy title of *A Land I Saw in My Dreams: One Hedonistic College Grad's Personal and Political Journey Across the Excoriated Landscape of the American Dream in the Final Years of the Reign of Bush.* I sent it out only out of inertia, not knowing what else to do except, in the words of the immortal Tupac Shakur, keep hustling. Of course, I believe it's good, that after a few rewrites and a polish or two, it will have a lot of value, but I only finished writing it a few months earlier, and all but the first chapter is unedited. The rest is a rambling, absurd mess that takes all the worst aspects of a diary and combines them with raging profanity and a laundry list of illegal behavior divided into easily digestible chapters.[60] If I have to send this guy anything other than the material he already has, the best-case scenario is that I'll be laughed at. In other words, this book is not yet what one might call "readable."

My second and predominant reaction is: *aw hell yeah, I'm gonna be rich.*

I go home that night, and the two reactions conspire to bring my mind to a state of focus so intense, so driven, I can barely keep myself from banging out a 70,000-word screed on how much I'm going to kick this book's ass the second I sit down at the computer.[61] During my ride home on the Brown Line, I formulate a plan. First, I email J— the following unctuous note:

---

60   Sooo *not* like this book.

61   Markley, Stephen. *Watch Me Beat the Shit Out of This Book* (HarperCollins, 2009).

From: s_____@yahoo.com
To: j—@_____.com
Subject: Re: Query

_____

J—,

Thank you for your interest in the book. I do have all the
materials I sent you available electronically and can email
them by tomorrow, including the excerpt from Chapter 5,
which is available on my website. As for the full manuscript, it
would take me a bit longer to pull it all together, but if you let
me know I will certainly get started.

Best,
Stephen

The next step of my plan is bold: I'm going to edit, rewrite, and
revise this entire book in two weeks. I figure given enough caffeine, time, energy, booze, and commitment, I can turn my road
trip memoir into a masterpiece in two weeks. It may not be ready
now, but I believe in this book, especially now that J— might,
too. It was the first lengthy piece of nonfiction I'd attempted, and
while rereading parts of it, I saw what it could be: in the prose
I'd captured the wild, freewheeling anarchy of that cross-country
journey. Even if it was a mess, it had soul. Surely, I figured, if it
falls into the right hands, that person will recognize what they have
found, right?

My plan involves arriving at work already two cups of coffee down
and banging out everything I need to do for the day before lunch,
so I can spend the rest of the afternoon working on the book. I will
return home, make a quick trip to the gym, and then launch myself
back into it until I pass out at two or three in the morning. Hell,
this process may even be beneficial to the tome—give it a feverish,

dreamlike quality that you find in prose written by frantic, sleep-deprived, caffeine-shocked beasts.

Obviously, this is the closest I've ever come to real hope that I'm cracking the wall, that some editor at some publishing house is about to lose his shit over me and go to his bosses and say, "Hey, bosses. I just totally lost my shit over this kid. Where's that emergency book contract we keep for the big finds?"

Then the bosses will grab the little hammer and smash the glass of the compartment where they keep the aforementioned emergency book contract.

"Make sure he signs it in blood," they will say.

And in the meantime, I have completely forgotten about *Publish This Book*. Now that I'm about to hit it big, I think back over my quaint little experiment to write a book about publishing a book the way one thinks of a child who cuts two eyeholes in a box, puts it on his head, and calls himself an astronaut. I relegate *Publish This Book* to my Abandoned Idea Bin on my laptop along with other nonstarters, such as the novel about the eight-year-old who rescues his elementary school classmates from terrorists a la *Die Hard* and the group of twelve-year-old boys who rob a bank a la *Reservoir Dogs* (begun when I was eight and twelve, respectively).

I go to James and tell him what happened.

He looks up from his book, some turgid thing by Marcel Proust. His glasses, held together almost entirely by Scotch tape, are making a rare appearance on his face. "Whoa, dude. That's cool."

"I know. So look, if I need an emergency edit of between, say, fifteen to two hundred and seventy pages, would you be down to help me out? I'd owe you, big."

He leans back in his desk chair. James lives in our basement surrounded by his books and posters of Miles Davis and Jack Kerouac. The entire situation has the look of a less-handsome Colin Farrell hosting *Masterpiece Theater* in his underwear. "I don't know, man," James says. "My schedule's kinda crowded. Right now I'm reading

Proust, and this weekend I was going to go to a bar and try to do shit with chicks."

"Yeah, that is a full plate."

He nods. "I know, I know. I wish I could help you out, but *The Guermantes Way* ain't gonna read itself, and I don't think chicks are about to do shit with themselves…"

This entire conversation is James's way of saying, "No problem." I leave him the first two chapters and return to work.

• • •

For two days, I tear through my work, silent, efficient, and blood-and-gore deadly. With my trusty red pen, I slash and burn prose, annihilate paragraphs, relocate whole sections, rebuild entire vanquished chapters from the ground up, only to machine-gun to death individual words and punctuation.

Editing may be my favorite part of writing. When you write the first draft, you spew, but when editing, you craft. It's the difference between walking up to a pretty girl in a bar and running your game and actually convincing that girl that you're interesting.

I send J— the chapters, outline, and query by email, attaching a sycophantic little note about how this could be the start of quite a partnership. I figure it will be a day or two before his partner reads them, another for them to discuss, and then I should have an answer before the end of the week.

In my mind, this is a done deal. The next three chapters I'm going to send to J— are not only interesting and funny but read effortlessly in a single sitting. I figure he'll be halfway through the entire thing before he realizes he *has* to represent me.

I've already mentally spent the money I'm going to get from my advance. First off, I'm having a party. A big-ass, booze-soaked bash where I will buy everyone in the bar a shot and go home with only the prettiest girl in the joint.[62] Next, I'm going to donate a huge chunk of that cash to SaveDarfur.org. No more jettisoning small increments of my paycheck to the cause of ending the first genocide of the twenty-first century, I'm writing a check that's going to blow some minds. Those beleaguered aid workers are going to look up from the deserts of Sudan and say, "Jesus Christ, who's this guy who just sold this book? He not only single-handedly stopped the slaughter but there was cash left over to haul Sudanese president Omar al-Bashir before the International Criminal Court to be charged for his heinous war crimes! Right on!"

And then finally, I'm going to get a tattoo. But not like my other tattoos. This one is going to make people wonder how a guy like me with a tattoo that badass can possibly be a writer. They'll think I'm a Hell's Angel or a pickaxe-wielding vigilante psychopath ready to cleave in half the skull of any authority figure who dares step in his way. This tattoo will slither, snakelike, into entirely different quadrants of my body. It'll start at my back and move across my shoulder and up my neck and down to my bicep but not before flirting with my left buttock. It will be the most epic tattoo anyone has ever seen—the *Apocalypse Now* of tattoos, the *Born to Run* of tattoos, the *Roots* of tattoos.

Yes, for two days, I rain terror and enlightenment on my manuscript, and then—not forty-eight hours after sending the agent the material electronically—I receive this communication while sitting in my cubicle at work:

---

62 And not simply the prettiest one who will agree to go home with me, which was my strategy for the first twenty-four years.

From: j—@_____.com
To: s____@yahoo.com
Subject: Re: Attachments

Stephen,

Thanks for sending us your materials. We've had a close look, and although we think your writing is strong, there's not enough here to differentiate this from other books of its type. And while there's a lot here to recommend, we are going to take a pass. We wish you the best of luck in your search for another agent.

Sincerely,
J—

My immediate internal reaction, if displayed by a visual medium, would look like Godzilla sodomizing the Hindenburg.

I'll save you the mountain of letdown I ate—one bite at a time—for the rest of that week.[63] But perhaps this experience is worth a few words of explanation as to why the life of a writer is so frustrating.

I certainly don't want to wallow in cynicism here, but what exactly does this example demonstrate about the process of getting published? Essentially, this J— character asked me to send him *exactly the same materials he had already read in hard copy.* There was nothing new. Everything he asked for was already in his possession. Sure, maybe his partner, S—, did not like the chapters as much, but

---

63 Ah, fuck it: Letdown like a motherfucking earth-swallowing void of despair! Despair like a twenty-five-foot ogre bringing his club down on me so that all my bones and organs turn to dust and jelly in a sack of skin. Give up writing, I thought? I don't want to just give it up; I want to ban it from the face of the planet. I want to spend the rest of my life becoming Dictator of the World, so I can illegalize all forms of the written word and condemn to death and agonizing torture anyone who ever again thinks of writing anything more complex and artistic than a grocery list.

wouldn't it at least be worth his time to hear what was in the rest of the book? What tectonics of the publishing world shifted in those few days that sent my book proposal from "tell me more" to the discard pile?

Nevertheless, this is the process of trying to get published: mysterious, strange, frustrating. And I can make jokes about it. I can say to James, "I can pretty much guarantee that even if the manuscript was a discombobulated mess, there was plenty to 'differentiate it from other books of its kind.' Oil dependency? Jack Kerouac's ghost? Driving through the desert while hallucinating about armies of sand monsters? Show me another book with chapters on all three!"

But the truth is that this hurts, and it hurts for very acute reasons. Spending the advance in my head was fun, but I would've written the book for a dollar. I would've written it because I wanted the adventure of writing it. When I got that terse email from J— it gave voice to my doubt—the Fear, I sometimes think of it—that this is truly not in the cards for me. That like Sisyphus, I will push this boulder my entire life only to have it roll back down the hill as soon as I near the peak. This thought keeps me up at night, staring into the ceiling well into all those cold Chicago mornings. *I mean*, I say to myself those nights, *what the hell else am I supposed to do?*

• • •

A week later I come home after work to my laptop, my little white iBook G4. I sit down on my lawn chair and boot her up. I drag back out from my folder of Abandoned Ideas a file titled "PublishThis. doc" and drop it into the In Progress folder. I stare at the file for a moment, meeting eye-to-eye that little icon with the blue header, dog-eared corner, and the lowercase "a".

"Hey there," I say. "What's up?"

The file is silent.

"Yeah, I just thought... You know, maybe you and me could try to work on things."

Still nothing.

"I got a little carried away, I know. But I promise this time it'll be different. I want to see things through, I really do. It wasn't that I liked that other book more, it's just *other people* seemed to like that book more."

I move the cursor over the file. The little arrow rests gently on the icon.

"Come on, I wouldn't have kept you on my hard drive if I didn't think there was some hope that I might someday write you, you know? We all make mistakes. If you give me another chance, I'll write you the way you want, the way you deserve, so hard and so long and so fierce, book, I promise."

I hesitate. I click once. The file becomes highlighted with blue. I click again. The document springs open. There is the title. There is the byline. There is the first chapter.

"Thank you," I say. "I promise you won't regret this."

SEVEN

Autobiographical Digression #1: Leaving Behind the Skin from Your Knees

i[64] warn you that the following chapter has little to do with writing a book about writing a book. I was going to write a revealing chapter

---

64   all right, stay calm. You've probably noticed that I did not capitalize the first pronoun of that sentence. I know I've totally thrown your sense of balance and belief in an ordered universe into complete disarray, but do not throw this book down and run outside shrieking and clawing your eyes out and begging a merciful god to save you while the jelly runs down your cheeks. Bear with me, is what I'm saying. You see, as a reader of literature, I often notice novels and "serious" nonfiction in which certain authors inexplicably ignore some standard grammatical rule. For instance, they will not use quotation marks or they will randomly capitalize words for no apparent cause or they will use
   indentation in the middle of a sentence for no discernable reason. I suspect this may be part of some kind of ego trip cloaked as a symbolic device. Not to be outdone, I've decided to not capitalize the first word of each paragraph in this chapter. Why, you ask? What purpose could this possibly serve other than to senselessly distract the reader and annoy him or her with my gimmicky arrogance? That's the beauty of it: The symbolism is yours to interpret. Are you reading this for a class right now? A book club? If so, be sure to discuss the rich symbolic texture I've just added to this chapter. Do you think that maybe, because this chapter recounts my youth, I am signaling a philosophical mistrust of the importance of any single moment in one's life? Perhaps I am theorizing that every moment has its place in a vast web of memory and experience and therefore singling out certain letters for special treatment—placing extreme importance on one word simply because it begins a sentence—is anathema to this ideal? Or maybe I've done away with the capital letter because it is a constant reminder of structure and hierarchy, while the purpose of this chapter is to demonstrate how I learned that occasionally rejecting such paradigms can bring a great deal of emotional and intellectual freedom. Or perhaps the stark, childlike tapestry created by a page free of capitalized words on that left-hand side lends itself visually to a distanced reflection of one's youth—a way of catapulting the reader back to adolescence with the simple aesthetic makeup of the prose. Or maybe I'm just fucking with you. In the end, it's up to you to decide, and I doubt any of us will ever truly know.

on my beginnings as a writer: my formative experiences, and the
forces that led me down this road. You know, a deep look into the
mind of a young boy who liked to tell stories and arrange words
and who would one day grow up to write a truly derivative, mind-
numbing, painful-as-a-skull-fuck chapter in a book about his experience becoming a writer as a child.

i suppose if I devoted an entire chapter to horticulture or international copyright law, I could bore one or two people more efficiently,
but on the grand list of all things obnoxious and uninteresting, a writer
bitching about how hard it is to be a writer tends to be up there.[65]

my professor's advice in the second chapter made a lot of sense
once I got around to thinking about it. So this chapter is about basketball, but really it's not. It's about writing. But it's not really about
writing, right? Because it's about the dreams we have and the lengths
we'll go to to secure them. It's about reaching an understanding, a
détente, with your vast unshackled hopes and ambitions. The key
for you as a reader is to decide how the allegory works (And isn't it
helpful that I'm telling you it's an allegory up front?).

my infatuation with basketball began when I was living in
Portland, Oregon, with the near-championship run of the 1992
Portland Trail Blazers. It is no understatement to say that this group
of overpaid athletes effectively changed my life, and to this day my
knowledge of that team remains preposterously detailed. I'm certain
one day I'll have to remember something really important like my
daughter's blood type and it will be blocked out by Buck Williams's
jersey number (52).

during the Blazers' '92 run to the finals, which culminated in
a heart-breaking six-game loss to Michael Jordan and the Chicago
Bulls, I became infatuated with basketball. Suddenly, I was begging
my father to take me to the nearby elementary school where I would

---

65   oh, shit! That's what this entire book is about! Ignore the glaring contradiction I
just made!

hoist lay-ups with two hands and try to dribble the ball between my legs just once without nutting myself.[66]

shortly thereafter my family moved to Ohio, where the game came to dominate my life, both in the form of my own participation and the hours upon hours I devoted to watching, reading about, and analyzing it. I'm fairly certain there was a point in my life, maybe around 1994 or 1995, when I probably knew more about NBA basketball than some NASA rocket scientists know about physics. You could have named any player on any team and there was an 85 percent chance that ten-year-old Stephen Markley could have told you his average points, rebounds, assists, all the teams he'd played for in his career, where he played his college ball, and how many illegitimate children he was known or suspected to have fathered.

i stuck with basketball, mostly because I was good at it. Not LeBron James good. Not Steve Nash good. Not even Danny Ainge good. Obviously there is a reason why professional ballplayers don't come out of small, all-white rural towns. No one ever made it to the NBA playing against his five-foot-nine father from academia. But I was decent. I tended to beat most of my peers in games of one-on-one, rack up the most points for my YMCA team, and even hold my own when I played against the older kids.

i enjoyed the cerebral nature of the game: judging your options in three dimensions, seeing lanes of movement and spacing, interpreting direction, intuiting your opponent's reactions before he even knows them. This was the part I was good at. My shooting, defense, and left hand all needed work.

in middle school I went from YMCA all-star to simply another body in a crowded group of kids vying for time on the seventh- and eighth-grade teams. I met kids better than me, which was a big blow to the ego. Occasionally, I felt a bit of resentment toward them, not

---

66 as it so happens, most of my childhood seemed to revolve around a constant vigilance to not "nut" myself during various activities. I like to think I met with more success than failure.

only because they were more naturally gifted shooters or had hit puberty sooner than I had but also because I knew when they got home from practice every night they showered, watched TV, and went to bed. I, on the other hand, had my hour of writing.

i would get home every night after practice and sit down at the family computer and make myself write. During those days my projects consisted of a novel about an assassin with amnesia (I had never read the *Bourne* series, and my idea was better because the twist at the end was that the assassin was hired to kill himself!) and a novel about a pterodactyl eating people in a Texas national park (I still have hopes for that one).

how, at age thirteen, I had the discipline to sit down and write nearly every night, I have no explanation. Here was what I did know: my warped little thirteen-year-old mind was interested in three things, and since girls didn't pay attention to me, I really only had writing and basketball—and I was a junkie for both.

• • •

in eighth grade I came under the tutelage of Coach Miller, who selected me and my friend Ian to be his double-headed point guard. To a fourteen-year-old kid, all authority figures seem more or less the same, but as that season developed, a part of me began to realize that Miller was different, that I should keep my sugar-amped, hormone-addled mind trained on him for as long as I could manage.

miller was this dry, brusque guy with a quick mouth[67] and a curly afro of jet-black hair. He had the requisite Mount Vernon beer gut fitted over a thin frame and eyebrows slanted to a scowl even when he smiled.

---

67   example: one time someone defecated on the floor of the girl's locker room, and Miller walked into a gym class of sixty kids and said, "How hard is it to not shit on the floor of the locker room? You guys don't like rules, that's fine, but here's one that doesn't get broken: Don't shit on the floor of the locker room." Our fragile teenage minds were completely blown.

he won the respect of his basketball players by telling us frankly who was going to play and who wasn't. He won our hearts by telling us jokes with cuss words. He won my admiration by putting his trust in me.

we had eighteen kids on the team that year, and only eight were really getting substantial playing time, so he devised a system where three of the bottom ten players would take turns not dressing for games. Midway through the season, he pulled me aside during practice and asked me what I thought about this.

my initial instinct was to say, "I have no idea. You're the coach," but from the way he was looking at me, I could tell he wanted a truthful answer.

"i don't think the guys like it," I told him. "I think they'd rather dress and never get in than sit in a shirt and tie all game."

the next practice, Miller announced the new policy.

years later, I would begin to learn there was more to Coach Miller than a sense of humor that slayed fourteen-year-old boys. To begin with, he had gone to Kent State and had been on campus when the National Guard cut down those kids. On the twentieth anniversary of the slayings, my high school newspaper quoted him for a story. I recall how he described the hyper-reality of waking up one morning in 1971 and knowing that four of his classmates had been murdered and the country wasn't going to be the same for a long, long time. He said little about the politics of the situation, but years later I spotted a quote in his office that said, "Terrorism is the war of the poor against the rich. War is the terrorism of the rich against the poor." There are always layers to people—layers you'd never suspect.

long after I graduated from high school and left Mount Vernon, I returned to the middle school to read from one of my short stories for an English class. I wandered down to the gym between periods to say hi to my old coach.

in his office, he showed me a photograph he'd framed from his time coaching my eighth-grade team. "Won't lie, Markley," he said, "that was probably one of the best teams I've ever coached. You, Thompson, Justin, Ian, Jimmy—you guys were great kids. Serious, selfless... and smart. One of the smartest groups of kids I've ever worked with."

i didn't really know what to say. I guess I could have told him about the real and profound impact he'd had on me that year, but that would have required a step outside of my comfortable emotional box, so I remained silent. I handed the picture back to him, our young, clean faces all full of mischief and distracted by the girls nearby who were watching as the photographer arranged us.

"it was one of those times that allowed me to say I honestly had no regrets about my choice of profession," Miller said. A heavy sentiment from a guy whose job was supposed to be tossing volleyballs to kids so they could peg each other for forty minutes.

years earlier, though, he had just been my basketball coach. I liked him, and I played my goddamn brains out for him, but that was all I thought of the relationship. It's hard when you're fourteen to be on the lookout for those moments—those unforeseen instances when Important Shit goes down. I know I certainly missed this one at the time.

the Mount Vernon middle school eighth grade boys' basketball team was good that year. Our friend, this kid named Thompson, who would go on to play division three ball in college, was busting out of himself, playing like he wasn't a five-foot, eight-inch white kid from rural Ohio. We lost only one game during the entire regular season, which included an incredible comeback win against our rival from the Columbus suburbs, Worthington Worthingway. On the verge of our tournament, you would have thought we were starring in our own Disney movie about the plucky undersized basketball team that could. The practice before the game, Coach Miller sat us all down in a line on the first row of bleachers after practice. Naturally, we were all expecting a go-get-one speech, something to pump us up before we went into battle the next day.[68]

instead, Coach Miller told us a story about how he grew up.

his family was poor. The kind of poor where your old man is an alcoholic. The kind of poor where he spends an entire paycheck on liquor and beer and hands you a dollar for your own entertainment. As Miller told us this story, I could see the perplexed faces of my teammates, all of our young, skinny bodies draped in those Mount Vernon practice jerseys, our eyes following this man as he slowly paced up and down our ranks.

"the point," he said when he finished, "is that life has a way of never letting you know what's important. You guys need to remember what it is to be where you are—to remember that you're lucky, that what you have is something worth having. You never know what's going to happen. You never know what will come the next day or the day after that. That's why we're here now.

"make sense?"

we all nodded solemnly, but of course it didn't. We were probably thinking about boobs. To tell you the truth, at the time I thought Miller's speech sounded trite—this word wasn't in my vocabulary then, but like a platitude. At fourteen years old, how was I supposed to know his words would stick with me? That I would hear this speech all the time in those quiet moments when I needed courage?

• • •

---

68 incidentally, one of the teams we defeated on our march through the tournament was Dublin Coffman, which starred a short, skinny kid named Chris Quinn. Quinn went on to play his college ball at Notre Dame and eventually ride the bench in the NBA behind Dwyane Wade on the Miami Heat. If I had known that at the time, I would have made better friends instead of noting to my teammates before the game that he looked like a goblin. Chris, if you ever read this, I'm sorry.

high[69] school saw the introduction of a man who I named Coach Stahl when I fictionalized him in the first novel I ever finished. Stahl took over the varsity program the year I arrived in high school, which meant that he was in control of the entire basketball program the way George W. Bush had control of the United States government after 9/11. While nominal checks and balances to Coach Stahl's authority existed, he ruled with near absolute power.

to get an idea of this guy, simply view any clichéd high school sports movie with a raging, overzealous, red-faced, short-tempered, two-faced head coach. I suppose stereotypes exist for the very reason that occasionally real people fit them shockingly well. He was a man of rectangles. His head, his torso, his limbs—they all appeared as short, blockish parallelograms attached to each other by unseen joints. This man of solid, uninterrupted mass appeared to be driven by a cacophony of competing demons that thrashed and clawed and bit at each other so much, it drove him into delirium in unpredictable intervals.

i remember the first time he stuck his face less than an inch from mine during a practice and barked, "Markley, you couldn't set a suckin' screen to save your life. Quit setting picks like a suckin' puss!"[70] while his spittle peppered my face.

---

69   so we've reached the halfway point of this chapter, and it seems as if I'm sticking with the lowercase thing for better or worse. A few thoughts on this: 1) It is really hard to type a document in Microsoft Word using intentional errors. The autocorrect knows to capitalize the first word of a sentence, so I have to spell out the whole word, let the autocorrect do its job, and then delete the word and write it again. 2) I have to ask myself, is this gimmick really working? Or is it just that, a gimmick? In order to succeed, it must transcend itself and prove its value beyond merely distraction and show-offishness or risk becoming a disaster. Then again, now that I've doubled-down on the technique by including this footnote, you have to ask yourself: Is it meant to be a disaster? And if that's the case, do you need a bowl to collect the fragments of your skull from me just blowing your mind yet again?

70   the list of allowable cuss words for high school coaches when deriding their players is of great mystery and sociological interest to me. Based on his vocabulary, I gathered that Coach Stahl saw "fucking" and "pussy" as unacceptable but not "sucking" and "puss."

i can't recall if I was called a puss more or less often than anyone else, but I do remember my extreme, untempered desire to never have him do that to me again. These days it's hard to recall the dread that man instilled in me with any accuracy, but he did, and small-town basketball became consequential in explaining my core as small and petty and bizarre as that sounds. This is a man whose life was coiled so tightly around boy's high school basketball that a simple play executed incorrectly during practice could send him into a screeching minute-long tantrum. Yet back then, when I was deep in it—when basketball dictated my life, was my passion and my agony—I lived and died by the pitch of his voice. Coach Stahl stayed with me; my own highlight reel of intense, fury-driven performances. When it happened to someone else, I could only stand quietly and thank Christ it wasn't me. When it was me, I could only nod, nod, nod and hope it would be over soon.

slowly then, over a number of high school seasons, my friends left. The day my friend Justin quit, I knew we'd all reached a turning point. He came strolling through practice that day with his shoes in one hand, jersey in the other. His face was proud, even defiant. Justin had other things—a hell of an arm for one—and was looking for a scholarship that would let him pitch in college a few years down the road.

the coaches hadn't called us to the center of the court yet to stretch and warm up, so I stopped to talk to him.

"i guess in baseball you don't have to be able to jump over a Dixie cup," I said. "You just run around in the grass and giggle and grab each other's asses."

he looked around and did not try to mask his contempt, especially when his eyes landed on Stahl. Of course, I didn't know all the things that waited down the road for us then, but his words gave me a strange chill nonetheless. "Have fun," he told me.

• • •

when I got my driver's license, I spent a summer borrowing my mom's minivan and hauling half the team around to summer shoot-outs and basketball camps. Stahl would take one half of the team in his minivan, and whoever was lucky enough to call it would cram into mine. Starting at six in the morning, we'd drive three hours across the state to Muskingum and play loosely refereed scrimmages until our legs felt like they might fall off. I was still at the bottom of the totem poll when it came to court time, so I made the most of my moments. I guarded the other team's star players, drilled into scrums of bigger, taller guys for rebounds, scraped half the skin from my knees and elbows retrieving loose balls, and just generally beat the shit out of myself.

once at a summer scrimmage, I took a nasty elbow to the back of the head and lay dazed on the floor long enough for my man to streak down the court for a lay-up.

"markley," Stahl shrieked from the sideline, a look on his face like you would give a dog if it jumped up on the table and pissed all over dinner. "You still asleep? Did you wanna show up today or did you wanna stay in bed back in Mount Vernon?"

thompson came over to me on the court during a foul. "You all right, Steve?"

"god, felt like that kid put a dent in my skull."

"yeah, I saw."

at this point it was clear Thompson was a soon-to-be star. He took far more abuse on offense than I ever did just because the other team dogged him all over the court. By senior year, the basic play in Mount Vernon basketball would be "everybody block for Thompson," a methodology that had the kid running off screens for two hours a night.

"i do not like him," I said, motioning my head toward Stahl, who had his hands on his hips, eyeing the free-throw shooter as if he had just found the dog that had ruined the family dinner.

thompson shook his head. "Remember when he was following

me back into the locker room that one game? After I missed both free throws just before half time? He was screaming in my ear the whole way, 'you fuh-hin puh-y, you fuh-hin puh-y.'" Thompson was a good God-fearing kid who didn't have it in him to repeat the language used, but I remembered the story and I told him so, recalling one of Stahl's few moments of such volcanic anger that he forgot to make his word substitutions.

"yeah," he said, "well, Purse was in my other ear the whole way back. I had Stahl saying all that stuff in one, and Purse[71] in the other going, 'Just ignore it, man. Just ignore it, Thomps. In one ear, out the other, man. In one ear, out the other.'" Standing there at mid-court with our hands on our knees and sweat cascading off us like the whole state had been swallowed by the Ohio River, Thompson laughed out loud. "Now whenever Stahl gets going, that's all I can ever think about."

i concocted fantasies in my head, grand scenarios where in the middle of getting ripped by Coach Stahl, I would stage a walkout and the rest of the team would follow. I would be the Che Guevara of Mount Vernon basketball.

fantasies like this have a powerful influence. You daydream about a scenario enough times, and sooner or later it's bound to take on firmer, grander proportions in your mind. As a burgeoning writer, I internalized this angst, and from it was born the first novel I ever completed. I was sixteen when I typed the final word of the last chapter.

at first I called it *American High*, and then *The Last Days of Living Young*, and then simply *The Last Days*, and it was basically a multi-character, multi-narrative revenge fantasy including everyone who

---

71 incidentally, "Purse" was the name of an older kid who started at point guard our sophomore year—the year Thompson moved up to varsity and the year I took more elbows to the rib cage guarding Purse than a Guantanamo detainee. He was like a better-looking, more athletic version of me. At least girls from his grade often told me that I reminded them of him, but always in a way that let me know they were referring to my goofy sense of humor and not my athleticism or looks. In an unrelated note, Thompson dated and eventually married Purse's younger sister.

had ever wronged me in high school, from Stahl, to specific peers I loathed, to every girl who had ever shot me down. Writing it was cathartic, even if it was a spectacular piece of shit.[72]

still, I was sixteen years old and had managed to finish an entire novel without provocation. That had to say something about the future, right?

• • •

naturally, there is more to this story than I'm letting on. Basketball relates to some other things, as well. Over four years the Mount Vernon High School class of 2002 had to deal with some heavy shit. Suicide. Car crash. Cancer. After one of these, I went to what might have been the most awkward, awful practice in the history of the Mount Vernon, Ohio, basketball program. This practice stood as a testament to the line, thin as a hair split length-wise with a razor, that represents the separation of the utterly mundane trappings of life and a hard, dark look into the abyss that follows any tragedy.

i remember pulling my practice jersey over my head in the locker room, the shoulders stiff with dried sweat. I never washed it. I thought to myself, *Is this actually happening? Am I really about to go out and play basketball right now?* And then on the court— doing the three-man weave, guarding the varsity guys in half-court scrimmages—all of us quiet, shell-shocked.

and in the days that followed, I had some of the best practices of my life. I'm thankful for them in a way I wasn't thankful for much else at the time. I could take that basketball in my hands and suddenly everything was gone, everything that had happened, so bright and glaring in my mind that sometimes to think of it felt like holding my eyes directly on the sun even as my retinas screamed in protest.

---

72 i showed it to my professor, Steven, not long after I took my first class with him, and he was blunt in telling me how unreadable it was.

during practice all I needed to think about was the positioning of my defender as he shifted his weight, and the swift roll of my feet as I pushed past him, driving to the basket. All I had to feel was the sticky, pebbled texture of the ball on the pads of my fingers and the river of sweat streaking endlessly from my body. Just a bit of respite was all I was after, a little shelter from the storm. And the game was there for me in a way no person could be. Even if it was just me alone in that gym, the thud of the ball on hardwood was as consoling as any empty prayer to a fictitious omnipotent god.

• • •

eventually, I quit.

this is not to say I quit basketball. I could no more quit basketball than I could quit watching television or writing self-referential books. But I did quit its organized high school version, and I did so one week before the first game of my senior season, ceding my starting position, no less.

sometimes I reflect on how long it took me to get to the point where I was a starting guard on the Mount Vernon basketball team. Essentially it was all I had been working toward for seven years. Yeah, I guess I was in school and still ostensibly wanted to get into a good college and get an education and all that bullshit my parents wished I mentioned more, but school was easy. Girls and basketball: that was the hard shit.

there were a few factors. There was Coach Stahl, whom I had grown so tired of that I was literally having a physical reaction every time I saw him, whether at practice or in the halls at school: his taut, glossy face, his curled snarl, his shit-shoveling grin—no matter his mood, I could not look at him without feeling a psychic ennui matched by a sinking in my gut.

understand that high school athletes spend more time with their coaches and teammates than they do with their own families. During basketball season, Stahl became my de facto father, and like any boy with his father, my desire to please him ran deep even as I simultaneously held a gutter-dwelling opinion of the man. This dichotomy was as frustrating as it was demoralizing. Every success, every pleasure I had in life was colored by basketball. Any success meant absolutely dick if I turned the ball over one too many times or missed a couple of jumpers or let my defender take me off the dribble.

the day I quit, I went to the locker room and stood staring at my locker for about twenty minutes. We had practice later that night and I had gone down there with the intention of either putting new laces in my shoes or quitting the team. I knew Coach Stahl was in his office, so I crept past it and positioned myself in front of my locker, running the factors of this decision through my head. One of the ones that popped up, seemingly from nowhere because I couldn't remember it having ever occurred to me before, had to do with writing. *Isn't it time to get serious?* I thought. *I'm not going to the NBA; I think we all know that. I do, however, have the first forty pages of my second novel written.*

i tried to imagine all the time I would have on my hands if I quit basketball. The sheer number of hours overwhelmed me, but I dismissed this thought at once. I wasn't quitting basketball to become a famous writer any more than I was playing basketball so I could get to the NBA.[73]

so I stood and stared at my locker, an orange row of mesh metal, the entire apparatus reeking of stale sweat. An inventory of my locker revealed a reversible practice jersey, shorts, shoes, and a water bottle with my name written on a piece of tape. Not a whole lot to clean out. I felt something sacred in that room, where my friends had joked, had endured shouting tirades from coaches, had prepared, racked by nervous energy, had felt disappointment, had

---

73   of course, as it would turn out, I would spend 95 percent of that free time with my high school girlfriend either fawning, fighting, or fornicating, and only the minimal hour a night actually writing.

filled with glory. I made my decision in a random instant with no particularly decisive factor swaying me. I turned, knocked on the door to Stahl's office, and quit. The entire conversation lasted less than three minutes.

"my heart's not in it anymore," I said.[74]

"i thought something was wrong," he said. "I saw it in your body language at the scrimmage last week. We'll all be sorry to see you go."

i really wanted to say something more. If twenty-four-year-old Steve Markley could have stepped into the body of scrawny eighteen-year-old Steve Markley, having had six years to think about this moment, I presume he would have said something like, "I hope one day you coach a group of kids who make you think of all of us as more than just collateral."

instead, we hugged and said good-bye and I felt a troublesome, almost frustrating indifference when he walked me to the door. I went home and called my teammates to let them know I'd be rooting for them.

later that winter, I was putting gas in my car when a stranger in a Carhartt jacket and a mustache approached me and said, "I'll miss watching you play this year, Steve. It's a shame the way they let you walk away like that. No lie."

i thanked this man, who I did not know and did not recognize. This is how it works in small towns where people have time to be preoccupied with the high school basketball team. Still, it didn't stop me from using his words as a kind of talisman to stave off regrets when I watched Thompson and the rest of the guys win the division that season.

i still feel it was the right decision. I needed to outgrow my

---

74 when you play high school sports, you often find it easier to speak in high school sports clichés, and sometimes that vocabulary—gleaned from movies like *Hoosiers* and *Varsity Blues*—is all that comes out of your mouth. So you'll talk to a girl and say, "I gotta be ready for the big game, Shelly Ann. If I don't play my heart out, I might not get that scholarship that's gonna get me outta this town." And then she'll say, "My name is Megan."

juvenile dependence on the praise and acceptance of people whose opinions I did not respect in the first place.[75]

nevertheless, while it may have been the right decision, it is still one that bizarrely haunts me.

i have this particular recurring dream. It's my senior season again; only this somehow means it's my fifth year of high school because in my dream I always remember having quit. I did not play for a year, but now I've decided to come back. I want to win a conference championship with my friends before we all graduate. And in this dream I'm always preparing for a game, either in a practice the night before or in the locker room just before we take to the court. I'm nervous as hell. My stomach has filled with flaming, gasoline-drenched butterflies, and I keep tying and retying my shoelaces. I sweat in my warm-ups. I make nervous jokes with my teammates. I pound a basketball back and forth through my legs and try to imagine how this upcoming game will go. It's been a year—will my skills have rusted? Will my nerves get the better of me? Will the adrenaline rush be there, coursing, the way it always used to—that nearly narcotic sensation of energy and fuel and youth that burns brightest for those who know that these small-time high school games are as far as their athletic glory will ever take them?

whenever I wake up from this dream, I always have the exact same muddled, confused thought: *this time it's real.*

i wake, and I know that I've had this dream before, that I've had it dozens if not hundreds of times, but *this time* it's the real deal. I'm back in high school, and this is my chance. I need to get ready. I need to prepare. Jesus, I need to at least stretch for Christ's sake, because this is my chance, this is my opportunity to change the story, to transform the narrative so that this time it will make some sense...

and then the world always seeps back in. I'm in my college dorm

---

75   until I need to publish a book, when I will seek all that again...

room, I'm in my girlfriend's bed, I'm sleeping in my car at an Oregon rest stop, I'm on my floor-mattress in my room in central Lakeview, and once again high school basketball seems as distant and inconsequential as my severe childhood addiction to string cheese.

the day after Coach Miller gave us that speech, we met our rivals, Worthington Worthingway, for a rematch in the championship game of our eighth grade tournament. There are some losses you never get over. Blazers in '92. Buckeyes in '06. Kerry in '04. Abby Harmann in fifth grade. This was one of those losses.

a player from Worthington Worthingway named Kevin Anderson—a kid whose name I will never forget for the rest of my life—had the ball with ten seconds left and the game tied. He took two dribbles past the three-point line, hoisted a sixteen-foot jumper, and hit nothing but net and wind, and the sound of the ball going through was what my little fourteen-year-old heart sounded like when it ripped itself in half at that very moment.

with less than a second left, Justin tried to find Thompson at half-court but the ball ended up in the bleachers and we walked off the court and back to the locker room. I punched my fist as hard as I could into a locker, resulting in my immediate need of a medium-sized Band-Aid, which strangely failed to heal the cut properly, leaving the faintest little scar on my knuckle.

although this might be one of the most vivid memories in my entire life, I understand its place. I understand now—and maybe I even knew it subconsciously back then—that I was never going to the NBA and that basketball and I would have to be, at best, old lovers who reunited every once in a while for a fun little romp.

when you play a sport in school, it completely dominates your life. As I said, it demands more time than your homework, your friends, or your family. There were certainly days when I would rather have nutted myself on a pole of barbed wire than gone to practice. Nutting myself on anything would have seemed like a small price to pay to escape the dreaded drills, scrimmages, and "stingers"—that infamous Mount Vernon basketball punishment that for the rest of my life will make me recoil inwardly at its very mention.[76]

writing isn't all that different. You sit down and you write no matter what. Sometimes you suck, just like sometimes you suck during practice when you keep screwing up the play or you toss the ball into the bleachers and the coach rips you a new asshole. Still, you don't walk out of the gym after you mess up. No, no, no you run your stinger (or five) and then when you're at your most fatigued, you step back onto the court, and if your defender is still checking you with his arm to keep you from getting a pass into the post, then you bust his face with your shoulder 'cause there ain't no fucking way you're running another stinger.

similarly, when you hit your stride, when you're in that zone, you find yourself with that essential feeling of escape, of life melting away to be replaced by worlds that normally just drift and flitter on the periphery of things. Whether it's a concrete court or the stranded, struggling characters of a novel, you find these worlds taking prominence while the steel trap of reality turns to smoke and fog.

so I gave up one impossible dream for another. I took what I had learned from that time that had so dominated my youth—what I'd learned about myself and the people around me and the way all lines of travel never end in the places you'd expect but still somehow manage to cross and tangle—and pocketed it for whatever good it can do: a small private moment when Kevin Anderson missed that jump shot or I'm back in the locker room tightening my laces for my glorious senior year or the winds of time have crossed and I'm marrying my high school sweetheart and settling down in the distant farmlands of Knox County, Ohio, to teach scrawny high school boys how to pin a defender in the post.

---

76   for those readers who did not play Mount Vernon basketball, a stinger is when you start at the baseline and—as fast as your legs and lungs can manage—sprint to the foul line and back, half-court and back, the opposite foul line and back, the opposite baseline and back. It is unpleasant.

now what I have left of basketball are memories and abandoned dreams. That's why when I was standing in that locker room alone trying to decide whether or not to quit I thought of writing: because it was my dream-in-reserve, and once basketball was gone, it would be filling the starting position. When you're locked into a hunt like this, you think of why we chase these dreams with such tenacity.

it's simple enough, really: because they give us hope. Because they give us power. Because we want to have that feeling where everything in life melts away and all you have is a pen, a paintbrush, a guitar, a lump of clay, a basketball. We chase these dreams because, in the end, it's all we know how to do.

How to Get Rejected

As I sit down to write my book proposal, I must consider this: it cannot be anything like the proposal an agent would expect. Book proposals are clunky, awkward creative objects. Unlike a magazine or short story query, they cannot just be interesting—they have to aggressively explain why this project will make money.

For instance, if you're just querying the *New Yorker* with a short story, the methodology is pretty simple: include an autobiographical paragraph. This paragraph must include who you are, where you live, what you do, where your work has appeared previously, and whether or not your name is Alice Munro, George Saunders, or someone else who has already appeared in the *New Yorker*. This is imperative, as real literary journals have very little interest in writers who have not yet appeared in the *New Yorker*. However, do not send your story to the *New Yorker*. Do not waste the *New Yorker*'s time with your dreary, pontificating bullshit—the *New Yorker* also only accepts stories from writers who have already appeared in the *New Yorker*.

For a book proposal, on the other hand, there are only two basic steps as far as I can tell:

Step 1: Write a book or get an idea for a book and send the idea to an agent or publisher.
Step 2: Receive rejection notification.

Your rejection notification will sound something like this:

Thank you for sending us/thinking of us/burdening us with your story. Unfortunately, it did not fit our needs at this time/had a bizarre subtext that made us think something went wrong during your oral fixation stage/was not authored by anyone who has previously published in the New Yorker. *Please excuse the impersonal nature of this response, but due to the volume of stories we receive, we cannot reply to each individual submission/no one read this/ our intern Hanna folded the manuscript and used it to properly balance a restaurant table. Good luck placing it in the future.*
    Sincerely, the Editors.

Congratulations! You've now completed the work cycle of an active author. All that's left is buying a pretentious-looking notebook that you scribble complete nonsense in two to six times a day and drinking in large quantities to properly prepare for your alcoholism, and you'll be ready to go!

To avoid this fate (yet again), I need a new game plan. Therefore, when it comes to the proposal for this book, I decide that this is what I need: to have fun, to come out swinging for the fences with tactics as brash and unapologetic as I can get away with. Grab the situation by the balls, so to speak.

Mere weeks after the crippling disappointment of my flirtation with a literary agent, I am living again with purpose, with a ferocious electricity and a wound of youthful hubris that I do so enjoy. With this in mind, I package together a query letter, proposal, and the first two chapters of this book. What you read next is exactly what lands on the desks of over fifty literary agents across the country.[77] This is my last stand. This is me at sundown in the middle of town,

---

77 It includes all the errors, misspellings, and typos, so feel free to tabulate them (hint: there's a particularly glaring one in the chapter outline).

gun hanging from my hip. This, I tell myself as I send each proposal off, had better work.

Jane T. Agent
Jane T. Agent Literary Agency
225 Book Deal Street
New York, NY 11111

Dear Ms. Agent,

I'm obviously writing to pitch you a book, but before I get to that, let me break with the standard of query letter format and begin by telling you a bit about my background and slim bona fides. I'm a Chicago-based freelance writer, who currently supports himself by writing content for Cars.com's blog KickingTires and publishing interviews and columns in RedEye, *the Tribune Company's free daily. In addition, I publish my own column at www.stephenmarkley.com, which caters to a network of readers who have been following me since my days as a campus firebrand at a college newspaper. My other credits include* Private Investigator's Magazine, Midnight Times, The Progressive Populist, *and most recently* Weber Studies Journal.

Those are my successes. My failures include an unpublished novel and a nonfiction road trip memoir, which has flirted with representation but likewise never found a home. Why do you care? Because that is what my book is about. Publish This Book *is the story of its own publication. In other words, the entire book is about my endeavor to publish the book. Subsequently, this letter itself is part of the book, as is your response whether you send me a contract ("Cool!" I will write in the book) or a form rejection letter ("Not cool," I will write).*

Of course, I understand what a ridiculous, self-serving concept this is. However, it's obviously not just a book about publishing a book. It's a scathing look at a young writer in pursuit of his dream—the travails of taking that road less traveled, the pitfalls and angst of beginning a life from scratch, of dropping into Chicago with no money, no job, and no prospects. It's about politics and religion and friendship and an unexpected pregnancy and unrequited love. It's about the journey to publication, but not just my publication. Because it's a book about writers, it will include my encounters and interviews with writers from all across the spectrum of success. I will mine them for their stories, using my journey to publication as a backdrop for their accumulated wisdom. The more well-known authors I've secured for interviews include NBA winner Richard Powers, science fiction author Kim Stanley Robinson, bestselling mystery writer Phillip Margolin, pop culture critic Chuck Klosterman, and first-time novelist Heather Skyler. I've already interviewed High Fidelity *author Nick Hornby for the book, although in the interest of full disclosure, we spent more time talking about Bruce Springsteen than writing.*

Yes, the idea is high-concept and unusual. And that's exactly what will set it apart and make it so much fun to read. In addition to the opening chapter, I've included a proposal and an initial chapter outline. However, I encourage you to take a look at my website or even meet with me in person to get an idea of how serious I am about this project. Look at my work with an eye toward opportunity, possibility, or both.

Sincerely,
Stephen Markley

Proposal: *Publish This Book*

How do you market a book that is essentially about itself? A project like Publish This Book *would have broad appeal to a number of different reader constituencies. First and foremost, it has the appeal of any quirky, book-about-nothing-yet-everything. Think Dave Egger's* A Heartbreaking Work of Staggering Genius *or Chuck Klosterman's pop culture rants. There are always large audiences for a strong, humorous voice—one which a reader will follow anywhere, no matter the topic.*

I'm fortunate to have demonstrated such a voice with a core following of readers. My column in the Chicago Tribune's RedEye has quickly become one of its most popular, and the columns that run on my website continue to attract a faithful readership of thousands.

In addition to this scythe-like wit (as demonstrated by my ability to ironically refer to my wit as "scythe-like"), I have a pretty fantastic concept. What the idea of this book allows me to do is travel within any genre—from interviewing famous writers, to telling the awkward story of how my friend got in a fight with Larry Bird, to losing the love of my life to indecision. The book is not actually about nothing. *It is a bizarre, perplexing, occasionally downright silly journey.*

As a member of the so-called Millennial generation (or DotCom or Generation Y or whatever you want to call it), I have seen the chasm that exists on bookshelves for people who came of age during these twisted times of Bush, Iraq, and Paris Hilton. The closest anyone has come to properly describing it is Jon Stewart of The Daily Show, *and he is nearly twice the age of most of his audience.*

Furthermore, aside from some fairly big names I've already secured commitments for interviews, this book has opportunities for cross-promotion. I'm looking to feature conversations with writers as a major part of my "journey" to publication. Why couldn't a few of those writers be selected from among your clients or other writers a publishing house is trying to promote? It's never shameless synergy if you admit it is shameless synergy.

Last but not least, I urge you give me and my project serious consideration for this reason alone: I'm ready to explode. With two books under my belt that no one wants to touch because I don't have a strong enough list of credits to my young name, I'm in a position to come out of nowhere. I'm young, charming, good-looking (enough), and primed to tear a white-hot streak across the face of the country. I can't make you understand through a simple query letter and proposal how serious I am about this book and about my future as a writer. Any risk I represent because of my youth is well worth the upside. I'm the kind of writer who is willing to quit his job, pack his bag, and drive from college campus to college campus to promote himself (in fact, I've already done that—minus the book tour).

None of this will convince you, however. Read the sample chapter, peruse my website, and if you have questions or would like to get a better feel for the direction of the book, feel free to contact me by phone or email.

Chapter Outline (So Far)[78]

1) The Gist—Serves as an introduction to protagonist (me). Sets up writing aspirations, concept of book, thinly veiled narcissism giving way to even less thinly veiled fear, self-doubt, and scatological humor. Theme: Entitlement to fame and fortune.

2) Where to Begin—Begins linear narrative of year spent writing said book. Introduces major characters including Justin, Cleveland, and old professor, i.e. the Mentor. Theme: Self-awareness.

4) Dear, Chicago—Continues linear narrative of year spent writing aforementioned book. Introduces character of Dudeman, who also

---

78 *All subjects of chapters subject to change if reader (you) does not like them and/or can think of better ones.*

appears in parts of Epic Road Trip. Details initial occupations, which include freelance writer for the Tribune's RedEye *and temp at a temp agency. Details soul-crushing aspects of both. Continues development of Cleveland, the narrator's Love Interest, while foreshadowing Life-Changing Moments. Theme: Foreshadowing.*

5) About a Hornby—Describes protagonist's interview with High Fidelity *author Nick Hornby. The two men discuss Bruce Springsteen, Hornby's newest novel, and surreality of having succeeded at writing. Protagonist shamelessly plugs self. Theme: British.*

3) How to Get Rejected—Describes in-depth, the process of getting rejected by every category of the literary world. Describes sense of futility and hopelessness attached to publishing. Describes narrator's two near misses with landing literary representation for a novel and a non-fiction book. Begins backstory of Epic Road Trip. Describes encounter with girl who claimed to have had a reverse orgasm while tripping on acid. Theme: Desperation.

6) A History of Basketball—Takes a look back at narrator's short-lived basketball career as Metaphor for the travails of becoming a writer. Chapter includes no capitalization, and several suggestions for how the reader can interpret this choice symbolically. Theme: Symbolism.

7) Art of the Workshop—Recounts the narrator workshopping the first two chapters of said book for an all-female audience. Comments include similarities to Klosterman, Eggars, Max, to the resentment of author. Written comments include: "Parts of this book that belong in the toilet." Theme: Gratuitous profanity.

8) And In the Meantime Life Goes On—Recounts narrator's en-counter with long-time best friend and drinking buddy, Justin, who reveals he is going to be an (unplanned) father. Recounts narrator's pants-soiling shock. Recounts amusing anecdote involving Justin and NBA superstar Larry Bird in a gas station. Recounts visit from Cleveland and explores narrator's uncertainty regarding his firm commitment not to love her. Foreshadowing grows ominous. Theme: Inevitability.

There is some accomplishment with sending this proposal off, in and of itself. Coach Stahl used to tell us that all you could do in a basketball game is put yourself in a position to win in the fourth quarter. Well, simply by sending off proposals, I was putting myself in a position to win at the very least. Naturally, I told no one. I simply slipped away at work during my lunch hour, strolled over to the post office a few blocks from my office, and ponied up the dough to send three proposals each day.

This leads me to step 1.5 of sending out book proposals, which I neglected in my previous summary.

Step 1.5: Forget you sent the story. Yes, just erase every action—from writing to editing to mailing—that you took to send out this proposal. Don't bother imagining what it would look like in print. Don't envision an agent reading it and gradually nodding his or her head as your lucid brilliance becomes clearer by the paragraph. Take your healthy little ego and your precious little heart, put them in a box, lock it, and then forget the box even exists.

• • •

Sending off the proposal for *Publish This Book* is my most aggressive search for literary representation to date, but it is not my first. That would be the novel I wrote for my senior thesis at Miami.

In my youth, I'd cut my teeth on Crichton and King, creating a smorgasbord of half-finished monster novels with antagonists ranging from a bloodthirsty pterodactyl in Texas to a genetically altered shark with arms savaging an undersea research station.[79] By the time I was a sophomore in college I had written two "what I now think of as" practice novels, each of which, as I said, could go by the alternate title *High School Sucks and My Basketball Coach is a Dick*. By my sophomore year of college I was ready to get behind something with some heft to it, something starkly and unashamedly real.

I won't go into the details of the novel's story because I hate brief, glib synopses of novels enough without trying to force that kind of reduction upon my own. Suffice it to say, the novel I chose to write was a bleak, unrelenting story that dealt with some fairly vicious male-on-male sexual abuse. It was about survival and alienation and was thoroughly unlike anything I'd ever written before. I don't know why I wrote it, except that the idea was there, burning a hole in my dreams until eventually it seared through to the world.

I used this novel for my honor's thesis, so I could graduate with lots of arrogant-sounding honors that have all the real-world application of a Slinky on a football field. This turned out to be a lot of work. Whereas most of my peers were writing theses of thirty to fifty pages, I was playing with a manuscript that ran over three hundred. Through some arduous sessions with my advisors (including Margaret and Steven), I slowly honed the novel over the course of a year.

I promised them that come the fall I would start sending the book to agents—maybe see if a small streak of luck could rocket me past the immeasurable hurdles involved with getting a novel published. I knew full well that countless writers struggle their entire lives to publish just one novel or collection of stories, yet I felt that youth

---

79 Which I wrote in the fifth grade, well before the Thomas Jane–LL Cool J vehicle *Deep Blue Sea*. I'll take that check for the plagiarism settlement now, thank you, Duncan Kennedy and Donna Powers, screenwriters.

and arrogance were on my side. Only a cocky twenty-two-year-old kid would have the audacity to think he could make it so easily, that he could run out four months after graduating from college and conquer the fucking world, but this was all I had.

While on my Epic Road Trip across the country, I spent two weeks in Portland putting together a package while simultaneously researching my markets.

I knew going in that most agents and publishers find new writers through contacts. Like anything else in life, publishing seems more who you know than what you know. I was thus pinning my hopes on dumb luck because connections have never been my strong point. Ninety percent of the people I know either have nicknames that double as words for various parts of the female genitalia or they have bizarre penchants to try to dry-hump my face in excitement when Ohio State wins a close football game. These were not the people who would vault me to literary success.

At that point, I also had very few publishing credits. My only successes included Miami's literary magazine, a nonfiction piece in *Private Investigator's Magazine*, and a story in an online horror, science fiction, and fantasy magazine called *Midnight Times*.[80]

While in Portland, I spent the bulk of my time putting together these packages, but Portland is also my old hometown. I lived there until I was eight and still carry a fondness for the place (not to mention that die-hard commitment to the Portland Trail Blazers). I hadn't been back in years and wanted to take a look around.

---

80   I found out my story had been accepted to *Midnight Times* just before I left for Florida on spring break of my senior year in college. It was in a Sarasota bar that my mentally deficient friend Jack (proud owner of one of those female genitalia nicknames) brought up my literary "success" to the girls we were talking to.

There I was, trying to chat with one, when Jack broke in, "You know, Steve's going to have a story published in an online horror, fantasy, and science fiction e-zine."

"Ha ha," I said. "No I'm not."

"Yeah, he is," said Jack.

These girls gave us a look—you know, the look that says "Did this guy really just try to impress me with a publishing credit in a horror, fantasy, and science fiction e-zine?"

I made it up to the Rose Garden and down to the river walk. I spent a misty gray day walking through downtown, recalling fragments of sights and locales. I went to see an old childhood friend named Stuart. I met Stuart and his older brother, Jeremy, when we were all around the age of four and my family lived in a small rented home across the street from them. Driving back through the old neighborhood was nostalgic in a manner so distant it was like wandering onto the set of a TV show I'd watched years ago—kind of like if I suddenly found myself in Monica's apartment in *Friends*.

I hit up Powell's, the city's breathtaking bookstore, where I lost myself for the better part of the day. Bookstores are incredible things, and every time I step inside one, I am immediately overwhelmed by a sense of purpose. The sheer volume of stories and ideas waiting to be read, the depth and breadth of possibility—it always makes me want to run home and bang out five to twelve books in a single evening. If in your average Borders, this feeling resembles the influence of a minor narcotic, then stepping into Powell's—an endless maze of book-crammed rooms with shelves that soar to two-story ceilings—is like smoking crack with my eyeball. By the time I wandered out, I realized I hadn't had food or fluid for five hours.

I also met a girl in a bar.[81] I was just sitting there, sipping a beer, watching the Iowa–Ohio State football game (mere weeks after the Ohio State-Texas game when I told Jared Padalecki his girlfriend gave me herpes), and ended up getting in a conversation with several Iowa fans, one of whom was a quietly sexy redhead. After Ohio State crushed the Hawkeyes and I'd had my fun at her expense, we struck out across the city, ending in her bedroom that night happily exchanging some fairly foul language.

This girl and I hung out for the rest of the two weeks I was in Portland. We saw *The Departed*, drank a lot of beer, told our stories.

---

81 For those of you wondering how any of this—let alone meeting a girl in a bar—has anything to do with writing, you need not worry because it doesn't. Just relax and remember that life is like a hammock: The threads are all connected.

She recounted a path that took her from Iowa to Vegas to Portland. She worked at the Portland Art Museum and was simultaneously thoughtful, demure, and surprisingly world-worn. She reminded me of a friend who had probably never existed. Without warning, she said things like, "My car was stolen at gunpoint." Or "You always just know when you're doing coke too often."

I told her I was a writer, and she asked, "What does that mean?"

"Mostly nothing," I said, telling her about my three months spent tracking down opposing viewpoints on the Yellowstone wolf controversy. I told her that I was holed up in Portland for two weeks while I mailed proposals for my novel.

"What's it about?" she asked.

"Mostly sexual violence."

"Really?"

"See, that's like the best pickup line ever. I go up to women in bars and tell them I wrote a book about brutal sexual violence. It's better than being rich."

"So then it sounds like you are a writer," she said, a smile dipping her cheeks back.

"I guess," I said. "I'm only a writer in the sense that I'm not anything else right now."

She tilted her head and long curls of reddish-blonde fell sideways. "Do you ever plan to be anything else?" She said this—as she did everything—with a kind of detached amusement. Everything in life seemed like a joke to her to varying degrees, from Iowa's defensive line to our brief, unhinged acquaintance. Only the joke was never simple. It was cosmic, and only she understood it.

I answered her truthfully. "Not really."

I remember my last night in town when I sat on the edge of the bed in her tiny one-room apartment, still feeling her hands and mouth all over me, and asked about the tattoo on her foot. There were others on her body, including a crescent moon on her back, but this one was particularly curious. I can't remember it very well now, except that it was dark green and looked vaguely like a misshapen face. When I brought it up, she smiled and said there was a story. Of course, I asked to hear that story, and here it is, filtered through my unreliable memory.

"Oh, this?" she said with that same bemused smile flitting across her face. "I was tripping on acid and outside it was raining.

"Someone had turned on the stereo and it was playing a familiar CD—maybe U2, something we'd all heard a million times before and would hear a million times again—only I'd never heard it like this. It was in my entire body, you know? Strumming and grasping and pulsing. Then outside it was raining, right? But not just raining; it was a thunderstorm. Lightning flickered on and off in the sky like a child playing with a light switch just to piss off his parents. So some friends and I watched the rain and the lightning and listened to the music sweeping in and out of us until I honestly didn't think I could take it any more—like having a melancholy song playing inside of your eyeball. And all I could do was collapse on the carpet and let it ride through me like a friendly demon who didn't take to exorcism; the rain and the music frightening and sensual, a creature of sex and blood and love that just swallowed me even as it burrowed deeper beneath my rib cage, a jumble of mixed metaphors and soaring birds and winter-tinted dreams filling me up and out like an orgasm in reverse."

"Oh," I said. "Cool."

I never figured out what rain and U2 and an LSD-induced reverse orgasm had to do with a tattoo that looked vaguely like the Napster symbol, but her answer was so poetic I didn't want to ruin it.

I tried to think of something transcendent to say, maybe a carefully worded soliloquy on the nature of life and time and moments of power, shared and in solitude, that would fit nicely into a book I would someday write about this experience and that frighteningly beautiful thing she had just told me, but rarely do you think of the good shit to say right at the moment when it would work best to say it.

"Guess I'll see you when I see you?" I said.

The bemused smile deepened and faded; it was like the corners of her mouth were always trying to say more than the rest of her face. "Keep me updated," she said. "Let me know where life takes you."

And then I was gone, bound for Reno, Nevada, the next day, my wanderings continued, this girl and her tattoo slipping into the recessive fog of memory.

• • •

Months later I found myself in Jackson, Mississippi, sleeping on a friend's floor and recovering from a bizarre night that involved waking in the Marriott hotel downtown with no recollection of how I got there. I woke to my phone ringing, and I answered it groggy, sweaty, and disoriented. It was an agent's assistant asking me if I was the author of the novel he had in front of him. I said that I was. He said that they liked what they had read so far and would like to see the rest of the manuscript.

In my head, I planned to say, "Oh, great! Absolutely. If you give me the details, I will have the manuscript shipped immediately," but that ended up coming out in the slightly less eloquent: "Fuckwhatthebook—Who?"

After a moment of stutters and slurs, I recovered with a promise to send the complete manuscript.

Several weeks later when the agent sent me his vague, uninterpretable rejection letter (he thought I was an "excellent" writer but that the book did not seem "marketable" at the present time—the readership for male-on-male rape really having peaked in the late Nineties, I guess), I could not help but wonder if the man's decision was at all influenced by his assistant saying something to the effect of, "When I talked to this Markley guy, he sounded like he was halfway through a violent heroin withdrawal."

After that, I put the manuscript in a proverbial trunk, and more or less tried to forget about it. I had been warned by enough people: publishing a novel, especially a novel that proposes to be challenging, is hard, dirty work and takes immeasurable amounts of luck. I won't dispute it: too many things have gone right in my life for me to think I deserve luck.

Fate is a trite, stupid word, but occasionally I wonder about the vast store of circumstances that set people in each other's paths. I wonder if we have any measure of control. As it turned out, my enduring memory from my time in Portland would not be the launch of my writing career, which imploded without anyone really noticing, but a stranger I met in a bar who loved art and Iowa football and had once been carjacked at gunpoint. Occasionally I'll think of her and wonder what she's doing, if she's maybe creating inadvertent poetry as she explains to a stranger how to change buses. I'll remember her and her tattoo, and hope that she still finds life as secretly amusing as that night of mixed metaphors, winter-tinted dreams, and the occasional orgasm in reverse.

NINE

And in the Meantime Life Goes On

After finishing the book proposal, I begin the arduous process of sending out queries, accompanied by the two now fully work-shopped sample chapters. And in the meantime life goes on because it is callous and does not care about my dumb idea to write a book about trying to get the very book I'm writing published. Life cannot appreciate a good post-modern screed.

[Author's note: Since this book is something of a cautionary tale for aspiring writers, I thought it would be useful to offer some instruction in the craft. This way I can demonstrate some of the day-to-day decisions of a writer by using a narrative-advancing chapter as an example. We will see how to juxtapose scenes, inter-rupt prose with asides, mesh dialogue with description—all that shit. I thought about using the footnotes to do this, but they're already pulling all the weight they can handle just keeping up with my incisive wit and extraneous anecdotes. That's why you'll get these lovely blocks of italicized interruption. Count on all this to lead somewhere thrilling.]

My break from this book comes in the form of Thanksgiving and a trip home to Ohio for the holiday. I set out from Chicago and wait patiently through brutal traffic on the Dan Ryan and, later, cross the empty fields and small towns of Indiana and western Ohio while belting out every word of Bright Eyes's *Cassadaga*. Thanksgiving with the family passes uneventfully, and the next morning I prepare to set out for Cleveland to see my Love Interest while she is home from Boston.

Remember how way back in the first chapter, I went through five rites of passage to adulthood all in the same weekend? I've since discovered that's how life works: you go through long periods of emotional and psychological stagnation only to have the shit hit the fan all at once.

Before I leave, I get a call from my friend Justin. He wants me to come see him before I take off. I protest, "Justin, I can't. I gotta get up there. I haven't seen her in months."

He won't have it, though, and he won't tell me why he needs to see me. "I'm at my grandparents' house," he says. "Just stop by."

[Next we have the scene where the Primary Action will take place. It is best to set scenes in interesting places like deserted Anasazi ruins, the White House, or a rough neighborhood boxing gym. In this case, what I am writing actually happened. And although it was at Justin's grandparents' house, it would suit my restless imagination better to set it in a space station circling a black hole. In fact, let's try that.]

"Computer," I say, as I arrive at the dock of the space station. "Calculate gravitational intensity."

The pleasant female voice responds from a trapezoidal black speaker set into the wall. "Gravitational pull at 66 percent. Have a nice day."

"Thanks for coming," says Justin, meeting me at the air dock.

"Your levels are a little high. That hole seems hungry."

"They're within range," Justin says confidently. "As long as we get those reinforcing solar processors out here in the next two months, we'll keep this baby afloat long enough to send the exploratory craft in with the anti-gravity buffering system."

"You think you've got all the kinks worked out?"

Justin nods. "The system is designed to form a protective bubble of tightly condensed space-time. This should not only keep the spacecraft from being pulled apart infinitely as it's dragged into the vacuum of the hole, but should also keep it intact long enough to spit it out on the other side."

"But the other side of what?"

Justin raises a daring, half-mad eyebrow. "That's the question, now isn't it?"

[How fun was that? Now let's reset the scene on the precipice of a cliff overlooking a river of lava in some alternate-dimensional hellscape.]

"Grolthar will have the IronStriker's key!" screams Justin as beads of sweat collect on his brow. His eyes blaze with fury and all around us the lava spews chunks of ashen debris.

I hold my ground, my sword-scythe at the ready. "Grolthar knows not the power of the IronStriker's key, Justin! Don't you see? The key gives men the power to rule worlds! It is the ultimate corrupter and debaser of souls."

"Markley, I will have that key or I will have your bones as a necklace and your intestines as a meal for my dogs."

The river of lava rages below us. Justin advances, and I take a step backward, rocks and sand tumbling off the cliff, their echoes vanishing into the bright molten orange of another world. "Take no further steps, my friend! We were once Brisbians of the Inner Circle, but now you have betrayed the Crux of the IronStriker in your quest for unlimited power. Grolthar promised you worlds, but you shall be delivered unto your own eternal misery by the IronStriker himself!"

Justin roars, *"Say not his name!* The IronStriker cannot save you now!"

*[So cool! Still, we should get the actual events recorded for poster-
ity, and it's hard to do so if we're playing around in cool fictional
locales. The real scene will follow if I set it where it actually occurred: boring Justin's boring grandparents' house in boring Mount
Vernon, Ohio.]*

Pissed off that I have to drive upwards of two minutes out of my
way, I go to see Justin, who is waiting for me in his grandparents'
driveway. They live on a quiet back road on Mount Vernon's edge
where a development of small-fry McMansions has sprouted in the
last decade. Their more modest home has managed to escape the land
grab, and I can see out over the dull field of grass that stretches away
into forest. I'm thinking this is about our plans to see a Cavs game
over Christmas break, or our upcoming trip to Europe that summer,
or maybe, as I suggested over the phone, that "cute cuddly Justy just
misses his bestest friend? Does he? Could that be it? Does he wanna a
raspberry? Aw, I bet he just wants a raspberry, doesn't he, Justy?"

"How's it going?" I approach him and prop myself against his
red Jeep, just soaking in a breath of November's unseasonably warm
air and looking out over a browning grass field with the rising sun
burning off an early morning chill as it ascends to the sky.

"Good. Yourself?"

"Just swell. What's going on, man?"

"Well, Markley," he says, hands on his hips, chewing the inside of
his cheek. "You were right. Loren is pregnant."

*[In order to know what he means by "You were right. Loren
is pregnant" (although, I think you can infer pretty well), we
will need to go back in time. Luckily, in writing there really is
no such thing as screwing up the chronological order of things.
Every mistake can simply be attributed to literary license and
soundly executed and buried with various "literary devices" that
can basically appear anywhere, including right in the middle of*

a conversation. Writers discover early that if they ever need to defend something, using the term "literary device" cannot hurt (if I'm ever brought up on manslaughter charges, for instance, I will definitely cite the use of some literary device). So let's back up.]

I consider Justin a brother. Not a brother in a good way necessarily, but the kind of brother you play grab-ass with while you're waiting in line at the grocery store with your mom; the kind of brother who gets more satisfaction from draining an eighteen-foot jumper in your eye than almost any other accomplishment in life; the kind of brother who can get you to drink more by calling you a "twat." More that kind of brother.

Here's what happened after my Epic Road Trip: I moved back to my college town of Oxford, Ohio, for four months with our mutual friend Phil, so the two of us could drink heavily, deliver pizzas, and chase unsuspecting young girls. By all accounts this period was a resounding success. Justin was out west teaching at the time, and Phil and I wanted to share with him a taste of this amazing rules-free existence we had carved for ourselves. Phil and I missed the big guy and convinced him to fly into Cincinnati and visit us for a weekend. Because he was going to so much trouble, we offered to pay for one night of his drinking[82] and resolved to try to pair him with a nubile college coed.

This did not work, as we had made weed brownies that weekend and spent most of our time in and out of a dream fugue populated by spritely angels and barbarous demons to rival the entire catalogue of Revelation. We *did*, however, introduce him to a girl named Loren, whom we had both befriended that semester.

Now I want to avoid saying anything bad about my friend and the mother of my best friend's child—but when I met her, Loren was batshit fun-crazy.

---

82 In Oxford, Ohio, this can be as little as twenty dollars if you pre-game with forties and get four-dollar pitchers at Mac 'n Joes. Forgive us, for we were young and really didn't know any other way.

Loren, Phil, and I once spent a Sunday night going on a "super-senior pubcrawl" where she sucked down something like four hundred cigarettes, and the three of us drank to the point of blackout while cataloguing for each other the most vile, disgusting, deviant stories from our sexual histories. (Let's just say the conversation included a long line of extemporaneous debate on whether or not the activity of "anal ring-toss" is socially acceptable.)

Cut to three months after they met, and Justin's back from Arizona and dating Loren. The two seemed quite happy together, and everyone was more or less pleased. This continued into the fall until I went to visit Justin at Miami where he had started working on his master's. Over pitchers of Pabst Blue Ribbon at our favorite dive,[83] Justin told me that things had cooled between him and Loren. He said she was acting strangely.

"Maybe she's pregnant," I joked.

That is what Justin is referring to when he says, "Well, Markley, you were right." He had only known her for six months.

[Cool. So not only did we find out the reason behind Justin's initial comment, but we got the sum total of Justin and Loren's relationship very swiftly while also discovering that I eat weed brownies. Not bad at all. Now let's pick up after I ask him why she wasn't on the pill.]

"She was on the pill," Justin says.

"Dear." I suck wind. I think of all the times I've had sex based on the assumption that medical science had figured that little egg out. *"Fucking."* I try to breathe. The implications here are as vast and bottomless and unfathomable as the empty eye of a black hole. *"God,"* I say.

---

83   Mac 'n Joes (see previous footnote).

"Yeah. Found out a couple of weeks ago. I just told my family. I told Phil."

"Um," I say.

"I went to see her in Columbus and we went out to dinner. Then afterwards we were in her car, and she just turned to me and said, 'Markley was right.'"

"Shit," I say. "Oh my…" I try to think of an appropriate word. "Shit."

"So I looked at her and I asked if I was the father, and she said yes. So I asked her if she had been to the doctor yet."

I stare at him waiting for more. My tongue is not tied; it is a dead, skinless fish in my mouth. There is so much I need to say, to ask him…

"She said no, so I said first thing's first, and we got a doctor's appointment. Well, sure enough…"

"Um," I say.

"And I just told her, I'd be there for her. Whatever it takes, whatever she needs. I'd be there for this kid no matter what, and that's all she had to know and didn't have to worry about anything else."

I haven't said anything other than cuss words for a minute or two, and I'm not really listening to anything Justin is saying anymore. My shock, fear, and individual insecurities have gotten the better of me. My Id must have slipped out and handed me a piece of a paper before my producer could take a look at it. Even as I open my mouth, I know I'm about to say something incredibly insensitive.

As you might imagine, an insensitive person would say something presumptuous like, "She's getting an abortion, right?" Luckily I am not that person. I am not just insensitive but Incredibly Stupid and Insensitive, so instead, I say, "So are you going to kill yourself?"

Justin gives me a tired look, as if he were stranded in the desert and God asked him if he'd prefer to be transported to the middle of the Pacific Ocean. "No, Markley, I don't think I'm going to kill myself," he says.

Again in my defense, this is the kind of shock when you can no longer feel your blood circulating, when every function of your body feels suspended and your gut feels queasy like you just drank a cup of gasoline. The black hole has swallowed us. The key of the IronStriker is lost.

Slowly, though, Justin pulls me back into orbit. He lays it out for me real simple: he is twenty-four and both he and Loren have college degrees. This is not like getting your girlfriend pregnant after prom. His parents had him at the same age—granted they were married, but having a child at this age is not completely out of the realm of human behavior. "All it does is speed things up a bit," he says calmly.

I feel sick. I have no idea what to make of Justin. He has known this for two weeks, so he has an excuse to be this placid, yet I find myself wishing I could share that initial moment of discovery with him. He's a hard enough guy to read as it is. Since we were kids, he's always played his cards so close to his chest, the events that rock his world, those life-cleaving triumphs and heartbreaks, not even registering as twitches on his face.

"How did you take it?" I ask, and here is where he betrays himself.

Arms folded tightly as if holding his own guts in his belly, he spits into the gravel and says, "Not gonna lie: after she told me, I didn't sleep for about two days. Just…" he shakes his head. "Just stared at the ceiling and thinking—just…" (This is the third time I have him saying the word "just" but he may have gone through five to fifteen more.)

"Just thinking about everything that could have gone differently," he finishes.

Justin has his original speech about being there for Loren. He has this front, this calm that I know he doesn't really feel, so I indulge myself by being scared out of my goddamn mind for him. Forget any question of "love" here—no one's asking if he "loves" this girl. There are other considerations, and it's not just that Justin is a student still, waist-deep in loans, and that Loren has no health insurance, which is kind of key for the whole pregnancy thing. It's not just that she and Justin have known each other for less than half a television season.

It's that we are just kids. We are children ourselves.

He scratches that thick stubble that started popping in on his neck when we were only in seventh grade and bites at the inside of his cheek like he has a dip in. His blue eyes betray nothing. They only say what he says to me now, "Just one of those things, man. It happens."

"Jesus, dude," is pretty much all I can think to say.

[Phew. Heavy stuff. So after introducing our conflict, what some people would call "what the story's about," we can reflect on the larger implications of all that has just occurred. I find the best way to do this—to really calculate the impact that this previously minor character has now had on the narrator's life—is to turn to the Flashback. Fortunately, in literature you don't use actors so we don't have to make Tommy Lee Jones look like he's twenty-four again to play Justin and we don't have to make Screech from Saved by the Bell *look less heterosexual so he can play me. Nope, I just take you back in time full throttle to the days of my Epic Road Trip, for which I have no need to change the setting.]*

I had just left Las Vegas, where I'd managed to rack up a surprisingly small amount of sin considering the opportunities I'd had at my disposal. I had spent the night at the Grand Canyon, wishing I had time to throw on my backpack and venture down into the valley to dip a hand or foot into the snaking Colorado River. But I had to meet Justin, and in the morning I struck out for Many Farms, Arizona, where he was teaching on a Navajo reservation.

My drive took me across both the Hopi and Navajo territories where the desert turns from a drab brown to bright red sandstone that could double for the surface of Mars. Along the way, I saw towns consisting mostly of trailer homes or dilapidated shacks that were tapestries of junked cars, children's toys, hubcaps, rusted wind chimes clinking in the stillness, Mardi Gras beads hanging from door knobs, ripped-out motor parts, abandoned tools, and a thousand other examples of life's trinkets lost just outside the homes to which they belonged. I knew that across the country reservations have always been in rough shape,[84] but there is a difference between reading about a thing and actually seeing it. For instance, I knew rampant alcoholism plagued these communities, but that is different from walking into a gas station and seeing that they keep the hairspray behind the cashier's station along with the cigarettes because the cans can be cracked open and the liquid cut with water. In a stretch of empty desert—nothing in either direction for miles except rock and sand—I passed a man sitting by the side of the road, thumb cocked back, grinning madly to show off a mouth that looked mostly empty of teeth. He seemed to be shaking. I slowed, naively thinking I might actually stop for this happy drunk, until I saw that in his other hand he held a spoon. Just a spoon clutched tightly with the concave side facing the sky. I kept driving, and as I passed, I could see he wasn't shaking but laughing.

Many Farms, as Justin had warned me, really was out in the middle of nowhere in a way that's hard to comprehend until you've driven a straight hour without seeing enough buildings clustered together to form even the most desolate outpost. When I pulled into the small town sandwiched between a few mesas, I felt as if I'd suddenly landed in Times Square.

I parked at the dormitory and wandered over to the high school where four hundred Navajo kids get an all-American education. I found Justin in his classroom grading tests. He'd grown a beard. My own hair was shaggy, wind-battered, and five months without a cut, so our reunion was one of double-takes.

---

84 Ever since that—whattayacallit? Oh yeah, genocide.

"I like the growth," I told him.

"You look like shit," he said.

Over the course of the next week, Justin explained the workings of the reservation and the high school: the low graduation rates, the lower college attendance, and the military recruiters who stalked up and down the ranks of young Navajos.[85] I met Justin's roommate, Kevin, who may as well have been the black version of me (or I the white version of him, I guess). The conversation between us might as well have gone like this:

Kevin: *I like basketball and making sexual references about my friends' mothers.*

Me: *Wait, I like basketball and making sexual references about my friends' mothers!*

Kevin: *The politics of the last six years have basically turned me into a socialist. I'd like to see our president and most of the cabinet water-boarded until they admit their daddies got them all out of facing combat in Vietnam.*

Me: *Let's be friends!*

Kevin: *I talk about sex more or less nonstop. It is on my mind at least every fourth second of every moment of my entire life.*

Me: *While you were saying that, I attained and lost and re-attained an erection based on a picture of a girl I saw in an Abercrombie & Fitch catalogue in 1998.*

Kevin: *For as long as we share living quarters, making fun of Justin is my number one intellectual pursuit.*

Me: *You're dreamy.*[86]

---

85 And to think only a century earlier that this military was tasked with exterminating these people off the continent. Times sure do change!

86 The only time Kevin and I found ourselves in disagreement occurred in a bar when we began talking about Barack Obama. I was of the opinion that Obama had a very serious, very immediate future in politics. My exact words were: "The day Barack Obama decides to run is the day we prepare to elect our first black president."

Meanwhile, Kevin believed that White America would grow even paler at the prospect of leaving its daughters alone with a black executive. Kevin's exact words were:

I watched Justin teach, and he had me speak in his class. I used a Bruce Springsteen quote as my jumping-off point for the discussion. He told me this was something he tried often: he would write a quote on the board and have the kids discuss it. "You know, just to get them thinking, just to try something different."

It did not take me long watching Justin teach to see that the kids completely revered him. He moved with an easy confidence and commanded their attention, even among a group of kids that was supposed to be all but uncontrollable. I knew Justin best as a belligerent fool whose face turns red and whose laugh sounds like a flyswatter hitting a wall repeatedly. It's strange how the more time you spend with a person, the easier it becomes to forget their raw likeability, the things that give them power and that remind you of why you formed a bond with them in the first place. I shouldn't have been surprised to see how good Justin was at this, but I have been so close to him for so long, I was anyway.

All of this was well and good—enlightening, edifying, and all that—but the highlight of our trip came when Justin and I drove out to Durango, leading another car of his friends.

Alone in my car, the two of us finally took some time to catch up. I filled him in on my trip, and he described his future plans. You have to understand at this point, life had taken an abrupt turn for both of us. Only months earlier, Justin was all but married to his longtime girlfriend and thinking about moving to Columbus to teach. I was dating my Love Interest, trying to make amends with her for all

---

"White people won't vote for him. They say they will, but when it comes down to it, and they're faced with a choice between him and some acceptable white Republican like McCain, they're gonna bitch out."

To which I replied, loudly, drunkenly, "Don't get me wrong, Kevin. I hate white people with a slow-burning fury that could probably serve as a source of alternative fuel—"

Kevin shushed me. "Dude, look at the people in this bar! We're in goddamn Durango, Colorado. You're gonna get me lynched."

"What? I'm the one who said I hate white people."

"Yeah, and I'm the one who's black."

my various fuck-ups, and only beginning to understand that I was serious about fleeing madly and recklessly across the country.

And there we both were, hauling ass over the mountains and watching the gray sky descend over Shiprock, New Mexico, where millions of years ago an uprising of lava solidified into an enormous rock wall like the gate from Skull Island. Life had seriously jumped the script, but I figured sometimes the script needs a rewrite. I glanced over at Justin, who had his elbow propped on the edge of the window and his Duke hat tucked low over his brow to shade his eyes from the sun. Justin was about the last kid I expected to find on a Navajo reservation in the middle of the desert. He was something like fourth generation Mount Vernon, and to look at him and hear that sliver of country in his voice, you'd never peg this kid for someone who was looking to challenge his own perceptions of the world. I saw him change in our years at school, and this was the result. Now he talked about the reservation in terms of the graduation rates, stereotypes, economics, alcoholism.

Speaking of alcoholism, in Durango, we had one of those perfect day-drinking shitfests. We got bloated on Himalayan food and hit the bars to watch the Buckeyes play Illinois. We called some of our buddies back in Ohio, who of course were also drinking and watching the game because that's just what us Ohio kids are good at, and in between rounds of nine-ball, I dredged up all the embarrassing stories I could think of for Kevin and Justin's other friends, including the one time he basically said he would bone NBA bench-warmer Chris Quinn.[87]

"You guys want to hear something else?" I asked the group. "Justin used to have this thing he said all the time. He would always

---

87 You remember Quinn from Chapter 7 as the NBA player who once faced us in middle school. Basically, one night during our senior year of high school, a bunch of us were sitting around reminiscing about past athletic glories, at which point Quinn's name came up and we started making fun of him. Justin rushed to Quinn's defense, saying, "Come on now, Quinn's a decent ballplayer. I'll give it to him. I'll give it to Chris Quinn." Try to guess which phrase of Justin's our eighteen-year-old minds fixated on and found unbearably funny.

make a statement and then follow it by saying, 'True or not?' So say we'd be talking and he'd say something like, 'The Buckeyes have the best defensive line in college football. True or not?'"

Kevin laughed at this.

I continued. "It was like you were on a fucking game show every time he opened his mouth. 'Markley, Arizona has some awesome deserts: true or not?' 'Look, Chris Quinn has a long, flavorful penis that would fit nicely in my mouth. True or not?' Every time he said it, we were all like, 'I don't know, true? I guess?'"

Everyone was laughing except Justin, which I took as a good sign. "Me and our other buddy, Phil, used to rag on him so much for it that eventually he stopped saying it all together."

"I'm gonna have to remember that," said Kevin. "True or not?"

Justin shook his head. "Yeah, Markley. Real fucking hilarious. You're a riot."

I offered my beer for a toast. "To our future brides," I said. We clinked glasses.

Earlier that day the two of us had found ourselves standing alone outside of a thrift store while we waited for the others. I had my hands stuffed in my pockets, kicking at the curb like an impatient child and occasionally brushing the shaggy hair from my eyes. Justin leaned up against a wall, chewing a toothpick to splinters.

"Justy," I said.

"Markley," he said

"Something occurred to me the other day."

"What's that?"

I looked off into the deep shadows cast by the western sun. "Well, think about it: when we get married, the two of us have to be each other's best man because all of our other friends have brothers, and brothers get priority for that kinda thing."

Justin did think about it. Out loud, he rattled off every one of our good friends from high school through college. "Wow," he said. "You're right."

"I know. So the only way we'll get to be the best man in a wedding—ever—is if we make a pact right now."

He nodded his appreciation of this momentous truth. "You're right." He stuck out his hand. "Deal."

"I can't believe I agreed to that," said Justin in the bar as we both drained our beers. In an hour I would be arguing with Kevin about Barack Obama. In a day I'd be playing my guitar on a quiet street corner in El Paso. In a month I would be lying in a bed in a cramped apartment in Charlottesville, Virginia, watching the eyes of my Love Interest flutter as she slept. And in just under a year I would be standing in the driveway of Justin's grandparents' house in Mount Vernon with my jaw hanging open in shock. But right then the deal was simple: just the two of us having a drink, our shit-eating grins on wide display, youth and hunger in our eyes.

"Justin," I said. "I'm your best man now. True or not?"

[Backstory, consider yourself filled in. Looks like we've covered all our bases and now have an excellent reason to be invested in this unexpected pregnancy, in which the author (me) is so heavily invested. We've now reached the denouement of the chapter, which will seem completely unrelated to all that we learned previously. It will take place in a different setting, require a different backstory, and involve a different character. Yet the two incidents are related, linked by a common frustration. Because no matter how badly you want to stick to the set of tracks you've chosen, there's always a drunk at the switching station who fell asleep and set you off on another line. Because in the meantime life goes on, no matter how much you want to stick to the route you'd planned. With this in mind, I present to you the Foreshadowing.]

After seeing Justin at his grandparents', I drive to Cleveland, obviously unable to stop thinking about this development. One of my best friends in the world is going to be a father. Justin, James,

and I had been planning a trip to Europe that summer to backpack for six weeks, which now is so obviously out of the question
that the question has been changed to some kind of weird floating
gerund with a quote mark and a pound sign randomly attached.[88]
He is going to have a kid. Like, for forever. He'd shown me a
picture of the sonogram on his cell phone. He had been sitting in
class when Loren sent it to him with the text message "due june
2nd" attached.[89]

This is wild. This is out of bounds. This is one of life's incalcu-
lable curveballs that has no precedent, so when you see the pitcher
throw it, you can only stand there with your jaw slack and wonder
what the hell that was whizzing past you into the catcher's mitt. "Oh
right," you say, "it was a fucking baby."

"No!" says my Love Interest when I tell her.

"Yes."

"NO!"

"Yes."

"Justin?"

"I know."

Man, does my Love Interest look beautiful. When you go a long
time without seeing someone, it's easy to forget the kind of impact those
simple features—eyes, nose, mouth, cheeks, hair—can have on you. It's
been over three months since I last saw her. She has a new haircut, the
sleek blonde shortened, revealing her slender neck. Her eyes positively
glisten in the light coming through her kitchen window.

"You look amazing," I told her before dropping the bomb
about Justin.

---

88 **My mom:** So are you guys still going to Europe this summer?
    Me: Cooking"#

89 Although reality had deserted me momentarily, thank God my sharp wit did not.
Upon seeing this grainy baby-shaped image, I wryly commented. "Well, I can't see his
dick, so at least we know it's yours." To which Justin replied, "So predictable, Markley.
If it were your kid, I would've come up with a much better small dick joke."

"Thanks," she said. She looked me over and shrugged. "You look okay."

I grabbed her and pulled her face to mine.

"How did it happen?" she asks now.

"Well, you see, when a boy and a girl like each other very much—"

"Oh, you're funny. Steve's so funny. He has such good jokes. Why wasn't she on the pill?"

"She was on the pill."

"No!"

"Yes."

"NO!"

"Yes."

"Well," she says, "that's not something a girl likes to hear."

I first spotted her at a party in college, and when I caught sight of her eyes—eyes like a mojito with a splash of dark rum—and they danced over mine only briefly enough to sell me and move on, I remember thinking that I was going to get this one no matter what—no matter how much I had to lie, cheat, or steal. I pined after her for two years before she broke up with her boyfriend, giving me the chance to ask her out.

I remember our first date. When the check came, we both reached for it.

"No, I got it," I said.

"No, come on," she said, reaching into her wallet. "This place is expensive."

"Okay, this is the part where I say, 'No, no, I got it' and you say, 'No, come on let me help out' and we go back and forth for minutes. Let's just cut to it: I'm gonna pay for this, and you're going to owe me a sexual favor later."

She threw back her head and laughed so hard that people in the restaurant stopped eating to look at her. I knew right then I was onto something.

Three years down a treacherous road, and the exact state of things cannot be quantified or described. I own all of the mistakes made in our relationship, beginning in college. Occasionally, I'm aware that I stumbled upon plutonium when I found her. Meanwhile, she bartered for a friend and a partner and got an emotionally selfish and star-crossed love interest who could satisfy her deeply only in the moments when his attention hadn't wandered, when he was behaving himself and trying to scale an outsized temperament back to suit her. After being so reckless with her heart, I hesitated to ask her to insert me back into her life full-time, and as long as we didn't live within a thousand miles of each other, this seemed like the best way. So in the meantime we'd steal away and see each other. She is my best friend, I realize, the person I've trusted most in my life, even as I proved entirely unworthy of her.

So we maintain a mirage of a relationship. "Casual" is the word. Fleeting weekends and road trips. How do you define something like that? So you once shared a joint with her and laughed uproariously at the television because Don Henley kept singing the same ridiculous lyric over and over again on an ancient episode of *Saturday Night Live*. So she once made you laugh until your stomach hurt when—the first time she ever undid your belt—she had the audacity and comic timing to say, "Aw, great. Now you're going to tell all your friends I'm a big slut." So you showed up at her door unexpectedly in Charlottesville a year earlier when she thought you were in San Antonio, and she was so surprised she couldn't stop shaking, yet she still had the audacity and comic timing to point to her gym outfit and say, "Well, I hadn't planned on ruining this moment by sweating balls in this outfit, but now that I have, I've got to say, this should teach you a lesson." So she challenges you and goads you into the uncomfortable realization that life is infinitely more complicated than you ever could have imagined.

"What are you thinking about?" she asks me, as we sit on the couch in her living room.

And because it's easier (and often the truth), I say, "You sitting on my face."

She nods. "Good. I've trained you well."

Two years spent pulling visits to each other's respective locations whenever we had the time and financial wherewithal—visits that only protract and worsen this strange limbo. When we part, we are both back to our vague, difficult realities. We are college graduates of an uncertain generation, and the world we live in is not the one we expected from our childhoods.

[Before we proceed with this, let's change scenery. A suburban living room is just about insufferable, so let's move the action to the Creator's Garden, which is a circular ring of foliage and forest overlooking a pool that contains the universe. The grass is a more vibrant green than your imagination can conceive, and the fruit that grows from the trees would make your head explode if even a drop of the sweet juice ever blessed your tongue. And at the center is the universe: spiral galaxies and elliptical galaxies shaped like footballs and quasars and red giants and white dwarves and, yes, black holes locked in a swirling, infinite cosmic dance.]

We sit on the silky grass of a hillside looking down into the pond of creation. "Do you remember the bar in Charlottesville?" I ask her. "The Band was on the jukebox. We were talking about Michael Caine?"

She doesn't, but that's okay. I explain to her that this is the last time we ever had a serious conversation about the universe.

"What about the universe?" she asks.

I shrug, my eyes locked on a nebula of space dust unraveling into a rotating galaxy, being swallowed and absorbed. "What is the state of the universe? Where is it going?"

She shakes her head, runs her hands through those vibrant green blades, breathes in the scent of the garden, which makes her dizzy with the odors of rain and sea and cake and flowers and sun and snow and rivers and grilled lake trout cooked in tequila over an open flame. "I don't know," she says slowly. "The universe has always been a complete mystery to me."

"It's like it's forever locked in this strange limbo."

She shrugs. In the pool of the universe, worlds are sucked into holes in the fabric of space-time, and this makes her eyes well with tears. "What's a girl to do?" she says.

There was no answer when we were in that bar and The Band was singing about the night they drove old Dixie down, and there seems to be no answer now. Just this tapestry of cosmic forces at the center of the garden—complete with all of its suffering and joy and bitterness and wonder. I think of Justin and now I can smell the truth: limbo can only be limbo for so long. Life waits for no one, so you either get on your ride and let it take you where it takes you, or you can only stand there with your ticket in your hand like a timeworn shmuck as all the things that frighten you careen off into the dusk on the ride you should've taken.

The universe is one beautiful fucking mess.

"I guess, for now, this is enough," I say.

She looks at me and smiles, those eyes—eyes like the Northern Lights trapped in a marble—leaving me hopeless.

[So there we have it: A sprawling story that outlines an event, delves into the various properties and realities that event affects, and delivers a nice ambiguous ending that forewarns of things to come. All in all, a pretty good deal. Sure, had I not written this and was instead the reader, I would have a few gripes: "First of all, more tits, please. If I wanted to read Under the Tuscan Sun, *I would have borrowed it from my divorced aunt." Another contention might be: "How exactly does this relate to the book you're writing, which is supposed to be about you publishing the book?" To which I say, Excellent question: let's set my response in the form of the next fourteen chapters.]*

TEN

Chicago Cold

The rejection letters for *Publish This Book* begin to trickle in and with them that familiar disheartening drag on previously effervescent spirits.

As I said, I'm used to rejection. I don't mind the letters. They're part of the process, and you have to let them slide off you or you'll go mad. But the first couple of rejections you get after querying for a new project are the worst, the pits of hell.

You've just put together this package—this fresh, sparkling collection of brilliance and insight that you pored over, edited and re-edited and shaped and smoothed and buffed and refined until you had it shining like the Grail. Then to get back an email or letter only days later that says simply: "Not for me. Good luck with this elsewhere." It doesn't matter how thick your skin has grown, how calloused, you still feel despair like a punch in the gut.

The rejections for *Publish This Book*, however, have led me to an interesting realization: it's no longer my Ego I fear for. With previous projects, I always had this overriding fear that I simply wasn't good enough. This is now gone. I'm aware I have some minimum kind of talent, at least. What worries me is how many more times I can go through this process—how much more jaded I can afford to become before I simply tell whatever talent I have to go fuck itself as I settle into an existence writing ad copy.

Still, even a rejection is better than hearing nothing. I always hated it when I went out with a girl and she just stopped answering the phone in order to get rid of me. I much prefer the women who tell me I'm an unattractive borderline narcissist with a drinking problem. I like to know where I stand.

Earlier in the year, I met a kid on the staff of the satirical newspaper *The Onion*, who recommended that I apply for a freelance position with them. I thought this was a superb idea because it would mean another paycheck and a writing gig where I got to curse. *The Onion* is one of my favorite news sources, an outright middle finger to the established order, constantly reminding us that life—even at its most depressing, violent, and chaotic—is entirely farce. I was so psyched about the prospect of writing for them that I set aside *This Book* and spent two weeks working on my submission and writing sample. I sent a letter with my résumé and a handful of short fake news articles to the editors.

But I never heard back.

I admit, if I worked in the offices of *The Onion*, I would probably smoke more dope than the glaucoma wing of a major Bay Area hospital and, because of this, not respond very promptly to freelance submissions. Still, it was disappointing, even though I knew in my heart that every wannabe satirist in North America sends an application to *The Onion* immediately upon graduating from college. And as soon as they realize that they'll never hear back, they promptly return to smoking weed out of a pop can and letting those great *Onion* headlines they come up with while stoned vanish into their THC-addled dreams.

Well, this wannabe satirist ain't about to let his hard work go to waste. That's why I've decided to replace all space breaks in this chapter with samples of my *Onion* stories that I never heard back about. Keep in mind, these have nothing at all to do with the chapter. They are glorified asterisks. Like so.

Osama bin Laden to join cast of hit Fox show *24*

LOS ANGELES—Sources report that Osama bin Laden, the reclusive al-Qaeda leader and mastermind of the shocking terrorist attacks of September 11, 2001, will put his global jihadist ambitions on hold for the coming spring in order to focus on his new role as a secret agent for the fictitious Counter Terrorist Unit on Fox's hit drama *24*. Sources say that in a twist, bin Laden will play a loyal friend to the show's main protagonist, super-agent Jack Bauer, played by Kiefer Sutherland.

"It's a true pleasure to work with such a serious, devoted individual," said Sutherland in a phone interview. "I'm really looking forward to playing his foil in some pretty intense scenes."

Although the plot of season 7 of the runaway television phenomenon remains under tight wraps, rumors abound of a possible love triangle involving Bauer, bin Laden's character, and long-time Bauer squeeze Audrey Raines.

Bin Laden, who remains the world's most wanted fugitive and currently resides in the ghostly, treacherous nightmarescape of northern Pakistan, could not be reached for comment.

I send most of my queries for this book by email, simply to save on postage and trips to the post office. I know this is not ideal (it feels as if it's much easier for an agent to disregard an email than a physical manuscript), but if I plan on sending out between eighty and one hundred of these packages that include fifteen pages from my first two chapters… Let's just say that's a lot of paper I'm going to have to steal from Cars.com.

Paper and ink have always been an issue. Back when I was in school, I used to work at the circulation desk of the main library, and I'd print out all of my material there. There's no way I could estimate how much money I cost Miami University creating hard copies of my literary aspirations. Suffice it to say I couldn't have afforded it myself.

Here's an important tip for aspiring writers: find a job where you have easy access to a communal printer. You have no idea how much time, effort, and money this will save you in the long run. In fact, when I left the SoulSuck Agency to pursue my car-blogging career, I spent my last two days smuggling out reams of printer paper in my bag because I knew when I arrived at Cars.com I would be hesitant at first to print out thirty pages a day.

I have my puny college printer at home, but it's a dinosaur that I've been hauling around with me for three years. It etches out each page at a snail's pace, and I must vigilantly watch for paper jams, smudged ink, or other printer-related disasters that occur with shocking frequency. It's difficult to send out stories and queries regularly when printing seven pages can feel like the psychological equivalent of cooking a gourmet meal with a hair dryer.

I rarely use this printer, as it is a depressing reminder of my continuously loose and insubstantial existence. Sometimes I feel like I can almost hear my printer encouraging me, but I can't tell if it's being sincere or incredibly condescending.[90]

To escape my printer and claustrophobic living quarters, I spend the remainder of my free time enjoying basketball and *The Daily Show* on a big-screen hi-def TV with my roommates. Like them, I have signed a mutual nonaggression pact with adulthood and therefore think it's okay to eat cereal for dinner regularly. None of us

---

90 "You keep it up, buddy!" says my printer. "I know things seem rough now, what with not being able to afford a desk so that I, Inkjet 3000, don't have to sit right on the floor. But hey, no worries! After all, guy, even though you seem to have staked all your hopes and dreams on this one unwieldy idea that you have me chugging out pages for like a cancer-stricken smoker hacking up painful, phlegmy breaths, what do I know? I'm just a silly-goose Inkjet 3000! I love your passion, pal! It's written all over you, even with the bumper stickers on your little trunk! 'End the War'? 'Big Media' with a slash through it? Wait'll the Powers That Be get a load of that!"

knows what we want out of life or anything about women or God or how to stop the sewage from bubbling up in the basement when we run the washing machine so that the entire house does not reek of shit.

Weather saves man from awkward racial tension

TACOMA, WA—Sources report that Gerry Teager, 37, a financial analyst in Tacoma, Washington, was saved this past Tuesday morning from an embarrassingly silent elevator ride with an African American. Teager arrived to work at his building, as he does every morning, with a mentally prepared small-talk script to exchange with Hank Grifford, 54, who heads security at the office park. "Usually we talk about the Seahawks or the Mariners… You know, 'cause I figured he likes sports," said Teager, who is Caucasian.

According to Teager, everything was going perfectly well until Grifford left his post to step into the elevator with him. At that point, said Teager, "It all went to hell."

After gazing at the lighted numbers for a moment as the elevator ascended, Teager was able to avert a complete social disaster when it dawned on him to say, "Boy, is it a scorcher today or what?" The ensuing conversation sparked by this observation took Teager and Grifford through the remainder of the elevator ride.

"I wanted to let him know that I'm cool with the whole affirmative action thing," said Teager. "But I figured he could tell because I was so interested in talking to him. People sometimes can just sense good things about others."

When reached for comment, Grifford said. "It was 65 degrees. I don't know what he was talking about."

It's also winter in Chicago, which is like winter in Hell, except for in Hell you can at least meet interesting historical figures. Every morning, I stand out on the platform at the Wellington Brown Line stop and pray for a train to either arrive and take me to work or jump the tracks and grease me; my dying thought would be something like: *All right, three-day weekend!* Winter here is soul-crushing, never-ending, unrelenting. I've lived in the Midwest most of my life, but a Chicago winter is somehow different. It's not just the bitter cold, the skin-stinging wind ripping gruesomely off Lake Michigan, or the endless snow that piles ever higher. You think nothing can be worse than this until the snow melts and the streets and sidewalks become unforgiving swamps of slush and water, which is the new Worst Thing Ever right up until that slush and water freezes into a hull of ice coating every street and sidewalk and you risk a broken arm every time you step outside.

And then it snows again.

One night during that first winter I spent in Chicago, I find myself in a bar in Boystown, explaining to a friendly gay man just how much I hate winter right now.

I got to this crowded labyrinth of dim blue light and overbearing techno music thanks to SoulSuck people. I went to a party at the apartment of a girl I became friends with while working there, and in the course of events that followed, befriended a gay guy named John who, along with a few other people, convinced me that it would be a good idea to head to this nearby bar with no shortage of guys who are better looking than me.

This fits perfectly into my philosophy involving the gay lifestyle and attending gay bars. James once told me that he doesn't mind when guys think he's hot. "It's just like if an ugly chick thinks you're hot. You're flattered but not interested."

Well said. However, I also feel (or have convinced myself after drinking an entire punchbowl of highly alcoholic spiced cider at the party) that a gay bar will be the perfect place to attract low-hanging fruit—women who have tagged along to the bar and find themselves longing for heterosexual attention. This was my plan when I left for this bar: to find a quick bit of comfort and assurance. Now my only plan is to bitch at my new gay friend about the weather.

"This ain't the same city I moved to. This is something else. This is a nightmare, a vision of Hell. And you know what I'm going to do? Trudge outside and just fucking take it!" I think about my choice of phrasing. "Was that offensive when I just said I'd take it?"

"Chicago cold," he agrees, as if he didn't hear my last question.

Before I can continue, he asks me what I do.

"Oh," I say. I'm prepared to give him the usual spiel about being a writer, working for a car website, maybe you've seen my column in *RedEye* (and at this point that is no longer an unrealistic possibility). Then I think of my queries bouncing back at me. I think of the general ennui I've settled into about my future. "I'm a gargenflargle," I mumble.

"Come again?" he asks over the pulse of the music, which seems completely out of tune with the strobing blue lights.

"A gargenflargle," I say louder, but not much. If you're young and in a loud bar, you can get away with telling people what you do in nonsense words. They'll just assume you're talking about finance or PR or something. "I work with vrision-pace, jousticks, and a lot of phenymoore cooprers. You know, cadenceville."

"Oh, right," he says. "Cool."

When I leave the bar at two in the morning, I make the trudge south to Belmont and then west to my house. The snow is piled thigh-high at some curbs and on the sidewalks my boots disappear with every step, even as I try to follow the prints that came before. It's Chicago cold outside, and every step reminds me not of how much closer I am but rather how far I still have to go.

Man disappointed to finally see singer, songwriter Ryan Adams

NAPERVILLE, IL—Upon seeing his favorite new musician for the first time, Jim Dearborn, 25, could barely contain his disappointment in Ryan Adams's physical appearance.

"I couldn't believe it," said Dearborn with a sad shake of his head. "Seeing him for the first time was like finding out Pamela Anderson has a penis."

Dearborn pointed to Adams's bizarre bedhead hairdo, his clear lack of thought about his clothing, and rather plain, unremarkable facial features. "All I'm saying is that this guy makes great music," said Dearborn. "Jesus, when he sings 'Easy Hearts' with Whiskeytown, it makes me want to rip my fucking heart out and squeeze the blood into my eyes. Then I finally see a picture of the guy and he looks like my friend Tom. And Tom's a total douche bag."

Dearborn only recently became a fan of Adams's music because of his girlfriend and had figured the singer would look appropriately dark, yet gritty, with a handsome jawline and between two to four days of stubble. "But no," said Dearborn. "He looks like Dana Carvey playing Garth from *Wayne's World*."

While my book proposals don't seem to be landing with agents, at least my columns in *RedEye* have begun to garner a smidge of attention. Every now and then I'll get an email or Facebook message from a stranger telling me how amusing a particular piece was. One guy asks me for a copy of a column in which I confessed my love for John McCain's daughter, Meghan. A young woman Facebooks me to say that she too hates text messaging.

My content at *RedEye* is fairly innocuous, though, leading to rather weak hate mail. The only really juicy one comes from a gentleman who berates me for several hundred words for noting that Republican presidential candidate Mitt Romney "looks like a guy you'd like to punch in the face." My final word on the matter is that all it takes is one look at Romney to see that this is not a subjective statement.

It lifts my spirits somewhat to see that I'm finally sparking a reaction, albeit an isolated one. Yet I already feel myself growing restless with where I can go at *RedEye*. Am I going to write silly columns about being hungover on January 2 when I'm forty? I think back to when I arrived in Chicago and recall that landing a column in this paper felt like scoring a Pulitzer Prize. I'm like the little kid who cries for months to get the robot action figure he wants, only to decide it's a lame, unimpressive toy as soon as he has it in his hands.

Area youth harbors growing fear that 'surge' may not have worked

GREEN BAY, WI—Ryan Jones, 18, reportedly continues to shelter a sense of dread that the so-called "surge" has failed.

"I look in the mirror and I say to myself, 'Is this all a lost cause?'"

Beginning back on mid-Tuesday, Jones found an insurgent pimple on the lower part of his brow that he could clearly see was going to develop into a full-fledged zit if not attacked immediately. "You gotta fight 'em when they're blackheads," said Jones. "So you don't have to fight them when they're whiteheads."

The purpose of the surge was to allow so-called "breathing room" for the surrounding pores, so that the freshly expunged pimple could scab over and begin to heal. Still, Jones refuses to set any kind of timetable for the zit, saying only that as the Cetaphil facial scrub stands up, he will stand down. Although he refuses to set an artificial deadline, friends and acquaintances know that mid-Saturday is Becky Chambers's party and as one senior member of Jones's friend group put it, "There's no way he's gonna get into her pants with that fucking growth on his forehead."

I've considered failure before—what it looks or tastes like—but never like this. I've never had this much free time to stare it in the eye. I continue to interview bands for the Chi-Tunes feature, chasing down bland punk groups who could all put their songs into one big mix tape and none of them would be able to tell which were their songs and which belonged to the other lyrically glib Smashing Pumpkins impersonators.[91]

These interviews become disheartening because it's hard to talk to band after band, musician after musician, all of whom think they are sitting on the cusp of breakout success, of massive, overwhelming popularity, of having all of their dreams come true. Then to an outside observer like me—well, all I have to do is listen to their stuff and understand that a lot of these guys[92] will be going back to school in a year or settling down in that office job in two. It seems artists—musicians, writers, and actors alike—never understand that one in a million means there are 999,999 failures waiting to happen, and yes—you, I, we—are likely among them.

I interview a rapper named Ill Eagle, who earns my respect almost immediately by saying the most intelligent thing I've yet heard from any of these almost-entirely anonymous acts. After talking for a while about his youth growing up in the devastated factory town of Gary, Indiana, just south of the city, his affinity for grunge rock, and his experience as an unheard-of underground musician, we talk about how he promotes himself and his album. "You can understand," he says. "You're a writer. We're the same thing. You know as well as me, all you can do is put your shit out there and hope someone notices."

---

91 Seriously, I interview the lead singer of a band, and he literally cannot name another musical influence other than Smashing Pumpkins. Sure enough, when I check out the band's music on their MySpace page, all eight songs sound like Billy Corgan after a lobotomy.

92 And why are they always dudes? Don't women ever pursue dreams in the face of sucking so badly?

By phone, we talk well beyond the normal parameters of one of these interviews, and he tells me about growing up in the hardscrabble industrial town of Gary while being a black kid whose favorite band is Nirvana. The rapper speaks with a smile in his voice of how he never exactly fit anyone's expectations of what a black kid from Gary should do and say and feel and believe. I spend the rest of that night listening to a particularly haunting song of his called "Burn Out/Fade Away" and thinking about all the truth and sadness of that statement: you put your shit out there and hope someone notices. Then you keep going until you can't take it anymore and maybe even after that.

Iraq war, Darfur causing serious distraction to Spears's unraveling

LOS ANGELES—Media analysts, politicians, and citizens alike cried foul this past week as the dual escapist spectacles of the Iraq war and the ongoing genocide in the Darfur region of Sudan robbed the spotlight from pop singer Britney Spears's mental breakdown.

On the very same week that saw Spears's audaciously poor performance of her new single "Gimme More" at the MTV Video Music Awards, the pop star's travails were overshadowed by the continued rape, pillage, and slaughter in northwestern Africa and Gen. David Petraeus's much-hyped report on the success of the military surge in Iraq.

Connecticut senator and presidential hopeful Chris Dodd voiced his dismay. "I know what citizens of Connecticut and of this country need to see when they turn on their TVs, and it's certainly not careful, reasoned debate about how to extricate ourselves from Iraq without leaving a dangerous power vacuum and chaos behind. In light of this performance, we need to know what's going on with Ms. Spears. For the love of God, she looked like a retarded whale."

Spears's personal life has been a topic of much speculation and

interest ever since her marriage to dancer/rapper/tank-top aficionado
Kevin Federline. Unfortunately most people feel as if it's not enough.

"Sure, we saw the pictures of that caesarean scar near her vagina,
but have we ever gotten video images of the inside of her uterus?"
asked professor of political science James Whithoff of Columbia
University. "We hear about this place called Darfur with stunning
regularity, but I'll tell you something: that place isn't even in the
United States. Britney Spears is. She lives somewhere in California."

Hillary Clinton is on our enormous big-screen television after
losing the South Carolina primary. But instead of acknowledging
that she lost that contest, she has chosen to launch into a standard
stump speech about health care.

"Oh fuck you, Hillary Clinton," Erik tells our TV.

"I'm so fucking sick of health care," I say. "That's it: no one gets
health care. You all couldn't stop being annoying about it, so that's
the end. No health care for anyone."

In case you couldn't tell, our house voted Obama.

This is the favored pastime in our house now. We watch the news
and analysis from the most dynamic, history-making, ground-breaking,
air-conditioner-shaking election of modern time and then bitch about
how dumb the whole thing is. We are junkies on a binge that will last
months, until either Clinton or Obama finally cries uncle.

I've been an Obama backer ever since 2004 when I picked up his
memoir, *Dreams from My Father,* and was shocked to find it thoughtful, intelligent, and well-written. I was sure he was too smart to ever
be president.

I do take some shit from Democratic friends who say I'm voting
for Obama because of my white guilt,[93] or because I think he's the
second coming of Jesus, the savior of the country and the world, or
because he's an egg-head, latte-sipping, limousine liberal elitist. No,

93 Although it is overwhelming.

he has my vote because he has successfully demonstrated that he can a) form a coherent thought longer than a paragraph and express that thought in a way that is not condescending to the intelligence of the average American and 2) because he comes at policy looking for "what works" rather than from an ideological straitjacket.[94]

Obama appeals to us—a generation that grew up in the laid-back chill of the Clinton years only to rudely awaken to a far different reality during the days of Bush—because he offers the Promise even if no one can quite describe what that is.

We also have a peculiar tolerance. By this, I mean that in the United States, ours is the most tolerant generation yet. People my age are less likely to care about race, gender, or sexual orientation than any previous generation. Listening to NPR[95] one day, I hear a commentator refer to us as the "Whatever" generation. As in, "Obama's black?" Shrug. "Whatever." Our generation sees promise in Obama that we've never seen in any other politician in our lifetimes.

As Erik puts it: "He can be a progressive Reagan. A transformative figure."[96]

And as James puts it: "I just want to kiss Barack. All over his cute face."

I agree with this, even if I don't agree with Obama's every policy right down the line. He has the potential to do greater things than any of his rivals. Our generation sees this in him because I think we occasionally see it in ourselves when we aren't watching *The Hills* or contracting venereal diseases.

Yet after South Carolina, the Clinton machine begins to bring the heat. Even when Obama fights Clinton to a draw on Super

---

94 I know this doesn't sound like a shocking idea—unless you follow politics at all, in which case it's crazier than a clown growing knives out of his face.

95 Oh my god, I'm such an elitist! Gimme my latte! Line up my limousine! Granola, abortion, raise taxes!

96 Full disclosure: Erik says this to us while lying splayed out on the couch in his boxer shorts and a T-shirt, a homemade bean burrito in one hand and his testicles in the other.

Tuesday, I have my doubts that he'll be able to pull this thing out. Just something else in life to stress out about all day.

Area woman thinks of perfect *Onion* headline

ATLANTA—Jess Slayer, 42, an ad executive, claims to have come up with the perfect headline for the satirical newspaper, *The Onion*.

"I was just taking a shower thinking of what I'd have for lunch, and suddenly it hit me," said Slayer. "The most perfect *Onion* headline you've ever heard."

A longtime fan of the publication, Slayer believes that the headline is perfectly irreverent, witty, and urbane.

"It's not one of those where you read the headline and it strikes you as hilarious all of a sudden. It's one you've got to think about for just a second, but then... Eureka!"

All Slayer will reveal is that the headline has something to do with shampoo brands and the uncertain political future of Venezuelan leader Hugo Chavez.

My roommate Elliott sums it up for me in one word.

Elliott, as I said, alerted me to the job at Cars.com, and once I'm employed there, he and I spend 20 to 40 percent of our day talking via Google Chat about topics of the utmost importance to the company. Issues like:

- The hot tub on craigslist we should totally buy for the house

- Nina, the hot chick on his floor, who is *soooo* fucking hot

- How bored we are at work right now

- If I think Nina would like it if we had a hot tub in our backyard

Yes, we are a crack team. Rarely a day goes by when I do not see this message pop up on my screen:

Elliott: fuzzy man
Me: what dude?
Elliott: nina just looked at me. oh man she is sooo hot.

Fuzzy indeed, Elliot. Fuzzy everything. Fuzzy politics, fuzzy this goddamn living situation, fuzzy my perpetual lack of sleep, fuzzy this frustrating book, fuzzy my Love Interest living so far away, fuzzy my lame job, fuzzy this never-ending winter weather that sucks the life-force from my soul, fuzzy my unrealized dreams, but most of all fuzzy these rejection letters.

The key is to disregard the letdown. I keep telling myself that I have to press forward, that getting discouraged and fed up will not help in any way. But if existential dread could be a doctoral topic, I would have a PhD by the end of the week.[97]

Writer's exploration of self, world in self-referential tome found unbearable

CHICAGO—Writer and self-proclaimed "voice of a generation" Teven Sarkley, 24, claims to have written a moving and epic book about his quest to become a published author.

"It's funny; it began as a little joke with myself," said Sarkley, a blogger whose daily writing responsibilities consist of less than five hundred words on esoteric functions in automobiles. "But now it's ballooned into so much more. I'd call it a 'howl'—the epic of a generation yearning to find an identity."

Sarkley began the project seven months earlier, at which point he was unemployed and packing boxes part-time. He now has over

---

97 But not a published book on the subject.

50,000 words of what he describes as *On the Road* meets *Naked Lunch* meets *Beloved.*

"It's supposed to just be about publishing this book—you know, that's the funny little hook, but then I come around the back and make it all about love and life and friendship and dreams and stuff," said Sarkley.

Friends and loved ones have been reluctant to tell Sarkley that his "once-in-a-generation masterpiece" is a circular, self-indulgent writing exercise gone horribly awry.

"From what I can tell, it's mostly about him bitching about things," said friend and confidant Ted Donner. "I mean, there's an entire chapter about how he hooked up with a chick in Portland. Yeah, well, I made out with a girl in Milwaukee once, but I'm not about to write a book about it."

We throw a New Year's party and my Love Interest flies in from Boston. We drink and dance and I rap to her every lyric from the 2Pac song "Thug N U Thug N Me" while she cackles wildly.

She sleeps beside me on my floor mattress for those few fleeting nights, out-muscling me for the center of the bed like she always does. In spite of the fact that she is half my size, kind, and even-tempered, sleeping beside this slender young woman is like bedding down with the German army on the Russian front circa 1944. It feels like I'm cannon fodder every time she makes her move for the middle. I often wake to find myself on the verge of tumbling off the mattress or sometimes with my shoulder resting on a bedside table for support. Meanwhile, she will be on her stomach, occupying more physical space than is mathematically possible given her petite figure. Quantum physicists should study her just in case this contradiction of the basic principles of physics might someday open up an errant black hole and threaten Earth's existence.

Upon waking, I always try to move her back to her side of the bed and regain some of my territory. My Love Interest, however, is one of these people who always wakes up slightly confused and doesn't always make sense when she first speaks. So I'll nudge her awake to tell her that she is yet again dominating the bed in a way that would make Napoleon's conquest of Europe look relatively tame, and she will inevitably say something like, "Huh? That cat was named Molasses…"

On her last night in Chicago, I wake to find myself in this familiar territory, thrust to the side of my small floor-mattress. I don't care much though. This trip of hers has been deeply needed. I feel things slipping, a part of me knowing that this state of affairs—not together, but together when we see each other—cannot last forever. But I've missed her in the last few months, more than usual, and I'll take every moment I can get—even this one, with her drooling on what had been my pillow when we fell asleep but is now clearly her pillow.

I say, "Baby, wake up." She stirs, smacks her lips. Her eyes are slits as they open, and even in the dark I can see she is confused and troubled by this interruption of her dreams. "You gotta scoot over." I nudge her. "Come on."

"Wha?" she says sleepily. "Turnips didn't invent peanut butter."

I finally manage to shove her to the side of the bed, but when I slip back into my original position, she greedily turns, slides her hand over my chest, and pulls herself onto me so that her head rests in the notch between my pec and shoulder. Her hand combs at the hairs on my chest for a moment, and then she is still and breathing. I can just barely make her out in the dark, her silhouette the color of silver in the light that has slipped the boundaries of the window shades. We lie there, and like with so many things, this is the way it goes.

And the Good News?

This is the part of the story where we are surprised to find that our humble narrator is not doing so well. What should I shell out first, the good news, the bad news, or the really bad news? I like to end on positive notes, so I'll start with the really bad news: my Love Interest tells me she no longer wants to see me.

Here's the thing: I went to see her in Boston and knew something was wrong. She acted strangely the whole time—quiet when she would normally have roared with ideas, somber when she would have lit the sky on fire with laughter. Walking along the bizarre dodecahedron-shaped buildings of MIT, she didn't even flinch when I broke out my faux-pet name for her.

"Something wrong, Sugar Nipples?"

To which she *should have* responded something like, "You aren't playing with my girly parts." Instead, those eyes—eyes like a translucent alien swallowing a whole lime—avoided mine and she simply said, "Nothing."

Before I left, I bit my tongue and it bled for five hours. On the latter end of that ordeal, she told me she wanted to know where this was going. This led to the typical two-hour conversation about life and love. For a quicker example, see any *Friends* episode where Ross and Rachel fight.

But to know what was really behind the discussion between us, take a look at this sentence she once said to me: "Steve, I'm afraid that you're the love of my life."

Have you ever heard someone say that to you? And he or she wasn't fourteen? I was terrified that this was true for me as well but for an entirely different reason.

Luckily, after I got back from Boston, my Ego had command of things. I found him snorting coke off the thighs and buttocks of vapid, blonde Northside Chicago girls and telling me, *Whoa, Markley. Slow down. Just hold on a sec. You're not goddamn John Cusack, man. You've got places to go and shit to chase down. Isn't there a harbor in Auckland you wanted to get a look at? What about those cliffs they got in Dover? You think she's gonna wanna put all her shit on hold? Her ambitions, her goals, her dreams, her life just because you've got a little too much wanderlust? You're gonna move to Boston and live in a little apartment with a whole bunch of furniture that the two of you will bang your shins on during the move when you finally upgrade to a brownstone and then some house in the fucking suburbs? Are you kidding? What part of this sounds like anything you're capable of? Face it, my friend: you weren't designed to take on freight. You're built for speed.*

We finally speak on the phone weeks later, and before we're past the hellos, I can tell everything is shot to hell. I know this because my Id shows up. I'm sitting on the Throne of Genius under glittering white Christmas lights and the watchful gaze of six different Bruce Springsteen albums, when suddenly my Id is sitting on my floor mattress with his ankles crossed. He winks at me.

My Love Interest says, "I can't do this anymore. I'm not a girl who needs to justify herself by being in a relationship, but after a while, after long enough… I mean, I can't get by on a visit with you every two or three months."

Oh, she might be talking, sure, but I'm not really paying attention to her. I'm watching my Id in the corner of the room. My Id looks a lot like me, only he has better facial hair. I can't grow a decent beard, but my Id can, and he demonstrates this with his perpetual two-day stubble. His hair is a ragged mess, long and spiky and sinister. He wears a faded leather jacket, blue jeans, and heavy cowboy boots, which I motion for him to get off my bed. He gives me the finger and then felates that digit while rolling his eyes back in ecstasy.

"Every time I see you," she says, struggling heavily with each half-sentence, "I have to start all over again. I have to fall in love with you again, I have to leave again, and then I have to spend however many months telling myself that this is not something I can afford to invest in. That you're not a person I can put my faith and my trust and my future in."

My Id claps his hands together once, and finally, speaks: *Fuckin' A, finally!* he cries. *She's doing it! It's done!*

"Shut up," I tell him.

He pantomimes crying. *Suck it up, Markley, you little fucking queer. I've had some good shit saved up for this disentanglement—and that's how you gotta think about this shit: a disentanglement.* He produces a legal pad and a pencil, which he licks the tip of. He slips a pair of reading glasses over his face. *You ready for this, or what? I've got some good material here!* He riffles through the pages. *This bitch is toast!*

"Don't call her that," I say.

Bitchcunttwatslutwhore. Grow a fucking dick, Markley. You knew this was on its way, even if you didn't. Now are you going to blubber or are you going to make this chick regret this moment for the rest of her life?

I stare at his grizzled visage. God, I hate this guy. I say, "Yeah, yeah, okay. What do you got?"

Fuckin A right, you little cocksucker. He begins to list off his points in an authoritative voice, like a professor giving a lecture. I just repeat it line-by-line to the girl I once thought I loved.

"If this is the way it's going to be, then we probably shouldn't speak any more," I snap. "After all, if you've got to cut off your arm, better to do it quickly with the axe than slowly and painfully with the saw."

She is silent. "I don't want to do that," she finally says.

Now, with a note of aggression: Yeah, well I don't really fucking care, says my Id.

"Yeah, well I don't really fucking care," I snarl. "How exactly will we do anything else? We're not from the same town, we won't end up in the same place anytime soon for any reason. Hell, it might literally be years before we have a common excuse to be in the same city, let alone the same room."

Oh shit, says my Id, slicking back his hair with a comb he's just licked. He hears her through the phone. *Tears already? Wow, that wasn't even hard. Okay, let's go out on a bang now.*

"I only ask three things," I say, repeating after my Id, who's reading from his notepad. "No hooking up with each other's friends or enemies."

You see, growls my Id as he chews on the pencil thoughtfully, *what this will do is establish the fact that you will probably salve your pain by hooking up with as many girls as possible as quickly as possible. I like this line. It shows promise in making her feel sad and insecure.*

My Love Interest is flustered, angry already. "What? Why would you even say that? That's ridiculous."

"Well, I have a lot of both," I shoot back. "Number two is: I don't want to look on your Facebook wall and see some fucking guy all over there making retarded inside jokes to you. I don't want to see pictures of you at parties with some chachbag draped over your shoulder, and I sure as fuck don't want to see your Facebook status as 'In a Relationship' ever."

Ah, brilliant, says my Id, congratulating his own suggestion. *The beauty of this remark is that it will make her feel guilty if and when she starts seeing someone new. However, the added benefit is that she will assume that you will abide by this rule, when in fact, the first hot girl you hook up with—well, you can immediately write on her wall, so as to ensure that she will write on yours. This will inevitably find its way to your Love Interest, who will then compare herself to this girl in every conceivable way based on 1) looks and b) whatever inside joke of your own has appeared on said Facebook wall. I don't want to be immodest here, but I'm the smartest, greatest, most badass motherfucking unorganized personality structure ever.*

She is flustered. She starts and stutters over the phone. "Why would I—What are you talking—Steve—"

"And finally," I cut her off.

My Id leaps to his knees on my floor mattress, tossing aside the pencil and legal pad. *This is it,* he snarls, his eyes like murder. *I've had this on hold since the day you got your first date, Markley. Time to draw blood.*

I say, "I want you to be careful. Okay? Just be careful. There are a lot of cruel, mean spirited guys out there that don't deserve you."

Nice. Good. Very condescending.

Then suddenly I think of how the blonde of her hair feels, the chiseled slice of nose, and of her eyes—eyes like a ship lost at twilight in the Arctic Sea—and have no idea what I'm saying: "I can't think of anyone who deserves you, me included."

What the fuck are you doing? my Id demands. *That's not the shit I said.*

"You are just—you are the most amazing person… There's something about you, something truly good and kind and genuine, and I don't think I've ever met anyone who doesn't see it in you."

Markley, what the fuck are you doing? my Id shrieks. *You dumb cunting pussy; you ragged dicksucking piece of shit! You're ruining everything!*

I ignore him and continue. "I think that's why I always felt different around you. I felt calm. You had a way of bringing out the best parts of me. When we were together, I always felt the capacity to be the person I think I can be."

My Id is apoplectic. He hurls himself around my bed, thrashing the sheets, screaming the foulest cuss words he can devise. He lowers his pants and defecates on my pillow. He cuts his tongue with a razor and spits blood in my face. He wails and moans and orgasms on his own misery.

I say good-bye to my Love Interest before he can calm down and get a word in. "I'll see you when I see you," I tell her.

Her voice is small. "Don't say that."

"I'm sorry." And I hang up.

My Id stares at me from my bed, foam all over his mouth. *Well, I hope you're happy, you funny little bitch.* I get up to leave. *Where the fuck are you going?*

I give him the finger.

Straight to the neighborhood bar I go, a little joint called Wellington's. This is not a good way to react to negative developments in one's life, I know, but sometimes you have to compound your misery. I sit at the bar and alternate beer with shots of tequila. I pretend to watch a meaningless NBA game being played on the West Coast. I steal glances at the bartender, who is gorgeous, and make up little fantasies in my head where she asks how I'm doing and I tell her not so hot, so we get to talking and finally she says wait for her shift to be over and then she takes me home and asks me to specifically do to her anything and everything this other girl would never let me do.

Of course, she doesn't say a single word to me the entire time I'm there except, "Another one?"

I get bored with my own self-pity and leave. I'm in an awkward zone, having drunk too much to be sober but not nearly enough to blind away the night's conversation. I walk in the wrong direction on purpose. I turn down alleys and dash across streets, weaving through the grid of Central Lakeview as if I could possibly lose myself in a simple square where I know all the street names.

I know I'm not unique. I know that this dissolution of a relationship, a friendship, feels devastating the way they all do. I know that years from now, I'll look back and understand that I was young and imprudent and fell in love too easily with everything and everyone. I know one day I'll go twenty-four hours without thinking of her, then forty-eight, and then finally she'll just be another name on a list. She'll be a joke between me and my wife. "Which one was she again?" my wife will ask with a sly, bemused grin to remind me that my life before her sounds like that revolting show with Flava Flav. This will be our joke, and the Love Interest will be just another notch, and I won't miss her, and I won't think of her, except maybe on her birthday when I call to wish her my best, and we'll be distant, unhinged quasi-friends, and the world will be at peace. I know all this, but it's cold in Chicago, and the city feels hard and strapped down, like every surface and maybe the air itself is frigid concrete, and I find myself in an alley, kicking a trashcan to death.

One moment I'm just walking along, hands tucked in the pockets of my jacket, weaving slightly, my eyes and heart as hard as I can make them, and then the next my foot is out, my boot crashing against the side of the last large black plastic bin in the row.

I end up with coffee grinds and eggshells on the cuffs of my jeans, the plastic bin cracked and trash spilling everywhere, but I like kicking it and barking incoherently something like *"FuckingFuckMotherfuckerFuck!"*

Then I'm done and breathing so hard I have to bend down and hold my knees. I stare at the mess I've made. I spit into a crack in the bricks on the ground.

"Fuck you, trashcan," I say.

I don't sleep that night because deep in the back of my mind I have to wonder a terrible, wicked thought: *Am I letting this happen because it will fit nicely in the book?*

This is, of course, on its surface, insane. Letting a perfectly wonderful girl walk out of your life because you think it will be a nice thematic fit for a narrative in need of a little hurt, a little pain, a little conflict, a little trouble for the not-so-humble narrator? Not even a book that is going to be published, mind you, but a book that is nothing more than five or six rambling chapters on a hard drive and sitting on the desks of a few dozen agents (probably to be returned as soon as they whittle down the slush pile). Therefore, I have to ask myself if the book is now driving my life rather than the other way around?

That is fucking crazy. However, there is no way around the fact that I will write about this moment. There is no way around the fact that the book, which started as something else but has morphed into a kind of meditation on these fast, reckless years following college, is in part about the Everyman aspect of leaving school for the real world, dealing with realities that before did not seem real and owing things to people you care about yet not having the currency to pay.

In this fevered state, I can only think of her with a halo. Back I go to the good times because that's the way memory works, fogging over the problems and turning the nostalgia into a slideshow. I can only think of her huddled next to me in the cramped bed of my apartment, her naked skin under my fingers like heat and velvet in the dark. I can only think of watching her as she searches for her clothes in the morning, pulling underwear over her small, tight little butt and slowly reaching for the rest of those strewn garments as I stare at her and measure within myself the differing capacities for love and fear.

• • •

So that was the really bad news. Now for just the everyday, oh-am-I-still-worrying-about-that? news.

My queries and proposals for *Publish This Book* are being returned en masse, waiting for me in our homey Lakeview mailbox.

The letters are the same as all the ones that have come before, and as usual, I'm taking it from all sides. Sometimes I'm surprised I'm not getting rejections from small children, scribbled in crayon on oversized paper, that say, "I have yet to decide on a career path or even which binkie I want right now, but should I choose to become a literary agent in the future, I would just like to let you know that your project does not fit my needs at this time… Poopy."

I'll admit up front, much of my failure with this book is probably my own fault. With this project, I've taken an approach to querying the same way a duck hunter does—a scattergun, aimed in a general direction, trigger pulled, with the hope a big juicy duck will just fall out of the sky.

Also, I may be on the receiving end of some karma for having, let's say, "unapologetically tweaked" my original letter and proposal. Let's take a look at some of the few minor—let's say—discrepancies between "truth" and "not as much truth."

Things I Embellished, Obfuscated, or Flat-Out Lied About in My Letter and Proposal

The Letter: *"In addition, I publish my own column at www. stephenmarkley.com, which caters to a network of readers who have been following me since my days as a campus firebrand at a college newspaper."*[98]

"In other words, the entire book is about my endeavor to publish the book. Subsequently, this letter itself is part of the book, as is your response whether you send me a contract ('Cool!' I will write in the book) or a form rejection letter ('Not cool,' I will write)."[99]

"Of course, I understand what a ridiculous, self-serving concept this is.[100] However, it's obviously not just a book about publishing a book. It's a scathing look at a young writer in pursuit of his dream—the travails of taking that road less traveled, the pitfalls and angst of beginning a life from scratch, of dropping into Chicago with no money, no job, and no prospects. It's about

---

98 This "network of readers" essentially consists of twenty to thirty of my closest friends and perhaps a few strays who still remember me from *The Miami Student*. I stopped looking at the average number of hits on my website after the number became too depressing, but if I had to hazard a guess, I would say it's no more than 200 to 400 per week.

99 One of the rejection notes was simply my own query letter with the words "Not Cool" circled in black pen. I saved that guy's response because someday I'm going to toilet paper his house.

100 I chose the words "self-serving" without thinking that they would fail by a mile to describe the self-indulgence I was about to have an orgy with in this thing.

*politics and religion and friendship and an unexpected pregnancy
and unrequited love.*"[101]

"*The more well-known authors I've secured for interviews include
NBA winner Richard Powers, science fiction author Kim Stanley
Robinson, bestselling mystery writer Phillip Margolin, pop culture
critic Chuck Klosterman, and first-time novelist Heather Skyler.*"[102]

"*In addition to the opening chapter, I've included a proposal
and an initial chapter outline. However, I encourage you to take
a look at my website or even meet with me in person to get an idea
of how serious I am about this project. Look at my work with an
eye toward opportunity, possibility, or both.*[103]

*Sincerely,
Stephen Markley*"[104]

The Proposal: "*There are always large audiences for a strong,
humorous voice—one which a reader will follow anywhere, no
matter the topic.*"[105]

---

101 At this point, I truly had no idea what this book would be about, but I did know
that it would more or less include everything and anything of interest that had happened to me from the time I thought of it until its conclusion. As of the letter, I knew
only that Justin was having a kid, and that I like to do shit with chicks and sometimes
rant about politics. It seemed like I could base a book off of that.

102 This is the part where I should probably explain how I can manage interviews
with all of these relatively accomplished authors. The truth is, when I sent the letter
out, I had no idea if I could or not. I knew my dad vaguely knew Kim Stanley
Robinson and that he worked with Richard Powers at the University of Illinois, so
I figured, Shit, I could probably talk to them if I really had to. Phil Margolin I met
while I was in Portland on my road trip—a mutual friend thought he might enjoy
hearing about my novel (he didn't). I'd met Heather Skyler through Steven, so I figured that encounter was real enough, and finally, Chuck Klosterman—well, I based
my ability to interview Chuck Klosterman entirely on the premise that Katie, from
my all-female writing group, had once hung out with him backstage at a reading,
which is more plausible than, say, interviewing Kim Jong Il.

103 Now that I read this line I wonder: What the hell does that even mean? "Opportunity, possibility, or both?" Aren't those the same thing?

104 I probably forgot to sign at least 40 percent of the letters I ended up mailing.

105 With this book, I've certainly put this assertion to the test.

"I'm fortunate to have demonstrated such a voice with a core following of readers. My column in the Chicago Tribune's RedEye *has quickly become one of its most popular[106] and the columns that run on my website continue to attract a faithful readership of thousands."[107]*

"Furthermore, aside from some fairly big names I've already secured commitments for interviews,[108] this book has opportunities for cross-promotion."

"Last but not least, I urge you give me and my project serious consideration for this reason alone: I'm ready to explode. With two books under my belt that no one wants to touch because I don't have a strong enough list of credits to my young name, I'm in a position to come out of nowhere. I'm young,[109] charming,[110] good-looking (enough),[111] and primed to tear a white-hot streak across the face of the country."[112]

"None of this will convince you, however. Read the sample chapter, peruse my website, and if you have questions or would like to get a better feel for the direction of the book, feel free to contact me by phone or email."[113]

---

106   This is just patently untrue in every single way.

107   Again, this is such an exaggeration, it makes James Frey look like a drug addict.

108   Again, the only thing I've secured is that I'm a lying liar desperate to get a book contract so that I will not have to work for a living and perhaps attain some kind of revenge against my high school basketball coach, because he so frequently called me a "suckin' puss."

109   True.

110   Depends who you ask.

111   According to my mom.

112   Or ready to work in a cubicle for the next forty years, marry the first girl who doesn't mind that I occasionally drink too much to perform sexually, and have kids, who I will resent every time they succeed in any way that I did not—but "white-hot streak," yeah, sure, right.

113   I'm surprised I didn't add: "Please, please take me, I'll do anything: bribes, solicitations, debasing myself at private parties. You know that scene with Jennifer Connolly in *Requiem for a Dream*? I'll re-create that with my own grandmother if you be my agent oh please oh please oh please."

Following the revisiting of the query and proposal, I actually go back and read the sample chapters I've sent to fifty different agents. You have to understand that I've been at this for months. Having forgotten what these chapters said almost entirely, I wanted to know what an agent would see with a pair of fresh eyes. To my disbelief and appalling dismay, I realize within the first half-page that I had chosen to open my book with the story of my college roommate, Scott, explaining his shitting/shaving contraption.

No, I thought. *Why would I do that?* I don't even admit to people that I *know* Scott. Scott is an idiot.[114] Why would I choose to start a book with him saying one of the dumbest things I've ever heard? What have I done?

As if I'm not distraught enough, it has dawned on me that this book may have set me on a path to stark-raving madness. After all, the only way this goddamn book will ever end is if it gets published. That's the only logical ending. Nothing else works. Therefore, what if it never does get published? What if I'm just collecting anecdotes and unconnected, irreverent thoughts for the next fifty years—my entire life revolving around the absurd narrative of a book that has no narrative other than itself? The problem is that when I began this project, I had more or less envisioned myself publishing it after about a year. Why, you ask, after I have discussed previously just how hard and unlikely it would be that I'd ever actually publish anything, would I still secretly harbor this sentiment?

I begin to have visions of myself, thirty-five years old and living in Naperville, Illinois, with three kids and a fat wife, still writing and editing for a car blog because I have a mortgage, a car payment, and three college tuitions coming up quick. Old friends will come to visit and they'll ask, "Hey, how's the book going? The one about publishing the book?" And I'll forlornly think of the 2,346th page

---

114 To be fair to Scott, he is simultaneously earning a PhD and MD from an Ivy League school.

I've just written that morning. Likely by this time I'll be down to cataloguing interesting things I've picked out of my teeth after meals for material.

An Excerpt from Future Stephen Markley's 2,300-plus-page Epic *Publish This Book* Circa 2023

It was just after lunch and Ted from marketing had given me the second half of his hoagie, claiming he couldn't eat both halves because that much meat would wreak havoc on his colon. I chomped away at it delightedly, only to realize that it was heavy on the salami. This being the stringy, gristly salami where the threads of meat tend to implant themselves between your molars and canines, exerting some fairly unpleasant pressure on your gums. After finishing the sandwich, I realized my teeth were now packed with left-over salami gristle. I went looking for a toothpick, but the restaurant didn't have any. Sweet Jesus, I wondered. How the hell do you not have a toothpick? Then Linda called to say I needed to pick up Elmer's Glue on my way home for Tiff's school art project. I asked her why she needed me to pick up the goddamn glue, weren't there stores all over Naperville with glue? And she said, "My ass might be enormous, but you are the biggest gaping asshole I've ever met." And having had that delightful conversation with the wife, I procured from the coffee room a plastic fork. After freeing it from the plastic, I began needling a single tine into the gaps between my teeth in attempt to get at the salami. One particular bubble of refuse popped out with a satisfying trail of muscle rending out of my gums. I stared at it for a moment, dangling from the single fork tine, a glistening gobule of processed meat that vaguely resembled a single dead spermatozoa. Smiling, I popped it into my mouth and swallowed it down. Then I opened my mail and got more rejection notices for this book...

Whoopdi-goddamn-doo isn't this a great original meta-concept?
Blahblahblahblahscatalogicaljokehere.[115]

If this theory plays out then this book could just end up a catalogue of my entire life—the raving commentary of a verbose lunatic. Perhaps one day, my grandchild will unearth it from the attic and show it to his friend in the ebook uploading business, and this young man will leap to publish it as the tragic, bitter study of the twenty-first-century writer at the death of print media. It would only be read by cretinous twenty-second- century scholars uploading it to their iRead or Kindle9 or whatever moronic contraption people in the future will use because they're too lazy to separate paper pages with thumb and forefinger.

What a fate.

• • •

So what exactly is the good news? That's the question of the moment, and the one I ponder as I trudge back and forth from defeat to defeat, rounding out my days with *The Daily Show* and a beer, creeping between bars on the north side of Chicago, meeting people who don't interest me, debating concepts I don't believe in, trafficking in myths I once found distasteful.

What exactly is the good news?

One night I find myself sitting beside James on our living room couch watching Fox News. Erik is off with his new girlfriend, Liam may be riding his bike, and Elliott surely exists somewhere in the same dimension as us. But for the time being it is just me and James watching *Hannity and Colmes*, which, in our state of detached ironic distance, appears to be the story of a bold American hero standing up to a black guy and a woman while a sycophantic Igor mutters and twitches to his left.

James and I like to watch Fox News for sociological purposes.

---

115 Not bad, right? Looks like Future Steve Markley's still got it!

It's like being at a zoo-cum-mental asylum where you get to watch all the inmates rant about interdimensional mothmen and bite each other's ears off. You know you're safe because there's a pane of glass separating you from this madness, but still it's discomfiting. I'm having trouble getting into it tonight though. James knows this but waits for me to say something.

"Dude," I say.

"Dude," he says.

"Dude, I was meaning to tell you: have you gotten the—" I launch myself at him, kissing the air by his neck furiously as he staves me off with his hands. I keep it up for a minute until I finally sit back on my side of the couch.

"Feel better?" he asks.

"A little."

"Dude, what's up?"

I shake my head. "I dunno, man. I'm losing my shit lately."

"Because of you-know-who?" he asks. I look at my friend. Occasionally I'll tell James that as a human being, he makes no sense. Born into a highly religious, highly conservative family in small-town Ohio, the quarterback of his high school football team, he has no right being at all cool, yet we are essentially the same person. I remember one of the first times we hung out while studying in Italy. I was wearing a shirt that said, "This Machine Kills Fascists." James took one look at me and said, "Woody Guthrie. Cool." I should've known then that we'd probably end up hanging out for a while.

"Yeah, that too, but that's not all of it. I don't know. I just feel stuck. Like everything has gone static. My job… winter."

"Winter sucks," he agrees. "And jobs suck."

James has since moved from the SoulSuck Agency to a construction trade publication where he calls contractors all day to confirm information. He hates it there, too. He says, "I have mastered the technique of doing exactly the bare minimum to get by and then reading online the rest of the day."

"What do we do?" I ask. "I don't have money to go anywhere. I can't quit my job because it looks like they're not going to make any more jobs ever again."

"We'll go out this weekend," he suggests. "We'll do shit with chicks."

He says this like it's a novel idea. Like it isn't what we do every weekend. Still, the prospect of meeting a pretty girl who will laugh at my jokes lightens my mood by a degree or two. "I guess that has potential."

We watch Hannity interview a guest who agrees with everything he says. *Hannity* smugly questions the guest in a way that lets you know the question he is asking is not his but the scum-sucking Marxist media's.

"You know what's fucked up?" I ask James.

"What's that, man?"

"We are such a couple of little crybaby bitches." I shake my head. "Seriously, think about it: of all the people in all of human history, we are among the luckiest .0000001 percent. I mean, Jesus, we could be living in vacant apartments shooting smack on the South Side right now."

"That's true."

"We could have been born women in a Nordic village in the tenth century and spent all our time getting raped by Vikings."

James nods thoughtfully and says, "We could have been accused witches during the Inquisition and had the skin stripped from our back until we admitted we practiced sorcery."

"We could have been any worker in any city anywhere during the Industrial Revolution," I add.

"We could be political dissidents in North Korea."

Now we are on a role.

"We could've been villagers in My Lai," I say.

"Gay lovers in 1938 Berlin," James says.

"Bird-watchers in Nagasaki."

"Black activists during South African Apartheid."

"Haitian children subsisting on bread and water."

"Persian infants tossed live into a pit of tigers by Alexander's army."

"Iraqi civilians."

"Sudanese civilians."

"Congolese civilians."

"Republicans."

"I mean, let's face it, man," I say. "In the course of human history we have completely lucked out: white men born into middle-class families in the United States of America during the twenty-first century."

James happily agrees, bobbing his head and grinning, perhaps just glad to see my mood improve. "We have nothing to complain about. Nothing to worry about," he agrees. "The biggest problem we have is that once we get through the *New York Times* and *Slate* during work, we get kinda bored."

The two of us nod, grinning at our little exercise. I realize that when James said, "Gay lovers in 1938 Berlin," I laughed out loud for the first time in what might have been days. On the TV screen, the guest has turned to Colmes, who is sniffling questions at him that he firmly rebuts as if Colmes were asking him why babies shouldn't be tossed into pits of live tigers.

I say to James, "You're right. We should do shit with chicks this weekend. If I wasn't terrified of my latent homosexual urges, I'd totally hug you right now."

"Ditto, man," says James. "Totally ditto."

• • •

James was right: I am not a nineteenth-century wage slave breaking rock in a New York quarry for sixteen hours a day. Yet life has still managed to lose some of its gleam in recent months.

I've piled up twenty-three rejections for this book. My Love Interest is gone—over a month since I last spoke to her, nearly three since we parted ways at Logan Airport. My job has become a series of mundane tasks, so redundant that my every movement throughout the day is choreographed—even down to the precise moment I quit working so I can read online. The world is rife with brutality, whether it's genocide, failed governments, civil war, or the U.S. presidential election. I can feel something familiar in my heart: a slow-burning anger mixed with ennui and dread. I begin spending large swaths of my day clicking around the Internet, checking the prices of plane flights to Singapore, New Zealand, Vietnam. On a notepad I begin to carefully calculate how much money I would need to drop off the face of the earth for a year. (I decide it wouldn't have to be much. A few thousand dollars, and I could spend the rest of 2008 and much of 2009 hopping trains, planes, and buses around South Asia.) This restlessness—like a twitch in my foot that can't keep me from tap, tap, tappin' away—is a beast. And the sum of events has combined to pick the lock and let the beast loose.

Then I find out an old friend of mine will be deployed to Iraq in a few months. I speak with him on the phone, and I can hear an uneasiness in his voice that makes me tremble internally. I can't think of anything worthwhile to say, so we hang up with a promise to see each other before he leaves. I walk outside of the house to sit on the stoop. I consider finding a trashcan to kick apart, but that seems like a cliché now. All I know is that the beast wants to move. I want gone.

To counteract this dip in my fortunes, I begin drinking more, which is always productive, and fill the rest of the void with the affection of women, whose names are always foggy to me even as I speak them. I basically have no control over my penis at all. He leads me on a wild goose chase across the city of Chicago, only in this case when the goose is captured it turns out both the goose and I are mutually disappointed with each other. The details of this period are simultaneously revolting and uninteresting, so I will spare you except to say that my nadir comes when I go home with a blonde young woman because she looks remarkably like the girl I want to get off my mind.

After a grueling night, I wake up the next afternoon and am filled with a chunk of self-loathing so unwieldy, it's like trying to carry a hundred-pound hulk of jagged concrete on the El during rush hour. To make things worse, Fox News is on, and my new blonde friend is watching election coverage and calling Hillary Clinton a cunt.

"Excuse me?" I say.

She smiles, and in the light of day I can see that the resemblance I was looking for was woefully false. "I just hate that woman," she says through a happy grin.

"Oh Christ, you're a Republican?" I ask.

"Of course," she says, as if the years 2000 through 2008 never happened.

When I get outside, I look up to see that I've spent the night in a rather glitzy high-rise. I look around at the street signs and don't recognize any of them.

"Please don't let me be in Milwaukee," I say.

I'm walking toward what I think is the city, but I don't recognize anything. I wander directionlessly for five minutes, turning left at an Italian restaurant (because Italian restaurants are good things to turn left at, obviously) and right at a dry cleaner. When this method fails to mint me as a modern-day male Sacajawea, I start calling my friends for help. James is not near a computer and cannot use Google maps to track down my whereabouts, so I call Elliott.

"Jesus, man," he says. "You're practically downtown. How'd you get down there?"

"It's a fairly long story," I tell him.

"You hooked up with a chick?"

I tilt my head in thought. "Okay, so it's a short story."

"Fuzzy."

I find my way to the Red Line and spend half an hour traveling back home. As the train rumbles out of the earth to the above-ground line, I watch the city slip by through the window, cold and gray and faded like a pair of jeans that have been through the wash too many times.

TWELVE

The Call

The next week, I'm at work vaguely worrying about sexually transmitted diseases and trying to think of how best to describe my mental state in prose: like I'm slowly being beaten to death with cotton? Like I'm watching the same TV show and eating the same cereal and drinking the same glass of lukewarm water over and over again? Like I've discovered that predestination is real and nothing matters because Free Will is a complete illusion? While I kill time thinking of analogies, I open my email.

There are notes from two agents.

The first is hesitant but interested. I read it with more trepidation than excitement (I am going to leave his name and most of his identifying information out for reasons that will become clear later). He asks to see the next two chapters of my book.

The second is from a woman named Julie Hill.

From: j___@aol.com
To: s___@yahoo.com
Subject: Re: Query

Hi Stephen, (Steve?) I like the proposal... read it on a plane on Wednesday, (no distractions, save the occasional pretzel and juice), and like it. I think it may intrigue editors. I couldn't

help but react to your mentors' thoughts... Have my 2 cents...
I laughed, I got mad, all the good stuff. Getting me to email
or write back more than a few words is a sign... Are you still
looking for an agent? My website is below. Let me know.

    I "have" a couple of Chicago authors, have strong affection
for the Midwest as well as your proposal.

thx

j

I'm at work when I read these. I have just spent an hour eating
oatmeal, scanning car blogs, and building web pages. I was only
checking my email out of habit, and here it is: a viable, highly interested response from a member of the publishing community.

My Ego wants to leap up and scream, but I slam him back down.

My Id throws himself at the electrified fence I've erected around
him, giggling insanely as he thrashes and foams at the mouth.

But I have not forgotten what happened with my road trip memoir,
A Land I Saw in My Dreams. I refuse to believe this is real and allow
only the smallest increment of hope to creep anywhere close.

I write back to both of them, and as I type the emails, I feel glar-
ingly, overwhelmingly like a phony. I want to sound professional.
I know that I am smart, that I am capable, that I can write an engaging book, but with each tap of my fingers on the keys, I can't
help but feel like a poser—not a writer but a twenty-four-year-old
jerk-off whose primary interests include bizarre and debasing sexual
escapades that last longer than the film *Lawrence of Arabia*.[116]

---

116 Or at least now that's one of my interests. Thanks a lot, blonde Republican girl.

From: s___@yahoo.com
To: j___@aol.com
Subject: Re: Query

Ms. Hill,

Thank you for your response. I took a look at both your website and some of the authors you represent and would definitely be interested in speaking further about "Publish This Book." Up front, I think it's only fair to tell you that I've gotten word from another agent as well, who has requested to see more materials, but—as you can tell from the nature of this project—I am mostly a novice at this, so feel free to take advantage of/exploit my naivety.

Just to give you a better feel for what I'm proposing, let me outline how I see the rest of the book developing:

Essentially, everything in the chapter outline I sent you is complete (if not immediately ready to read, than certainly close). The way I see the remainder of the book is a contrast between the struggle to get the book published coupled with the narrative drive of strands from my personal life—relationships, my best friend's unexpected fatherhood, etc. (Please note that these will not be maudlin "oh I can't believe we're growing up so fast" clichés; the purpose is to subvert those stereotypes... Also, so that I can include a truly fantastic anecdote of my friend's encounter with basketball legend Larry Bird).

Finally, I see the the greatest strength of this book as it's "pliability" for lack of a better word. Because it confronts exactly what kind of book it is up front, it will allow me to travel in genres, to experiment, and to stay irreverant and thoughtful simultaneously.

At any rate, I don't want to take up more of your time. Let me just say, as a parting shot, I'm young, single, and a tireless self-promoter. I think that puts me in a position to work for this book a lot harder than many other writers who have to balance family and a day job. I'd love to speak with you further about this, so let me know what the next step might be.

Sincerely,
Steve

I read and reread this response five times before I actually hit "send" and still manage to miss two spelling errors, use "than" when I should've used "then," repeat the word "the," and say something as self-important and faux-intellectual as, "the purpose is to subvert those stereotypes."

I sit back at my desk, return to blogging, and try not to get my hopes up. I know it will likely be a few days before I hear from this woman again. Until then, I plan to carry on with my life, act accordingly, and generally just try to—

My cell phone buzzes in my pocket. I remove it to find a number I don't recognize with an area code I've never seen before. *No fucking way*, I think.

I hope I don't sound out of breath when I answer, "Hello?"

"Hi, Steve?"

"Yes."

"This is Julie."

No longer am I concerned that I might sound out of breath. Now I am concerned that this woman can hear me shitting myself from her office in California.

"Oh… heyyyyaaa," I say, dragging the sound out because I want to say hello but realize I already said hello when I answered the phone and thus try to change it to "hey" halfway through, only to confuse my vowels and turn it into the hook from Andre Benjamin's hit on *The Love Below*.

"So you had a chance to look at the site?" she asks.

"Uh," I say, thinking, *What site? Whose site? Her site? Right, her site!* "Yes," I say.

"And you are still available? You're not being represented?" Her voice has a flat, Midwestern emptiness, and she sounds vaguely middle-age. I picture her eyes darting to other projects as she speaks to me.

"No," I say, "not currently."

Nice, Markley, I think. *Good use of industry lingo.*

"Well, I just wanted to call and let you know that I loved your proposal. Like I said in the email, I had a chance to read it on the plane and I just found it so engaging and readable and glib but in a way that you know you're being glib."

"Right," I say, as if this is exactly the combination of words I myself would have chosen to describe my book, when in truth, she could have said, "I thought it was archaic, banal, and overwhelmingly Faustian with a hint of equatorial disillusionment," and I would have readily agreed that this was the most sound, brilliant assessment of my work I'd ever heard.

"You have a really strong voice, and it's a voice that you can't duplicate and you can't fake, and I really like that about your writing. Now you say you have more of it finished?"

"Yeah, everything in the chapter outline is done."[117]

"Well, I would love to see more of it."

"Sure, absolutely. I did mention that I'm sending it to another agent as well, right?"

---

117 It's difficult for me to say if this is an outright lie, a white lie, or the truth. At this point I do have "writing" that "exists." However, the problem is that because I'm writing these chapters so quickly and essentially adding to this book entirely by the seat of my pants, the first draft of every chapter is more or less me bitching about things and people and circumstances I don't like. It takes two or three rewrites just to eliminate all the derogatory insults I use to describe the majority of everything and everyone in existence in the universe. "Ah, let's cross you out," I say as I delete the slur, "scum-oozing pustule on the asshole of a roach." Can't say that about my own mother, I figure.

"Yes, and I thank you for being forward with that, but I would say, don't sign with anyone until you talk to me first. The next step for you would be a contract, and once you've signed on, that's that."

A contract, I think to myself. This woman is talking about a beloved-Jesus-honest-to-fuck contract. My empty bowels somehow find their reserves, and I'm soiling myself all over again.

"Right," I say. "Of course."

We speak for over fifteen minutes. Julie asks me where I went to college, tells me she has very fond associations with the Midwest, asks if I was in a fraternity,[118] and tells me about her own three sons. When we finally hang up, all I can think in bright neon lights is: *Uhh*.

• • •

Strangely, the contact from Julie and the other agent could not have come at a more ideal time. Not two days after she calls me, I head back to Oxford because I'm speaking in one of Steven's classes.

Steven teaches a class each year about the nuts and bolts of the literary marketplace. He takes a group of young writers and instructs them in the murky, mysterious ways of the publishing industry; essentially how one goes from a zit-faced creative writing major bemoaning the tragic cruelty of the literary world to a published, self-supporting writer. He likes to bring in an actual writer (aside from himself, that is) to talk about how that person found his or her way.

---

118 Okay, let me make this categorically clear: I was not in a fraternity in college. I never considered joining a fraternity. I never rushed. I never thought of rushing. Apparently because I like to drink and fornicate and use foul language that must mean—to most people—that I was in a fraternity. Well, no. I drink and fornicate and use foul language because it amuses me, as it does many people. Fraternities did not invent amusement. Why anyone would pay money to associate with people who suck when you will inevitably spend most of your life trying to temper the amount of time you have to spend with people who suck has always been beyond me. Or, as James once put it to me, "Phi Tau for life, bro."

When I took the class my senior year, we were introduced to Heather Skyler, the author of a sweet, melancholy little novel called *The Perfect Age*. In her description of how she went from a college creative writer to an MFA student to a published author, Heather was demure, humble, and informative.

I, of course, am the opposite of all these things (we'll get to that momentarily).

Before the class, I meet Steven for lunch at Oxford's best restaurant, the High Street Grill. It's a ritual of ours dating back to when I was a student, which I enjoy because a) it gives us a chance to bullshit and 2) he always buys.

"Mr. Markley," he says wryly upon seeing me, that faint smile always dancing on his lips—as if my very existence still amuses him like some kind of inside joke.

We get into it immediately, discussing the election and Barack Obama. Steven—your typical far-left-of-center academic—hates Barack Obama. He may not say he hates him, but our debate stretches for several minutes. If I could summarize Steven's opinion: Obama is the natural product of a society and a generation fueled by a narcissistic tendency to believe that it is special above all others. His candidacy is the result of unabashed self-worship by the "Me" generation, and he will get his brains beaten out by John McCain because he is a snobby liberal whose close personal friend and pastor is a ranting lunatic.

My position: back off my boy.

But this is why I like Steven so much: he simply does not care about your feelings. Like he's backing up a truck, he'll come at me, and I can either step aside or simply choose to get hit by the truck. I love getting hit by the truck.

Lively debate aside, I quickly segue into my exciting development.

"Two agents contacted me," I tell him.

He blinks, his eyes popping wide. "That's fantastic. For your novel?"

"No, for that other thing I told you about. *Publish This Book*."

"Now," he says carefully, brushing strands of white hair back from his forehead. "What did you get the reaction to? A proposal? Or have they seen chapters?"

"Chapters," I say. "The first two chapters, which incidentally you are in. In fact, this one woman, Julie Hill, seemed to think you were brilliant."

Indeed Julie had repeatedly mentioned how helpful and wise this "Steven fellow" sounded. She asked if he would return in later chapters of the book, and I said yes, knowing full well that I was about to see him and would have to describe in agonizing detail every word she had just said to me and then pump him for information and advice with only slightly less frenzy than the CIA interrogating high-value al-Qaeda prisoners.[119]

"Well, first I would say, you have to send me these chapters immediately."

"I will."

"Secondly, have you looked into her agency?"

"Yeah, checked out the website, checked out the other books and authors she's represented. She's legit."

"What about the other one?"

"I don't know," I say. "He was interested, too, but he only emailed me, whereas she called. And I gotta say, just from his emails, he sounds… I don't know… pretentious as all hell."

"Why do you say that?"

I try to think of how to properly describe the second agent. "Well, when I mentioned that Julie was in California, he kind of brushed that off, saying, 'Oh well, you have to have an agent in New York.' And he just sounds like he thinks he's this hot shit commodity, but

---

119 Yet again, I find myself confronted with the bewildering question of whether my life is driving this book or if now the book is driving my life and I am simply concocting situations to include in later chapters. I know for certain that this is not the case with Steven because I would undoubtedly not make a move in any major aspect of my writing career without consulting him first. Still, one wonders…

then I looked at his website and he's not exactly representing the height of the literary community. He mostly does coffee table books from what I can tell."

What I don't tell Steven was that this man told me he found my idea interesting but only if it was in the vein of "Some Fucking Writer Guy." Why aren't I telling you who this "Some Fucking Writer Guy" was? I'm pretty sure it was because he didn't exist. If both Google and Amazon couldn't find him, I wasn't about to try to write a book like him.

In fact, in all my interactions with this man, my primary emotion was helplessness because this guy knew I wanted his attention, yet if I met him in any other circumstance—say as the professor of a class—I would have no respect for his opinion. I would visualize every word boomeranging backward to suck his own ass before eventually zipping to my ear.

Steven listens to my description of both agents before asking, "What did each of them say?"

"They both wanted to see additional chapters, but Julie sounded like she wanted to talk contract right then and there."

He nods. "That's great." Typical for Steven, however, he immediately launches in to all the reasons that this is not great.

"There are some things you should think about."

"Ugh. I hate thinking. Such as?"

"Well, first of all, this book: it's not you."

I know where he's going with this, and I'm glad. I want to hear him say out loud what I've been thinking ever since I got that phone call. His hands form a box as he talks, framing his argument.

"I'm assuming this book is in the voice of your columns, but that's not you. You're a fiction writer. I've read enough of your stuff to know that that's where your talent is and that's where your heart is."

I nod. This was exactly what I had been thinking in the mid-to-slightly-mid-rear of my mind ever since the day of Julie's call.

He continues. "So say you write this book, it comes out, and it's a sensation. Smash hit. Then suddenly you find your editor wants another book along these same lines. You want to publish a novel, but no one's interested in that. Then pretty soon you've been pigeon-holed into this category. You're a snarky chronicler of politics and pop culture without any depth beyond."

I nod some more. "Sure, but at the same time wouldn't that be an okay problem to have?"

"Oh, absolutely. I'm not going to sit here and tell you not to sign with this woman because of that. No, that would be insane. It's just something to keep in mind about yourself."

"You know," I say, "no one actually asks anyone for advice so they can be talked out of something. They just want to have the decision they've already made affirmed."

He grins. "Absolutely then. Consider it affirmed."

Our meals come, and I resist tossing my silverware aside and immediately burying my face in the plate. This is the first meal I've eaten in roughly a month that costs more than ten dollars and does not involve me supplementing it later with Kashi Go Lean Crunch cereal or peanut butter and bread, which are my two primary dietary staples.

"How much of the book do you have done?" he asks.

"About half. Maybe. Depending."

"And do you know where it's headed?"

"I guess I have some idea."[120] I sigh. "To tell you the truth, this entire thing has been such a fly-by-the-seat-of-my-pants operation… I'm just so stunned anything actually happened with it, I haven't had a chance to take a breath and think about the repercussions."

"Something to consider," says Steven.

We drive across campus to Bachelor Hall, where I spent half of my undergraduate career hauling heavy tomes to the second and

---

120 I say, as I carefully memorize this conversation to put in this book later. *Oh good, I think, now I don't have to think of anything for Chapter 12.*

third floors. I sit in front of his class, which is packed (it's impossible for me not to notice) with improbably attractive young women.[121]

I go through the story for them, the one I've told here already: how I started young wanting to be a writer, how I worked at it with bizarre ferocity, how I landed my various successes, and how I learned to ignore the many failures. Mostly, however, I just crack jokes.

"What do you think would happen if you suddenly did publish a book?" a kid asks me.

"Hopefully improve my sex life," I say.

One girl asks a question but she is wearing a shirt that says "I [heart] the Female Orgasm."

Instead of responding, I point to her shirt, "Come on, everyone knows the female orgasm is just a myth."

And a moment later: "Okay, maybe it's not a myth. After all, just because I've never seen a yeti doesn't mean a yeti doesn't exist." Man, I am so clever.

After the class, as we walk to his car, Steven gives me a bemused look. "The Stephen Markley stand-up hour," he says.

"What?" I look at him. There is not disappointment on his face, but maybe disappointment's slightly more respectable cousin. "I don't know," I say. "I just don't want to take myself too seriously in front of them. I don't want them to think I think I'm hot shit because I've published a short story in an online science fiction e-zine."

He asks, "Have you ever heard of a defense mechanism?"

He drops me off at the library, where I plan to work on this book for an hour while I wait for Justin to get out of class.

"Let me know what you decide," he says.

"I'll probably have to call you before I do anything."

---

121 Every time I'm away from Miami for a while, I always forget that every corner of campus is slammed with a high number of improbably attractive young women. I know you're thinking right now, "Well, my college had hot young women, too." And I'm sorry but you're wrong. It's like if the Beatles broke up, but Paul McCartney, John Lennon, and George Harrison all formed their own band. Your college was Ringo Starr's band.

"Absolutely."

I nod. My masculine box keeps me from expressing the gratitude I'm feeling at the moment. "Thanks for everything," I say.

He smiles. "Enjoy your weekend."

• • •

Oh, and enjoy it I do.

Oxford seems like she's missed me as much as I've missed her, and while Justin won't admit it, I can tell he's reveling in the opportunity to catch up. After dropping my meager luggage at his apartment, he and I head "uptown" as it's called at Miami. Justin and I hit our stride immediately over beers at the greatest bar in the entire world, the previously mentioned Mac 'n Joes (and yes, it is strange that the greatest bar on Planet Earth is conveniently located in a filthy alley in Oxford, Ohio). Some things have changed at Mac 'n Joes in the time I've been away. For instance, the proprietors have painted over the graffiti in the men's bathroom where—among other things—someone had written "Steve Markley sucks cock." Also, the cheapest pitcher is no longer Pabst Blue Ribbon for four dollars but now Natural Light for four dollars.

"I forgot how goddamn cheap it is to drink here," I tell Justin. "Four bucks is the average price for an entire beer in Chicago."

Mac 'n Joes is all wood paneling and hard-backed booths and random sports paraphernalia lining the walls without coherency. This is the bar where I made most of my college memories. Miami University has an almost unspoken segregation—not between black and white people[122] but between Greek and non-Greek. Fraternity and sorority members often congregate on the other side of High Street in bars like Brick Street and Church Street. To stereotype, they often come from money and do not have to seek out four-dollar pitchers of beer. They are also better looking than

---

122   That would first require Miami to have more than three black people.

us. The cool kids, however, congregate at bars like Mac 'n Joes and Steinkellers (where a stein of PBR would run you about three dollars, and two of those would get your night thrumming like a turbo-charged hemi).

Justin and I crawl into a booth with our pitcher.

I shake my head as we sit. "So, less than two months, huh?"

"That's right, Markley. I'm gonna be a daddy."

"How's Loren?" Loren is working in Columbus and living with her family while Justin visits her on the weekends.

"She's good. Things are going really well."

"And you're naming him Jaxson with an X?"

"Jaxson with an X."

"You trying to get him beat up?"

"Markley, I can't wait till you have a kid. My kid is going to beat on your kid."

I grin madly. "I ain't having kids, Justy. Unlike you, I'm going to look into this whole 'condom' thing that's all the rage with the kids now."

"She was on the pill," he says to me for probably the four hundredth time since he first told me back in November.

I laugh. "Yeah, too bad your sperm are like motherfucking Green Berets or something."

"Superman sperm. Sperm of steel."

"They've got like jet packs and lasers and shit."

"And grappling hooks. They don't know how to quit."

"Rocky Balboa spermatozoa."

It's a good thing my friends and I have each other because I don't know who else would put up with a conversation like this.

Of course, all of our discussions can't be this fun. Over the course of the night we pursue this single line of thought: *What the fuck happened?* We carry it with us from Mac 'n Joes to Steins, to Buffalo Wild Wings, to 45 East, and even though we're trying to fit in time with all of the old friends we've managed to corral into Oxford for the weekend, we essentially return to this thesis at every opportunity, picking up the thread as if we'd never dropped it.

"Ex-girlfriends suck," I say. We've been talking about Justin's. Loren and the baby have put the final nail in the coffin of that relationship, it seems.

"I wish her the best," Justin says of his ex. "I really do."

"No, you don't," I tell him.

"Of course I do. Why wouldn't I?"

"Everybody says that, but no one actually means it."

Justin shakes his head. "You're wrong, Markley. I'll always have a lot of love for her, and I hope she finds someone who makes her happy."

I stop and stare at him. He scrapes the stubble of his beard and looks back at me in that earnest way he has, like I'm the one who just said something clichéd and untrue. "Justin, just admit that you're full of shit."

"Is this about you-know-who?"

"Of-fucking-course it's about her," I say.

"When's the last time you talked to her?"

I think about it. "About a month ago we had a brief conversation when I told her I didn't want to speak to her anymore. Other than that it was…" I shake my head as I realize it. "Jesus, it was February. Over two months."

He nods. "And you can honestly say that you don't wish her well?"

I moan and roll my eyes. "Well, I don't want her to be miserable or anything," I say, downing my Natty and pouring another helping into the little white plastic cup that still has the Pabst logo from the glory days when Pabst was the cheap-o beer. "But look, do I want her to meet someone better than me? Hell no. I could say I did. I could be like you and pretend for myself or the sake of others that I do, but it would be a lie."

"That's pretty selfish, Markley."

"Oh fuck you, you self-righteous piece of shit. Do you honestly hope that she," I say, referring to his ex, "finds someone better than you? Who makes her happier than you did? Who makes her forget about you? Are you fucking delusional?"

Justin sighs. "Markley, Markley, Markley."

"Okay, I do hope for her happiness. I just don't want her to meet a guy who's funnier than me, or makes her happier than me, or who's better in bed, and he sure as shit better not have a bigger dick."[123]

Justin mulls this over. "Okay, I see your point, I guess."

"Jesus, man," I mutter. "I'm all over the place. What am I doing with myself?"

"You could get someone pregnant," he suggests. "That seemed to focus my attention."

• • •

We meet up later that night with our friend Dave and his fiancée, who've driven up from Cincinnati where he goes to law school. If there is a god, then surely he must have invented Dave for my amusement and no other reason—how else to explain Dave's interest in basketball, creative writing, and progressive politics? Surely, his parents' values couldn't have anything to do with that, so it must have been God wanting me to have a playmate. He is the second person I tell about the possibility that I might soon have an agent.

"Whoa," says Dave. "Congrats, man!"

"Well, it hasn't happened yet."

"But still, man, that's like a huge step. Someone's actually giving your stuff a shot. What is it? The novel?"

Before I go on, I should tell you this story: I met Dave freshman

---

123 Women, pay attention: If you really want to get down to brass tacks, the truth is that the only thing straight men really care about at all, in any capacity whatsoever, are penises. We are completely obsessed with penises—our own, others', it doesn't matter. Penis size is essentially what our half of the species focuses its entire conscious thought on. So if you're dating a guy and he ever asks how he compares to past boyfriends, just tell him he's the biggest. Even if he's not and knows he couldn't possibly be, even if your last boyfriend was Shaquille O'Neal, just tell him this anyway. Trust me, I know of what I speak.

year when he lived down the hall from me in the honors dorm. He was a boxer, so I figured him for a meathead until I found out he wanted to major in creative writing (along with a pre-med focus, which, I often told him, was the strangest combination of interests I'd ever heard of).[124] Dave, it turned out, was a pretty good writer, and we often shared our stories and gave each other criticism and encouragement. After I wrote that novel for my senior thesis, I held a reading in Bachelor Hall. A few days later, Dave and I were sitting on the stoop. The stoop was our favorite. Over the course of two years spent living in this apartment on the most traversed residential street in Oxford, my roommates and I had grown to love the stoop outside of our place where we often drank or smoked cigars or just shot the shit for hours on end. It's incredible how much fun you can have just sitting on a concrete step.

Dave and I were out there along with our other friend, Jeremy, mulling over the end of college and the various decisions we each had to contemplate when Dave said—almost completely out of the blue—"I don't know, man. I really think you're going to make it."

"Come again?" I said.

"With your writing. At your reading I was just thinking to myself, I've never known anyone who goes after something with that much dedication. That much focus. I'm like the most skeptical person about anyone ever actually becoming a writer, but I really think you're gonna get somewhere with it. I just really think you'll make it."

I'm sure at the time I responded with some offhand self-deprecating remark or perhaps attacked Dave, maybe implying that his intelligence was sub-par or his mother of questionable genetic origin, but I remember when he said that, I felt my stomach become light as my nerves lit on fire. Even now just

---

124 It turns out I was right, and he has no defense because he did not go into medi-cine and thus wasted four years of his life freaking out about biology exams and the MCAT. No one has ever put more effort into a never-pursued career than Dave.

sitting here in my Fifth Third lawn chair, I can feel the slightest lump lodge itself in my throat and threaten my eyes. Sitting on that stoop, though, it would have been wildly inappropriate for me to tell Dave how much what he said meant to me.

Two years later we sit in Buffalo Wild Wings, and as I tear into a basket of spicy Caribbean jerk wings and a basket of chili cheese fries, I tell Dave, "No, not the novel. Remember *Publish This Book?*"

Dave's eyes narrow as if he's trying to figure out if I'm joking. "*That's* what she's interested in?" he exclaims.

I nod. "I sent her a proposal and the first two chapters, and she said she loved it."

Dave laughs. "I think I told you that was a dumb idea, didn't I?"

"Yeah, asshole, you did. So now when I'm rich and famous, I'm hiring a hitman."

"You're going to kill me?"

"No. He's going to break down your door, shoot you in the foot, and then cuddle with you."

"How embarrassing."

"Right. I'll have him take a picture."

After Dave heads back to Cincy, Justin and I return to Mac 'n Joes to meet up with our friend Luisa and her boyfriend Gordon. Luisa was my first real girlfriend, and we dated from our senior year in high school until midway through our freshman year at Miami. We remain close, and she is overjoyed to hear my news but has a few questions about the book. By now these are questions that I'm used to answering, but at the moment they have become slightly harder because Justin and I are, as he puts it, "Not in a frame of mind where I'd talk to my mother."

"Wait," says Luisa. "So what's the book about? What actually happens in it?"

"Well, this happens. This right here. And a whole bunch of other shit." Getting all these words out is kind of like sucking molasses through a straw.

"Here's my question," says Gordon. "How do you sell the book if it doesn't have an ending? It doesn't have an ending, right?"

"Right. Because the ending is me signing a book contract. But the publisher who buys the book—if anyone does—these assholes are gonna just have to take the book on spec and trust that I can finish it. They'll pay me an advance too, which," I throw my head back and howl, "would be sweeeeet!"

"So you'll write the ending later?" he asks.

"Yeah, exactly. The publisher says, 'Okay, cool. We like what we see. Here's some money. You go finish it and then we'll give you the rest when you bring us an ending.' Then they just have to hope that the ending is as good as the first part and not about Nazis raping babies or something."

"Do you have an ending?" asks Luisa.

I shake my head. "I don't have the faintest clue of an ending. I'm hoping it'll come to me."

This is approximately the time I spot Roger. I forget this conversation and yell across the bar like I'm competing with the invasion of Baghdad, *"Roger!"*

He turns. He yells back, loud enough to drown out the cluster-bombs, *"Markley! Fuck!"*

Roger is another writer, two years younger than me. We met in Steven's literary marketplace class and developed a passing, if steady, friendship based on our mutual desire to write for a living. He arrives at the booth a few minutes later, bringing two pitchers of Pabst with him. Justin's eyes go wide in disbelief. "This is gonna end badly," he says as he tops off his plastic cup.

I introduce Roger to the assembled gang, but as soon as he hears what we are talking about—namely, this book and the possibility that I have found an agent—he forgets anyone else is at the table. And trust me when I say this, he speaks only in italics with many, many exclamation points.

"What? Are you fucking kidding me? Markley, motherfucker! Fuck

yeah, man! Fuck!" Roger is drunk, maybe even drunker than Justin and me. His face is bright red and in his excitement he knocks over a cup of beer and couldn't care less. *"What's the book about, man? Whatizzit, a novel?"*

I quickly explain the concept and say, "It's called *Publish This Book.*" Roger's lip curls into what looks like a snarl. He slams his hands against the table and brays laughter. "Publish This Book! Publish This-*motherfucking*-Book. *Like Abbie Hoffman. Markley, that's fucking genius. I wish to fuck I'd thought of that. Holy shit, man. Fuck. That's fucking great. That's fucking wild, man."*

"You might be one of the only people to get the Hoffman reference."

"Genius, man. You're fucking crazy. You've always been crazy. Fuck, man. Fuck yeah. I'm so happy, man. I'm so fucking happy."

And suddenly Roger is hugging me in the booth at Mac 'n Joes.

"Thanks, man," I tell him. "Although, I gotta warn you, after this little display, you're probably gonna be in the book."

"Fuck, man. You say whatever you fucking want about me, man. This is fucking great."

"Okay," I point at him drunkenly. "But it's probably going to be that you're a baby-raping Nazi."

"Fuck yeah, man. Fuck yeah."

My nights in Oxford turn into a blur of time and dim light and an alcohol warmth in the pit of the belly. The days turn warm the nights cool they blend they coagulate they suffuse. There are delicious steamed bagels from the world-famous Bagel & Deli and more cold beer and some warm beer and March Madness basketball and our good friend Mark shows up with his girlfriend and we talk about his brother and the war and his fourth or fifth deployment and we talk about his girlfriend and we talk about my Love Interest we stand outside in the cold at four in the morning and I take a drag from a cigarette for the first time in my life and Roger's words ring in my ears and I think of Julie reading over my errant thoughts and declaring it worthy of championing and there in the night I realize my Love Interest's old apartment is right next to Justin's place and I can see the window to her room while I stand holding that cigarette, the room where I spent so many nights where I watched her cross the floor in her underwear and this is my home but not any longer not really and so I pour another drink and another and this might be the warning shots of a love affair with booze and I'm really okay with that but Justin has that kid so he's probably not going to be able to go down that road with me he's probably going to need a job ASAP with a salary and health insurance and whatnot and his damn kid will probably have me speaking at his wedding as the best man several years sooner than I'm ready for and I hand that cigarette right back to Mark because the last thing in the world I need is to start smoking but in the end it all comes down to me and Justin at four in the morning in the parking lot of his apartment complex, standing outside screaming at the moon.

We are past the fun kind of drunk and on to the angry belligerence. We've bounced from bar to bar all night and we've seen the people we needed to see and said the things we had to say, but now it is just the two of us, leaning against the wooden railings in a warm Ohio night and basically picking up the conversation we were having hours earlier. His ex-girlfriend. My ex-girlfriend. The mother of his child. His son.

"And the fucking thing of it is," I say—no, I don't say. I yell. It is four in the morning and we are having this conversation at maximum volume. Anyone at any of the three apartment complexes in the immediate area who is still awake at this late hour can certainly hear both of us. "And the fucking thing of it is, I know she's with someone. I know she's seeing someone because there's no other logical explanation. She's moved on. She's got her little life in order, and in two years I'm going to hear from a mutual friend who's gonna tell me he just got a wedding invitation from her in the mail. I'm going to hear about her marrying some douchefuck Red Sox fan and that's going to be the sorry world I'll have to live in."

"Markley, you're one to talk," barks Justin. "I don't think there's anyone who's on your side on this."

"Oh, you think I don't know that? You don't think I know I'm the one who's responsible for this?" I shout back. "Yeah, I know exactly what an asshole I am, but unfortunately that doesn't exactly make it better."

"I'm saying you had two years to figure things out, to put things right—"

"So did you."

"And I tried," Justin snarls. "You have no idea, man, how. Fucking. Hard. I tried."

"Of course I have an idea."

"But you know what? Sometimes things just aren't meant to be. Sometimes—"

"Bullshit!" I leap in the air and smack my hands on the railing as I come down, stinging both palms. "There's no such thing as 'meant to be.' That's just the garbage people tell themselves to take away the worst of it, to take the edge off." My eyes feel as if they are straining at the sockets. Justin turns his empty face from mine, and I move into his line of sight because I want him to look at me for this. "There's no plan, there's no 'supposed to,' there's no 'meant to.' You have what you have in this world, and either you make something of it or you don't."

"And now I have what I have," he says, and finally his voice is calm, which just makes me even angrier. I want to leap at him and grab his face and shake it and smack it until he hears what I'm telling him. "I have what I have. And you know what? I'll be the first to admit that it's not what I expected." He kicks at the ground, his foot drawing little lines in the dirt. "It's not what I planned for at all. But now that it's here and now that it's coming… I'm going to love this girl and I'm gonna love this kid, and I'm going to work my ass off for both of them."

I shake my head. "It's not Loren and it's not the kid that bothers me, man. It's the way that those things work. None of this…" I pause and suck some of that Ohio night into my lungs. Those drunk tears, those tears of rage are collecting at the corners of my eyes, and I have the fiercest urge to rip the flesh off the world with my bare hands. "None of this was supposed to happen. This is not how things were supposed to turn out. It's all wrong."

He shrugs, his face placid now. "But this is the way it is. All you can do is do the best with it, Markley."

I think of the two of us over a year earlier, clinking glasses of beer in a bar in Durango, Colorado. I think of how wildly life has jumped the script since then. Here we are, and I don't feel young anymore, and I don't feel strong. I stuff down the tears, but the feeling lingers anyhow, a feeling like if you had a war criminal tied to a tree in an empty forest, a monster you knew had raped women and executed children, like if you had him there at your mercy. *All this anger, all this drunk madness and carnage,* I think, *and I'm stuck here with stupid Justin trying to peacefully accept the things we cannot change.*

I don't remember when we went to bed, but when I wake up, Justin is in the kitchen.

"That was an interesting night," he says.

I blink. "Oh yeah, what did we do?" I joke. "And when was it that I got hit in the face with a battleaxe?"

We both laugh. Justin is making coffee while studying a problem from his stats book with a kind of lackadaisical intensity. "I think it was bound to happen," I say.

Justin shakes his head. "Yeah, but did it have to happen at four in the morning with us yelling as loud as we could? I'm surprised no one called the cops."

"'Yes, officer, I think there are two drunk guys having an existential crisis in the parking lot. Yes, it seems as if they're mourning the loss of their innocence and the fading promise of youth. No, I don't think either of them realizes that his problems are annoyingly typical.'"

Justin and I both chortle and snort with hung-over laughter. I rest my head on his coffee table and close my eyes, still laughing.

• • •

The week following my trip to Oxford, I spend in a minimum of communication with anyone. The shadow has lengthened and now the questions have moved into so many different realms and the threads of my life have tangled in so many different knots I have difficulty deciding which I should work on first. I know I need to figure out the agent situation, but some of the things Steven said to me during our lunch have stuck in my mind and festered.

The question that has begun to truly gnaw at me is this: do I really want to write this book?[125]

As Steven pointed out, this book is not me. I mean, it is, but it isn't. This isn't who I set out to be as a writer. It's not what I thought of when I set out to grab this dream of mine and wrestle it to the ground. I read back over the first nine chapters and what I see is self-indulgence and irreverence and anger and the thinnest fiber of wistful hope.

By this time, I belong to two Chicago writing groups. Besides the girls of the Thousand Fibers writing clan (the lovely ladies you met in Chapter 4), I hang out every other Tuesday with a group that meets under the authoritarian banner of Literary Writers Network (also a craigslist discovery). I have not yet shown this group any piece of *Publish This Book*, mostly because I don't think I can stand to think about it anymore than I already do. Yet it is this group that helps me make up my mind.

Sitting in a coffee shop on Chicago Avenue just west of the Dan Ryan, we spend the last twenty minutes of our two-hour meeting discussing the group's publishing goals for the summer. Or rather they are talking. It seems like I don't say much of anything to anyone anymore, whether it's my closest friends or six other aspiring writers

---

125 Because you're holding it in your hands and reading it, I understand there is a fairly limited amount of drama to be mined from this.

I see for a total of four hours a month. As I sit there silently, the group discusses an online magazine called *Toasted Cheese* and the merits of submitting to it.

This publication looks like it's run by four MFA dropouts from a basement room in Wicker Park. On their website, the editors suggest that if writers do not hear back about their submissions they should perhaps email an inquiry periodically to remind the editors. One of the group's writers, Denis, brings the conversation to a grinding halt when he says, "Look, I know none of us is going to appear in *Zoetrope* or *Glimmer Train*[126] in the immediate future, but at the same time, if you're not proud of where your stuff is published, what's the point? And frankly I don't think anyone here would be proud to see a story in *Toasted Cheese*."

Denis is right, but not the fun kind of right: no, he's the ennui-inducing kind of right.

I leave the meeting and truck down Chicago Avenue so I can catch the bus east. The night wind slithers and tucks into the creases in my jacket, and while I wait, I think of the road to becoming a fiction writer. It feels like years ago that I was young and simply figured I would run out and conquer the world, publish my first novel to critical and financial ecstasy before I was old enough to rent a car without paying the young driver fee. Out there on the street corner in the cold waiting for a bus that will be loaded with lost-looking people listening to iPods and staring blankly through windows that only show them their reflections, I wonder where I will find myself: thirty, thirty-five, forty years old and still licking envelopes and hoping I don't need to send another email to the editors of *Toasted Cheese*?

I arrive home that night and trudge immediately up to my room. In my Fifth Third lawn chair, I sit and read the first nine chapters of

---

126 For those who are not short story writers, *Zoetrope* and *Glimmer Train* are two of the premier publications for short fiction. They are considered a couple of Holy Grails in creative writing circles.

this book from start to finish. My Ego stands silently to the side, his solemn eyes reading over my shoulder.

He pats my back. *Full steam ahead. Eh, Markley?*

"Guess so."

He cackles madly. *Atta boy, you big sopping vagina.*

• • •

The next day I call Julie.

There was never really a choice here. The other agent turned me off thoroughly with his emails chock full of vaguely intellectual jargon that had very little to do with anything I was saying. He has yet to reply to my last email, and I figure we'll end our relationship on those terms. In the meantime, Julie had said just about everything right.

After calling her from one of the dark meeting rooms in the Cars.com offices, I say to Julie, "A semi-brilliant person once told me that you make some decisions with your head and others with your heart and the trick is figuring out which organ to use for which decisions."

"Yes," she says. "Good advice," and I wonder from the way her voice falls if she thinks I am going to tell her I'm choosing the other agent. I quickly correct my tone, impressed that I actually was in the position to professionally disappoint someone.

"I just have a good feeling about you," I tell her. "I just get this feeling that I'm onto something here, and that you've seen what I can make it… If that makes sense."

"I understand. And I would have understood if you had gone with the New York base, but I'm glad you didn't. I also think you happen to be right. We are onto something here."

"So what happens now?" I ask.

"I send you a contract. You read it, sign it, send it back."

"Right. Yeah."

"Then," she says, "you write a book."

THIRTEEN

Autobiographical Digression #2: Confessions of a Campus Firebrand

There is a reason I chose to write this book in this voice, in this way. We've heard snippets in the last chapter, clues from Steven and myself. "This isn't you," he said.

Now obviously there has to be a story behind that, right? After all, if this isn't me, then who the hell is it? It certainly sounds like me: the foul language, the delightful similes, the lovely bouts of narcissistic alcohol-laced fury and willful misuse and subjugation of an otherwise honed intellect in favor of baser impulses.[127]

I am at heart a fiction writer. But even as I have pursued that path over the course of my short life, a series of circumstances came along and knocked me in a different direction. I warn you: what follows is not entirely pleasant. This chapter will be quite a journey. There will be anger. There will be fury. There will be wild, unhindered digression. You will frequently wonder what the hell I am talking about. But hey, it's my book, so shut up. The problem is that in order to understand some things (writing, life, wastewater management, etc.), you have to first understand others (politics, grammar, the mechanics of an orgasm, etc.).

---

127 Incidentally, "Narcissistic alcohol-laced fury with a willful misuse and subjugation of an otherwise honed intellect in favor of baser impulses Dude" was my nickname in high school.

• • •

After my Epic Road Trip and after Phil and I spent four months living off the fumes of our own notions of invincibility and the love of sweet young women, I found myself idling around back home as I prepared to move to Chicago. It was still weeks before I'd dreamed up the idea for this book, and I felt emotionally and intellectually drained. I had lived my dream as hard as I could for as long as I could, but when I woke up, I found myself adrift, uncertain of the next step and weary from my lack of direction. I thought of all this as I wandered around my childhood home in the middle of the afternoon.

I moved without purpose from one room to the next, glancing at errant family photographs, striking a few keys on my mother's piano, generally wishing for someone or something to drop out of the clouds and tell me what the hell I was supposed to do with myself now. That's when I stumbled upon the weathered, yellowing stacks of old Miami University student newspapers in a cluttered corner of the living room.

We had dozens, maybe hundreds of copies of these lying around, most of them containing columns, stories, or editorials I had written during my tenure at the publication while I attended Miami. Seeing these old copies now brought a rush of nostalgia followed by a crashing wave of remorse. I never lied to myself about how much I missed college—my friends, my girlfriends, the classes, the professors, the campus, the bars, and most of all working as the editorial editor for the student newspaper.

I picked up the top copy and flipped to the editorial page, only to frown when I did not find my own goofy face staring back at me from the column picture. Strange, I thought. Then I realized why I had kept this particular issue. It was the last of 2006, my graduating year. And it included a fan letter. Standing in my living room as shafts of mid-afternoon summer light decorated my sticky, sleep-worn body, I read the final word ever printed on my career at *The Miami Student*.

Smutty column didn't deserve publication

I am unbelievably disgusted with Steve Markley's "letter" printed in
the Tuesday, April 25 issue. This year I've continued to read his opinions, even though I get ridiculously angry every time I do. His conservative bashing (often on unfounded, uneducated bases) infuriates
me, but I endure it because I believe in letting other people have
opinions that differ from my own. The column this week, however,
crosses the line. I wish it were a political column, but the smut that he
wrote is absolutely disgusting. I don't know Mr. Markley as a person,
but the implication that he has personal experience having "anal
sex with (his) friend's dog" or that whores in Amsterdam showed
him "vaginal muscles of Herculean strength." I don't know what the
editorial staff was smoking when the [sic] decided to let this "article"
be printed, but I'm disgusted that an institution at our distinguished
university, the oldest school paper in existence, would print crap like
this. Frankly, I'm happy to see Mr. Markley graduate, if not for the loss
of his uninformed liberal opinions and libelous remarks toward the
right, then most certainly for getting rid of crap like this in our paper.

—Nathan B.

I had read the letter before (recalling the very poor sentence construction), but seeing it with fresh eyes gave me a chance to read it
as if it had just come off the presses. I reached the part where young
Nathan quoted my own words, and like a child hearing his first dirty
joke, I couldn't stop giggling.

In order to understand the origins of this book, I'll have to
take you back to my college days—those breathless, seething years
when young minds put that first hesitant foot in the real world and
straddle adulthood; when those minds learn how to love, how to
hurt, and how to safely ingest recreational drugs and still finish a
ten-page paper.

Like millions of other middle-class kids who grew up in the nineties facing little to no adversity, this was my typical college experience, which makes the one glaring difference in that experience all
the more stark.

I was a campus firebrand.

Yep, at Miami University, I was kind of famous. This is not to
say people knew my face. The grainy black-and-white photograph
that appeared beside my column in *The Miami Student* rendered me
mostly unrecognizable. However, people knew my name. In bars, at
the gym, in classes, I got this quite a bit: "So *you're* Steve Markley."

The "you're" always came off their lips with a mixture of antici-
pation and disappointment, as if these strangers had long awaited
the day they would meet the crass, sophomoric, left-wing campus
writer, but now that they had me in front of them, they couldn't
quite get by the fact that I looked more or less like any other dude in
a school of fifteen thousand.

This mild fame was simultaneously fun and perplexing. I never
really understood it. All I did—all I ever did—was write what I
thought about certain things on the editorial page of the lone campus
newspaper. I tried to be funny, I tried to be interesting, but I never
went looking for trouble intentionally.

You'll undoubtedly question the veracity of that statement before
you reach the end of this chapter.

• • •

It was the beginning of the 2004 school year, and Miami students—
like college kids all over the country—arrived back on campus just
as election season was gearing up, and you could sense there was
something in the air.

Now that we are several sorry years removed, it's hard to describe
the mood then, the frothing zeitgeist that was visible even on Miami's
insulated, conservative, white-bread campus. In August of 2004, it
was clear that battle lines had been drawn. Bush-Cheney bumper

stickers could be spotted on every other vehicle crossing campus. Kerry-Edwards stickers were a little less common but still prevalent. In every class, in every discussion, the ideological war was there, lying just behind everyone's words and arguments.

Then there was me, for whom this election was like giving crack to a Rottweiler and tasering him in the balls.

It was my first year as a full-time columnist for *The Student* after having written for them sporadically my sophomore year. I was still green, still getting lines and paragraphs cut by timid editors, still opening the paper and finding that they had changed this or censored that. I had made waves the year before with pieces about a dispute over the Ten Commandments controversy in an Alabama courthouse, the Miami workers' strike, a dinner with Ralph Nader and Alan Keyes, and Mel Gibson's snuff film *The Passion of the Christ*.[128] I wrote almost exclusively to amuse myself and my friends. I cared more about writing something entertaining than actually trying to convince anyone of my perspective.

Yet when 2004 began and my first column hit campus, there was that electricity in the air. Maybe I didn't realize how easily I could tap into that vein of ideological fervor that was gripping the country in the wake of the first term of George W. Bush.

I wrote my first column viciously criticizing my peers who would choose not to vote that fall. I wrote, "[This] means, God help you, that you are dumber than our president, George W. Bush, who will almost certainly vote (presumably for Ralph Nader in an effort to detract votes from John Kerry)."

The emails came, both angry and complimentary, but in both cases

---

128 Incidentally, that film was one of the first times my Love Interest and I ever hung out (we went in a group with mutual friends, who were also interested in this film everyone was talking about). When we left the theater, brushing past people with tears streaking down their puffy red faces, I remember saying, "Mel Gibson is a fucking lunatic." She looked at me with relief and said, "Thank God you said that. I was afraid you had just been awed by the power of his Love." I did not know if she was referring to Gibson or Jesus, but either way I was impressed.

with an inherent intensity, a drive behind them that identified the authors as foot soldiers in the trenches of some larger conflict. I didn't realize it then, but I was being drafted. As it turned out, Ann Coulter would come to town, and soon I would be serving with pleasure.

• • •

I had beef with the College Republicans before they brought Ann Coulter to campus. The year before had been the second anniversary of the attacks of 9/11, and the College Republicans took the opportunity to plaster the campus with fliers that read "For Those We Lost" and then below that, in font just marginally smaller, "Sponsored by the College Republicans."

In my column on this I said rather undiplomatically that this was as self-serving and exploitative as if I had gone around on Martin Luther King Day posting signs that said "Civil Rights: Sponsored by Stephen Markley." At any rate, the column never ran, and I was afraid to ask why for fear I would be fired. There had been previous clashes over my columns, and I decided to play it safe (if not a bit cowardly) and just let the piece die.

But the fall of 2004 was a different time. Iraq was beginning to catch fire, not a single WMD had been found, and people had begun to notice something funny happening with the income gap in the United States.

Therefore, I thought it was hilarious when the College Republicans chose Ann Coulter as their speaker... That is, until I realized they weren't doing it ironically.

The College Dems brought Howard Dean that year. Say what you will about Dean, but he was an elected official, a governor, and a serious presidential contender. Coulter, on the other hand, is a shrieking bigot, who either intentionally says the most offensive things she can think of for attention or, worse, believes what she says and is therefore psychologically disturbed. When I sat down to write a column prior to her arrival, this was all I wanted to point out.

In my column I outlined a fairly standard fantasy:

> I have a dream to have sex with as many female right-wing pundits
> and icons as I can. Why, you ask? Because I want to wake up the
> next day, tell them I'll call them soon, and then immediately delete
> the phone number from my cell… There's a lot of you aging but
> mildly bone-able right-wing nutjobs out there whose feelings I
> have to hurt.

I then pointed out, however:

> I've decided Ann Coulter is where I draw the line. If I wanted that
> experience, I'd simply dip my genitals in a jar of acid… There aren't
> enough left-wing revenge fantasies in the world to get me to have sex
> with Ann Coulter.

Oh, and I pointed out her camel toe.[129]

While it was certainly not the most eloquent thing I ever wrote, it
served its purpose, which at the time I felt was fairly obvious: satiriz-
ing Coulter's own technique of saying something cruel and outrageous for attention and dressing it up as political commentary.

I was surprised to find my column in the paper completely
unedited and with the stilted, awkward title "Enacting revenge
through sex." Usually, my editors cut out everything I liked, but
here was every word in the paper verbatim. I remember thinking
there was a chance the piece might ruffle some feathers, which was
so fantastically naïve I now want to recall if I also thought that eating
a slice of rainbow might have me pooping gold.

---

129   In an interesting side note, the reason I pointed out the camel toe was because
only weeks earlier I had not known what "camel toe" was. My friends Jeremy and Dave
were telling me a story that involved camel toe, and I had to stop and ask them what
they were talking about. After that, I basically couldn't stop seeing camel toe. Everywhere I went, every girl I saw. It was like one of those Magic Eye pictures: Once you
see it, you can't unsee it. Jesus, that was a rough couple of months.

The day the column ran, my email inbox exploded. For the four days following its publication, I couldn't check my email without seeing subject headings that said things like, "Where do you get off?" or "Constructive debate please" or "Liberal shit-bag cockskunk." My editors kept forwarding me the letters coming to the office from students, faculty, and administrators. The bulk were not positive. One called it "a misogynist rant with no redeeming political value," and that was from my mother.

Two days after the column ran, I was on my way to class when I bumped into the editor-in-chief of the paper, Leah, who lived only a few houses away from mine. She sat on her porch smoking a cigarette, her unwashed hair pulled back against her scalp and her sharp eyes erratic and blinky. When she saw me, she simply said, "You."

"Hey, Leah."

"You motherfucker."

"How are you?"

"Oh, I'm fucking glad to see you, asshole. I'm so glad to see you." Her hand danced the cigarette about in the air. "Do you know the shit I've had to put up with because of that goddamn column of yours?" I tried to say no, but she wasn't looking for an answer. "I have alumni calling me," she went on, "saying they're ashamed of the school. They say they'll never read another issue of *The Miami Student*. One of these assholes told me, 'Mother Miami hangs her head in shame.' That's what this motherfucker said: 'Mother Miami.' What the fuck does that mean? Steve, I have administrators— *motherfucking Miami administrators*—leaving messages on the office phone saying I should fire you."

My stomach sank. "Are you going to?"

Leah blasted a jet of smoke from between her pursed lips. "Fuck no! I told those assholes, it's called 'freedom of the press.' It's called 'satire.' And they can kiss my ass if they don't like it, those fucking holier-than-thou pricks."

So at least my editor stood by me. Kind of.

Ann Coulter came and went, exceeding any predictions of right-wing lunacy beyond my wildest dreams (for example, she championed racial profiling at airports by suggesting that paint chips be used to identify the skin color of men who should be detained and searched). But long after Coulter had vacated Miami's campus—on to plant her bile-drenched seed elsewhere—the debate around my column continued.

Emails began to arrive from people without "@muohio.edu" addresses, places like Philadelphia, Tucson, and Ann Arbor. I emailed one of them back to find out how he'd seen the column and discovered that someone had posted the entire piece on a conservative website called The Free Republic. There, under the title "Campus Columnist Makes Sex Threats against Conservative Women (My Title)" I found over 160 enraged postings concerning my column. The following are actual posts in response to my article. I pulled them directly from the site and edited out only the most extreme grammar and spelling errors.

"Funny? More like disturbing and sick. Although, this column will get him a job at the *NY Times* when he graduates."

"Any chance that we could get a picture, and/or other useful information about this bum? In case law enforcement is curious, that is..."

"I would think that most women, not even conservatives, could spot this loser a mile away. It also strikes me that many of the most hateful, visceral, and banal liberal men out there are also gay."

[Concerning the jar of acid I said I would prefer to dip my genitals in rather than copulating with Ms. Coulter]: "It would have to be a shallow jar."

"I think a thimbleful would do..."

"Miami University has a Police Dept., and I gave them a phone call. But the potted-plant that answered the phone kept saying it was 'free speech.' I asked the plant what he would think if some[one] fantasized in a perverted way about his daughters on the Internet, and the plant said that it would still be free speech. After reminding him that it was all over the Internet, plant said that he would report it to his superiors."

"This calls for faxes and emails."

[One of the emails mentioned above]: "Dear Editor Leah R—, As a conservative, if I were to mimic Steve Markley's comments (about conservative women in your 'America's Oldest College Newspaper') to you and your female staff, I'd be investigated, castigated, eviscerated, and obliterated as a hate-filled sex-offender preying on good-intentioned liberal women, with the only power I had, the power of the penis."[130]

"I am pretty sure little Stevie Markley is a plump pimple-faced loser that has about as much chance of scoring with right-wing women as Michael Moore has to run up a flight of steps. Little Steven most likely has never had sex with anyone other than Rosey Palmer and her five sisters."

"Well, for many years to come any potential employer he's interested in will hopefully type his name into Google and this column will appear. And perhaps future girlfriends will do the same. And his children... He just screwed himself royally! How ironic!"

"The rambling power-fantasy of a disturbed gay."[131]

---

130 Upon reading the words "the power of the penis" my friend Phil launched into a fit of laughter that consumed most of his day.

131 This is surely the title of my next book.

In addition to these comments, other people posted pictures of hydrochloric acid, pictures of women with guns, all of my personal information from Miami's database, and the occupation of my mother (ironically, she is a professor of women's and gender studies).

Incidentally, The Free Republic is the same "grassroots" conservative organization that instigated the boycott and CD burnings of the Dixie Chicks after they said publicly that they were ashamed George W. Bush was born in Texas. Other than being a fellow Texan,[132] I admit I never thought I'd have so much in common with the Dixie Chicks.

• • •

I sent the link to everyone I knew, and then sat with Phil and Justin for an hour reading all the posts out loud.

"God, Markley," said Justin. "Why you gotta be causing all this trouble?"

"These people really don't like you," said Phil. "They want to call the cops on your column."

"They want to call the CIA on my column," I said. We were sitting in Justin and Phil's closet of an apartment, which was below my own. It was the middle of a Saturday afternoon, and as usual we had all the important bases covered: homework safely stored away undone, beer cans littering every surface, college football on the television, and Justin and Phil's girlfriends being carefully ignored with each ring of their cell phones.

"'Markley should know that most conservative women carry concealed weapons,'" Phil quoted from his laptop. "Holy shit."

"I know! They act like I said I wanted to rape Ann Coulter. I specifically said I did not want to have sexual intercourse with her."

---

132 Born in Lubbock, bitches! Which makes me more of a Texan than George W. Bush, who was born in Connecticut, educated exclusively in New England prep schools and universities, and learned how to talk like a functionally retarded hick so he could be president.

"Yeah," said Phil. "I think they're kinda missing the point, which is that you want to hurt their feelings, not like, tie them up and have sex with them."

"They say you're gay, a rapist, impotent, and sex-crazed all at once," said Justin. "I like these people. I think I may log on and add something of my own."

"Thanks, buddy."

"Dude, I don't know," said Phil. "Anyone with a Miami email account can get online and look up your address and phone number."

"You think I should change them?"

"It might not be a bad idea."

I looked at Justin. He shrugged. "You gotta get your mail from Miami, though. If you change your address you won't get your bills and crap."

"What if I change it to your guys' place?"

"Oh great," said Justin. "So some fucking whacko comes and dips my dick in a jar of acid because he thinks I'm you? I don't think so, Markley."

• • •

Needless to say, the attention from Free Republic was dynamite material for a slew of columns. In my next, I wrote:

> I suspect these people took umbrage at my claim that I'd like to hurt the feelings of certain conservative women by having sex with them and not calling back. I guess I should have explained that I was experimenting with this radical new concept I've decided to term a "joke." The way this so-called "joke" works is sometimes you say things that you don't mean and/or are not true. I refer you to a previous paragraph where I said I had an abortion. For those of you using all the parts of your brain and not just the one that loves war and hates poor people, you can look at my name and picture and reasonably conclude that I have not had an abortion. Further proving

my theory that conservatives have no sense of humor, a guy on Free Republic who goes by the moniker of "areafiftyone" missed out on the irony of calling me a loser.

What really scares me is that these right-wing geniuses like our pal "areafiftyone" are not on the fringe of society anymore. They're running the damn country. "Freedomlover23" is probably Defense Secretary Donald Rumsfeld. "IluvBushbutnotinagayway(gaysscareme)7897" is most likely Supreme Court Justice Antonin Scalia.

The end result of this entire episode (other than feeling so very flattered) was that I became a topic of conversation around campus. With each new column the hate mail poured in, now matched (almost) by fan mail.

And rather than getting fired, at a staff party Leah offered me the job of editorial editor (admittedly, she was kind of drunk). I had never had any aspirations to work as an editor. My entire goal with *The Student* was to make a few people laugh, get in a few jabs at our idiot-child president, and work less than a total of thirty minutes a week. Here now, I was presented with an actual paying job, real responsibility, and most importantly, a level of editorial control.

It's harder to censor someone you work with, who can come back at you time and time again and generally wear you down until you have no choice but to include a reference to "Michael Moore's swamp-sac."[133] If you can't beat 'em, join 'em, right?

• • •

Of course, Bush won the election of 2004.

I got home from class that Tuesday afternoon positive Kerry would beat him, so I went running. I was tireless. It was raining, a light drizzle, the sky overhead a brilliant gunmetal gray. This was

---

133 You may not believe that I managed to fit that into a relevant policy debate, but if you're writing about the need to expand gay rights, it makes a certain degree of sense in context.

still during the furor over the Coulter column, and the entire experience had given me a strange sense of invincibility. I was bulletproof. My words were bulletproof. And George Bush was a lame duck in another six hours. I had honestly never been more certain of anything in my life.

I spent election night embarrassingly inebriated and insane with rage. I yelled at strangers on the street and screamed from the windows of our apartment. Never had I felt like I understood the world less than in the week following the election of 2004.

Following this setback, my columns took on a more somber tone, but the fire never died. If anything, trouble seemed to have set a bull's-eye on my forehead, even when I steered away from politics.

I wrote a column about my experience at a sorority semiformal, to which a friend had been kind enough to invite me. Basically, these things are like seventh grade dances only with alcohol and a far greater likelihood that the participants will end the night doggy-style. My observations earned me a scathing letter from a sorority representative.

I tried to back up from politics even further, publishing a column about my job at the circulation desk of the university library. Surely, I thought, there was no way I could get myself into hot water when writing about the day-to-day grind of checking out books, laptops, and study rooms. Yet sure enough, four days after it was published, a friend told me that my name had been at the center of a meeting among library administrators, some of whom wanted to fire me.

I was incredulous but this time, I admit, a little scared. I would not start at the paper until the following semester, and I basically survived on my minimum wage job at the library. I even went so far as scanning the Internet for a free-speech lawyer.[134] I hastily published a preemptive column describing the situation.

134　Which means I Googled "free speech lawyer" and was immediately daunted enough by the results to go find friends to do drugs with.

Puritan oppression is alive and well here in America. We'll all stand up for that quaint little document, the Bill of Rights, as long as it's convenient for us. Maybe we should go back and revise Voltaire's statement to "I'll defend to the death your right to say it as long as you write about nice things like popped collars, how hard finals week is, and don't evoke various parts of the human anatomy for crude humor.

I really was mystified. I got the reaction to the Coulter column. Even if I thought it was hysterical and nonsensical, I could at least understand it. But now I felt as if things had spiraled a bit out of control.

In my heart of hearts I felt that I was not just being an obnoxious rabble-rouser. I knew people must be reading my stuff and enjoying it because I watched their eyes light up when they realized who I was. I went three months in an English class before the gorgeous blonde who sat to my right turned to me at the beginning of a class and said, "Holy shit, I didn't realize you were the kid who wrote the sorority semiformal column."

"Umm… Yeah. That was me."

"That was one of the funniest things I've ever read. I just never could have envisioned you as being at all talented."

I squinted, trying to decide if that was a joke, but she was already back to underlining passages in one of her books.

"Oh, um… cool," I said to myself.

• • •

Luck was on my side again, for when Pat Buchanan and Andrew Cuomo came to campus as part of the lecture series in 2004, I won a seat at the dinner table with them through a raffle for members of Miami's honors program.

I sat across from Buchanan, along with five other students and a couple of professors. The conversation was genial and enlightening. Pat Buchanan has always struck me as one of the most forthright and intellectually honest of the hard right. I agree with almost nothing he has to say, yet find myself at least capable of swallowing his argument.

The dinner conversation involved talk of the upcoming election and Iran. Cuomo and Buchanan acted incredibly cordial to each other. Buchanan commented on how much he respected Cuomo's father, Mario (the governor of New York who did not buy a prostitute). Both men demonstrated a surprising amount of candor when talking about both Bush and Kerry, Buchanan voicing his distaste for the Iraq war, and Cuomo his concern that Kerry's war vote had been politically motivated.

I, of course, asked Buchanan about Jon Stewart and his appearances on *The Daily Show*, and the former presidential candidate called the guy "brilliant."

After dinner, I had to walk over to the lecture hall for the debate, but first I stopped in the bathroom to relieve myself. This is where the fun began.

Lo and behold, upon entering the facility I became aware that none other than Patrick J. Buchanan was occupying the only stall. I knew this because I could see the tail of his jacket hanging below the door, and because I had passed Cuomo, Mrs. Buchanan, and the woman in charge of the event waiting outside the restroom as I went in.

Naturally, my first reaction was, "Oh my God, this is the closest I've ever been to a celebrity taking a crap; I probably have to write a column about this for the paper," with little idea of how I would stretch an incidental bowel movement into six hundred words. Oh, if only I'd known.

As I prepared to do my business, Buchanan started his. Loudly.

It sounded like he had lost all control of his colon. You know that scene in *Dumb and Dumber* with Jeff Daniels? It was like that—like lumpy oatmeal being poured into a bathtub.

I completely froze up. I was in shock. I could hear an ex-presidential candidate grunting in exertion, moaning like he was forcing out something the shape and size of a toaster oven. I'm man enough to admit that I couldn't handle it. I could no more have performed under that set of circumstances than I could have if on my wedding night, my parents were sitting in the corner of my hotel room doling out helpful advice. I zipped up, pretended to wash my hands, and got the hell out of there, knowing I'd be hearing that sound in my dreams later that night.

And this, I discovered after writing my column about the incident, is the great thing about the dual nature of the politically conscious American. We can all disagree. We can passionately pursue truth, freedom, and justice. We can hate the other side for their narrow-minded views and simplistic, unintelligent opinions. We can rail against their greed or self-righteousness or stupidity, but at the end of the day we can all agree on at least this: Pat Buchanan taking a noisy shit is hilarious.

The Buchanan column seemed to both cement my status and put my critics at ease. The letters slowed after that, I think because people knew they could afford to take me a little less seriously. I felt I had plateaued, found myself a comfortable niche to occupy, and I could go on writing in relative peace without hearing that I should be fired every three weeks.

That is, until the "Europe Column" appeared.

The very first piece I wrote for publication my senior year was a simple recap of my time spent studying abroad that summer in Florence, Italy. I had done all the typical things college kids do in Europe, which is to say drugs, sex, drugs, art history, and drugs. I figured my experience was no worse than that of any other twenty-one-year-old cut loose on the continent and probably a whole lot tamer than most. For the column, I simply recapped my visits to Interlaken (semi-drunk tandem skydiving), Amsterdam (live sex shows and mushroom hallucinations), and Prague (a warehouse strip club with midget strippers).

But after this column hit campus, shit just blew the fuck up—worse than the Coulter spectacle by a long shot. Outrage, umbrage, horror. Leah, who had since moved on from her editor position, chewed me out thoroughly. The head of the journalism department wrote a letter to the editor bemoaning the low standards set by our editorial page. The dean of the School of Arts and Science wrote a four-hundred-word rebuttal castigating me for—these are his words, not mine—"being an enemy of Enlightenment principles." And, no surprise, my email inbox was slammed for weeks.

"What is this?" people demanded. "You ingested narcotics? You bore witness to copulation in exchange for money? You drank alcoholic beverages? Such violation of the student-institution compact I have never seen!"

The difference this time, however, had nothing to do with politics and was entirely generational. The Europe column was apolitical—strictly for laughs. To this end, I succeeded, and I had the proof in the student response.

Then on the other hand, I had emails from professors, who across the board seemed to think I was a disturbed, anti-intellectual cancer—maybe a sexual deviant, a racist, or both. I found myself in more than a few sniping, back-and-forth email battles with various provosts, administrators, and professors. I admit, my only goal during these exchanges was to force them to continuously quote lines like "smoked a cigar with her vagina" over and over again for my own amusement.[135]

Students reported bizarre anecdotes to me. One kid told me that his German professor had spent an entire day in class ranting about this columnist and his smutty garbage column. This professor claimed that he had called the president to ask why I hadn't been

---

135 The problem with email is that it lets you respond instantaneously, and boy, do I like to shoot from the hip without thinking about what I'm saying.

fired. I had a friend who worked in the Study Abroad department and she informed me that they had begun referring to undesirable study abroad candidates as "Steve Markleys."

All this over a few jokes you could find any night on basic cable. Other than the 2004 election, perhaps this was runner-up in the "I really don't understand the world" sweepstakes.

• • •

Not long after the furor erupted over the Europe Column, a trial began for an ex-Miami student who had raped and nearly killed a young woman. The trial was, obviously, big news on campus, and the case seemed open and shut to everyone, including the editorial board of *The Student*. We had been following the developments for months, and no one for a second suspected this guy had any chance of getting off.

I was sitting in the newspaper office working on putting together the editorial page for the next day's paper, when Allison, Leah's successor as editor-in-chief, got a call. There were about six of us sitting around that tiny basement office with its rows of glowing Macintosh computers and general newsroom clutter. She looked out over the staff, said the guy's name—a stark, one-word sentence—and then: "They acquitted him of the rape charge."

Our sports editor, JD, said, "Are you fucking serious?"

"Yeah. The girl I have on it just called. He was convicted on lesser charges, but it was not guilty on first-degree rape."

"No fucking way," I said. "No motherfucking way."

Then the whole lot of us were basically just yelling all the details at each other.

"The girl nearly fucking bled to death!"

"—Bled to death from vaginal tears—"

"You don't go to the goddamn hospital and get a blood transfusion after consensual sex!"

"That motherfucker nearly killed her! She almost died."

"Who is on this fucking jury? How the hell does this happen?"

This went on for about ten minutes, and then I said, "We've got to scrap the editorial and write about this."

"Do you have time?" asked Allison.

"I do now."

"We don't have all of edi board here."

"I can piece it together."

I outlined the editorial for the six staff members there. Essentially it was, "This is bullshit."

"Write it," said Allison.

I did, and it was cathartic to put some of that rage to paper. Allison came over to me after she read it for edits and said, "This is really good, Markley. This is exactly what we had to say."

"Thanks."

"Why don't you—" she began, only to have her words grind to a halt.

"What?" I asked.

She shook her head, as if to clear a thought. "Nothing. You're a talented guy."

Allison, like Leah, frequently told me I was better than I pretended to be—that I had a passion about life and could be more than the licentious, hedonistic child I made myself out to be. *Why don't you do this more?* her eyes asked.

After that, the staff of *The Miami Student* sat back and waited for the campus to react.

The only word I can use to describe that reaction is "nonexistent." All the angry professors, students, administrators—they all sat that one out. I couldn't believe it. A vile, harrowing criminal incident in a small, tight-knit community, one of the most unacceptable outcomes imaginable, and the collective feeling of Miami University was, "Meh."

In my next column, I wrote, "My stupid, juvenile tract on sex and drugs in Europe elicited dozens and dozens of outraged letters.

Guess how many letters we received over the acquittal of this rapist? One. One solitary letter."[136]

This, I think, speaks to something larger about the American character, something that bothers us provocateurs both large and small. People tend to be far more outraged by indecency, by obscenity, by deviations from the status quo than we are by actual societal injustices. In other words, African Americans continue to face overwhelming institutional racism that leaves millions stranded in this country's decaying ghettos, but what really upsets people? Jeremiah Wright saying, "God damn America." A hypocritical philandering racist serves in the Senate for half a century and no one thinks much of it, until one of his senate buddies says he should have been president. A thousand people drown in their living rooms in New Orleans, but oh my, did you hear what Kanye said? Out of line!

These are the things that wake people up, that make them stand up and say, "Now that pisses me off!" What gets people to write letters to the editor? Not the rape of their land by corporate interests; not kids dying in a distant country over a body of lies; not the economic injustice that strands millions in poverty while the richest 1 percent of the country showers in obscene wealth. No, the average American citizen can get by just fine muttering under his breath about these and a host of other problems. What he cannot put up with, however—what he just cannot tolerate and will not abide—is seeing Janet Jackson's tit during the Super Bowl. That requires a call to arms.

• • •

There were two people who I met through my duties at *The Student* who have stuck with me in the years that have followed. The first we'll call "Jasmine."

---

136 The author of that letter—a sophomore—impressed me so much, I hired her as a columnist and then made her my successor as editorial editor the next year.

Jasmine is the print nickname I devised for this kid who I saw applauding wildly at a speech given by John Ashcroft. After he began sending me nasty Facebook messages, I used him as an example in the paper, where I took to calling him "John Ashcroft's Skid-Mark" ("JASM"), or Jasmine for short.

Basically what happened is this state representative named Tom Brinkman came to town. Brinkman is the guy who came up with an initiative called "Issue 1" that went on the ballot in Ohio during the 2004 election. Issue 1 made it illegal for gay people to marry or for any institution to support gay couples with "marriage-mimicking" benefits. Miami University, a public school, offered same-sex couples partner benefits as it would to heterosexual couples and continued to do so after the legislation passed. Brinkman, not satisfied with being a homophobic bigot, sued Miami to make them stop.

Needless to say, I thought Brinkman was a cretinous asshole who—if he's right, and there is a Heaven and Hell—will justly deserve to sit on Hitler's cock for all of eternity. I said as much in my column, and understandably the response was extreme.

This was how Jasmine introduced himself to me. I sat down at my computer one day, opened Facebook, and found the following message from this guy.

> hey man sweet article about brinkman! [*sic*]... but a least youre scoring points with all the fags and losers of our school [*sic*]. you must have like... 800 new boyfriends by now huh!? anyone one of which you could get domestic benefits with... until Miami LOSES the lawsuit of course! [*sic, sic, sic, sic*].

I had been in these little online spats before. I had pretty much traded bitter, jabbing emails with the entire leadership of the College Republicans for two years, and I tended to know how unproductive these kinds of "fuck your mother" debates could get.[137]

Jasmine was different, though. Here I had my own little scrap of tangible evidence that I had not been wrong about my targets for all of these years. There were people out there who had sick and cruel things inside of them that they wanted to codify and legislate—the remnants of a certain backwards moralism that lingers openly across the country and throughout the world.

And if this is who I was up against—if they had the power and the money and the representation and the Fear and all I had was a nerdy three inches of column space in a student newspaper—well, I figured I'd better bring the heat.

Then there was Kevin.

By the halfway point of my senior year, I had begun to write feature articles so that after I graduated, my portfolio would contain more than just caustic screeds. I wrote a retrospective about the Miami workers' strike of 2003, about the recovering drug addicts from Cincinnati who sold candy on street corners. And I wrote about the impact of the Iraq war on Miami's campus. This impact was, of course, slight. Miami does not churn out the kinds of kids who go to die in wars. It churns out the kind of people who send them there.

Yet in the corners, on the periphery, I found them: a professor whose family had been permanently altered by a wounded nephew. My friend Mark, whose brother had served four tours of duty in Iraq and Afghanistan. A girl whose good friend died in Iraq—his

---

137   Although quickly I'll mention two of my favorites. The first was a girl who chided me for my misplaced values only to end up in the Police Beat the next week after she was arrested for a DUI. The second was a kid who wrote to tell me what a liberal faggot I was and that I had no idea what I was talking about because his brother was in Iraq right now. Months later, when I was working on a piece on Miami and the Iraq war, I contacted him and offered an olive branch. I wanted to talk to him about his brother being over there and how it was affecting him and his family. He wrote me back to say—not very apologetically—that he had lied about his brother being in Iraq. I wrote back, pressing him for where his brother was serving, but he never responded after that. I'd actually be surprised if the guy even had a brother.

name was Mike Cifuentes, and he was killed in 2005 when an IED exploded under his Humvee. He was twenty-four and engaged. His mother worked at Miami.

My last interview was with a criminology major named Kevin. Kevin had served in Iraq from March to October of 2005 as a team leader and machine gunner in the 325th battalion of the Marine Corps Reserve. He had spent his time in the wildly volatile and dangerous Anbar province, working his way up and down the Euphrates River, clearing cities of insurgent pockets, going house to house, living in a constant blur of firefights and roadside bombs and his own raw, exposed nerves.

I spoke with Kevin in his apartment on the southern tip of Miami's campus. There was a Marine Corps flag on his wall, a row of DVDs beneath the TV. I took a seat on a chair and he relaxed into his couch, a tall Ohio kid with short blonde hair. He could have played on my basketball team or sat behind me in chemistry. He looked so unbearably average.

We talked about his day-to-day life over there. He described how he spent his time, how he got by on a daily basis, what he did to unwind. I asked him how it felt to be home.

He shrugged. "Everyone tells me I haven't changed. I think I jumped right back into the civilian world. I think there are two extremes of people when you come home: the ones who are really appreciative and the ones who think it's not that big a deal. But I guess everyone's been supportive."

"Does that bother you?"

He gave that little half-shrug again. His movements were all slow, very relaxed, as if he felt like he had to force a nonchalance. "I like giving people an understanding of what's going on if I can, but no. It doesn't really bother me. It's hard for people to imagine if they haven't been."

"How do you feel about it now? Are you glad you went?"

"Oh yeah. Generations of my family have served and I wanted to step up, make that sacrifice, you know? I always wanted to be in the military. I have a fiancée, though, and that's the reason I didn't want to go another tour. It was hard on her and she was going crazy while I was over there."

"Do you feel—" I searched for the right words. "You say you don't feel different, but do you feel changed at all?" I hoped he would just ignore the fact that "different" and "changed" were exactly the same word.

He shook his head. "When you see dead people, mangled people—you think it would affect you, but people handle things in different ways. I'm the kind of guy who can get shot at and laugh. It's exciting and fun as long as you're not getting hit."

As I jotted this into my notes, I tried to reserve judgment. I definitely would not consider getting shot at "fun" in any sense of the word, even if the bullets were landing forty feet away. But then again, I thought, what the fuck did I know? Statistically, the most dangerous thing I'd ever done in my life was get into an automobile.

Then came the part of the interview I had been dreading, but it would have been cowardly not to ask him this question.

"You knew Mike Cifuentes," I said simply.

He nodded. "Yeah. We actually grew up two streets away from each other in Fairfield. We didn't really know each other until we both joined up, though."

"You were friends?"

"We were real good friends. We were going to be each other's best men. He was engaged, too, you know."

"Yeah."

"We'd be out on post together at night and talk about going on double dates in Cincinnati. Going to Hofbrauhaus down there. We wanted to make T-shirts when we got home that said 'Back from Iraq.' He was getting married first, so we talked a lot about his wedding."

Every once in a while I do know when to shut up, and sitting there in Kevin's apartment with the shades drawn and a sliver of sunlight setting fire to the dust in the air, I did. He leaned forward on the couch and his hand absently fell on his coffee table where his thumbnail began to dig a groove in the wood.

"I was two Humvees in front of Mike," he said. "We drove right over that IED. You know when you're there, you think about dying all the time, and when I heard that thing go off, I thought, 'If it's ever gonna happen, this is when it would.'" He looked down at the coffee table, and in his voice there was nothing but that same matter-of-fact tone. He was just relaying information.

"I could feel the heat on the back of my neck," he said. "I didn't pray too much over there, but that night I did."

I wrote the piece and it was well received. A number of people wrote to tell me that they liked it, including Mike Cifuentes' mother. I didn't know what to say to her, and I can't remember if I ever wrote her back.

When I put together the story, I looked over a few pictures of Cifuentes, not surprised to discover that he looked like any other guy I knew or hung out with. Broad grin, short black hair, nondescript. I had never met him and I never would. But occasionally, starting a few months after that, I would dream about him.

Of all the things I've written in my life—the novels, the short stories, the columns, the editorials, the papers, the essays—this thousand-word piece on Iraq is the one that has haunted me with the most dogged persistence. Every time I watched the news or read about the war in the paper or saw a member of the Bush administration on television, I thought of Kevin and Mike talking about a double date in Cincinnati. Whether or not either of them agreed with my political views, from their stories bloomed a darkness in my perception of the world. I felt a rising, cancerous panic that the age of Bush was an aberration, a mistake in Time's trajectory—and it had cost certain people things that cannot even be described. That conversation with Kevin has stayed with me in a way I never imagined it would. Now I have to assume that it will stay with me forever.

• • •

With this measure of distance now, I admit that after I discovered how fun and satisfying it felt to be controversial, I wanted more of it. I wanted to antagonize people. Partly this was a reaction to the times. On a campus as conservative, complacent, and homogenous as Miami's, I almost felt I had a duty to inflame and incense, to get under people's skin, to arouse in them the frustration and helplessness that our government aroused in me.

I have a feeling that in a few years it will become hard to remember just how uncertain a period this was. These were heady, freakish times we were living in. A person could get on TV and say that up was down and left was right, and not only would people believe him but they would become enraged when you pointed in the other direction.

This long psychic raping of the country felt impossible—a period so stupid, ugly, and brutal as not to be believed—but it was real, and over half the country was complicit in it or complacent about it.

My bludgeoning rhetorical methods were a direct reaction to the complacency. Here I lived in this insulated reality: a college town bubble, and while the country raged and the times grew darker, I felt as if nearly everyone was more preoccupied with the fates of Britney and Lindsay and Paris, those three sluttish harbingers of complete American idiocy.

I wanted to stand on the biggest soapbox in town and shout as loud as my lungs would allow: *Wake the fuck up!*

If only that alone was enough of an explanation.

But there were people like Kevin with his story about feeling the heat on the back of his neck. There were the kids I knew from Mount Vernon who came home from Iraq and Afghanistan and within thirty seconds of seeing them again, you could tell they were changed people. Then there was the TV telling me that up was down and down was right and left was a triangle.

That's why I found ways to amuse myself when confronted with a sick bigot like Tom Brinkman or Ann Coulter or Jasmine. It was why my columns began to read like a madly giggling snarl. It was just my way of staving off the darkness, the sensation of rot I felt at the core of those strange, disturbing days. We all had our ways of coping. This was mine.

My legacy from that period, then, is this voice, the one I've brought to bear in my book about publishing a book. That frustration simply never left. At the time, the humor, the aggressiveness was simply the only way I could think to grab people's attention, and maybe it was over-the-top and senseless, but at least from time to time I felt like someone had heard me. Two years down the line, I can look at these episodes with a bit of clarity and distance. Of course, now when I reread what I wrote, I can see that sometimes the message was off, my tactics brutish and unnecessary. But like I said, bless the agitators. Bless the profane. Bless those who are never happy with the status quo.

And if you don't like it, well, bite my fucking cock.

Whose Opinion Counts

I try to keep the news about signing with Julie silent. I don't want to jinx this in any way, and even after I sign the contract and send it back to her in the mail, I feel as if at any moment my phone will ring, and she will say from the other end, "Hey, sorry, kiddo, got some bad news: looks like I just found out I was actually interested in this guy 'Steven Markly,' you know, with a 'v' and no 'e' in the last name… Yeah, he's really good. He's got this transcendental lesbian Korean War novel that's just out of the ballpark, but hey, good luck to you!"

But no, when Julie and I speak on the phone, it's about how best to craft the proposal she will send to publishers. She has me buy *Jeff Herman's Guide to Book Publishers, Editors, and Literary Agents*, and use his model. This proves difficult because the example Herman gives is for a nonfiction book on cardiovascular health. My book, as you have no doubt discerned by now, has very little to do with cardiovascular health. In fact, most of its recommendations fly in the face of conventional cardiovascular health wisdom.

Thus I find myself scratching my head thoughtfully as I try to decide—as Herman suggests—what makes me an expert on my topic like his author is an expert on hearts.

This much becomes clear: I must lie.

I can't very well write: "*Publish This Book* is fraught with instances of Freudianesque homoerotic humor between supposedly hetero-sexual men. My bona fides in this field are impressive, as I often walk halfway down the stairs when I know my roommates are in the living room, saying in the gravest voice possible, 'Hey, guys I have something kind of serious I need to talk to you about…' And then bound down the rest of the way, leaping onto the couch where they sit, screaming 'Kiss attack!' as I try to mouth their necks and faces."

Clearly a paragraph like this cannot make it into the proposal.

To decide what should go in the proposal, I must consider whose opinion I am courting here, whose approval I seek. Who will buy this book? Who will review it? How little or much will I care about elite opinion? The opinion of reviewers like, say, Michiko Kakutani of the *New York Times*?

It's funny, but after I wrote that throwaway line at the end of Chapter 5, I suddenly found myself completely obsessed with what Kakutani might think of me. I began to read her reviews and articles religiously. Even in the ones with which I disagree, I find myself engaged and compelled by her arguments. She is a one-woman car-nival for my brain. There are days when I spend my entire afternoon searching for her old work. What did she think of Fareed Zakaria's *The Post-American World*? What about Tim O'Brien's *The Things They Carried*? When she writes a piece on the brilliance and influence of *The Daily Show with Jon Stewart*, I am almost apoplectic with glee.

I no longer care what Kakutani thinks of my book, what kind of review she would write about it, or how she would find the infantile humor. I don't just want Kakutani to review my book, *I want to fucking hang out with her*. Therefore, I'd like to revise my previous proposition that Kakutani review my book. Now I'd like to say, Michiko, we should totally get a beer sometime.

As much as I admire Kakutani, however, I know that hers is only an elite opinion and does not sell books. As we now know from the McCain campaign and Fox News, the *New York Times* is a propa-ganda tool for Marxists.

No, there is only one person who can actually help my book and that is the woman who is single-handedly propping up the entire publishing industry: Oprah Winfrey.

Oprah's Book Club sells books in a way no other vehicle ever invented has done. She puts her stamp on *Your Little-Known Book* by Poor Disregarded Writer and Mr. Disregarded Writer had better buy himself a bigger bathtub because you can't bathe in money unless you got something at least the size of a Jacuzzi.

Yes, it would be nice if I could ingratiate myself with Oprah—after all, she is a Chicagoan herself—but short of camping outside of Harpo Studios, I can't really think of a way Oprah and I would end up shooting the shit.

I give it my best shot by writing a column about her in *RedEye*. (To be fair, I actually do think all of the following.)

You'd think that she would be my natural enemy.

After all, she's always out empowering women, which can't be good for my dating life. But I still love her.

She's just so cool, funneling untold amounts of her private fortune into helping people whose needs are genuine and immediate, bringing her influence to combat injustice and inequity in a country that sometimes is a little too okay with those things.

You won't believe what I recently did: I was on the Internet at work and I actually looked up tickets for her show.

Do you know how bad it would be if any of my friends were to find this out? Do you understand how long they would make fun of me? I wouldn't be able to sit down in my living room without a conversation like this taking place:

One of my roommates: *Hey, dude, Oprah's summer weight loss episode is on.*

Me: *[Bleep].*

Roommate: *Your thighs are looking a little beefy.*

Me: *[Bleep].*

Roommate: *Have you caught up with the book club yet?*
Me: *[Bleep, bleep, bleep].*

The problem with modern literary opinion is that, other than Oprah, there is no surefire way to the hearts of the masses. No one knows how books become hits, and publishers (not to mention authors) have yet to develop any reliable method for picking the winners. It's certainly not book reviewers who are setting trends or helping people decide what to read. This leaves a rather large vacuum, and unfortunately one entity has stepped in to fill that vacuum.

His name is "A Customer" and he writes on the venerable website Amazon.com. He had this analysis of Richard Wright's *Native Son*:

> This book was the most boring book that I have ever read. There are one or two scenes in the book that are interesting, but overall the book is boring. BORING. BORING. BORING. Oh yeah, its [*sic*] about a black dude who accidentally murders a white girl. Things like that happen every day. He murdered the girl out of fear, just like many people in the world today who do things out of fear of something. I don't understand why so many people like this book...

Or take this review of Harper Lee's classic *To Kill a Mockingbird*:

> I started reading this book because I heard so much about it. It sounded interesting—the south, racism, a murder trial. It seemed to have potential. The beginning was o.k... [*sic*] After 50 pages I started wondering where was the ground breaking story? why [*sic*] should I care about any of the characters? This book is so boring! Nothing is going on. Until you get to the trial piece, you have to go through pages and pages about Atticus's childrens' [*sic*] lives which have no relevance to the supposedly main idea—racism in the south... Does anyone have any idea why this book even won a Pulitzer?!?! If you want to read a really good book about life in the south why not "the color purple" [*sic*] or even "A time to kill?" [*sic*] this is not a masterpiece. I don't know how this bad book on such an important subject ever got published in the first place.

Or this take on my favorite novel of all time, Vonnegut's *Slaughterhouse-Five*:

> Kurt Vonnegut is not a writer. He is someone who was able, through his contacts with governmental money provided to academics in the 30s, to foist is [*sic*] sloppy, humourous [*sic*] (lacking actual literary ability) cheaply and dishonorably written work upon us. As a student I was forced to read this monster. His books are not writing, they are pure tom foolery [*sic*]. This book, lauded to be the capstone, the beggining [*sic*] for an exploration of his touted literary genious, [*sic*] is actually probably only useful as toilet paper. So it goes... Kurt Vonnegut uses this disgustingly cheap segway [*sic*] to work himself out of every situation. His book wastes pages and pages of precious ink talking about aliens and splicing in images of WWII. Its pure trash. [*sic*] Up their [*sic*] with Michal Moores [*sic*] 'stupid [*sic*] White men.' [*sic*]

Yes, three of my favorite novels got destroyed by those esteemed reviewers of Amazon.com. (I take particular issue with the comparison of *Slaughterhouse-Five* to a Michael Moore book.)

So, controlling the first five to ten reviews on Amazon.com is becoming increasingly important to an author's critical appeal and ability to sell. Customers only tend to read the first five reviews, so even a fourth-grader's critique of *Jude the Obscure* can become one of the most widely read reviews of that book. As Amazon comes to dominate the market for selling books, getting those citizen reviewers on your side has grown far more critical than getting Michiko Kakutani on your side.

I confess, even I have fallen victim to the habit of reading the first three Amazon reviews to determine whether or not I want to invest time in a book. I borrowed my dad's copy of *White Noise* and didn't read it for five years because an Amazon reviewer called it "incoherent." I fear *Lolita* remains on my bookshelf because I am still subconsciously putting it off due to an unfavorable Amazon reviewer who found it, and I quote: "Loooooooong."

Of course, I have no proof that the rise of the Amazon review is stupefyng the American reading public, but it's something I sense intrinsically in my gut. The publishing industry has been fretting for years that it is hemorrhaging readers as the country grows ever more illiterate. People who do buy books buy ones about dogs helping people find themselves or moving to a fix-me-up house in Tuscany to find themselves or having drug addictions so they can find themselves (unlike writing a book about oneself to find oneself[138]).

Whatever the case, I can already predict exactly what my Amazon reviews will look like. It's not too hard: just imagine people from all walks of life with way, way too much fucking time on their hands.

116 of 171 people found the following review helpful:

★★☆☆☆ **Self-indulgent mess**, January 5, 2010

By **Jasmine** (Omaha, NE) – See all my reviews

I don't normally read biographies but I'm a creative writing major and a friend told me to pick this up and I can't believe I actually finished it. Markley spends the entire book insulting his readers, telling them they're "poor bastards" and generally mocking his audience, and then he wants us to like him at the end because he's got problems too? Please. He said it best himself: "completely self-indulgent." There's a good reason this guy never got a book published and it's because he's completely obsessed with himself. He reminds me of the kid who always raised his hand in class to answer the teacher's question and then made some idiotic comment to make people laugh. Don't buy a copy. You'll just encourage him.

---

138   Ah, goddamnit, those first three ideas are totally more profitable. Would it require too much of a suspension of disbelief if I suddenly reset all of this in a tiny village on the outskirts of Florence with a scruffy furball named "Ruskers" by my side as I overcame a heroin addiction?

78 of 110 people found the following review helpful:

★☆☆☆☆ **gross**, November 23, 2009

By **Susan R. Wilder** (Urbana, IL) – See all my reviews

This book is vile. In the very first chapter he describes how he thought he had testicular cancer. First of all, that's not funny at all. My cousin had testicular cancer and he almost died from it. That's not a joke at all. Then from there it just gets worse. From what I can tell it's not about being a writer but trying to sleep with girls, do drugs, and have disgusting conversations with his friends. I couldn't even finish it. This guy needs help, not a book contract.

12 of 58 people found the following review helpful:

★★★★★ **HILARIOUS**, November 2, 2009

By **Svenk** (Irvine, CA) – See all my reviews

Markley is hilarious!!! You have to read this book, it made me laugh so f***ing hard people would look at me! where does he think of this sh**!

45 of 97 people found the following review helpful:

★★★☆☆ **Better stuff out there**, April 9, 2010

By **JoannaD** (Concord, NH) – See all my reviews

It was okay. I like Tucker Max better because he doesn't worry about sounding smart or like he's being really intelligent. There's a lot of stuff here about politics and books that just gets in the way. Still, some funny stuff. Read it if you've got nothing better to do.

233 of 311 people found the following review helpful:

★★☆☆☆ **So this is the voice of a generation?**, May 12, 2010

By **Kevin Horenstein** (Ithaca, NY) – See all my reviews

We hear so much about millennials, and frankly if this guy is their mouthpiece, it's no wonder Barack Obama got elected. I hope that millennials reject being labeled like this—as aggressive, hedonistic, infantile misogynists who only care about their own vainglory. Markley represents just about every negative trend in this country. Actually, he doesn't just represent it, he embodies it. The only reason I'm not giving it one star is because I will admit (begrudgingly) that it made me laugh a few times, which is not to say that I liked it. Even a blind squirrel finds a nut every now and then.

165 of 201 people found the following review helpful:

★★★★☆ **Reader Beware**, December 13, 2009

By **Jason Cross** (Eugene, OR) – See all my reviews

In the tradition of vaudevillian memoirists like Eggers, Klosterman, and Sedaris, Stephen Markley has taken the postmodern autobiography to an entirely new plateau as he explores his own career, life, insecurity, narcissism, and redemption in this spastic and seemingly extemporaneous account of his year spent attempting to publish his first book. To say that this book is all over the place hardly does justice to just how unaccountable Markley is to standard narrative form. If Eggers and David Foster Wallace and their disciples tried to play and reinvent the standard narrative form by tearing it down and rebuilding it brick-by-brick, Markley seems content to take a barrel of dynamite to the entire notion and walk away wiping his hands in self-satisfaction. This is not to say that "Publish This Book" is a failure. Far from it. To even offer a critique of the book is pointless since Markley has long ago anticipated any and all criticism that one could level. His humor is all over the place, from sophomoric rejoinders ("That's what she said" recalls the work of Steve Carrell on "The Office") to positively juvenile discussions with his friends that usually include some kind of thinly veiled homoerotic humor (is it homophobic? Hard to say, as Markley himself does not seem to bear any particular prejudice toward anyone's sexual orientation; he simply mocks his own supposed dogmatic adherence to hetero-normative behavior).

Yet when Markley steps away from his "crutch"—as one character calls it—he reveals thoughtful, even insightful moments. Who, then, is the real Stephen Markley? As one purveyor of controversial social commentary that Markley likely listened to as an adolescent once said, "Will the real Stephen Markley please stand up?" Alas, this confusion of tone and voice detracts only partially from the unfolding narrative. Suffice it to say, Markley manages to stay interesting throughout. Whether it's random satirical news pieces rejected by "The Onion" or footnotes that go on for half a page, he keeps the surprises coming and the reader engaged. I doubt Markley will ever qualify for literary brilliance, and it seems unlikely that he will somehow grow into a storyteller with any real depth the way that Eggers has, but he should maintain a relatively determined following—for those at least who are willing to forgive his constant excess. It makes one wonder what Henry Miller or Hunter Thompson would have made of Markley. Likely they would have recognized a kindred spirit in the booze-soaked womanizing excess but would they have also re-calibrated those initial judgments to find a true and serious author underneath (the way many did with them)? It seems unlikely but I could be wrong. Needless to say, a following will emerge for this book, albeit a small one, and likely the twin pillars of the Establishment—popular and critical opinion—will have to determine if there is anything more here.

7 of 167 people found the following review helpful:

★★★★★ **Awesome**, December 29, 2009

By **TankHammer** (Fort Worth, TX) – See all my reviews

ahahahaha Shit/shaving machine! Classic!

• • •

Of course, all this speculation about Kakutani, Oprah, and TankHammer is purely academic. Up until now I've hesitated to reach out to people in my life for fear of jinxing this sudden strike of fortune, but I realize I'll have to tell them eventually. After all, I need some kind of guidance in all this—I'm slowly creeping out onto a limb with this book and I may not fully understand all the implications just yet.

More immediately I must look to these people who I remain closest to
in my life. If this book is about different shards of my existence, then
they are the glass over which I'll walk. I have to throw this out there
and see what comes back. Therefore, here are some of their reactions—
in no particular order, set everywhere from Chicago to Ohio to New
York with no over-arching conclusion to be drawn:

My Dad (Chicago O'Hare airport)

When my dad and I are together, we usually rotate through the
same three topics, and since the first is strictly how crazy my mom and
sister are, I cannot count that as legitimate.[139] For me and my father,
this leaves sports and politics. Bitching about our favorite sports teams
always leads quite naturally to bitching about politics. We don't even
have subjects; just random thoughts that spark our ire:

> **My dad:** *Bush, that fucking idiot.*
> **Me:** *Cheney, that fucking leech.*
> **My dad:** *[While driving by a radio tower] See, why can't that
> be a wind turbine? How fucking hard could that be?*
> **Me:** *Why bother when we can stuff another couple billion
> dollars in the pockets of oil executives, those slimy fucks?*
> **My dad:** *Oh, Joe Lieberman, that fucking piece of shit.*

It's a language all our own.

On this particular occasion we are sitting in the O'Hare airport
preparing to fly to Connecticut for my grandfather's ninetieth birthday when I break the news about getting an agent.

"For a novel?" asks my dad.

---

139 Because likewise, when I'm with my mom, we always begin with how crazy my
dad and my sister are, and of course when I'm with Hannah, my sister, our prime
target of disdain and pity is our parents, who, in Hannah's words, "lost their minds
sometime before the two of us even hit puberty." There is very little ill will involved in
all this; I think it's just how your average nuclear family operates these days.

"No, nonfiction." I explain to him the concept of *Publish This Book*. His smile slowly fades to a bemused frown. "Oh. So is this written in the vein of your columns? Is that about right?"

I nod. "Hits the nail on the head, Dad."

He shakes his head. "Jesus Christ."

I laugh.

"Is this going to be one of those things where I have to wait until most of the extended family is dead before I start telling people about it?" he wonders.

"Yes. Probably." I think about Chapter Four. Then Chapter Sixteen. Oh, and Chapter Nine, Lord have mercy. "Definitely," I add.

James (Chicago Fitness, our neighborhood gym)

Chicago Fitness blends a strong boxing/kickboxing/mixed martial arts culture with a heavy Chicago Police Department influence[140] with a streak of poor college grads who just want an affordable gym in Lakeview. The majority of Chicago Fitness members have multiple tattoos including the telltale sign of someone who doesn't care about getting hit in the head, which is neck ink.

I tell James the good news while a meaty life support system for two enormous biceps pounds the tape off a bag nearby. James reacts with a congratulatory, "No way!" followed by a high five.

After I give him more of the details, he says, "Oh no, man."

"What?" I ask.

"You're accomplishing something."

"No, I'm not, man. C'mon, I wouldn't do that."

"No way, you are." He shakes his head as he selects a couple of

---

140   Once while taking a piss, I overheard a conversation between two that went, "So this jagoff tried to make off with Tommy's gym bag right out of his locker."

"So what the fuck'd you do?"

"What do you think we did? We caught up with the jagoff and beat him in the ribs for a while."

"Fucking jagoffs."

sixty-pound dumbbells from the rack. He wears a black T-shirt he's hacked the sleeves off of and a pair of blue mesh shorts splattered with paint. Nearly half the clothes James owns are covered in paint. "Dude, you're doing something with your life. Hardly 'mediocre,' wouldn't you say?"

"No, I'm still a mediocre renaissance man. That hasn't changed."

"Unh-huh. You're achieving well above mediocrity now. You're out of the club, man."

He takes his weights and huffily shuffles off to find a bench.

My friend, Alberto, visiting from California (In the bar at the top of the Hancock, Chicago)

A twisted Ecuadorian socialist who drools on himself when he laughs too hard, Alberto asks, "And when does the book come out?"

"I don't know," I tell him. "I've gotta find a publisher first, then I'll let you know."

He shrugs. "No, that's okay. I'll probably just wait for the reviews."

Phil (By phone from California while I stand outside a shitty Thai restaurant on Belmont, Chicago)

Obviously I'm not an idiot, so before I go and sign any contract with an agent, I want to have my lawyer look at it. I don't have a lawyer, but I do have Phil, who is just finishing his first year of law school out in California. While it sounds like Phil has mostly been jamming his body full of illicit substances and cavorting with SoCal girls, I assume he has gleaned some kind of insight into contract law.

"Markley," he tells me after I make my request. "You've gotta get out here. Man, the girls—Jesus, man. I would say it's like shooting fish in a barrel, but that's not really fair to the fish. Maybe retarded fish."

I try to steer the conversation back on course. "So did you get that contract I sent you?"

"Oh, I'm sorry, I thought I was talking to 'Markley,' not my mom. You are 'Markley,' correct?"

"So I should move to Southern California."

"Frankly, I can't believe you don't live here already. It's like if the Pope had lived in Riyadh his whole life, and finally someone came along and told him, 'Hey, dude, you should really check out this place called the Vatican.'"

"Well, maybe if I sell this book, I'll move out there. How's the contract look?"

"Oh, yeah, sure. Fine."

He explains a few of the clauses in the contract, and we debate whether or not it was socially acceptable for a girl he has just met to send him naked pictures of herself via cell phone.[141]

"Wait, so what the hell is this book about? Is this a novel?"

"No, no novel. It's nonfiction. It's about me trying to publish this book, but it's also chock-full of stories from our youths—can youth be pluralized?—you know, you, me, Justin, Ian... Everyone'll be in there. I hope you don't mind me sullying your good name before you begin your professional career."

"No way, dude! No problem! Sully away, by all means. Just as long as none of our parents read it."

"Exactly, man. Our parents can never read it."[142]

---

141 I am not making this up: Phil met a girl at a bar, who he spoke to for all of five minutes before she asked for his number. It was late and he was in Hermosa Beach where he did not live, so he figured he would never see this woman again. By the end of the week he not only had pictures of every inch of her naked body, including a rather graphic one of her female parts (her gynecologist probably didn't have as good a view). The texts that followed had all the obvious, "I want your cock inside me," "I want to fuck right now," requests that one might expect from someone who would text naked pictures to a person she had only met briefly in a bar. Phil, to his credit, did not respond even once, but that did not stop this girl from sending more pictures over the course of the next week. If he had printed them, he would have had a pornographic flip book. Suffice it to say, weird shit like this happens to Phil frequently.

142 In a completely unrelated story that needs to be told, when we were seniors in high school and just becoming close friends, Phil and I discovered that we both had maternal grandparents living in Kettering, Ohio, near Dayton. Odd, but not too out of the ordinary. Then, one time my sister's full name appeared in *The Mount Vernon News* for an academic achievement, and Phil's mom saw that her middle name was the same as her maiden name. Weird, right? So then Phil and I began to dig around, and

My mom and sister (By phone from Ohio while I sit on the stoop of our house in Lakeview, Chicago)

"My baby's gonna have a book!"

"Oh, great. Like his ego needs this."

"I can't believe it! Oh, you're going be a published author. Congratulations!"

"Fantastic, now I get to listen to this for the rest of my life. 'Stephen got a book published when he was twenty-four! Oh my god, Stephen's so great! Oh, hooray for Stephen!' What an asshole."

"It was just yesterday you were just a little mush-faced thing— oh, you looked so much like Yoda—and now you'll have a book."

"So how many girls have you slept with so far? I mean, since you found out?"

"I figured this was going to happen sooner or later. You've always been so persistent! Oh, I'm so proud right now…"

"Did you at least leave them a note? Did you tell them which topical cream works best for your herpes?"

Elliott (In a shitty Thai restaurant on Belmont, Chicago)

"Just don't go around telling everybody," I say to Elliott. "I don't want to jinx this. The chances improved a little, but it's still so far from a done deal."

Elliott shakes his head. "No, man. You'll get it," he says. "I'm positive."

We're eating dinner. This Thai place—and I do not exaggerate when I say this—may be one of the worst Thai restaurants I've ever eaten at in either Chicago or the world at large. The food is so bland and uninspired that it is literally wrecking my entire weekend.

---

looking back down family trees, discovered that our great-grandfathers were brothers. No shit. Which means our moms are second cousins and we are third cousins, and this after having only met basically when we were freshmen in high school. Strangely enough, no one seemed to find this all that amazing, but they certainly did enjoy making comments along the lines of, "Well, looks like the two of you will have to stop having sex all the time." I think even Phil's dad made that joke.

"Why do you say that?" I ask him.

"Because, fuzzy man—God, this food is so lame." He tosses down his chopsticks. "What is this? A mussel?"

"I think it's a potato."

"That's not a potato. No way is that a potato."

"It's a potato, man, I'm telling you."

"Steve, I know what a potato tastes like, that's not a potato."

"Eat the fucker. I promise you that's a potato. Now what were you just saying?"

"Oh, I was saying, I just know you'll get a deal on this book because this always happens: my friends become really successful and rich and I just kinda…" He walks his fingers along the table to demonstrate his existential meandering. "You know, how my life is: my Internet always goes out when I'm downloading stuff, I never get the cool stuff from craigslist because there's *always* someone who's quicker than me, I can't ever seem to take a decent shit—"

"Well, the cigarettes and the eight cups of coffee a day probably have some—"

"And I know that because you're my friend, you're going to sell a book and get rich and then I'm gonna be in your book and all anyone will know about me is that my stomach hurts all the time and I spend all of my day surfing craigslist."

I shake my head at this. The waitress comes over and asks how everything was. We both lie and effusively praise the meals. When she leaves, I say, "You're kind of like a twenty-first century Job, Elliott. Only instead of God testing you with like swarms of locusts eating your crops or whatever, He just slows down Google when you're trying to use it."

Elliott shakes his head. "Fuzzy this shitty Thai food, man."

My old editor from *The Student*, Leah (By phone from Mississippi while I sit in the lawn chair in my room, Chicago)

"Oh, I hate you, Steve. I mean, congratulations and all, but I hate you."

"Well, I'm calling to thank you. You are one of the people who really helped get me started on this all those years ago."

She sighs. "If I had only known."

Ian (Visiting him in New York, somewhere in Manhattan)

"Shit, Markley, you can put whatever the fuck you want to about me in the book. It's all true. My life's an open book. Bring your worst."

"I'll keep that in mind."

"Except for the time I pissed all over myself and rubbed my pissy hands in Phil's face. I don't want to see that shit anywhere."

"I'll keep that in mind."

Dave (By email in the Cars.com office, Chicago)

Even though I already included his reaction in a previous chapter. He sends me this email, which is too true to not include. *I just realized something else*, he writes. *Markley, you might be the first person ever to be publishing a book about his life as a writer before having ever actually published anything as a writer. That's like running for president based on the executive experience you'll have after your term is over.*

Erik (A diner in Wrigleyville called the Pick Me Up Café, Chicago)

The Pick Me Up does not belong in Wrigleyville. It serves vegan milkshakes and vegetarian chili, has a population surplus of hipsters, and yet has set up shop at the intersection of Clark and Sheffield, the crux of Wrigleyville.

Wrigleyville, home to the despondent Cubs, is so chock-full of assholes you'd think you were at a colonoscopy clinic. They stroll down the streets all summer long, decked out in red, white, and blue with an overconfidence in their baseball team that borders on delusion. To be fair, the Cubs are not the reason all these privileged white assholes move to Wrigleyville; they just happen to be the sports team all these ex-fraternity and ex-sorority crowds pick up when they leave college and land in Chicago. The Pick Me Up Café is the complete antithesis of this attitude, and therefore you can always get a seat.

One afternoon James, Erik, and I are eating an early dinner and the subject of my book comes up. This is nearly two months after I sign with Julie, but Erik has been gone a lot, traveling, registering young voters, spouting his liberal propaganda.

After I explain to him the concept, he nods thoughtfully, chugging down a portion of his strawberry milkshake.

"Yeah, that's cool. That's a good idea. Have you thought about writing it as a short story first?"

James and I look at him quizzically. "Well, no, dude. It's a book," I explain. "That's kind of the concept."

He nods. "Maybe we could make it a short film, though?" He nods and gestures emphatically. "See, if we made it a short film, I feel like we could go to a lot of film festivals and screen it there. You know, kinda build momentum for it."

I am completely puzzled by the introduction of the word "we," but Erik's logic has temporarily blown a gasket in my head. "Wha—huh?"

James steps in. "I think he's saying that it's a book. The whole point of it is that he's a writer trying to publish his book."

Erik nods thoughtfully to indicate his understanding. "I know, I just think that if we start it out as—like—maybe a one-act play we'd really have something. Yeah, you know, if it was a one-act play we could put on performances. I think I know someone who would help us find the right venue."

My friend, Josh[143] (By phone to Atlanta while I wait for the El at the Belmont stop, Chicago)

Perhaps the most positive-thinking, optimistic human being I've ever known, madly in love with his girlfriend Lisa, and generally a humorous, life-loving kind of guy, Josh nevertheless says this to me, when I tell him: "Oh, great. Just what we need: Steve Markley with a national mouthpiece."

Liam (Near railroad tracks, Chicago)

"So am I going to be a caricature? Are you going to make me look like an absolute idiot and make yourself look completely sweet and badass?" Liam asks as he twirls the point of his mustache and finishes securing the young blonde virgin to the railroad tracks with a length of rope.

"No, of course not," I say, as I valiantly swoop down from the rock cliff, slash the knots of the rope, and whip the young woman into my arms just as the freight train goes barreling by us while simultaneously rolling into a defensive crouch and firing off one shot from my revolver that catches the bull's-eye right between Liam's eyes and sends him hurtling off the ravine yelling, *"Maaaaaaaaarkley!"*

Scott (By email, Cars.com office, Chicago)

Nice, Steve, he writes. *Now someone is going to steal my brilliant idea about a device that you can use to shave while you shit.*

---

143   This has absolutely no relevance to anything, but Josh had his dick pierced. That's right. He has a ring running right through the skin on the underside of his penis. Our senior year he went around showing it to anyone who asked (and some who didn't). So we'd be in Mac 'n Joes trying to drink our Pabst, and someone who hadn't seen it before would ask, and so we'd all have to sit there while Josh whipped his dick out. I probably spent an eighth of that year looking at my friend's cock. The best reaction was when Ian was visiting from Pittsburgh. We'd thrown a party and it was Josh's intention to shock Ian by whipping out his penis while they were playing beer pong. Josh did so, and Ian's eyes fell upon this bright loop of penile steel. "Oh my god," he said, and without missing a beat, "That is the smallest dick I've ever seen."

"Jill" (In a sketchy late night bar at 3 a.m., Lakeview, Chicago)

I won't use Jill's real name because she has a life and a future that presumably she would like to continue minus my editorial comments about the tumultuous yearlong period of our lives when we weren't quite sure if we had fallen in love.

Why haven't we heard of Jill before? Why is she now cropping up unexpectedly only to shortly disappear from the narrative for the remainder of the book? Maybe you'll understand, maybe you won't.

To explain what happened with Jill would require its own book. Suffice it to say, during college we fell into each other hard, only to fall right back out. This happens to young people because they are thoughtless and brash and full of a fire that can burst, scorch, and flame out as it consumes the oxygen of the surrounding world. I think this is what happened to us, although I may be wrong. I'm still not far enough away from events to tell what really happened. We met under less-than-ideal circumstances in a place that proved all too conducive to making poor life decisions. After a while, though—after the drama and the melodrama and the tears and the bitter words and the accusations and all that other shit we all know so much about—we calmed down.

By the time I see her in Chicago (where she is visiting a mutual friend, not me), it has been years since she last hated me or I last resented her. It has all melted down like a car frame into scrap metal, the original form unrecognizable. Now there is only mutual respect, admiration, and a lingering fondness, which is like the shell of the feelings we once had for each other.

When we get together we always like to talk about how awful it got.

"I hated you," she says, laughing, as we sip our beers at three in the morning in this shady late night bar called Big City Tap.[144] "Oh my god, I hated you so much."

"You told your friends they couldn't talk to me. It was a friend embargo."

She nods. "Total friend embargo."

"And that night when you showed up at my door."

She laughs and covers her face as she blushes at the memory.

"You were so drunk," I continue. "You weren't even making sense. You just stood in the doorway going, 'Oh. My. God. Are you serious? Oh my. God. Seriously? Oh. My God.' Like you thought me being asleep alone on a Thursday night was outrageous. I was wearing nothing but boxers and you just had that little dress on, and it was like two degrees outside and you wouldn't come in or go away."

She laughs hard, her face going pink. "I don't know what I was doing. That's so not me. I'm not that girl. You made me that girl, Steve. I was never that drunk falling-all-over-herself girl until I met you."

"I'll take that as a compliment."

"It's not."

We are both laughing now. I find it both strange and relieving that a period of your life that felt like the most epic tragedy can become something you laugh at only a few years later.

After Jill buys another round, she asks me about the book. I've told her only the barest essentials, but now I elaborate. I go through the concept again, tell her about my agent, tell her what the process of publishing involves.

"I don't know," I say. "It's a long way to go. After Julie signed me, I had this immediate reaction like, 'Holy shit, this is it. I'm actually going to do this, but…'" I look up at her, and she's looking at me with her head cocked onto her hand. Her small brow has furrowed

---

144 Otherwise known as Big Shitty, this joint may be the worst bar in all of human history. When you go there, one of three things happens: Either you hook up, get in a fight, or get your purse stolen—on a good night all three.

slightly, which it does when she's either curious or about to cry—both looks I know a lot about. "But I don't know," I repeat. "That wore off fast…" I trail off.

Her brow goes smooth and she takes a masculine swig from her Bud Light. "You'll get it published," she says like she just told me the capital of Ohio, like it's a fact already.

"Yeah?"

"Yeah. Oh, yeah." She nods like she's not even worried. "This is what you're supposed to do. Everyone knows it. And I'm totally gonna know a famous author. You better put me in your book."

"I'll see what I can do."

Jill once wrote to me on a birthday card that she had never met anyone as passionate as me, but she wasn't talking about romance. Rather, she was talking about the Fire, and she was the first person to ever point this out.[145] Admittedly, this was in the throes of our unrequited love phase, when saying such things likely substituted for mauling each other in stairwells and alleys and other inappropriate places. That birthday card was bad news: as much as what she said touched me, how can anyone live up to that?

"Oh shit," says Jill, followed by a belch. "We gotta go. I'm drunk."

We wander out into the night, packed and bustling in the hours of the quickly approaching morning. I help her flag down a cab, so she can get back to her friend's apartment. "How far is your place?" she asks.

"Not far. I can walk."

I won't lie to myself and pretend I did not see how the night could have gone. She reminds me of a time and place I can't get back to.

Instead, I kiss her on the cheek. Her skin is soft and cool at the surface but burning with warmth just beneath. "See you when I see you," I say.

---

145 The second was an Asian lady in Wyoming who spoke choppy English, but we'll get to that later.

She looks nauseated. "I think I'm going to throw up in this cab, Steve."

Then she is gone. Back to that other life where I only exist on the periphery.

I think of that time and place I once knew as I walk home through the Chicago winter that never fucking ends. The street-lights are yellow and as harsh as the glare of a rocket's blaze when it hurtles a spacecraft out of gravity's reach. Jill's confidence that this will happen for me—her matter-of-fact certainty that this is simply what I'm meant to do—is a strange thing. Yet her opinion—like Josh's or Leah's or my father's—is pretty much all that counts. It's a funny thing, I think as I trudge through the cold that glitters on the pavement, the way you build a web of people around you, the way each of them occupies his or her own hub, and just when you think you can't possibly care for any more people, they just come along, and pretty soon this new person has a view of the world that informs your own, that you want to cherish and protect.

My footfalls clap on the pavement, and I think to myself that even if I didn't owe Jill a spot in the book, she would have to be the stand-in, the placeholder for all the people and moments that matter but may not be part of the story.

Please Don't Fact-Check This Chapter

Now that I've done the hardest part and found an agent, my most pressing thought is: *Oh shit. I actually have to write a book.*

This comes as a rather rude awakening because, at this point in my life, pretty much the last thing I expected was any kind of success. Now not only do I have to write a book but—bummer—it can't just be incoherent babbling garbage.

Obviously, given my disposition, I cannot help but spend large swaths of time I should be writing instead envisioning the orgies I will no doubt have when I am a big published rock star (orgies that will take days and feature beautiful women wandering in and out depending on their commitments to various modeling shoots). But close on the heels of this pleasant thought is the dread that everything I write from this point forward will be insufferable because I will be writing it with the self-conscious awareness that it might actually be read. Every word will be charged with a level of "Should I say that? Will my second grade gym teacher think less of me?" Then again, I have to consider that I'm no longer just stringing together a rant of sex and shit jokes. I actually have to arrive at a point, a conclusion, a tangible statement on the nature of our absurd human world. This book has to, as they say, "succeed."

This leads to another conundrum: how is this book supposed to succeed when I don't know what it's about and can't define what that success should look like? Even if I want to make the book succeed, I don't necessarily know how.[146]

What I do know is that the focus of this book has changed drastically since its inception in the summer of 2007 and broken even from the vague initial categorization I tried to give it in the first few chapters. What it has morphed into is not entirely clear, but Katie, of my all-female writing group, may have had an insight into the book earlier than I did. She said, "It's a memoir, only 'memoir' is kind of a poofy word."

In one of our phone conversations, Julie says with a hint of worry, "What you have here is a memoir… of sorts—well, kind of—at least that's where they'd probably put it in the bookstore."

No sweat. Everyone knows that section in Borders: the Memoir of Sorts Well Kind of at Least That's Where We Think This Book Belongs section (just behind Spanish reference).

If this is a memoir, though, then I have a major problem: nothing has ever happened to me.

Sure, I have a few amusing stories, a few quirky anecdotes. After all, I *did* tell WB hunk Jared Padalecki that I gave his girlfriend herpes, and I *did* listen as former presidential candidate Pat Buchanan forced out a painful-sounding bowel movement, but I hardly think a publisher would be very receptive if I showed up at the offices and said, "Hey, I heard Pat Buchanan take a dump once, now give me my book contract!"

Overall, I have had a life of relative luxury and major convenience. I've never faced adversity or "beaten the odds" or done anything much of note whatsoever.

This dilemma is not unique to me. Many writers have faced this very same difficulty before, and I'm happy to report they overcame it.

---

146   My Ego, helpful as always, has at this point completely skipped out on the creative process. Where once we were creative collaborators and unshakable partners, now he mostly sits around huffing turpentine and declaring, *Whatever, man! Just cram it full of sex and shit jokes so we can get to the orgies. Time's-a-wastin'!*"

Mostly by faking their life stories.

For years, I have been perplexed by the fake memoir, and just as I wake one day and discover that I'm a twenty-four-year-old dumbass who must now write a memoir detailing his dumbass life, two additional fake memoirs rock the publishing world in a single week. I read of these debacles and suddenly all the issues involved with writing a memoir come bubbling to the surface. Never have the lines between truth and fiction, memory and invention, bullshit and made-up bullshit felt more consequential—and yet at the same time so frail.

First, it comes out that a geriatric Holocaust survivor named Misha Defonseca embellished a few facts in her book *Misha: A Memoir of the Holocaust Years*.[147] For instance, one of the minor caveats a genealogical researcher unearthed about the book: Misha did *not* kill a German soldier in self-defense; the scene was an invention of her imagination. I view this fabrication as forgivable, largely because it at least sounds plausible that an emaciated seven-year-old girl could kill a Nazi.

Oh, and there were a few other minor discrepancies in the narrative, such as: Misha did not journey 1,900 miles across Europe, alone, in search of her family, and she was not adopted by wolves that protected her from Nazi soldiers, and she was never trapped in the Warsaw ghetto, and she actually spent the war safely at her uncle's house.

Oh, and she's not Jewish.

But other than that, the manuscript's beyond reproach.

Reading about Defonseca's case in the *New York Times*, I am struck by the overwhelming urge to speak with the original publisher, just to ask if anyone's credulity was at all challenged when a seventy-year-old woman claimed she had been raised by wolves that

---

147   Holy shit! A footnote with a real, honest to God reference! (Eskin, Blake. "Crying Wolf: Why did it take so long for a far-fetched Holocaust memoir to be debunked?" Slate.com. February 29, 2008.)

protected her from Nazis.[148] Perhaps in an editorial meeting they should have had a conversation that went something like:

"Wow. How 'bout Misha's memoir, huh?"

"Powerful stuff."

"You think we should roll it out in November? Just in time for Hanukkah?"

"Hmmm, maybe we should check into the exact dates she specifies in the book, especially the Nazi invasion of Poland."

"You think she could be making it up?"

"No, I just want to make sure she's not leaving out a few months after she escaped Warsaw but before the pack of wild wolves raised her and protected her from Nazis. Kids have slippery memories, you know."

Following Defonseca by less than a week, I encounter the strange case of Margaret B. Jones.

Jones had written a stirring memoir called *Love and Consequences*, which detailed her life as a half-white, half–Native American girl growing up in the midst of predominantly black South Central Los Angeles with its culture of drugs, gangs, and everyday violence and despair. She ran drugs for the Bloods and watched a war with their rival gang, the Crips, escalate into madness. She saw an old friend gunned down in the street, and her adoptive older brother, Terrell, sent to prison and upon his release shot to death by Crips. She tells of getting a .38 pistol for her thirteenth birthday and of her foster mother, Big Mom, whose love guided her through her darkest hours. In the end, she tells of how she overcame it all—the drugs, the violence, the death—to wrench herself out of this spiral of hopelessness and attend college at the University of Oregon, where she graduated at the top of her class. Badass book reviewer for the *New York Times* Michiko Kakutani called it "a humane and deeply affecting memoir."

---

148 The book was even made into a French film titled, what else, *Surviving With Wolves*.

So now you're wondering: how much did she make up?

Everything. Including her name.[149]

It turned out that Margaret B. Jones was actually a woman named Margaret Seltzer. Seltzer's sister saw her picture in the Home & Garden section of the *Times* beside a profile about her rough-and-tumble life and her astonishing escape from the ghetto. Seltzer's sister called the book's publisher with some minor complaints as to the veracity of this story. Among them: far from growing up in South Central L.A., Seltzer sprang from the wealthy Sherman Oaks section of the city; she graduated from a private Episcopalian high school and lived her whole life with her biological family (including her turncoat sister!).

And she didn't actually graduate from the University of Oregon.

After she was caught and publicly humiliated, the story came out that she had written parts of the book as "stories" in a creative writing class. The professor of that class introduced her to a published author, who in turn introduced her to an agent, who encouraged her to write more of these supposedly autobiographical stories. She sold her made-up life story for—holy fuck—$100,000.

Grasping for an explanation as to why she perpetrated this massive, overwhelming fib, Seltzer told a *Times* reporter that the stories were true; they just were not hers. Apparently she had gang-member "friends" from whom the stories originated, and she wrote the book in a South Central Starbucks while "talking" to gang members. So she's almost an authority.

Seltzer said she wanted to get the stories out there in the world, so that these voices could be heard. Despite the unbelievable condescension of a privileged white girl claiming to speak for and about the injustices suffered by inner-city youth, it's not hard for a struggling writer to see what happened here: a B-student in a creative

---

149 Another reference! What am I, sick? (Rich, Motoko. "Gang Memoir, Turning Page, Is Pure Fiction." *New York Times*. March 4, 2008.)

writing class saw a quick path to publication, a leapfrog over the typical hurdles of publishing a novel, and she took it.

I have to thank Seltzer, however, because her story inspires me.

By no measure do I want to be Margaret B. Jones. I do not want my book to hit shelves only to immediately turn up on TheSmokingGun.com the next day. On the other hand, I can't write an entire book about getting drunk with my idiot friends.

The issue this raises is that I need more interesting things to happen to me, and I can't just ask someone in a Starbucks, "Hey, dude, what's the most fucked-up thing that's ever happened to you?" and then put it in my book. I can't risk any taint of falsehood lest I be Seltzerized by some Benedict Arnold family member. No, I need to do something tangible, something worthy of people's expectations, that will make them search inside themselves, that will leave them reevaluating the priorities of their own lives. There is really only one logical solution—only one path, which I must now travel.

I need to start hanging out more with my drug dealer.

• • •

My pot dealer goes by the name of Sergei and lives on the southern edge of Humbolt Park, where young black and Hispanic Chicagoans get shot at a rate high enough to be disturbing yet low enough to not divert the attention of the government as it happily tries to build sweeter aircraft carriers. Sergei's living room is a shrine to Al Pacino in *Scarface* and women with breasts that border on unethical medical practices by plastic surgeons. Other than the posters, you have your typical decorations of a super-expensive flat-screen television, thousand-dollar stereo system, and more empty pizza boxes and beer cans than Chicago's municipal workers could collect in one run. Also, for some reason the furniture always smells like burnt hair.

As Sergei separates a bit of marijuana, which I intend to buy from him, he starts in on how the increased violence of the warm weather has sparked a more vigilant police presence that has disrupted his business.

"A fucking socialist police state, man, that's what we're living under. People want out from under the Nanny, so then Big Brother comes along and clamps down. It's all about owning the means of production."

"What's that for?" I ask, pointing to the gun on the coffee table.

"Don't worry, Charles Markley," he says, focusing on the weed. "It only has one bullet in it."

"Oh." I nod. "Good."

Sergei claims to be from an ex-Soviet satellite, which is why he reviles communism in all forms, including the Democrats, even as he sells oceans of cocaine and dope to teenagers. He takes an agonizingly slow time completing my purchase because he loves talking, and the other people in his crummy apartment aren't in any mood for conversation. Currently, there is a young black couple passed out on his couch, a burly white guy sitting in a recliner across from us twitching and muttering under his breath erratically, and two white girls making out on a beanbag across the room. Playing on the TV is an episode of the Brooke Shields show *Suddenly Susan*.

"Let me ask you something, man," I say, because Margaret B. Jones is on my mind. "You think you could recognize if someone was lying in a book?"

"What do you mean lying in a book? Like that pinko, Paul Krugman?"

"I mean, if you read a book where someone was essentially making shit up, say about life in the projects, the ghetto—you think you'd be able to tell?"

Sergei nods his head and scratches his blonde buzz cut. I've never seen him wear anything but a white wife-beater and shorts that reach his ankles. He also has three visible tattoos: a purple dragon on his left shoulder blade, a sword with a cross on his right arm, and cursive words on his neck that say *Money Power Respect*. "Sure, I've lived the life. Here and in the Baltic." He is packing a bowl. He always makes me smoke with him. One of the girls across the room moans. Beads of sweat are beginning to spring out on the brow of the muscle-bound jock. "Every day I'm out hustling these streets, scraping to live, you know? Trying to save so I can donate every spare penny to the John Birch Society, right, Blaine?"

Blaine must be the guy passed out on the couch, but he says nothing, his arm draped lazily over his girlfriend who rests her head on his chest.

"Yeah," I say. "But if you read something and it sounded really convincing. Like this person had been living in the ghetto, would you rather read that or maybe like a book about publishing a book?"

"Book about what?" He lights the bowl and takes a hit.

"A book about writing a book."

"What? What the fuck does that mean? What's the book about?"

"About writing and publishing that book."

"What book?"

"The one that I'm—that I'm writing and publi—never mind." I take the bowl from him only to drop it on the carpet. "Shit," I mutter.

"Naw, man, that's good!" He picks up the spilled bud and repacks the bowl. "It landed on the carpet! That means we got carpet fibers in there. That shit'll get you high, man. Completely fucked."

"Really?" I am skeptical.

"Shit, yeah."

"Then why don't people just smoke carpet fibers?"

"'Cause, man, Nanny state wants to keep us safe. They don't want us to know about the means of production." I decide not to mention that the Republican Party would surely not advocate people selling narcotic carpet fibers. I am also beginning to question if Sergei actually knows what "the means of production" means.

I take the bowl and smoke it, hacking profusely as I pass it back. "Yeah, good shit, right? Good shit." He takes a hit himself. I feel high, but maybe not carpet-fiber high.

The big dude smacks a fist on the arm of the recliner, scuffing the duck tape that holds in the foam. *"Rod Stewart!"* he barks. *"Rod fucking Stewart!"*

I look to Sergei for an explanation, but he only shrugs his shoulders. Across the room, the beanbag squeaks as one of the girls pulls her shirt over her head.

"So what would you say if you read a book, and you thought it was awesome?" I ask.

"Man, I don't read much. Most books printed now are far-left propaganda. Last book I read was called *Hustler* and it was the titty-fucking issue."

"Okay, but say you read a book about your—um—this life. Life in the 'game,'" I say, feeling dumb as the word comes out. "And it's great, it describes your situation perfectly, but then it turns out the person who wrote it made it up?"

"Why'd they do that?"

"Because they wanted to make money and they wanted people to read their book."

"Well, shit, Charles Markley, that's just pure old-fashioned American capitalism right there. That's a cat trying to make a dollar—next caller, thank you! Seriously, man, there ain't nothing wrong with trying to hustle a bit. That's the American way."

"Yeah, but it's complete bullshit. It's—"

Just then the bathroom door flies open, slamming against the wall. A young Latino with a mustache on only the left half of his lip hastily scrambles out, pulling up his jeans and buckling his belt as he goes. He breezes by us, throws open the door of the apartment, exits, and slams it closed behind him without saying a word.

Sergei is still looking at me as if nothing has happened. "Man, what's with the talk? Aren't you here to get high? Do you wanna go places you've never dreamed before? Hit up your mind-pussy with the dick of truth?"

I sigh. Sergei is not interested in my dilemma. "Sure, why not."

He hops up and goes into his bedroom. I watch the girls, still sucking face on the beanbag. Blaine stirs, scratches his nose, and falls back to sleep. The big dude in the recliner is sweating profusely and has both of his hands clenched in fists so tightly that his knuckles are pale. "You can't get a free iPod Touch with a computer," he mutters. "That's fucking bullshit why do I fucking need the fucking iPod mini no one needs an iPod mini you need a fucking iPod that can play fucking movies and that you can move the icons around with your fucking finger."

I twiddle my fingers on my knees in nice-feeling rhythmic patterns. I think the carpet fibers are beginning to kick in.

Sergei returns with a bottle of rubber cement, a tube of blemish removal cream, and a turkey baster. He begins mixing the blemish cream into the rubber cement.

"What are we gonna do, eat this?" I ask.

"Not exactly."

"Smoke it?"

"Nah."

The girls are removing each other's bras. They begin rubbing their breasts together, manipulating them with their hands. Sergei begins to draw the rubber cement-blemish cream mix into the turkey baster. He hands it to me.

"I don't get it," I say.

"You ever heard of an enema?" he asks.

"Of course. What's that got to—oh, fuck that, man."

"Trust me, man, you'll never see the wild shit, the truly crazy, mind-bending, life-altering, fuck-your-cerebral-cortex-in-the-asshole shit unless you give this a shot. I swear, dude, you'll see a zebra on ice-fire flossing its teeth in a way that makes you hear Mozart symphonies."

"No way."

"You put that in your ass," he says of the baster.

"Yeah, I got that part."

"I swear you'll see rainbows driving cars and belt sanders giving speeches better than Ronald Reagan. You'll see nekked ladies coming down from the sky like snowflakes and little babies beating your enemies to death with chains and trashcan lids. You gotta try this shit, Charles Markley, you just gotta, man. Want me to go first?"

I hand him the baster. "Please."

"Will you help?" He begins to lower his pants.

"Absolutely not."

"Man, the angle's all funny. It's hard to reach."

Before we can argue further, the door to his apartment whips open and slams into the wall. It is the young Latino, holding a pistol. There are two others with him, also holding guns. "There he is," says one.

"Go check it out," says the one with half a mustache, who looks like the leader.

The other guy returns from the bathroom with a magazine and hands it over to the leader, who looks at it. "You think you could steal from me, Serj? You think you could fucking steal from me, man?" He holds up the copy of *Hustler*. "Man, this is the titty-fucking issue, too! All the girls are having sex with their titties."

"That's mine, man," says Sergei calmly. "You musta lost yours."

Before the leader of the Latinos can say anything, both of the girls previously making out on the beanbag are on their feet, shirtless and aiming sawed-off shotguns at skulls, one of the girls with a weapon in each hand to cover two men.

"Looks like we got ourselves an interesting situation," says Sergei. "Reminds me of when that pussy Kennedy couldn't pull the trigger on Fidel."

"*Transporter 2!*" snarls the jock, causing everyone to jump. "That movie made no fucking sense!"

"Oh, and you's gonna do the turkey baster without me," says the Latino leader. "Real fucking cool, Serj."

I am actually pretty close to the door, so I take this opportunity to pretend like I do not notice that half the people in the room have guns. I pick up my bag of weed. "Okay, Sergei, thanks, man. I'll see you in about a month."

"Yeah, Charles Markley," says Sergei, his eye on the coffee table where his gun sits with its single bullet. "Keep that motherfucker tight and strapped down. I'll think about what you said about the book."

I head to the door as the remaining players continue to eye each other carefully.

"What book?" asks the leader of the Latinos.

"A book about publishing a book," I hear Sergei say as I dash into the hall. "Like there ain't no fucking point to the book except for you got this shit in the book about how it's published, you know?"

• • •

My obsession with the fake memoir began in college with the author JT Leroy when a professor assigned "his" book for a modern American lit class. It found fuel my senior year in a bar in Nashville after my band, Full Bleeding Moon, had performed one of the hottest sets of our short career.

I read both of LeRoy's books, beginning with *The Heart is Deceitful Above All Things*. LeRoy's mother was a drug addict prostitute, and he spent his youth turning tricks with her at a West Virginia truck stop for vile old men. *The Heart is Deceitful* is a collection of short stories detailing his sexual abuse at a young age and his relationship with the truck-stop prostitute mother. Previous to that, he wrote a novel, *Sarah*, which is pretty much the same thing, only more sensational.

Reading these two works, I felt an acute sense of jealousy. LeRoy was a decent writer at best. What he had on his side was a compelling story. He had suffered horrific sexual violence, escaped, and now stood at the pinnacle of the literary world. He was celebrated by critics and contemporary authors alike. Dennis Cooper, Michael Chabon, and Dave Eggers all praised his work. His list of celebrity pals was even longer: Billy Corgan, Tom Waits, Liv Tyler, Bono, Courtney Love, Carrie Fisher—even Madonna had paid him a call. He had achieved ultimate cult celebrity. LeRoy also happened to be dying of AIDS, which only added to his tragedy and courage.

But it wasn't fair. Not at all. All I could do was make stuff up. This LeRoy kid had a gut-wrenching, heart-sickening experience to milk over and over again. He had crushing abuse and physical violation on his side. Jesus—how could I compete? How could anyone? If you experienced what LeRoy had, they probably handed out literary awards as long as you could put a coherent sentence together.

My jealousy was inexplicable, my contempt unreasonably cruel. *If I just got raped in the ass once,* I thought, *just once—I could write such a sweet book about it.*

But alas, my fate was to have had a mostly happy childhood with very few obstacles and zero heart-sickening sexual violence.[150]

I found myself reading *Sarah* while on the road with my band in Nashville. We were playing a weekend gig—just a few sets in this crummy bar on the south side of the city. One of my bandmates found me cradling the book in the back as we waited to play our set.

"Whatcha reading?" he asked me. I looked up from the magical powers of raccoon penis-bones, which, I'm not kidding, is a major motif in that novel.

"Nothing," I sighed. "Some guys have all the luck."

JT LeRoy was a mysterious celebrity magnet, a transgendered author, who had published his first book at the age of sixteen. He sold the film rights to *Sarah* for $350,000. He showed up, this five-foot-five waif, who spoke in a girlish voice, at some of the most exclusive events in New York where crowds flocked to him. Everyone thought he was brilliant, a towering literary figure for the twenty-first century.

Meanwhile, I was the lead singer of a country rock band that toured the Midwest and Border States when we didn't have classes. We sang a lot of covers: Dylan, Zevon, and Springsteen, with Petty and Creedence thrown in for variety. In our original songs, we explicitly ridiculed dumb pop country animals like Toby Keith, but our audiences rarely had the intellectual fortitude to realize we were mocking his jingoism

---

150 Thanks a lot, Mom and Dad, you pricks.

and railing against the stupidity of exercises in American imperialism. I mourned that I had not been born to a truck-stop prostitute.

Until I read the story in the *New York Times* titled "Lying Liar Tricks Literary Establishment into Thinking She is Sexually Tormented Transgendered Author When Really She is Just an Old Lady Who Sucks."[151]

Turned out—boy, is this a funny mix-up—there was no such person as JT LeRoy. The author of *Sarah* and *The Heart is Deceitful Above All Things* was actually a middle-aged woman named Laura Albert, and the "boy" appearing with all of these celebrities—this cult hero—was actually a young woman named Savannah Knoop in sunglasses and a blonde wig, the half-sister of Albert's boyfriend.

Turned out—oh man, is this nuttypants!—that Albert and her boyfriend Geoffrey Knoop concocted the whole story of a transgendered boy-genius author dying of the AIDS he picked up while being raped by truck drivers after his own mother pimped him out in order to *gain access to literary circles and celebrities.*

Turned out—hold on to your hats, this is getting whacky!—both of these books were the product of a failed writer and likely wouldn't have made it into print without the elaborate, exploitative, revolting "author" these three jerkoffs invented.

The *schadenfreude* I experienced after reading this *Times* article was off the charts. We were playing a show in Nashville that night, and our single "Wrap the Earth in Blood and Flag"[152] had just broken the top 100 on the Country Music Billboard Chart. I was running high from the news of "JT LeRoy" and launched into a stunning version of our other highly popular song, "Jesus (Was a Socialist)."[153]

---

151 That may not be the exact title, but by LeRoy Standards it's close enough. The actual article: (St. John, Warren. "The Unmasking of JT Leroy: In Public, He's a She." *New York Times.* January 9, 2006.)

152 A song that was wildly, *wildly* misunderstood by our fans.

153 We hid the "was a socialist" line under a thunderous guitar riff, so it sounded like I was just singing the Lord's name over and over with a really loud guitar piece in between.

During the show, I spotted a pretty young thing wearing a tight white T-shirt, jeans, and a Vanderbilt hat. I winked at her when I sang the line, *"Jesus told me, pretty darlin', to go and make you my pick/ We can go ahead and forget that we're all sucking corporate dick."*

Sure enough, after the show she was waiting for me, and as the other band struck up its first chords, she said, "I liked the songwriting. That you?"

"You betcha."

"I didn't expect to hear Noam Chomsky quoted in a country music bar."

"Finally, someone's listening."

We talked for hours while I downed beers and she sipped at vodka sodas. Her smile was wide, her nose impish, her eyes blue and clear. She had long straw-blonde hair and evident Nordic descent coupled with a tinge of Tennessee drawl in her voice. I figured I was falling in love, right up until the moment I told her why I was having such a good night.

"First I find out that LeRoy nonsense, and then I meet you."

"You like JT LeRoy, too?" she asked in excitement. "Oh, I think he's just brilliant. So wrenching."

"Wait, you heard that it's all fake, right? That there's no such person? It's actually this old woman named Laura Albert?"

"Oh yeah, I read that," she said dismissively, flipping that straight blonde hair back over her shoulder. "But still, it's so incredible what she did in those books. Magnificent."

I was completely bewildered. "Wait, you still like the books? *Sarah* and *The Heart is Deceitful*?"

"Oh my God, yes! Don't you?"

"What? No! Of course I don't! It's all bullshit. Every word is complete bullshit. None of it happened. Not only were the experiences not real, the person wasn't even real."

She tipped her glass toward me. "But that doesn't detract from the quality of the writing. If a book is brilliant, it's brilliant no matter its origins."

Suddenly I no longer found this girl that attractive. "Are you fucking kidding me? That's absurd. The entire reason either of those books exist is because they had this ridiculous backstory of this kid who was raped and abused only to escape and write coherent literature."

"They're both fiction."

"Driven by the fact that they're based on this kid's experience. Without that experience they're—" The implications dawned on me for the first time. "*The Heart is Deceitful* is just a squalid, gratuitous collection of lurid torture sequences without a point or purpose and *Sarah*—Jesus Christ—*Sarah* becomes this pretentious, silly, downright unreadable mess. For Chrissake, the narrator is babbling about magical raccoon penises for half the book. If Laura Albert had walked into an editor's office, instead of her boyfriend's half-sister dressed as this imaginary person, she would have been laughed at."

The young woman looked at me with a hint of condescension. "I actually have to go meet a friend," she said. "Good luck with your fake country band." She picked up her drink and hopped off the stool.

"Yeah," I shout after her. "Why don't you write your dissertation for Vanderbilt about the subtext of magic raccoon dick necklaces? I'm sure that'll vault you into the academy."

I turned back to the bar, where the bartender was staring at me as he cleaned a glass. "You know what the fucked-up thing is?" I said to him. "If Laura Albert hadn't thought up her little scam, I probably would have eventually."

• • •

Despite my experiences with Sergei and my near miss at becoming an ironic country rock legend,[154] I remain unconvinced that there is anything in my life worthy of documentation in a pamphlet, let alone a full-length book.

---

154 Our gigs dried up after a prominent country DJ figured out that our song "Hang 'Em High" referred to the global economic elites and not American flags or immigrants, as was thought by our audience.

In the end, it was a memory from a small brick-and-mortar classroom amidst the bayous of Louisiana that gave me strength.

I spent eight months during my early twenties teaching in a rural high school about an hour from Baton Rouge. They didn't ask for a teaching certificate in those parts, just a warm body to keep the kids out of trouble for a few hours. I was assigned to an eleventh and twelfth grade English class. I moved into a small house on the edge of a farm, which my landlord—a cranky old pig farmer—had converted from a chicken coop to rent out. It was cozy enough, with running water and electricity (although the rabbit ears on the television couldn't pick up a channel, and I had to drive into town to use the Internet).

Upon arriving in my classroom (a dilapidated closet with twelve desks and paint flaking off the walls like psoriasis), I immediately threw out the curriculum, which included Shakespeare, Fitzgerald, and a lot of other dead white guys. Instead, I threw together novels I thought might have more relevance for my students: *Invisible Man* by Ellison, *Go Tell It on the Mountain* by Baldwin, *Go Down, Moses* by Faulkner, *The Autobiography of Malcolm X* by Haley, *A Long Way Gone* by Ishmael Beah. Then—as a complete afterthought—I added to the end of the list *A Million Little Pieces* by James Frey.

I admit my reasons for adding this were completely selfish: I had just read it, formed an ironclad opinion of it, and wanted to see what my students thought of Frey's horrific but questionable experience.

The class progressed remarkably well. The students were far sharper than I had anticipated and provoked a lot of good discussion about race, class, and history. They had all the tools—they just didn't have the means. They needed someone to believe in them.

There were a few students in particular who stick out in my memory:

- **Kevin** was quiet, tall, and hefty. He played with his pencil a lot at his desk, twirling it in his fingers incessantly. I found out from another teacher that Kevin excelled in math. He had scored close to perfect on every test, and she was encouraging him to take the SAT.

- **Terri** was a short, saggy-faced young woman—not pretty exactly, but she had an honorable look about her, a quiet confidence. She was a literary marvel, writing poetry that rivaled anything I'd ever read or have since. I encouraged her to apply for writing contests, and I was sure she would win accolades rapidly.

- **Clyde** was a sly, graceful kid, whipping into his seat every day, studying relentlessly—a ferocious mind without the support it needed. Clyde could deconstruct complex philosophical texts, and he wrote dissertations on them in his spare time. I encouraged him to send these dissertations to the likes of Columbia and Brown to see if he could skip college and get his doctorate, but as he put it to me, "Ain't no one care 'bout the dissertations we writing out here. This place just another theoretical construct to them folks."

- **Buck** was stout and thick with muscle. He wore big round glasses and the same forlorn look every day to the classroom. Buck had won the MacArthur Genius Grant by figuring out how to engineer enzymes that could eat cancer cells in his science class. Unfortunately, his family was too poor to take him to Washington, D.C., to collect the prize, and the numbers on their mailbox had fallen off long ago, leaving them without a place to receive mail.

- **Jerome** was a happy-go-lucky kid with an easy smile and way of making his friends laugh. He had invented a mathematical theorem that proved the existence of God, but both his parents were gone, leaving him to raise six younger siblings by himself, and he simply had no time or means to publish it in the appro-priate peer-reviewed journals.

As we worked our way through the texts I assigned, the hot Louisiana summer gave way to the wet, muddy winter. When I finally handed out *A Million Little Pieces*, Terri aptly noted, "Oh, that dude Oprah smoked."

"That's the one," I replied.

For those not proficient in literary fakery, James Frey wrote a memoir about his battle with drug addiction and his time spent in a detox facility in Minnesota. The book is brutal, unrelenting, and judging from subsequent reporting, almost entirely made up.

After it debuted, Oprah chose it for her Book Club, and once that little seal was stamped on the cover and Frey appeared on her show looking like a distinctly geekier version of Jon Favreau, it catapulted Frey into the literary stratosphere.

When certain details were questioned by skeptical readers, Frey again appeared on the show to affirm that the book was almost completely true—at least 95 percent—but of course, he may have taken a smidge of literary license.

Of course! Literary license! Obviously! Haven't we all? Like the first time I cheated on my girlfriend, I took some literary license and said that I, in fact, had not. Or like the time George W. Bush and Dick Cheney said they knew without a doubt that Iraq had a nuclear weapons program. Literary license! What a gift.

"This is one lying-ass honky fuck," said Jerome during our first discussion of the book. After the class's giggling died down and I had rebuked Jerome for using foul language, he went on: "Sorry, Teach, but they say black people's lazy; this dude can't even get it together to lie right. Talking 'bout getting a root canal with no anesthesia. Ain't no licensed dentist gonna do that! Ain't no airline gonna let a dude onboard with hole in his cheek!"

The rest of the class murmured its agreement.

"Okay, good stuff," I said. "Let's engage now, let's mix it up. If you didn't already know that Oprah 'smoked the dude,' would you have been able to tell? Kevin."

In his husky voice, Kevin said, "I'd definitely have thought it."

"Why's that?"

"The book's too…" He struggled with the right word. "Too cinematic. Right, y'all?"

The class agreed.

"The whole thing with the mob boss mentor taking the cat under his wing. The confrontation in the crack house. I mean, come on, that's some stuff they'd put up in a movie, but it'd never go down like that in real life."

"Wow. Great stuff, guys. We're getting some real engagement—I knew you guys had it in you."

I handed out the Smoking Gun report[155] on Frey for the next day.

The Smoking Gun website features meticulous investigative reporting and exposes celebrities and politicians alike for various forms of hypocrisy and corruption. The unraveling of James Frey's life might stand as one of their finest moments. The report, roughly six web pages, details police reports (or lack thereof) and eyewitness accounts that put into question just about every story Frey brought up in the 432 pages of his memoir. From the supposed suicide of his rehab girlfriend, Lilly (police reports from Chicago—where she supposedly hung herself—never turned up a suicide even remotely resembling this scenario during the time frame Frey described), to the death of a childhood friend (it turned out Frey inserted himself into the life of a girl who was killed in a car-train collision, placing himself at the center of the tragedy, when in fact he did not know her). The Smoking Gun had trouble finding anything about Frey's story—outside of basic biographical information—that actually held up.

"C'mon, Teach, I know we ain't supposed to cuss, but this is some bullshit," said Terri in class the next day.

"Bullshit putting it mildly," affirmed Buck.

---

155 Another real citation! ("A Million Little Lies: Exposing James Frey's Fiction Addiction." TheSmokingGun.com. January 8, 2006.)

"Okay, okay," I said, knowing I had to channel these feelings into some kind of constructive discussion. "We all agree it's bullshit, but let's try to get a little deeper. Let's really mix it up and engage. I know you guys have it in you to discuss this book brilliantly, you just need someone who believes in you, right? What about the book itself makes you so angry?"

Clyde raised his hand. "Well, when I was reading it, I kept asking myself, 'Could this dude actually survive if he was doing this much stuff?' I mean if he's been an alcoholic since he's twelve or whatever and a crack addict for three years… I mean, I know dudes in my neighborhood who've died from less."

"Hell, my daddy," said Jerome. "Most of my family got smaller problems than this and they basically can't function or nothing."

"Great, we're really mixing it up now! So you think the description of his addiction sounds over-the-top?" I ask.

"Look at the Smoking Gun report," Clyde went on. "What Frey said was like his scraping-the-bottom-of-the-barrel flameout where he was messed up on crack and got arrested for fighting a bunch of cops—turns out he got a DUI 'cause he parked in a no-parking zone. I mean, a DUI ain't cool but no one's about to write a book about it."

"Hell, my daddy got DUIs," said Jerome.

Kevin raised his hand, and I nodded to him. "It's like this," he said in that post-puberty timbre. "Sounds to me like a rich white frat boy had a bit of a drinking problem and spent a couple months in this rehab place in Minnesota. After he get out, he goes and writes this shitty novel that he can't sell nowhere, 'cause it ain't no good—"

"Didn't become a hit based on literary merit," interrupted Clyde. "'Narrative feel willfully melodramatic and contrived.' That what Michiko Kakutani said 'bout it."

"Yeah," continued Kevin. "So finally dude just says all this BS be true, and what do you know! He selling more books than Jay-Z selling albums."

"Well, I don't know about that—" I began, only to be cut off by Clyde.

"It all point to narcissism, Teach!" he hollered, whipping his arm through the air to emphasize the point. "This whole book 'bout how 'bad' this dude Frey is, but really, he ain't bad 'bad.' Even his deepest, darkest secret is how he beat up some pedophile priest in Paris, but that ain't deep and dark. So he beat up a pedophile priest trying to grab his junk. So what? Now if he had been the pedophile or if he'd done something that the reader ain't forgiving him for, like pushing a pregnant lady down some stairs or something—that's how everyone should've known. He's writing this whole book about how bad he be, and he keep saying it. He's a Drug Addict and a Criminal—all in caps—but really the book just 'bout how good he is on the inside, and how badass he is to overcome all this. Self-aggrandizing motherfucker—"

I cut Clyde off because he probably could have gone on for ten minutes. "Great stuff, Clyde. I love the fire. That's why I believe in you guys," I said. "But here's my question, then: does the truthfulness of the story actually matter to the narrative itself? As a piece of literature, does it matter what the story behind the author is?"

The class erupted simultaneously into boos and catcalls. Someone threw a crumpled-up piece of paper at me, which I ducked.

"Come on, Teach!" cried Terri. "You can't be for real! You can't look at this and say, well, it don't hold up to the memoir threshold 'cause it's too full of shit, so let's call it a novel."

"Yeah," said Jerome. "Hell, my daddy could make up a bunch of junkie stories, do that mean he get a book deal, too?"

"Teach, the basis of whether it's a memoir or a novel change the whole game," Buck pleaded, his eyes looking pained behind his thick glasses. "If it a memoir and it all true, then all you can say is, 'Damn, that dude had a messed-up life.' But from what we read, almost none of it's true. This shady cat, Frey, just up and realized that when he was drying out in Minnesota, the clinic couldn't go against his story 'cause of a confidentiality agreement, so he wrote a bad novel and called it his life."

"'Zactly," agreed Terri. "Once you know it all lies, the 'courage' become cowardice, the 'harrowing' become pedestrian and pitiful."

"It be a disservice," said Clyde, "to a kid like Beah who actually had to live through some awful, awful stuff and then write it down in a book."

Clyde was referring to Ishmael Beah, a rehabilitated child soldier from Sierra Leone whose memoir, *A Long Way Gone,* detailed his harrowing experiences during that country's brutal nightmare of a civil war.

"Clyde, you're brilliant," I told him. "We're out of time for today, but you led me right to my next point."

"'Brilliant' just be a theoretical archetype applied by a ruling dictatorial minority to uphold the status quo, Teach."

I handed out photocopies of the article I had printed from Slate.com[156] that afternoon. I saw the looks on the faces of my students as the bell rang and they had time only to glance at the title: "The Fog of Memoir: The Feud over the Truthfulness of Ishmael Beah's *A Long Way Gone.*"

I stumbled upon the article while trying to learn more about Beah's horrific ordeal and what had happened to him upon leaving Sierra Leone. At first I didn't want to believe what writer Gabriel Sherman had to say. A couple of Australian reporters working for a Rupert Murdoch–controlled paper had come to dispute key facts in Beah's memoir. Most outrageously, they asserted that the two years Beah claimed he spent as a child soldier had actually been two months. They based this on a bit of chronology that Beah had seriously messed up: the takeover of a mine described in the memoir occurred in 1995, not 1993 as Beah claimed, which would have

---

156 Whoa! Actual citation #5! My head hurts from all this research. (Sherman, Gabriel: "The Fog of Memoir: The feud over the truthfulness of Ishmael Beah's *A Long Way Gone.*" Slate.com. March 6, 2008.)

made his tenure as a child solider two months long while he was fifteen rather than the two years he claimed.

Beah, his agent, and his publisher stood by the book and adamantly denied that such extravagant liberties had been taken. I stood with them. Of course I did. An African refugee writing about the horrors of war versus a media outlet owned by Emperor Palpatine himself? Not a tough call.

But then I reread the book, and much to my dismay noticed that under tougher scrutiny the middle section of his days as a child soldier were very slight, while the sections bookending that experience are much more vividly realized. Armed with the knowledge that Beah may have embellished the time frame, it was impossible to overlook the inconsistencies no matter how very much I wanted to.

When the kids halfheartedly stumbled into their desks the next day, I could see that they had come to the same conclusion as unwillingly as I had. Jerome sat with his arms folded sullenly. Terri reclined all the way in her desk, chewing gum and gazing without interest at the ceiling. I knew these kids needed someone to believe in them now more than ever.

"I know you guys need someone to believe in you," I said. "Now more than ever."

Only Kevin—waiting anxiously for me to rise from the battered desk tucked into a corner where the old brick wall was crumbling from water damage—seemed to want to know. "Did he make it up, Teach?" he asked before I even said a word.

I raised my hands in defense. "I don't know, guys," I said. "I really don't."

"Yeah, well clearly, he got some specifics to answer for," said Clyde, his gaze hurt, even betrayed. "It said he started them stories in his creative writing class. Said his professor encouraged him. That always the way, ain't it? When some motherfucker tell you you doing great with the lies, so just keep it up? Sign of the damn times."

"All right, easy on the language, Clyde," I told him. "I know you're disappointed, but—"

"It ain't even that I'm disappointed," he said, sitting up suddenly, boldly. "It's that if he got the balls to make up how long he was fighting for, why should we believe any of the rest?" He stared at me. "Huh?"

I shook my head. "I don't have an answer for that, Clyde. That's how mixing it up works."

"And it's like he taking away from all them kids who did have to spend they lives killing and raping and murdering for other people. They don't get to tell their story, but he just made his up."

"You don't know that," said Buck. "Ain't no proof he lied. Most all of that could still be true—what he saw, what he did."

"Sure," followed up Terri. "Just 'cause he made up how long he was in the thick don't mean the other stuff ain't what he saw."

"So where does the line between memoir and fiction and outright lie fall?" I asked them.

"That's just the thing," said Kevin, moving his bulk to look at his classmates. "It be like that Supreme Court justice who said that stuff about porno: 'I ain't know how to define it, but I sure as shit know when I see it.'"

"Is Beah's book memoir then?"

No one in the class answered. "Depends," Clyde finally said. "If the rest of it true, then yeah, it still a memoir."

The class seemed unsatisfied with this.

"I know Frey still pure bullshit," said Terri hopefully. "Know that."

"It's like to get at the truth," said Jerome, who had been quiet so far that day, "sometimes you gotta make a little up. Make up conversation or put two people together to make 'em one. Move some events around to make the book flow better, so it less like a diary and more like a poem—you need that." He paused. "But even when it's not exactly the truth, it still gotta be true, you know? Still gotta be true."

• • •

As winter writhes in its death throes in Chicago, I meet a semi-famous actress in a bar downtown. I am there by accident, trying to meet a friend, and wind up talking to her when she notices I'm wearing a T-shirt that says "Springsteen/ Jon Stewart '08." I recognize her vivacious, pouting mouth from a cancelled Fox drama.

"Is that your dream ticket?" she asks with a smile.

"Marry me," I say instinctively.

Spring is pushing hard but winter pushes right back. Every day of warmth, hope, or possibility gets hammered the next week by a brittle wind shattering the buds of the trees in lower Lakeview. Warm rains freeze. The days lengthen but the nights can still scar you with a chill.

The actress and I go on several dates. She is not famous per se, but she's at least had more than just the one failed TV show and has appeared on O'Brien and Kimmel, although she says she's still waiting for her publicist to get her on Leno so Middle America can get used to her face. She's in town for the next month shooting scenes for a small role in a big-budget, star-laden film that makes use of multiple Chicago locations. She is ambitious and pretty, so I know her interest in me is probably based on the fact that I have told her I am a "writer interested in getting into screenplays someday." I also tell her I have a book deal, a lie to increase the length of time she will keep seeing me.

She is surprisingly skinny, even more so than you'd think from watching her on television. I figure this must be a case of anorexia, although when we eat together, she puts down a very self-consciously appropriate amount of food. When we have sex, I feel like I'm handling glass, like she might shatter if I take hold of any part of her with too much force. I am relieved when she stops returning my calls—if for no other reason than she seems like an immensely sad individual. She speaks often of a father who ignored her and a mother with whom her relationship is so strained they cannot visit each other without bouts of tears over some long-ago sleight or argument. Our conversations often trailed off when she hit upon some dreadful-sounding occurrence from her past that she did not want to talk about, as in, "After that I met Randy, who I dated all through college, but that's a long…" [Avert eyes, fumble for cigarette in purse] "…He was about the worst thing I could've attached myself to at that point."

Still, the semi-famous actress is not without her unique charm and inner beauty. It is one of the last times we go out that I catch a glimpse of what is beneath the terrible self-image and longing.

We have a few early drinks in the observatory at the top of the Hancock Building. This is a popular tourist spot, and the drinks certainly aren't cheap, but it's worth it for the view of the city and Lake Michigan. The towering force of Chicago does not look proper from the corporate view at the top of the Sears, but from the Hancock it has a compact, nearly cerebral majesty, exuding the aura of an imaginary city like Gotham. Near dusk, the view is even better.

The semi-famous actress and I sit by the eastern window gazing out over Lake Michigan while a low mist envelops the horizon. "It makes me think of either the future," she says of the slowly burning gray light and the falling purple of twilight, "or the very distant past. Or maybe a combination of the two."

I sip my ten-dollar imported beer. I don't normally buy ten-dollar imported beer, but I don't want this girl of wealth and means to know that I drink Pabst at every opportunity.

"Did you want to get out of here?" I ask, hoping against hope that she says no, so I will not have to sleep with her and fear shattering her pelvis.

"Tell me about your book," she says. "You told me the idea, but tell me about what it's becoming. The part about you."

I sigh. Artistic people often ask absurd questions like this because they think they need to. "I don't know," I say. "When I started, it was just an idea, but frankly now I read back over it and I can't even recognize the first two chapters. It's grown beyond my plans and I think—just maybe—beyond my comprehension."

She laughs. "Artistic people always say absurd things like that. So now it's a memoir?"

I shrugged. "Kinda."

She sips her drink, a bewildering blue-colored martini. "But you're worried that it's crap?"

"Don't you worry that your performances will be crap?"

"Sure. But I'm not looking for my first Oscar yet."

"Here's the problem," I say, sitting forward but keeping my gaze locked on the sweeping view outside of the ninety-sixth-floor window. "I look at books people have written—memoirs, let's say—and they all have…" I think of how best to put this. "A reason to be written. You know? I don't have a reason. I'm a middle-class white kid with a college degree who hasn't really done anything of note."

Her eyes narrow, and she draws her fingers absently along the skin of her slender arm. "Isn't that why you're supposed to be a good writer? Even someone with a great story can tell it wrong, just like even someone with no story can spin it fabulously."

"I'm thinking of making a bunch of shit up," I say bluntly. "I'm thinking of saying I got caught in a gun fight at a drug dealer's apartment or I once sang in a country rock band or maybe that I taught a class full of troubled and disadvantaged but brilliant black Louisiana high schoolers."

"That's an idea," she says with a nod. "Or you could just be honest about your origins—however humble and uninteresting they may be."

"And maybe write a truly humble and uninteresting book."

She grins, and even though the tendons in her neck stand out rather obscenely, she is still quite beautiful. "You know what I think?"

"What do you think?"

"The best story I ever heard, I read in my hometown newspaper, right? It was about this—this couple that had been married for like forty years or something. And this old man had been overseas and lost his dad's watch in this Italian village while he was fighting for the Allies. Just a good American kid losing his dad's watch but otherwise coming home in one piece, which was the important part, right? Well, his wife, this lady of seventy or something, gets a look at this watch in a few photographs. She goes to his brother and sister and asks them to describe the watch. Then she pinpoints the exact store where the old man bought it, and she looks at different kinds of watches by different watchmakers in the 1920s, until finally, at long last, she identifies exactly what kind it was. So she goes looking in every antique store from Missouri to Albany, calling and calling until finally she finds the exact right watch in an antique store in Buffalo. She buys it for seven hundred dollars, has a professional watchmaker fix it, and gives it to her husband on their thirtieth wedding anniversary."

I look at her for a moment. "That's the best story you've ever heard? Did you ever see *Pulp Fiction*?"

"It's a good story—it's a very simple, sweet story."

"Yeah. I liked it better when it was an episode of *Touched by an Angel*."

She laughs. "The point, Steve, is that there's more drama, more emotion, more truth in the little victories, the small triumphs and defeats of people you've never heard of than you could ever believe. Sometimes those are the best stories, right? Just ordinary people figuring things out, running against the tide we all have moving against us."

She finishes her drink. "Will you kiss me while the view is still this nice?"

I lean in, and her breath smells vaguely of blue martini. The dark violet sky descends on our faces.

SIXTEEN

Expansive, Self-Critical, Honest, Jumpy, Surprising, Self-Confident, Cynical, Smart, and Very, Very Funny

I want to keep working. This proposal Julie's having me put together for publishers constitutes a whole new ballgame. It must reflect at least a modicum of professionalism, which is not one of my greatest talents—ranking somewhere between "keeping my opinion to myself" and nuclear engineering. This new proposal requires a chapter outline, overview, and market analysis, so I should really keep working (and "analyzing" "markets" is below nuclear engineering on my list of talents), but downstairs the results are coming in from the North Carolina and Indiana primaries. I can hear Elliott in the basement smashing apart his drum set. Liam is downstairs bitching about the beans Erik has left in the refrigerator. Like a Siren's call, I can't resist all the action.

"I mean, what part of his brain is completely impairing him from cleaning out these beans?" Liam rants when I hit the bottom of the staircase. "Look at them, man." He points to the bottom crisper in the refrigerator, which has one large dish with clear plastic wrap covering what was once refried beans but is now a colony of green and white mold so thick it envelops the entire meal. "How long have these been here? How long could he possibly have left these—"

"Since the South Carolina primary," I tell him. This is not all that surprising: Erik rented a keg for our New Year's party and it is still—probably as of the publication of this book—sitting on our back porch.

"I wrote that column. I thought it would help."

Indeed, I published in *RedEye* a column specifically meant to get Erik to start cleaning up after himself. Titled "The Democratic Party is like my roommate," it compared the sloppy and absurd nomination process of the Democrats to my slovenly and absurd roommate.[157]

I find James on the couch, watching the returns. Despite much media hyperventilation, it appears as if Clinton will squeak it out in Indiana and Obama will win big in North Carolina.

"I feel vindicated," I tell James.

"You should become a pundit, man. You called this months ago."

I wasn't the only one to say so, but after Barack built his early delegate lead, all it took was one glance at the remaining delegates and demographics of the states to realize Clinton couldn't catch him.

"She sure has beat the bloody hell out of him, though, hasn't she?" James exhales. "Are we gonna win this election?"

"I think so. McCain's full of shit."

"Maybe we should check out Fox News?" he wonders. "See what Hannity and O'Reilly think of the radical Black Power Muslim beating the ambitious femi-Nazi shrew?"

"I can't believe we didn't think of it earlier."

Hannity takes over our election coverage, and it sounds like the most dangerous, radical, corrupt leech in America may *actually get the Democratic nomination.*

"Amazing!" says James. "After we nominated that Islamo-fascist sympathizer, Kerry, we go and try to nominate an actual terrorist."

"I know! Come on, Democratic Party!"

I sit back down on the arm of the couch. Our living room is arranged for maximum enjoyment of the gargantuan big-screen

---

157 I would have worried about hurting Erik's feelings were it not for the beans, which he later removed from the refrigerator after we bitched at him enough—only to leave them in the sink where they stank for a day before Elliott cleaned the dish.

television at its center. The couch and armchair—matching pea-green—face the hi-def behemoth while a rickety papasan rounds out our attempt at furniture. We enjoy our meals over a sturdy coffee table where James now slurps large amounts of milk and Fruity Pebbles. He changes the subject and asks me about the book proposal.

"I'm writing the overview right now—the description, you know? But then I also have to come up with a chapter outline, and obviously—"

"You don't know all the chapters yet."

"Exactly. I'm kinda making it up right now, but without knowing what the end will be, I end up pretty vague."

James rubs the thick black stubble on his face and then his long, purposefully unkempt black hair. Like I said, he looks vaguely like the actor Colin Farrell if Colin Farrell went everywhere in cut-off T-shirts with "New Philadelphia Football" emblazoned across the chest.

"What else?" he asks.

"I have to write up a 'market analysis.'"

"What's that?"

"Exactly." I explain to him that a market analysis is a comparison of your book to other books currently on the market.

"Basically you're saying," says James, "'Hey, publisher, my book is about masturbating with sock puppets. You know people will want to buy it because of the success of the book *Masturbating with Regular Puppets*. See, a built-in audience and a unique hook.'"

"Exactly."

"So who are you comparing yourself to?"

I tick off the names. "Eggers, Klosterman, Sedaris... Maybe Tucker Max."

"Oh Jesus," he says.[158]

---

158 Here is a surefire way to know that a person of the Millennial Generation is an idiot: if he or she finds the work of Tucker Max funny. This is not a judgment on Max, who has every right to make money from not being funny, but readers who think that it is good writing or storytelling to simply relate an incident of getting shit on during anal sex should have tried living in any college dorm room between the years 1968 and TheEndofTime.

"I know. It was Julie's suggestion."

"Oh, Christ, dude. I didn't know you'd sell your soul that fast."

"Oh, I'll sell out, baby. I'll sell you and my mother and my future children down the river so fast, you won't even be wet by the time you're through. You think I won't exploit every advantage, every person, every mother-loving breath that anyone I know expels from their lungs? Please, I already have an entire chapter explaining how you once masturbated while smelling my boxers."

"As a joke," he corrects. "I knew you were walking into the room."

"Yeah, sure. Freud would have a field day with that."

He drains his bowl of milk and picks up his guitar, a deep oak-colored Virgin acoustic that has an Amnesty International sticker and another that says "Don't Be a Dick." He plucks a few notes, his fingers moving nimbly over each string while his other hand dashes along the frets.

I sit back and say, "The inherent absurdity of what I'm doing with this book is that I don't want it to be at all like any other book. Sure, I can see a similar tone when I read Klosterman, and as soon as I read Egger's *A Heartbreaking Work of Staggering Genius,* I got why Julie saw so much of that book in this one—you know, the self-referentialism—"

A quick tilt of the head. "Thatta word now?"

"Definitely not, but you know what I mean. Writing a book about writing a book and constantly referring to the fact that I'm writing a book. That what we're talking about now is going to be in the book and therefore—hopefully—someone out there will be reading the words that we are saying right now."

"Steve Markley masturbates to pictures of Jesus Christ, the one true God."

"What?"

"Now we can be sure everyone knows, 'cause it's gotta be in your book."

I shake my head. "The problem is that this book really doesn't have a comparable precedent, which makes comparisons tricky, but more than that—" I struggle trying to put into words what I'm feeling. It is wet and slippery, and every time I think I've got a grip on it, the thing goes shooting out of my hand like a slick bar of soap. "More than that, I don't know how to describe in the proposal what I'm trying to describe in the book. Which is that all of this— *all of it*—is about something larger. This," I point to the television where images of Bush, Clinton, Obama, and Iraq all vie for space on the Fox News telecast, "is part of it. This creeping sensation that the world's about three poor decisions or corruptions away from completely spinning off its axis, you know? It's about these weird, wicked times but also youth and promise and possibility and vigor and those times in your life when everything seems up in the air, but you kinda like it, right? But to describe that—to *summarize* it? How do you go about it? How do you put into easily digestible words that sensation of a gathering storm?"

James shakes his head. "'My name's Steve. I'm gonna sound *sooo* cool in my book.'"

• • •

Yes, I struggle with the proposal, but for the first time I see a ray of light at the end of the tunnel. Best get walking toward the light and worry about the rest later. I begin pushing my chapters through both writing groups—first Thousand Fibers and then the Literary Writers' Network (LWN). I have the first eight chapters done. The head of steam has been gathered. I feel good about the book, about life. I even get feedback from my old professor, Steven.

After telling him of my success of finding an agent in Oxford, Steven insisted I send him chapters as I worked on them, so I sent him the first two to start. What follows is obviously not really dialogue between us, but this is the twenty-first century and most of our communication (read: all) takes place via electronic mail. I thought it would be incredibly boring and pedantic to just reprint the emails, so instead, I will set the conversations in random locales of some kind of literary significance.[159]

The following dialogue is the exact language exchanged by email, minus a few small, easily identifiable rhetorical flourishes.

• • •

Steven and I pass the Plaza Mayor, walking through the shadows of the twin spires that overlook one of the most famous public spaces in all of Spain. During the Inquisition, the Plaza Mayor became the blood-drenched site of religious fundamentalism run amok. Accused witches were tortured, burned, and beheaded. Today it is regarded as one of the most beautiful public squares on the European continent.

We make our way to the nondescript entrance of the Sobrino de Botin, and I ask in clunky Spanish for a seat by the bar. The Sobrino was built in 1725 and looks as if it has gone almost without renovation since. Steven walks almost in a stoop as we pass under the low ceilings with exposed wooden beams. The entire restaurant is dim, the electric lights giving the impression of flickering candles quite well. The open kitchen has copper pots hanging from hooks and a charcoal fire hissing in a tiled hearth. The Sobrino is said to be one of the oldest restaurants in the world. It is also where Ernest Hemingway spent much of his time drinking and gathering material for *The Sun Also Rises*.

We sit at a small table in a corner, and Steven orders a coffee. I order roast suckling pig and the cheapest Spanish beer on the menu.

"As you can see, I got up extra early," says Steven. "Well, actually I was laying there in bed, awake, unable to go back to sleep, as has been my wont for the past two weeks. I don't know what this new

---

159　I know, I know: You'll say, "Didn't you already set a conversation in a one-act play? And didn't you use the people in your life as stage-dressing for various fictitious scenes? Isn't this all the same ploy, you lazy bastard?" To which, I would reply, "Your mother and I were once arrested for indecent acts in a public bathroom."

fresh hell is, but pretty much since you were in Oxford, I've been waking up in the 4:30–5 range, tossing and turning. A few times I've gotten back to sleep but mostly I've just gotten up. It hasn't been too bad. I've had time to read all the political postings and wonder anew at the vitriol in the two Democratic camps (as evidenced in the blogs), and sometimes I even get some work done."

I sip my beer. The charcoal fire in the kitchen must have my pig on it because something mind-numbing and beautiful is wafting from that direction.

Steven grins, his eyes wide, expressive, and filled with the mirth that breaks out in them from time to time when he is particularly amused or excited by an idea. "But this morning it's all about you. Last night I read the chapters from *Publish This Book* you sent me, and I wanted to respond right away. I can't for the life of me figure out why it's taken so long… I've been inundated with student work, and I guess I'm ashamed to say that (as usual) I put the stuff that I had to do (was required to do) in front of the stuff I wanted to do. Story of my life. Forgive me. It's not like you sent me the early pages of *Fear and Trembling*."

I laugh. "No, it's really got more of a *Concept of Dread* feel to it anyway."

"Anyway," he goes on, "it's pretty great. It made me laugh out loud any number of times, and was actually the most fun I've had in a while. The persona you're developing here is a side that comes through usually in public—not completely unlike the talk you gave to the Literary Marketplace class when you visited. It's at hyper-speed, on steroids, but slows down (unlike your visit to the Marketplace class) in places to enable you to allow yourself a more serious moment or two. I don't think it's too snarky in general, though there are a few moments I'd cut (if you ever asked me to). The voice is expansive, self-critical, honest, jumpy, surprising, self-confident, cynical (at moments), smart, and very, very funny."

I nod. "Okay, great. I mean, thanks. That means a lot. It really does. I'm waiting for the 'but' though. You always have a 'but' or a 'however' or an 'although.' Gimme the 'although.'"

"Here are my only concerns," he says. "The footnotes are too David Foster Wallace/Dave Eggers, or seem, at least, to be influenced by them, but knowing you, you've read about them but haven't actually read them yourself,[160] not knowing the meaning of 'erudite.' I'm think-ing ahead to critics who are going to flap their arms around saying your book is derivative, but I guess, who cares? You can't control what those critics will say or will want to say—and they all have their own neurotic agendas. Anyway, I started out actively wanting to dislike the footnotes and to tell you to cut them, but by the time I got to the one about Jared Padalecki, I was onboard; the ones that annoy me the most are those directly addressed to the reader ('I apologize in advance...'); the ones that work most successfully take the narrative in new and surprising directions. Or add an unexpected anecdote.

"I'd also go very lightly on the stuff dealing with young male twentysomethings' fascination with all things digestive: belches, fart, pee, and excrement. Sometimes you have to be there, and perhaps your book is not one of those 'theres.'

"But I'm totally happy and excited for you, though as I've said, you're playing a kind of literary roulette by going out with some-thing that isn't what you want to write (mostly). The danger is (as I've said) that you'll get known for this and it will therefore shape your career in unexpected ways."

I throw up my hands. "Hold on, hold on," I say. "This is a lot to digest—no pun intended. So you're saying that you didn't like the opening of the book with the shitting-shaving machine? C'mon, that's classic!"

---

160 How did he know this? How the fuck did he know that I had not yet read Wallace or Eggers when I started the book? Is this guy for real? He always seems to know what I'm thinking or guess at my angle before I even know what that angle is. I hesitate and decide not to tell him that the footnotes are probably most influenced by Dave Barry, who was my writing idol from ages eight to eleven.

The waiter arrives with my suckling pig. It looks browned and delicious, a chunk of meat so thick I can barely cut and fork away pieces. While I stuff the slick, sweet pork into my ravenous maw, Steven continues.

"Well, here you are, I don't know how many pages into this, and you've found an agent and signed with her. That's pretty great, but as we've said, might have its downside. The big existential question: how honest can you now afford to be in the book about the conversations we had and others you've undoubtedly had about the calculated decisions that went into signing? Though at first it seemed to me that the narrative of the project itself was po-mo and salable (and probably a good deal more than that), I don't think I really considered how—from this point on—the industry itself starts to become part of the narrative, the industry you're in a way seducing, and attempting to become part of. (Does publishing want to read about the analytic side of seduction, if publishing is the seduced?) In short, it's no longer Poor Struggling Writer Shows Off at Bars; it's New Initiate Makes His Way Gingerly Through the Bizarre Halls of Publishing c. 2008. How honest can you afford to be about your experiences with agents, about the conversations you're having with Julie, about your reactions to reactions from editors, about all the stuff that lies ahead? On the one hand, the book depends on your authenticity—on telling it straight. On the other hand, there lies madness."

During his soliloquy, I managed to stuff down about half of my suckling pig. All of the sudden my appetite is gone. "Jesus Christ," I say. "Way to bring a guy down. I hadn't thought of any of that. I never thought I'd get this far."

"New title," he says. "Cutting Off My Nose to Spite My Face."

I set down my fork and knife, no longer hungry at all.

"Anyway," he says. "I loved these pages. Actually, it was like spending time with you when you're at your smartest and wittiest; it's a great read; and it has many penetrating things to say about entering the workplace of the twenty-first century. There's so much more to say, but I'll leave it with this—cut 'gangly' on p. 11."

"Yeah, everyone thinks they're statuesque until they appear in a book, Steven."

I call the waiter over, ask for the check, and then down my beer.

"Ah. Great," I say. "You've given me an unimaginable amount of stuff to think about, as if this entire process wasn't already completely mysterious and out there enough already... Again, I'm mostly at the mercy of actual events. I think as far as the publishing end of things goes, the natural ending would be if I were to sign a contract. I would have to consider that the culmination of the dream, stated at the beginning, of publishing a book. Getting into any of the inside baseball of all that... I just don't know."

Deep breath.

"The problem is, I'm neck deep in the meat of the book, which involves actual things happening to me... Basically, I've just taken everything that's happened to me in the last year and crammed it into a narrative that follows me trying to publish this book. As I read over it, I'm beginning to understand the full scope of what I'm doing, but the problem is there's no other way to do it. It's gotta be honest, and this is the only way I can do that."

Steven foots the bill, even as I protest and try to pay for my suckling pig. We both have to catch flights back to Chicago and Oxford, respectively (the Oxford, Ohio, airport makes international flights only to Madrid and whichever third-world country stitches together North Face apparel). Parting ways at the front door of Sobrino, I stop. I call back to him, "Oh, also."

He turns, a tall white-haired figure on the verge of being swallowed by an encroaching mist rolling slowly over the cobbled bricks of the old Spanish street.

"I can sympathize with the laying awake thing. I don't sleep more than four hours in any given night and spend most of my time in bed staring at the ceiling. Among some of the reasons: my best friend is having a kid; another good friend is being deployed to Iraq; I think I may have been seriously in love with that girl in Boston; and I now have the possibility of realizing my only real dream with a book so unwieldy and slippery that I often just sit back while I'm writing it and wonder what the hell it is I've gotten myself into." I smile, look off down the road, and shake my head. "It's better than being bored, though, right?"

SEVENTEEN

Wrong-Headed, Condescending Toward the Reader, Self-Involved, and Unintentionally Revealing

Obviously, things were going far too well. I'm like the jock in the horror movie, so stoked I'm staying in this private beach house with all my best buds and my super-hot, unreasonably proportioned girlfriend—totally unconcerned that this is the tenth anniversary of the night we teased that nerd into going down into that mineshaft, only to never see him again.

Trouble for the book doesn't arrive all at once. Like in a horror movie, it creeps up slowly. In the movie, my dog would probably turn up with its head cut off. In real life, the trouble begins with Julie and the proposal.

We send this package back and forth several times, going over potential edits by phone. I find it strange that I'm working so closely with a person I've never laid eyes on before. All I know of Julie is a voice.[161] Other than that, I am putting as much blind trust into her as most people put into Jesus Christ. She wants the proposal as close to perfection as possible before she begins sending it to editors.

She can't decide what she thinks, though. "You have this part about Jon Stewart," she says, as I sit with my feet propped up on the desk of the phone booth. Cars.com's office has these awesome little

---

161 It occurs to me to ask her to send a picture, and then after that it occurs to me even more quickly how creepy that sounds.

booths for personal calls, which saves me the explanation of why I'm
not talking about upcoming diesel engines when speaking on the
phone at my desk. "But we need to know why you reach the same
audience. What appeals do you make to that audience?"

"Right, the whole Millennial humor thing again."

"Exactly."

Julie and I have mutually agreed that this book will be targeted
at Millennials, which is what I am, and who are apparently a group
that does not have an author to call their own. This got me thinking about which authors Millennials like. Since "oral sex" is not an
author, I came up with Jon Stewart of *The Daily Show*, who is as
close to the ringmaster of Millennial intellectualism as I could get.
At the very least, I thought, just maybe, I could get a spot on *The
Daily Show* to plug my book.[162]

"Also, kiddo, we need to pump up your bio. Do you know how
many hits your website gets?"

"Not many. Not enough that I'd be proud to put it into the
proposal."

"And you're working at getting your profile on *RedEye*'s site?"

"I'm on it."

"Good. Okay, get these changes back to me, and we'll keep going."

And I get them to her. But the proposal comes back, and it comes
back again. I am reading through it so frequently, some of the sentences have begun to melt like candle wax the way a word does if
you say it over and over again. Try saying the word "establishment"

---

162 Incidentally, I have had the story I will tell on *The Daily Show* planned out in my
head ever since Stewart first began hosting the show in like 1997 or something. I'll say,
"Jon, you know something? I've been watching this show since it was first on the air, and
I can prove it because one of the first commercials that went on when you took over the
show, well, you were smoking a cigarette and telling your producers you didn't want to
do this story or that story because they were boring. Then someone mentioned a porn
convention was in town, and you got all excited. That was the first commercial. Also,
your first guest was Gillian Anderson, and you did that stupid Craig Kilborn bit with the
five questions, but you weaned viewers off it by cutting the number of questions by one
per night." At this point, I expect Stewart to be frightened, and that's as it should be.

out loud one hundred times—pretty soon the syllables slip and you forget which ones go where and why such a strange concoction of sounds should mean anything in the first place. This is how my book proposal looks to me.

In the meantime, I send her additional chapters. I make the mistake of not running them through anybody in particular. I pushed them through my writing groups, but unlike with the first two chapters, no one had much to say. They made token corrections and suggestions but otherwise seemed satisfied. Bridget shrugged. Katie nodded. Suzanne raised both eyebrows. Chad chuckled. Denis bobbed his head. I took this to mean I had slayed them with my literary brilliance.

I am somewhat taken aback then, when I receive the following email from Julie:

From: j____@yahoo.com
To: s___@yahoo.com
Subject: chapters

Again, I LOVE the first two chapters. More from me when we talk (tell me when) about the rest. Not huge edits, but, Steve, a few of the chapters I find not terribly relevant, like you are trying to put too much into the book. I am unsure how some of the life experiences pertain to your experience toward publishing a book—Am I dense? Am I missing something here?

Jh

Immediately after reading this, I sit at my computer at work trying to digest it. Then I make the very stupid decision of letting my Ego out of his high-security holding cell.

Ladies and gentlemen! he proclaims, rising on a motorized platform in the shape of a giant roulette wheel with a fireman's pole sticking straight up from the center. He twirls around the pole, removes his top hat, and tosses it to the crowd. *It feels so goddamn good to be back. Did you miss me?* he asks his imaginary audience. *Oh, I know you little fuckers missed me. You always miss Daddy when he goes away.*

He shoves me out of the way, takes a seat at the computer, and starts typing.

"Okay," I say nervously. "But I want a final edit on this before you—"

Send! Okie-doke-artichoke, looks like we have ourselves an honest to Jesus retort!

I scramble to the computer screen. "Oh, Christ. What did you do?"

What? I just gave her an honest assessment of your talents. Isn't that why you let me out? My Ego kicks his legs up on my desk and lights a cigar, which he takes slugs of like he's just come up for air from the bottom of Lake Michigan. He blows the smoke in big, heaving breaths and claps his hands at my coworkers as they walk by, hooting and jeering.

I'm frantically reading the email he just sent to Julie. It contains phrases like,

> I'm bypassing the process of writing and querying with an ACTUAL idea because of frustration, impertinence, hunger (take your pick). The more digressive elements of the story are in place to give a fuller picture of how these emotions melded together to create the thrust of the book.

"Do you think you could have tried to make me sound like a little more of an asshole?" I ask my Ego.

He is not paying attention to me. He has spotted meat.

He sits up, purring, *Who in the holy hell of Jezebel is that?*

I glance up. "That's Lindsay. She's my coworker. We're going to start hosting this video podcast together for the blog."

My Ego jumps from his chair. *Oh, Markley. Oh, Markley, Markley!*

He is distracting me from the email. I have to keep reading. On the whole it doesn't seem *too* bad—mostly it's an explanation of what I'm trying to do with the book, even if it does come off as impertinent and hot-headed. I can't decide if I am missing the point or if Julie is.

My Ego, having squatted on Lindsay's desk in an attempt to lick her face, has completely forgotten that he even wrote the email, let alone that the book's future might depend on it.

"Hey, asshole, what's this shit you said to Julie about 'strings of perception'? What the hell does that mean? Are you just making shit up?"

Go away, he says, smelling her keyboard as soon as she pulls her hands away. *All I did was explain to that agent of yours what your book is about. If she doesn't get it, then what the fuck do you care?*

"I want to publish my book—that's why I care."

I read the email again—long, detailed, and maybe a bit impatient. My Ego explained that the different struggles—moving to Chicago, losing a love interest, discovering a friend's leap in life, wondering about one's own—all relate very specifically and importantly to the proposed story of publishing a book.

After a week, however, Julie has sent no reply.

I stuff my Ego back into the dungeon and promise myself that I will not let him out to write another letter to anyone.

• • •

However, I'll wish longingly for the tepid disapproval of Julie's no-reply after my next meeting with Steven to go over chapters three and four.

I pick the White Horse Tavern in Manhattan for our fictional location of powwow. When two or three of your favorite writers hung out in the same bar (but not at the same time), it means the place has good mojo. Since the 1880s, this wood-paneled bar has stuck out mightily in the midst of Greenwich Village's concrete jungle. It has one of those old-timey mirrors behind the bar with liquor bottles lining the length in a dense mass of light-reflecting glass.

Steven and I take a seat at the bar. He orders a coffee, while I ask for a Bud Light and a shot of whiskey to get my motor running.

"What kind of whiskey?" the bartender, a bored, ruddy-faced college student, asks.

"Whichever kind Dylan Thomas liked."

Generation after generation, the White Horse has played host to writers of every stripe. Allen Ginsberg and Jack Kerouac hung out here, as did Hunter S. Thompson, Anais Nin, James Baldwin, and Norman Mailer. With that literary pedigree alone, you'd be set, but the White Horse has an even better claim to fame.

In 1953 the acclaimed poet Dylan Thomas walked into the White Horse to celebrate his thirty-ninth birthday and the publication of his collection *18 Poems*. He took eighteen shots of whiskey, went back to his hotel room, slipped into a coma, and died four days later. It is said his last words were, "I've had eighteen straight whiskeys. I think that is a record." Now that is what I call raging, raging against the dying of the light.

The White Horse Tavern has me in a good mood. I'm feeling spry and cocksure. I down my shot, sip my beer to chase it, and turn to Steven.

"I wish," he says, "my response was as positive this time as it was last."

My heart sinks. "Oh," I say. "Hold on." I call the ruddy-faced bartender and order another shot.

I grimace as I swallow, but Steven is already calmly laying out his case. "I didn't like the chapter about moving to Chicago," he says. "It started okay, though the tone was snarkier than it had previously been, but went downhill fast on page two. Footnote 4 is an indication of what you clearly think is funny, and what I find off-putting if not wince-inducing. Whenever you get close to excrement, I want to shake you. What is so funny about shit?"

I'm motioning for the bartender to pour me another shot as quickly as he can manage. "Nothing—I mean, I don't know—I guess it depends—you know—on what you're talking about—or—"

"Nothing," snaps Steven. "Wretch. Vomit. Which is the last time I ever want either of us to use those words. I don't know who you think your audience is—and you may be aiming this at Generation Obama or the Millennials or whatever else your generation is being called these days, but you need to remember that your generation does not control publishing or reviewing, and you can take it from a Boomer that any time you mention shit, you are flushing yourself down the toilet."

The third shot goes down so smoothly, I whip my hand in furious circles to indicate that yes, goddamnit, while I'm getting eviscerated, barkeep, I'd like another.

Steven folds his arms, tilts his head, and stares at me coolly, as if trying to determine if we have ever met before.

"Things do not get better when you itemize the roommates who remain faceless or the lifestyle: 'throwing garbage on the floor of our kitchen.' Why exactly am I spending my money buying, and time reading, this book, I ask, when the author is clearly several steps below a Neanderthal, who always kept his cave clean, and proud of it?"

I choke down the fourth shot, slap the glass back on the bar, and gladly try to explain while the bartender tips the fifth. "Well, I don't know, I guess I just thought it was good to create a dichotomy between where I am and where I aspire to be or maybe, well—"

"I don't like the extended paragraph comparing your column and masturbation; I don't like your condescension toward grassroots organizers and political activists; I don't like the self-justifications offered for the appalling job you have; I don't like the extended 'rep-artee' with [James]—perhaps it was funny when it happened, but you clearly had to be there."

Fifth shot down. "Well, I certainly won't argue that being there makes all the diff—"

"And I don't like the exposé of your sex life."

Steven waits, perhaps collecting his thoughts or perhaps awaiting my response, but in the meantime I am yelling at the bartender. "You clown-faced bastard, where the hell do you think you're going?"

"Hey, man, maybe you should take it easy," he says.

"Maybe you should make sure you don't want a career requiring depth perception because when I come across this bar, I'm gonna take your eyeball out with my fucking teeth unless you pour me three—no, four!—more shots of whiskey."

Our red-faced friend lines up four shot glasses without saying a word. I tell him to make it five.

After he's poured, I take the first glass and hold it to my lips. "Okay," I tell Steven. "Go quick. Like you're ripping off a Band-Aid."

One.

"In short, I don't like the person who is writing this chapter, and I can assure you, it's the point where the editor stops reading and rejects the book."

Two. Yuck.

"But the problem is, see, the degree to which I recoil from those ten pages. I think back and ask myself what it reminds me of and I remember the way you acted in my class when you spoke, and I remember the tone of much of the road trip book and most if not all of your political columns, and I get the sinking feeling that perhaps I've been suckered... or been blind."

Three. Oh dear.

"Perhaps I've seen in you who I wanted to see in you, and when I tell 321[163] that this is all a persona you've developed to protect the vulnerable writer, I get the sick feeling that maybe it's the other way around: maybe the persona is the vulnerable writer and that the real Markley is this other guy."

---

163   He is referring to the class of his I visited, called English 321: The Literary Marketplace.

He tells me he had lunch with one of my peers, Ryan, who knew me at Miami through the English department.[164] And Ryan, says Steven, "said that his experience of you was that when you were hanging with your posse at the bars you were all about vulgarity, of varied sorts, which shouldn't have been a surprise to me, since you detail that stuff in your columns and other nonfiction but nonetheless was."

Ryan, you turncoat, I think as I slug back another shot. *More like,* I think sluggishly, *Benedict… Ryan. Or Ryan Arnold? No, that doesn't make sense.* I look up because Steven is still going.

"So: tell me it ain't so."

"It ain't—" I belch. Loudly. "Unghgrh," I say. "I don't feel s'good." Nevertheless the next shot hits nothing but throat.

Steven sighs. "I know I've never written anything like this to you before, but you write, 'He told me flatly when he thought what I had given him was crap.' I don't think this is crap (a telling word, perhaps, in your voice); I think it's polished, wrong-headed, condescending toward the reader, self-involved ('boy, am I cool and talented and funny'), and unintentionally (or intentionally, for all I know) revealing."

To dampen the brutality of this onslaught, I am anthropomorphizing each additional shot the bartender hands me, making them talk to each other, pretending they're at a party—a ball in my stomach!—and having a grand time. "Oh, Mr. Whiskey Shot? What are you doing out here?" I say to the glass in my hand. "It's cold and lonely out here, buddy! Get in here with your friends!"

"I also know," says Steven, ignoring my fun little game, "that now that you have made about every mistake you could make with the kind of book you profess to want to write, maybe you can learn from those mistakes."

---

164 Not incidentally, this is the same Ryan I referred to in Chapter 4, who I praised so heavily for his insight into my short stories.

Steven stands, gathering his coat. He has not touched his coffee. I try
to focus on him but my eyes have veered off in opposite directions.

"I guess I wouldn't blame you if I never heard back from you," he
says. "But I am assuming that what you want from me is my honest
and unvarnished response, and not a lot of false praise."

Then he walks out the door of the White Horse Tavern.

"No!" I call after him as he strides out through the door. "Are
you fucking kidding? False praise! Lots and lots of highly varnished
false praise!"

I sit back down at the bar. The bartender watches me with one
raised eyebrow. I pick up one final shot and toast him. "Well, that
was fucking brutal," I slur. "Not only did the writer I most respect
and admire in the entire world just tell me my book sucks." I hiccup.
"Buh he said I's faking the person I am for the last four years."

"Ouch," says the bartender.

I stare at his dumb bartender face and a darkness descends over
the fictionalized White Horse Tavern. The colors of the bar fade a
bit because this isn't a bar; it is an email, and the contents have cut
about as far to the bone as anyone could ever hope to cut me. Maybe
I'm not an amputee yet, but I'm bleeding everywhere—red droplets
even managing to stain and then cloud the liquor I hold in front of
my face.

"Eh," I say, drunkenly, bitterly. "It could be worse. It's like my
buddy and I say: I could be a… gay Nazi during the Inquisition."

I bring the shot to my lips, but the interior of the White Horse
begins to spin and I can't get the glass to match up with my mouth;
I keep missing. Before me are sixteen empty shot glasses. I manage
to say, "Shit. Beat by a goddamn poet," before crashing backward
out of my stool to black out for a lifetime on the grungy beige tiles
of the floor.

• • •

I discuss this development with the writers of LWN.

"How old is he?" asks Chad, smiling through a thin goatee.

"I don't know," I say. "Older. Sixties maybe."

"This might just not be his cup of tea," he suggests.

"I didn't find anything all that offensive in it," says Anne, meticulous in her critique as always.

"Yeah," says Denis, burst of reddish-brown hair beginning high up on his forehead and then exploding backward in tight wavy curls. "You have to keep in mind that this is one guy's opinion, and he may not even be your audience. Myself, I didn't find anything in here any worse than you'd find on cable television."

"Exactly!" I declare, feeling vindicated.

"I think it's funny, engaging," says Anne. "I can't wait to read more."

The women of Thousand Fibers are similarly dismissive of Steven's critique. "It's one guy," says Katie. "You can't please everyone."

"I know, but it happens to be the one guy whose opinion I count on more than most others—present company excluded."

Suzanne casts her eyes over the chapter I've handed in, the one detailing my exploitive interview with Nick Hornby. "I really wouldn't worry about it," she says. "I mean, has he ever seen *South Park*?"

The thought of Steven watching *South Park* brings a bemused smile to my face. "I would be surprised."

"Almost any episode is more offensive than this." She shakes the stapled paper.

"Stephen, maybe it's just that you need to let go of his advice," Bridget suggests. "Or at least let go of relying on it as the be-all, end-all of your writing."

Her comment shocks me. I sit back and take it in, drawing the idea inside like a breath. This is something I have not considered. Not even in the tenths-of-second way you sometimes consider punching a stranger in the face just to see what it feels like. I can honestly say that I've considered how best to murder a person and get away with it for a longer period of time than I've ever considered banishing Steven and his advice from my writing life.[165]

"It could be that this professor was very influential in helping you grow as a writer, but that he's kind of fallen behind where you're going and what you want to do," Bridget continues. "He might just not get this, and it might be that you need to accept that."

As I leave that meeting at a small restaurant called the Kitsch'n in Roscoe Village, I head for the Brown Line stop at Addison, footfalls echoing on the pavement and Fleet Foxes humming softly as they are channeled from iPod to ear. What both of my writing groups have said—well, it's been completely uniform. They have almost spoken in one voice. What they've told me is what I wanted to hear: that Steven is wrong. That he is old and humorless and behind the times and just doesn't understand what I'm doing. This is exactly what I wanted them to say.

And yet it wasn't, and I find myself wishing that they had echoed Steven, even if it meant I had dedicated ten months of my life to writing a hulking piece of shit.

"Oh God," I say, wincing at the scatological reference I had just employed *in my thoughts*. "Great. Now I'm going to be insecure about using my fifth favorite word for the rest of my life."[166]

---

165 Oh my God, I just had the craziest thought: What if this book comes out, and in ten years I'm falsely accused of murdering someone like my wife or my friend or my coworker, and one of the pieces of evidence the prosecution will point to is the previous paragraph in this book where I speculate that I've contemplated doing extreme violence to a person I barely know and murdering an individual simply to see if I could get away with it? They'll say, "Look! He was thinking about it even back then! He even put it in a book!" And I will desperately try to explain that, "No, no, no! It was just an analogy! It was a harmless throwaway analogy that I used to describe how very little I had contemplated this other, completely unrelated thing!" For the record, Future Me did not do it, and if the prosecution uses this footnote as a way to explain that I had already—even ten years back—anticipated that the previous paragraph would get me in trouble, and thus wrote the footnote to try to shield myself from further scrutiny and to explain away my homicidal tendencies, then they are being completely unfair, and I move that the judge strike it from the record.

166 Incidentally, my first four favorite words: 1) *Fuck* 2) *Goddamn* 3) *Scatological* 4) *Richard Dreyfuss*.

And the pile-on continues.

When she finally does reply, it's quite apparent that Julie's confidence in me has waned enormously—so much so that I begin to get paranoid. For instance, she suggests via email that I hire a professional editor to work on the proposal. This is pretty unrealistic considering editors who improve book proposals for a living run about sixty to one hundred dollars per hour. For a sixty-page proposal with chapter excerpts? I assume that will take longer than *one* hour, which puts it out of my reach financially. I'm managing to sock away a little money after the end of each month but certainly not enough to blow a grand or more to know what I already know: that I'm not doing a very good job writing the fucking thing. Then Julie suggests that she knows a very good editor, and my mind goes to work.

She's a con artist, I decide. She presents herself as a literary agent and tricks easy marks into signing with her. Then when she gets a young, naïve writer right where she wants him, telling him his voice is "unique" and he has a "marketable idea" and some publishing house will be lucky to have him for six figures, she springs the trap. Her "editor" accomplice collects a grand or two—whatever they can squeeze—before she hands back the manuscript and says so sorry Charlie this just isn't going to work out, better luck with someone else.

I walk around for a day absolutely convinced my theory is correct and trying to devise clever, *Ocean's 11*–esque ways to turn the tables on her. "You thought you had me in your sights, see," I would say. "But you weren't counting on the ostrich arriving by FedEx. Like a typical dame you thought more with your heart than your gut."

I go as far as looking up the other authors she's represented and cross-checking their names and books on Amazon.com and Google. After a thorough investigation that takes up most of my day at work (the rest of it being filled with frequent updates on the Clinton-Obama race and a good, hard look at the full statistical averages for all twenty-four players on the Cleveland Cavaliers and Portland Trail Blazers), it turns out that yes, Julie is in fact a real agent with real clients.

The next time I talk to her, I feel incredibly silly about my doubt. Julie sounds like a middle-aged woman with a maternal hum to her voice and wandering attention span. The thought of her plotting small-time rip-offs is a stretch.[167]

I am at work when Julie's next email arrives. I read it just before lunch and lose my appetite immediately after processing what she's saying.

From: j____@yahoo.com
To: s___@yahoo.com
Subject: RE: chapters

Well, I have been thinking about this a lot... Now maybe other agents liked the book as is, and certainly I did at first, but I may have made a mistake that it could be shaped as is into something pubs will die for. I certainly love the concept and much of the writing. *Publish This Book* is a story readers can enjoy. But we need to somehow tie into that more. Not necessarily a book about the business of writing, but a journey of one's identity, told around the anger, frustration, and rewards of the itinerant writer, who finds good success at one level, but longs for the coveted book published, and how you turned the tables on seemingly heartless publishers by putting what writers go through down on paper, without totally indicting them since you do continue to pursue the dream. That's what I keep hoping is in there.

One more thing: Other agents may like this for what it is. If there is one you think can do you more good with the

---

167 Although I maintain that when I do have to con the conners, somehow an ostrich will play a pivotal role in the turnaround.

book as it is, I am willing to set you on their course instead of mine. After all, this is your career and I'd never hold anyone back whose dreams clash with my thoughts. All agents can be wrong. I have been right more than I have been wrong, but I have been wrong.

J

Yes, this says exactly what I think it says. If I may translate:

Dear Stephen,

Wow, this is awkward. So when I got this proposal, I immediately had dreams of discovering the next Eggers/ Klosterman/Foster Wallace. What I did not anticipate was that I would then sign on with a much less talented, focused, and famous writer than I had previously envisioned. This puts us in an uncomfortable situation, as I do not want to represent this book and send this proposal to publishers (who I hope will want to hear my pitches again at some point), but I would rather not haphazardly crush your dreams. That seems mean. So how about this: let me give you this opportunity to be the offended artist. Just say to yourself, Well, she doesn't "get" me, and then huffily take your project elsewhere. Wasn't there another agent interested in your pitch? Why not try again with him. See? Are we all feeling better or what? Great!

Julie

That evening after work I take the El home, as always. The train crawls around the Loop, rumbling across rust-laden tracks that run at ankle height to Chicago's skyline. Just as it pulls out of the Loop and before it escapes into the northern part of the city, the Brown

Line train crosses the Chicago River. Riding above the Wells Street Bridge, you can see the rust-coated crossbeams of the others: the La Salle Street Bridge, the Clark, the Dearborn, the State. The city's buildings careen into the sky and frame the river. The Westin Hotel and United Airlines headquarters. A redbrick building on the waterfront called the Reid Murdoch that looks like a munitions factory from the early twentieth century. The pitifully phallic Trump building. The Marina City I and II that look like space stations with decks that serve as ejectable escape pods. Ancient and modern at once, I always look up from my book when I cross the river here. I remember to take it in, to capture the sight in my mind because one day I may need it to remind me of how I was a part of this city, how I was just one small thrum on an endless series of humming strings that made up a fantastic, soulful chord.

When I get home, I email Steven and Julie. I tell them to hang on, that I have to think about things besides the book, like maybe how the Chicago River looks when the sun sets and the skyscrapers begin to throw light from their endless crowded windows. I tell them, don't worry: they'll hear from me soon.

Never Start a Story with Dialogue

"Never start a story with dialogue. That's an ironclad rule... Unless you're brilliant and have a brilliant reason to start with dialogue anyway. I guess I'm saying my advice is: always be brilliant. That's easy, right?"

It was right around this time that Chad, a friend from my non-all-female writing group, offered me that advice.

Originally, I had envisioned a chapter in this book where I tracked down famous published authors and asked them questions about how they made it. I conceived this notion—I fully admit—as a gambit to attract attention from agents and publishers. I didn't so much care what Chuck Klosterman had to say about writing, but I figured if an editor or agent didn't care what I had to say, maybe they'd be tempted by an encounter with already-well-known writers.

As the book developed, I quickly realized how stupid an idea this was. Do I particularly care what Kim Stanley Robinson, author of the acclaimed sci-fi series about Mars, has to say about character development? Of course not. Now maybe he does have a few interesting insights into the craft, but his input would have been inauthentic and inorganic to my story. While writing this book over the course of the last year, I come to realize that—Nick Hornby aside—I am far more interested in the largely unpublished writers who populate my life. Great stories are often found in places you'd never think to look, and as I begin to talk to these writers, I'm reminded of why I want to be a writer in the first place.

None of these conversations take place in chronological order or even the timeline I've established for this book. In other words, I don't send an email to Julie telling her I'll get to work and redeem my book and then go out and interview a bunch of writers for inspiration. A few of the conversations came before this moment of crisis, most will come after. I've placed them here for a reason, though—they are the psychological breather I took as I contemplated how to fix this book.

• • •

"Wait, so the first film crew all gets killed, but one of them survives?" I asked. I was high and severely confused—but not because I was high. I was confused because the plot of Jared's screenplay was like explaining how NASA builds a spaceship.

"No, no. The whole first film crew disappears, but then ten years later the footage is found, and it kind of shows what happened but not really, and everyone thinks it's a hoax."

"Oh, so then people go back to the house?" I asked.

"Right, the second film crew."

"Nothing to do with the first film crew?"

"Right, they all disappeared. It's the family before them that got killed. The first film crew went there to make a documentary about it, but they disappeared. The film turns up and it shows that something crazy happened but people don't know what, and they think it's a hoax, so the second film crew goes to find out what happened."

Normally, I wouldn't have had this much trouble following the plot of a shlocky horror flick, but the screenwriter, Jared, and I had been passing a joint back and forth for about ten minutes, and apparently in California they just bake the angel dust and household solvents right into the bud. After two hits, I'd almost forgotten my own name, let alone who this guy was sitting beside me—this wiry, scruffy-faced dude with long, unkempt hair poking out from beneath a backwards UCLA baseball cap at angles as odd as the plot twists in his screenplay.

It was 2006, and I was on another leg of my Epic Road Trip. I had just left Portland and the girl of the infamous LSD-induced reverse orgasm. After spending a few days in Reno, Nevada, I made my way down the west coast to Los Angeles where I was staying with some high school friends in a small apartment in Brentwood. I spent my nights sleeping on an air mattress in their living room while by day we explored Hollywood, the Santa Monica pier, Venice Beach, and all the rest of those L.A. staples that are less impressive than their mythology.[168] One day while they were at work, I took the opportunity to hang out with their screenwriting neighbor. And by "hang out" I obviously mean "got really stoned."

Writers are funny people: even though they all recognize the same challenges and obstacles to becoming successful, they are all their own rugged individualists in the mold of Horatio Alger (or at least they think they are). Everyone's got their project, everyone's got their ideals, everyone's got their heroes, everyone's got the path they think is going to take them to the top. None of them are at all alike, but the pillars are familiar. In this way, they make for great and bizarre conversation—especially if they're into drugs.

"Didn't go to school. Well, went to school, but dropped out after a year to write," Jared told me.

"What do you do for money?" I asked.

He smiled and took a drag. "My parents kind of prop me up," he admitted.

---

168   We sat in the front row of a taping of *Jimmy Kimmel Live* for what may have been the strangest lineup of guests ever assembled on a late night talk show. This included Jennifer Tilly (of *Bride of Chucky* fame), who jabbered at Kimmel like she had inhaled a duffel bag of cocaine before coming out, a 104-year-old gentleman who was billed as "the world's oldest beekeeper," and the rapper Xzibit. I just wish I had been present for the meeting when the talent booker told the show's producer, "Yeah, Tilly and Xzibit are still good for the fifteenth, but Corbin Bleu had to cancel, so instead we got this really fucking old beekeeper guy."

Jared had seen some limited success as a writer of straight-to-video B horror movies. I had always wondered about those flicks, the ones that show up on the new releases shelf with titles like *Batz* or *Gravediggers* or *Dream Reapers* that you can't imagine ever being bored enough to rent. But the movies keep getting made, and I suppose guys like Jared are the explanation. I could hardly be critical either, since Jared had sold a screenplay and had played a bit part in his own movie, which made him 100 percent more successful than me.

I told him about my novel and explained that just the day before I'd received a response from an agent, asking to see more chapters (it wouldn't be until I'd reached Mississippi that he asked for the entire manuscript, as I mentioned before). Not realizing this dream would eventually be reaped, it was exciting to share the news with another writer. Then he started in on his screenplay, which, despite the convolution, mostly centered around "fucked-up shit" happening to the second film crew and ended with the revelation that a psycho with a rare hair-growth disorder is the killer.[169]

I decided it couldn't be any worse than *Batz*.

With the joint finished, I asked how he got into writing and he explained that it was just something he had always wanted to do, so he bought a screenwriting book and taught himself.

"How about you?" he asked.

"It's all I've ever wanted," I told him. "I think you just have to be stupid enough to believe you can do it in spite of the odds."

Jared frowned, and I saw that he disagreed. "I don't know… Sure if you knew the odds, you probably wouldn't like them, but you can't worry about odds. Ignoring the odds isn't stupid. That's courage."

---

169 For a little more depth on the plot of Jared's film—and if memory serves me correctly—it turned out that the psycho with the rare hair-growth disorder that covered his body in fur (an actual affliction) was the son of the family, their dirty secret, who murdered all of them and hid in the house for years, murdering the first film crew and terrorizing the second… You can tell how important it was to me that I get what was going on in this movie.

• • •

"Susan Orlean was a complete bitch."

"Whoa," I asked. "Can I print that?"

"Yes. Definitely," said Katie of my all-female writing group. "So I was in New York helping out at a reading for that Eggers nonprofit, 826, and the writers were Malcolm Gladwell, Chuck Klosterman, and Susan Orlean. I was a huge fan of Susan Orlean, so I thought we could have at least a basic what-kind-of-writing-do-you-do conversation—you know, I was clearly in awe of her."

"Right."

"But she had absolutely no interest, and she treated me like her secretary. Without even looking at me, she tells me she has a headache and to find her some aspirin. So—whatever—I go looking for aspirin for her and eventually find a janitor who has some Excedrin. He gives me two, which I take back to her, and she looks at me and goes, 'Why are there two of them?'"

"What?"

"Yeah, I guess you're only supposed to take one Excedrin, but I figured I might as well get two just in case. It was like she thought I was trying to kill her, so I ask, 'Do you want me to go back to the janitor and check the bottle?' And she just kind of flips around and says, 'It's fine. I'll just take one.'"

This story barely begins to explain Katie. She is laid-back and speaks with a slow, studied wit. I imagine if you told her you accidentally set her house on fire, she'd nod, take a second to ponder, and say, "All right. I guess we should get outside then."

Sitting in a booth in the Beat Kitchen on Belmont while we wolf down pizza and beer, she explains her philosophy: "I'm at the bottom, so what do I have to lose?"

She spent her youth getting beer bought for her by members of the bands Incubus and Foo Fighters. She once approached Junot Diaz to tell him about a project she was working on. When Diaz expressed interest and asked her to submit a piece for the *Boston Review*, he not only yelled at her via email for sending too much but also finished by saying, "Goddamn, these are good. You've got the chops, girl, but this just isn't what we do."

That hardheaded streak of fearlessness and luck landed Katie an unbelievable opportunity. After college, she found herself working as the chief feature writer for a magazine at the University of Chicago, where her duties included shadowing Michelle Obama for the annual report.

"I liked her a lot," says Katie. "She was very, very blunt. This was 2006, and people were just beginning to talk about Barack running for the presidency, and she sounded dead set against it. You know, 'He's already away enough as a senator; he has two little girls…' That kind of thing. Then you get her talking about the state of health care, and she would pretty much straight up say, it's complete bullshit. I had to stop her sometimes and say, 'Michelle, I'm writing this for a magazine.'"

Besides picking the brain of Michelle Obama, Katie also found herself assigned to write a story about a University of Chicago scientist named Donald Rowley, who basically invented the modern EKG and then all but faded into obscurity within the medical community. Donald, impressed with Katie's piece, asked her if she would write the biography of his wife, who discovered a cause of leukemia that led to the development of a drug that cures somewhere around 90 percent of the people to whom it's administered. The two of them have won awards, received honors from presidents, and suffered through the tragic loss of a child. And besides having this epic love story with a nerdy twist, they wanted to pay Katie $60,000 a year for two years to write the biography of their lives.

"Was it the right decision?" I ask.

Her eyes widen. "Hands down. We even signed a contract down on Wacker Drive that a couple of million-dollar lawyers drew up."

She was twenty-three years old when the Rowleys recruited her for the task. Now she not only has the burden of telling this couple's story in all of its breadth, depth, and warts, but she must find a publisher for the book as well.

See what I mean when I say that Katie is fearless?

That's why when she decided to start her own literary magazine called *Kablammo*, she took the bus to Minneapolis for a Chuck Klosterman reading, where she intended to ask him to contribute something trivial to the rag, just so the issue could have a name attached.

"When I met him in New York, he just seemed so down-to-earth. He's this guy from North Dakota; his writing makes him seem fairly chill. I just figured I'd ask."

After the reading, Katie broached the subject with him over a beer. "And he just flipped out," she recalls. "He said, 'Everybody wants something from me,' and I was like, You can just say no, man. That's fine. 'I don't have the time, sorry.' That would be fine. But then he goes, 'Maybe if I have something no one else will take.'"

"Was that a terrible bus ride back?" I ask.

Katie—tall, blonde, and extremely confident—said, "Oh, I think talking to my boyfriend on the phone at one point I burst into tears, but whatever. I was fine."

We ask the waitress for the check, and I offer to buy without really meaning it. Forty dollars on the old debit card is a sturdy hit. I turn to Katie in my time of narrative distress because she, like me, is a young writer trying to hurdle the typical stand-in-line-wait-your-turn path to becoming a published author. I recognize in her the bravado of a person who doesn't care to wait in line.

On the other hand, Katie's encounters make me think of us—we aspiring writers—as looking through a keyhole at all the people who've made it. We look into this room that we really want to get into, and we see the people in there and we want to ask them how they got into the room. But maybe once we're through the keyhole, once we're in the room, what if we see things differently? What if we see the stupidity, the uselessness of the young writers who clamor for wisdom and advice, and we just want to turn to them and say, "Look, kid, I don't know! Okay? This—all of this—it was an accident. I have no idea how I got here, but I know you can't come the same way. That road is now closed."

· · ·

"And so he says to me: 'That's courage.'"

"Yeah?" asks Denis.

"Yeah. Words of wisdom from a college dropout turned nascent screenwriter of B-horror flicks. So my question to you is, which side of the argument do you come down on? Stupidity versus courage, I mean."

"It depends on the day. Sometimes—when it gets difficult—I do wonder. How can you not? But then the rest of the time, I have the confidence. I've had enough small successes that I can say, 'There must be something there.' I'm not doing it blindfolded. I know it's a matter of doing the hard work, of actually sitting down, because that's all I do now. I don't have the nine-to-five job like you. Writing this novel—this is what I'm doing."

"Right. And where are you in it?"

"I'd say maybe 75 percent complete? I'd like to finish it in the next three to four months. You know, it's funny, when I was reading the early chapters of your book—the part about Hornby and the part about moving to Chicago, especially—it was hard not to think of myself. I basically moved to Chicago right after college and spent most of my twenties kind of fucking around. Then when I turned thirty—the day I turned thirty—that was a big deal. Like: *Wow.* So I made a list of things I wanted to do before I turned forty. One was make our business a success, two was to make a movie, and three was to write a novel."

"Hey, two out of three and closing in fast on the last one," I say.

"Yeah, well, I would like to actually have it published."

After meeting in the writing group, Denis and I went about four months without realizing that we were both products of Miami University (and, unfortunately for us, Browns fans), although he graduated nearly two decades before me. Denis came to his writing career late, having spent his twenties doing a bit more than just "fucking around." He and a few friends built from scratch an Internet software company. He also did make that movie[170]: it was called *Grave Matters,* and it got rejected by Sundance.[171] In 2005 he sold his stake in the company with the idea to spend a few years writing a novel. As his company grew and his workload decreased, he had come back to writing and even had some success, landing short stories in mid-level literary journals like *Wind River Press* and *The First Line.*

"So I had two things I wanted to do," Denis tells me as we sit in a nondescript bar in Bucktown sipping some kind of heavy German beer recommended by the bartender. "First, I love soccer, so I went to the World Cup. That was cool. And second, I wanted to spend two years in Northern California fly-fishing near Mount Shasta. I love fly-fishing. And while I did that, I wanted to write the novel."

I tell Denis how I have a picture of myself with Mount Shasta in the background. I passed right by it on my way from Portland to L.A.

"I definitely got a lot more fly-fishing done than writing, but…" Denis shrugs, maybe regretful, maybe nostalgic, maybe in love with a time in his life he'll have difficulty finding again. "You know. There's this river there—the McCloud River. They call it the 'River Cathedral' and there's a limited number of fishing licenses they hand out, so I stayed in this house and there were days I felt like I had the entire river to myself."

I nod and think of standing thigh-deep on a sparkling river, casting a rod all day, turkey sandwich for lunch, listening to the

---

170   From what I can tell of the plot of Denis's movie, it had neither a first film crew, a second film crew, or a psycho killer with a rare hair-growth disorder.

171   Fuck you, Robert Redford! You hippie Hollywood asshole!

wind, and the gentle rhythm-less ticking of nature. I've never been fly-fishing before, but the picture Denis paints makes my heart ache for other places, for that kind of quiet, wandering adventure.

• • •

"That was awesome, Steve. Just fucking awesome, man. You have no idea how awesome that article was," says Todd. "The last time we were in Chicago with the movie, my ex-girlfriend's friends didn't give a fuck. This time they were like, 'Hey, we saw the article about you in the *RedEye*! Wow, you really made it!' And I'm like, 'It's the same fucking movie that it was the last time we were here. Nothing's changed with the movie, but now it's in *RedEye*, so you're impressed?'"

"Ah, so it's about revenge," I say. "Giving the friends of the ex-girlfriend the finger."

"Fucking right, man. No one holds a grudge like me. Man, I will hold a grudge for years and years over shit I can't even remember."

His name is Todd Sklar, and he looks exactly like you'd expect a twenty-four-year-old independent filmmaker driving around the country in a van to promote his movie to look. Which is to say, he has a gnarly black shock of beard and wild, unkempt hair collected by a headband. He wears an outfit that consists of a T-shirt, button-up sweater, and brightly colored scarf, but none of these garments are attached to his torso with any comprehensible plan or style. As though he dove naked into a swimming pool of Salvation Army clothing and climbed out in an outfit.

I'd caught the assignment from my *RedEye* editor: check out these guys doing a cross-country tour with their slacker comedy flicks. I called Sklar, and he sounded so excitable on the phone, it was hard not to be intrigued.

"Man, I wish I had something better to say; you'd think this is the kind of shit a director and writer would think about and like have an answer for, but fuck, man, I'm coming up blank. I'll say something cool—hold on, let me check with the star of the movie." Try saying all of that in one breath, because he did. "Alex! Alex, wake up, man! It's *RedEye*, man, you got any good shit I can tell them? About the movie? About the tour? Shit, man, I don't know," he returns to the phone. "It's about passion, man. You know, we could go to New York and L.A. and screen this and then no one would ever see it again, but it's about connecting with an audience, you know? Like after you see a band at a bar, you just hang out with them and drink and that's like one of the best parts."

So I took the Red Line downtown and caught a viewing of *Box Elder*, a surprisingly hilarious ensemble college comedy made on a budget of credit card debt and starring various improv actors from the University of Missouri where it was shot and where Sklar and his crew went to school.

When I see him at the screening, the moppy-headed auteur grabs me in a bear hug. "Wow, man, so cool! So good to see you. Thanks for coming! Fucking awesome!"

And not long after that, I am hanging out with Sklar, his star, Alex, and a motley assortment of his college friends in a Wicker Park bar called Estelle's. They will not let me buy a single drink.

I explain my idea to Todd through a burgeoning haze of eight bottles of Pabst.

"This is what I'm saying: it's like this was meant to be, you and me meeting. It's like Hemingway and Fitzgerald hanging out. You make awesome movies with *Die Hard* references, I write books about writing books, and—Oh shit!" I nod gravely. "Now you're gonna be in the book." I look around the table. "All of you are gonna be in the book!"

Todd is clapping. "Yes!" he says. "Fucking awesome! This is great."

"To Steve's book!" someone says, and we all clink glasses.

Sklar found meager backing for *Box Elder* when he won a coveted spot at the Sundance Film Lab.[172] The application had a 450-word

---

172 All right, Robert Redford, we cool for now, motherfucker.

limit for all the answers to various questions. Sklar crafted every answer to exactly 450 words.

"So this girl calls me up and says, basically, 'I wanna know what kind of person thinks to type every answer exactly the word limit. And based on that, I got invited to the Sundance Film Lab.'"

We gab the rest of the night. We talk about how no one in Hollywood understands how to make a funny movie anymore, about how long-distance relationships suck, about how great a movie *Die Hard* is, about the idea for his next movie—a road trip comedy that follows three friends from Minneapolis to New Orleans, about my own Epic Road Trip, about the book, and based on this one night, I can sense that Sklar and I have pulled into each other's orbits, that this is just the beginning of a longer conversation. This kid is a whirling one-man dust storm, an explosion of exuberance and creativity that beams off him in near-tangible form.

I tell him about working on the docks at Jackson Lake, and how I once became embroiled in a conversation with a talkative older guy, mostly about running wild after college, sleeping in your car, camping in places you don't belong, and so forth. At some point, this old guy said to me, "Don't worry about money. Don't ever worry about money. There will always be enough money somehow—just go be with people who turn you on. That's the most important part. Be with people who turn you on."

I am not drunk enough to turn to Todd and his friends and tell them that they "turn me on," but I am smart enough to recognize what I've found when I find it.

• • •

"What you've got to do is work at it. Every day."

"Unh-huh."

"Get yourself in some classes. Practice. It's the only way you'll get better."

"Right."

"When I got started, I didn't know what I was doing. I sold my first book in 1978, and it ended up getting nominated for an Edgar Award. No way I could see that coming. I had been in the Peace Corps, decided I wanted to be a criminal defense attorney because of *Perry Mason*, but I always had a passion to write. You need to have that passion."

"I'm pretty good on the passion, you know? This novel I'm sending around is my third. I used it for my honors thesis at school, and it got a pretty decent reception…"

Phillip Margolin nodded, his smile tweaking slightly as he realized what I was about to ask him. He sat with his legs propped up on the sturdy desk in his law office in downtown Portland. It was only my second day in town, I had yet to meet the young woman I'd spend most of my time with, but there I was talking with an award-winning mystery writer. Margolin's office had sharp, modern edges of light-colored wood and sparkling clear glass. His computer had this enormous screen with what looked like a chunk of prose open in a Microsoft Word document—his next book, he said. How had I come to sit in the office of Phil Margolin, criminal defense attorney and bestselling, Edgar Award–winning mystery writer? Before I got to Portland, my parents had set me up with a place to stay: a couple of old family friends who lived in the hills of Multnomah County. These friends, an older couple with distant family connections, happened to be friends with Phil Margolin and his wife. When I mentioned that I was querying for my novel, they insisted that they set up a meeting with Margolin in his office.

"I guess what I'm saying," I told Margolin, trying to convey some semblance of professionalism, "is that I'm past the point of working at it every day. I'm now onto the find-an-agent-find-a-publisher kinda deal. That's what I'm actually asking for your help with."

I'm not sure if my intentions were wildly misrepresented, but as soon as I sat down in his office, Margolin was talking to me like I was a starry-eyed high school pubescent looking for advice—aw gee-whiz shucks—on how I, too, could become a bestselling mystery writer.

I thought about just sitting there and politely taking his kind—if slightly condescending—advice because I hated playing the role of aspiring writer asking for a favor. Yet I had driven all the way downtown and spent like three bucks on parking in stupid Greenpeace Portland, so I figured I might as well lob a grenade and see what happened.

Margolin's smile faded, his indefatigable jaw ground to a halt. He pointed to a stack of books in the corner of his office. "As I said, I'm judging the Edgar Awards this year, and I'm up to my eyes through January. Maybe if you send it then, I can take a look."

Not surprised but nevertheless disappointed that I'd wasted his time and mine, I thanked him and left his pristine office, stopping in a nearby Staples to load up on 9 x 11 manila envelopes with which to send more queries for the novel. It was a simple lesson I had sensed long ago, but which would be voiced perfectly by Junot Diaz to a young woman I had no idea existed at that point: no one is going to do the work for you.

In a rather sad corollary to this story, I found out from those family friends with whom I'd stayed that Phil Margolin's wife died abruptly from cancer in January 2007, less than three months after I spoke to him.

I reread my record of the conversation, recorded for my now-defunct book *A Land I Saw in My Dreams*. Because my assessment of him had been brief and unfavorable, I felt a sick twinge of guilt for taking the measure of a person so quickly. In looking at Margolin strictly as a means to an end—even if we had been introduced as little more—I had relegated this man's dreams, success, and joy into afterthoughts. I'd quashed them into oblivion in my perception of him—so wildly unfair.

There was so little to learn from that conversation, and yet it struck me that the very existence of the conversation itself was the lesson; art has nothing to do with Life's fickle intentions: write what you want. Draw what you will. Perform what you can. In the end, the unexpected twists—the mutated cells, the choked arteries, the swerving vans—will always tell the ending.

• • •

"I was way more committed to writing when I was single," said Chad, who had once recommended never beginning a story with dialogue—unless of course you could make it brilliant.

"Yeah?"

"Yeah. My wife is 'supportive'—in quotes. I'll tell her I plan to write on a certain night, and she'll say, 'Oh, yeah, you definitely should!' But when the time actually comes, she'll say, 'Oh. You mean now?' I don't write in bars anymore either, which is my favorite place to write. Was."

"Bars?" I say. "I can't believe that."

"I actually love the commotion. And at any time, you'll be sitting by a group of people, and one of them will say something—some random throwaway line—that's totally inspiring. Plus, there are a limited number of things I can do in a bar. I can write. At home there's a computer with Internet, a TV, a dog, who knows what else. I like to get away from that safe environment. No distractions because distractions are just all the stuff that's familiar. I write longhand when I have that energy and then can rough-edit when I type it in—transcribe it—later."

"But a bar?"

"Well, when I was single it was also a good excuse to meet people. You know, someone wants to know what you're writing, and it's an instant conversation starter."

Chad from LWN also has a major project under way, a novel called *Five-Man Fugue* that follows the intertwining journeys of several strangers through a mystic evening in Chicago. He has an even more frustrating tale of rejection than I do. In college, he wrote a poem, which became a short story, which became a novel. At a writer's conference he met an agent named Kim, who wanted to see that novel. He sent it to her, and she sent it back saying she liked it but she wanted to see edits. So Chad went through the book, implemented the edits, and sent it back. She returned it, asking for edits B. So Chad fixed edits B and sent it back. Kim returned it, needing edits C. Finally, after edits D, she said, so sorry, we've seen this too many times. Better luck elsewhere.

Chad shrugs off the experience. "Sure, frustrating," he says, in a wild understatement. We are in some Irish bar off the Montrose El stop, a joint where there are ruddy-faced, white-haired men muttering to each other in brogues and sipping Smithwick's and Guinness.

"You don't write for the money," he notes. "You write because it's a compulsion. Even if it's a compulsion that you fail to do all the time."

This is counterintuitive but true: kind of like a lifetime smoker having to force himself to get through that pack a day.

"Of course, some people do think it's a short road to cash. What's easier: writing the great American novel or working in a steel mill for forty years? Well, it turns out the steel mill, but most people don't realize that starting out." He pauses, taps his fingers on the table where we sit, and contemplates his beer. "I will say, I've had the thought before: if I someday make large amounts of money, it's going to be from this. Writing is Option A with no other options."

● ● ●

"It was very surreal. It felt so strange, mostly because after the book was accepted the editing happened really fast, and I don't write quickly. I have a very deliberative process, so I was anxious about mistakes."

"How did it feel to hold a copy? When you first got it in the mail or whatever and held it in your hand, you must have felt something," I say.

"Yes. I felt like it wasn't my book anymore. It was this pretty little object—and I still think of it that way; it is pretty—but now I feel very detached. Like these aren't my stories anymore."

My professor, Margaret, is talking about her first book, a collection of short stories called *If the Heart is Lean*.

"Did you read it after you got it? Your book, that is."

"Of course, but I'm a hopeless narcissist," she says, laughing. "I found some of the stories a little embarrassing. You know, some of them I first wrote, literally, years ago, and now I look at them kind of like artifacts. I read them and can't believe that I was into this thing or that thing—so much so that I had to write a story about it. I think it was Gore Vidal who said that his first book was awful and the attention it got embarrassed him, but at least it put him in a position where he could write things he was proud of."

We speak by phone. I have just called to tell her the details about my book, which, she says, she's interested to read—if for no other reason than to find out what I did to fill up pages after the initial concept. A middle-aged professor who dabbled in—among other things—music promotion before going back to school to become a writer, Margaret enjoyed success with short story publications in highly reputable magazines like *Tin House* and *Jane*. She fooled around with the manuscript for *If the Heart is Lean* for three years, querying agents and independent presses before finally landing a contract with the Louisiana State University's Yellow Shoe Press, a small but respected university press. As Margaret describes it, "A great place for short story people like me who have no commercial hopes."

Before we end the conversation with promises to buy each other's books, I ask Margaret about a slice of wisdom I plucked from an email she sent me nearly a year earlier, in which she told me about "redefining success."

"Ever since you wrote me that," I tell her, "I find myself doing it all the time. You know, when I started at *RedEye* I thought I'd hit on the mother lode, but now I can barely look at the thing. It's not enough—not by a long shot."

She takes a moment to enjoy her laughter. "I can't believe I'm responsible for wisdom that anyone still clings to."

"Yeah, be careful what you're saying to impressionable young people."

"I definitely feel it," she says. "I think right now it translates into me wanting to quit my job, to get out of teaching. Don't get me wrong, teaching is great, but it is so consuming with your time, with your energy… And every once in a while it's worth it when you're working with really talented students, but I have an intro class right now where the only books the kids read are *Twilight* or *Harry Potter*, and I keep wanting to ask them why they want to be writers if they don't even read. So to answer your question, I definitely feel that urge to get to the next level. I'm thrilled to get into good journals, but now I want the *New Yorker*. I don't know, do I even write stories the *New Yorker* would want? A higher profile, more money, a novel, a full-time writer—this is the stuff I think about."

• • •

"I like to have a structure because the way to overcome the blank page problem is to find a structure and then fill it up."

"Right," I say.

"So after this fairly dark chapter," says Josh (of the chapter I will eventually call "Wrong-Headed, Condescending Toward the Reader, Self-Involved, and Unintentionally Revealing"), "in which Steven, your mentor, has lost faith in you, you make it clear you don't want to become beholden to the conceit. And that's what I meant when I said, 'You seem to have found a vehicle'—because it doesn't matter what the vehicle is—whether it's a sonnet or a book about publishing a book—you want something that allows you to communicate ideas, humor, emotions, and then you fill it up, you fill out that structure."

Josh is one of the smarter people I've ever had a conversation with. Red-haired and red-bearded, he speaks in a voice that comes overwhelmingly through his nose. We creep along Western Avenue in his car as he drives me home from a meeting with my previously all-female writing group. Josh was a latecomer, but within two meetings I was extremely glad to have him on hand. His comments were always insightful if not dead-on. He articulated what I was trying to do in the book after reading only two or three chapters out of order. Sure, he's a writer in his own right, with published poems in *Slate* and *Potomac*[173] among others, but I include him here because he has hit dead on the nail what I've wanted to do from the beginning—and what I need to do now—to finish this book.

"It was my initial fear when I read those first few chapters," he says as we drive over streets slick with melted snow. The warmth of his car has just begun to melt the brittle chill from my hands and face. "That in following this conceit, it can take you in a direction you didn't want to go. That's happened to me several times."

"Right," I say, glancing at his profile. "The point is to stay in charge of the book. To drive it rather than let it drive me."

"And I think you've been aware of that this whole time, but I wasn't sure of it at first. Now I see that one of the main conflicts in the book is this internal struggle: you've let this guy—call it your Id or whatever, like you do in the book—out of his cage. You let him out of his cage so you can watch him dance."

Good analogy, I think. Wish I had thought of that.

"But you don't want to watch him dance while you sit there and weep because you can't get him back in the cage. That was what Steven was worried about, I think."

He turns down Belmont and I think about this as his car goes

---

173 Josh is also finishing up a PhD in material sciences at Northwestern where he studies nanotechnology. Publishing poetry in *Slate* and *Potomac* is his hobby, as was his MA from Boston University in poetry. Stupid Josh was also once a science advisor for the writers on *24* and is almost solely responsible for the detonation of the nuclear bomb in the desert during season 2. Also, I should mention that this is definitely *not* the Josh who has his dick pierced. That Josh not only is not getting a PhD in material sciences but I think there's an ongoing lobbying effort to have the federal government sterilize him in case he ever tries to procreate.

whistling past a tight-faced Latino who has walked straight into traffic despite the red hand telling him it was not his turn. The street swishes under the car's tires, a mist spraying up from the rubber. Josh makes it sound fairly simple, and in fact he has struck upon my intention throughout this book: let him out of the cage, get him back in.

Easy enough, right?

When faced with the enormity of tackling the rewrite of a project that itself must inherently be a first draft simply by definition, I feel as if I might buckle. I search my life for another time when I gave in—when I quit because something was too hard, too taxing, too much to handle, and certainly I can find plenty of examples—but not for anything I cared about this much. I don't have a choice but to make this work, and if this perseverance is all I have left at the end, then at least I'll have that. Writing is Option A with no other options.

The Chapter I Called "Wildheart"

On May 31, 2008, I get a typically terse text message from Justin that says: "Jaxson was born today. He's healthy."

I get Justin's voice mail and hoot and carry on into his phone until it cuts me off. I tell him we'll dance at his son's wedding. I call my friend Veronica who goes to school in Chicago and we make plans to drive back to see Justin and Loren in Columbus.[174]

Veronica and I leave on a Thursday in her Civic to make the six-hour trek to the Buckeye capital, where we meet Justin and Loren at her parents' farm just south of the city. In tow are three of our friends from Mount Vernon: Kdoe (down from our hometown as he feverishly plans for his upcoming wedding to his college sweetheart), Ritesh (down from med school near Kent), and Marie[175] (who attends nursing school in Columbus[176]).

---

174 In this vast web of complicated interpersonal relationships, let me try to explain how Veronica is connected to all this: During our brief time back in Oxford as pizza delivery men, my friend Phil began dating Veronica, who happened to be good friends with Loren (which is how we met her and, in turn, found her delightful and hilarious because she laughed like a madman and talked openly about the merits of anal ring toss). Now the whole lot of us are bound together by a failed birth control pill.

175 Their names are pronounced "Kay-doe," "Ree-tesh," and "Muh-ree."

176 And here, we run into a problem I've been grappling with the entire book: peripheral characters. The problem with writing about real life is that there are all these events you have to recount that involve scores of people, who nevertheless contribute very little to the eventual story I'm trying to tell. Do I leave them out, essentially striking them from

Before entering the house, I badger each of them about getting me a check for one hundred dollars. About a month before Jaxson was born, I was running along Lake Michigan trying to think of what the hell we were going to get Justin for a baby present. We decided that it was pointless for his best friends to buy him a crib or something, and when I asked Justin what he and Loren might need, he was not helpful. ("Golf clubs," he said. "I have a feeling Jaxson's going to need to work on his short game and his drive.")

During the run, it came to me—the perfect gift: we could start a college fund for the kid. If each of his six or seven closest friends chipped in one hundred dollars, we could put seven hundred dollars in an account with eighteen years to accrue. I ran the idea by some friends, and Ian said he'd join the effort: I would hassle people into getting together the money and a card, while he would collect the checks. I'm the enforcer; he's the banker.

Then I got the idea to reach out to other people, like Marie and Veronica, hence the badgering outside of Loren's house on a hot, sun-streaked morning.

We shut up as Loren greets us at the door. "Hey, guys," she says, smiling.

"Let's see him, let's see him!" I cry, bolting past her.

The five of us crowd into Loren's living room on this nondescript farm in the middle of rural Ohio, the flat green and brown pushing up against the summer blue sky just outside the window, and our jaws hit the floor.

Justin sits on a couch holding an honest-to-shit child. A baby boy. So small that the flesh of my friend's arms seems to swallow the tiny thing.

---

the history of the story? Do I add them in passing reference and senselessly confuse the reader? Or do I go to the effort of providing extraneous detail about a person who will in all likelihood not matter to the rest of the story? Unless, between this point and the completion of this book, we rob a drugstore together or drive a car off a cliff a la *Thelma & Louise* (in which case I'll have a lot of editing to do), let's just say that Marie and Veronica were present this afternoon, and leave it at that.

"Oh, weird," I mutter.

Justin looks up from his son, his face placid. "What's up?" he says.

We move in to surround him, staring incredulously at this minis-cule creature Justin made with an organ we previously thought was strictly for recreational purposes.

I look at this baby's small, squished face. "Oh, dude, he looks just like you." It's true. Even in that shrunken visage I can see the bulb of a nose that will someday resemble his father's, and the same dark blue eyes appear when his lids peel open ever so slightly.

"He does," Kdoe agrees. Kdoe, long and wiry with the body of a distance runner, is all sharp elbows and long knuckles. When he holds the baby, his arms look mechanical next to the small pink bundle, like the robots that whiz around putting cars together in auto plants. He laughs. "Look at him. It's Justin."

We spend the morning passing Jaxson back and forth.

When I hold him, I become even more amazed at how small he is, like a little loaf of bread. His hands move in spastic jerks, but otherwise he is mostly motionless.

I ask Loren how she feels.

"Pretty good. I was exhausted for about two days afterwards, but now I'm feeling fine."

"Was it crazy?" I ask.

"Oh, my God," says Justin. "Markley, you have no idea. Just this—it just comes right—it's crazy, man. You wouldn't believe it unless you saw it."

Ritesh giggles. He exists in a constant state of amusement, es-pecially at the stupidity of his white childhood friends, but he gets a special kick out of imagining Justin witnessing a delivery. (He's already delivered babies on his rotations.)

"Did you freak out, Justin?" he asks.

"No, man, I didn't freak out, but…" Justin's eyes go wide in a demonstration of how his face might have looked. "I just stood there with my mouth open and like… Are you kidding me?"

Everyone cracks up at the image.

"Does he cry?" I ask Loren as I cradle Jaxson.

"No, he's really well-behaved so far."

"Doesn't do much, I guess."

"Maybe he thinks you're boring, Markley," she suggests.

"Whatever. I'm the most fun uncle he has. Isn't that right, Jaxson?" I say to the nonresponsive infant. "Who else is going to teach you how to play basketball, buddy? Not Dad, that's for sure…"

We trade Jaxson; we take pictures. In one photograph taken by Veronica, it is just the four of us: Justin, Kdoe, Ritesh, and myself staring at him with a blend of amusement and wonder.

Yet there's a problem with this scene, with this moment.

Before my struggle with the book began, before I received Steven's criticism and Julie's hesitation, I had been formulating in my mind how I would end this book. If I was approaching a point at which I'd actually need to end the book so it could be published, I would need to wrap up all these disparate threads I had begun in the first ten chapters. I envisioned two scenarios that would have to be included.

In the first, I would call my Love Interest the day after I signed whatever book deal I had coming. It would be the first time we'd spoken in months. I would ask her how she was doing. I would tell her how I was doing. Then I would tell her about the book. I would tell her she was in the book, and I would probably not be able to help saying really nice things about her. Depending on how that conversation went, I would report how much losing her had broken my heart and accordingly, how hard it would be to forget about her in the years to come.

In the second, I had planned to use this scene: visiting Justin and holding his child. It would be an "All's Well That End's Well" kinda chapter. Jaxson would be this adorable little flesh ball that would melt hearts and make Justin see the inadvertent luck he had stumbled upon in the form of his newfound responsibility, and as for me, your not-so-humble narrator—well, I would understand the value of friendship and love and be transformed into a better person or some such Lesson Learned bullshit.

The problem, I discover, as I sit in this neat living room with a spotless carpet, carefully arranged furniture around a respectably large flat-screen TV, and so many family pictures it's like the photographs themselves procreated, is that it is incredibly difficult to cram Life into a preconstructed narrative.

The problem seems to be with Justin, who, aside from telling us how shocking he found the actual birth, is very quiet even by his standards. I needle him, try to kid him into a retort or two about what a moron I am, but he doesn't take the bait.

We go to lunch at Applebee's and order meals heavy with stuff your doctor warns you away from.[177] Finally, back at Loren's with her family gone, the women retreat to the back bedroom to feed Jaxson.

The four of us remain in the living room watching an unimportant baseball game: Justin on the couch with Ritesh beside him. Kdoe sits on the other couch, while I perch on a chair dragged from the dining room table. No one really asks him anything. Justin just starts talking.

"It's funny," he says, staring at the ceiling. "These beams. These beams are exactly the same ones from this other house where I used to spend a lot of time." I look up. Dark wooden beams, full of scuffs and knots for farmhouse authenticity, brace the otherwise pristine white ceiling. "The other night I was just sitting in here staring at them… thinking how they looked familiar. How I'm looking at them here instead of the other house." He pauses. Kdoe and I exchange a quick glance.

"Life's weird," I offer lamely.

Justin stares at the unimportant baseball game on TV. He sits

---

177 It is actually a rule that Ohioans must enjoy the native cuisine, which means they are required to eat at Applebee's, Bob Evans, or TGI Friday's at least once a month or risk paying a small fine.

with one leg propped up on the coffee table and his hands laced behind his head, relaxed. His face is completely blank. "I'll tell you what," he says, "I used to think I was a pretty strong person... pretty..." He chews his tongue. A clock ticks softly from a wall and the refrigerator hums from the kitchen. None of us looks at him, but watch the unimportant game where a foul tip careens into the stands. "Thought I could take whatever came along... That I could handle more or less anything."

The four of us sit silently. I stare at the ground. This isn't how the book is supposed to end.

Ritesh tries. "It's normal, you know, after birth... Not just the mom can get..." he hesitates at the word, "depressed. It happens to the dad, too. All the time."

Justin keeps right on watching the baseball game. "I don't know. Loren even called me out on it the other day. Asked me what was wrong." He speaks so slowly; I feel like my ear has to meet his every word halfway. "I didn't know what to tell her. Just said I had to get my head on straight."

Holding my chin in my hands, I mutter through my palms, "Look, dude, this isn't unexpected." I stop, trying to find the right words for what I want to say. "I mean, you can't be expected to not be down right now. You're living at your girlfriend's parents' house for the summer while you work in a shitty internship. It's weird—obviously, you just had a kid with their daughter... I'm saying, you have a right to feel like the world's fucked right now." I watch him. He says nothing, so I go on. "It's a few months, though. You'll get back to Oxford, you'll finish your master's. It's not like this is the way things are forever."

There's a long moment of silence. We wait, and then Justin says, "I told someone the other day... I said to them, 'I think I've fucked up my life.'"

And that is the end of the conversation. I tremble with guilt. While I wallow in self-pity about my stupid fucking book and my otherwise directionless life, my friend is worrying that he's lost things he could never have anticipated losing, things he can never get back, and that sometimes in order to carry on, we must erase whole chapters of ourselves—those wooden beams lost when his finger hit the Delete button.

Even when I see him off the next day, and remind him that we'll see each other soon for Kdoe's wedding—that we'll all be back together and things won't seem so insane—I realize that there are some moments in life that you can never come back from. There is a before and there is an after, and no matter how much you want to forget what someone said or did, you will always face a divide. I want to help Justin fix this. I want to tell my friend that it's all okay, that everything's gonna be all right, just like I had planned on it being all right when I put it in my book. But this situation, this fear, this uncertainty—they're all maddeningly out of my reach. I can't write him a happy ending.

We say good-bye and his eyes are empty, the blue faded so that they look less like his son's than I'd thought at first.

• • •

Spring comes to Chicago. Winter finally, mercifully begins to recede. I begin to run outside more frequently, taking my preferred route down Wellington to the lake shore and down to North Avenue Beach, where I smack the side of the outdoor bar, Castaway's, before turning around. On the good days, I go as far as the Drake Hotel, passing the men hunched over the stone chessboards, gauging each movement of pawn or rook with a severity usually reserved for the tactical calculations of wartime.

I write. I work. At the very least, it's a fascinating time to be writing about the automotive industry: soaring gas prices, American automakers beginning to shake at their very foundations. Sure, my beat has nothing to do with the big issues of the day, but I remind myself that it is better than nothing. I could be back at the

SoulSuck Agency listening as out-of-work candidates plead with me to help them find jobs that have all but ceased to exist as the economy continues to erode, sand spiraling into the bottom half of the hourglass.

Yet this is not what I envisioned for myself. Not two months ago, not six months ago, not a year ago, not five years ago. With the book stalled, the proposal in disrepair, and my future uncertain, I find myself suddenly wondering how long I will remain at Cars.com. Is this how it happens, I wonder? How a dream becomes complacency and one day you wake up and wonder where the last twenty years went?

• • •

Steven looks confused as he enters our third and final real-but-repurposed-for-fictional-conversations-that-actually-took-place-by-email locale.

"I don't get it," he says, looking around the spacious office. His eyes alight on a desk with a gleaming white Mac and dozens of notebooks crammed into the shelves, then move on to a guitar leaning in a corner and a table busy with recording equipment and a stereo system. Through the window, we can see a hard-scrabbled prairie that looks an awful lot like central Texas.

I shrug. "This is where Jewel wrote her book of poetry."

"Jewel? The singer, Jewel?"

"*A Night Without Armor*," I say, scratching my head as I look away. I finish off the subtitle, "*Poems* by Jewel."

"Why?" he asks.

"I don't know. I got flustered after the last time we spoke. I just picked the first place I could think of, and it *is* one of the bestselling books of poetry of all time."

"I guess the better question then is 'how.' As in 'How did you know Jewel lived here and wrote her book of poe—"

"You know, why don't we just get down to it?" I say, taking a seat on the carpeted floor and gesturing for him to sit in the desk chair. "I took a lot of time to think about what you said before responding to your response," I tell him. "First of all, of course I want your honest opinion and am fully capable of handling any and all criticism. Secondly, I would say let's not get too carried away with our indictments. Just because I wrote ten pages that you don't like does not make me a revolting Neanderthal masquerading as a soulful writer."

Steven sits straight in his chair with his legs crossed and his hands folded neatly over a knee, waiting for me to continue.

"One: This is a rough, rough work in progress that I have to feel out as I go. Keep in mind I started this without any idea of where it would go or how it would develop. The first seven chapters were written only with the idea that they had to be entertaining ('entertaining' obviously being in the eye of the beholder here) and catch the reader's attention.

"Two: I will gladly cede that the third chapter is likely all the things you describe, but some of those things, I think, are necessary now that I'm starting to see the bigger picture. There is intent here… When I first wrote it, I didn't necessarily see it, but now I do. Which is to say that when I began this project, my life was in a drastically different place than it is now… One of the funny things about choosing to write this book this year is that it is eerily aligning itself with so many very important things… I have to figure out a way to maintain the general reaction you had to the narrator (albeit perhaps not quite that strongly) while reevaluating what that entails."

He frowns, and I know he wants to interrupt, but I hold up a hand to ask him to let me finish.

"In part, it's about the reaction. One of the reasons I've stuck with this voice that you so dislike is because it's what has worked. At Miami and now at *RedEye* here in Chicago. For whatever reason, audiences react to this voice—whatever its deficits. Maybe you see that as selling out, but I think it can be harnessed for better purposes within the context of this book (at least, I hope, and I suppose that is my challenge). Even if my generation does not control the publishing industry, they do control what they find amusing, what they find full of shit, what they find tasteless, and what they find interesting. To a large degree, the book has to be geared to the people I hung out with in Mac 'n Joes on Saturday nights because—whatever else I may be and whatever else I want to do with myself—that is also who I am.

"Having said all that, have you had enough or are you up for chapters five and six in a few weeks?"

I sit back, and our eyes lock, neither of us willing to look away. A part of me feels like he'll stay in that seat and gaze at me until I blink, until he wins. The other part of me fears he will get up and walk out through the door right then and there, and that will be the last I will see or hear from him.

A bead of sweat breaks out on my temple. Just as I'm about to look away, the door to the office swings inward, and Jewel asks, "Steve, did you want 'Angel Standing By' as the last song on that mix or 'Pieces of You'?"

"What?" I bark. "What are you talking about? Do you mind? I'm in the middle of something, and plus, I've never even heard anything of yours except for that 'Save Your Soul' one on the radio."

She looks incredulous. "What? You sing 'Have a Little Faith in Me' in the shower every morning after your roommates leave for—"

I leap from the floor. "All right! Okay! That'll be all, Jewel!" I usher her out the door. "Don't need any crazy ladies interrupting my imaginary conversations!" I close the door and click the little button lock. "Sorry about that," I tell Steven. "Please, if you got something to say, just say it."

He nods. "Anyway, a quick response to what you said in response to my response: I'm glad you find this fun. That is not the word I would have imagined you'd use after my response to the last two chapters, but that's better than some ways you could have responded. For more of the same, try walking barefoot on thumbtacks.

"You have—in your words (or Julie's)—something that every agent and publisher and reader hasn't seen already. A niche, I guess is the word. Okay, but I thought what you had was the High Concept, not necessarily a fascination with feces. If you believe in Freud, you should have grown out of this stage, oh, about twenty years ago. As for your writing group, I wouldn't put TOO much faith in its members' response."

"Why?" I ask cautiously.

"These are people who are salivating about publication in *Toasted Cheese*," he explains. "And you took those chapters they resisted and found an agent. Right now they hate and fear you but are willing to curry favor. They would gladly trade various body parts for your position. Nevertheless, the word you used to describe their reaction isn't enthusiastic but resigned. You have thumb wrestled them into submission."

"Oh," I say neutrally. The writers I've gotten to know in Chicago do not fit Steven's description, but I understand the condition he's describing.

"As St. Paul famously put it, 'When I was a child, I spake as a child, I understood as a child, I thought as a child. But when I became a man, I put away childish things.' Childish things. Not juvenile things. Also, there is a change in simply moving from being a struggling writer to being a published writer."

I frown. "Right," I say, even though I have no idea what he's talking about or what the hell St. Paul has to do with anything.

Steven stands and walks toward the door even though I really wish he would say more. "Keep at it," he tells me. "You'll get there. But don't expect me not to try to ride herd."

And finally, I am encouraged. It's not even that I think Steven's criticism is 100 percent correct. It's true, I can't picture him enjoying the crudity of *South Park*, the unbridled violence of a Tarantino film, or feeling nostalgia for the Jay-Z and DMX song "Money, Cash, Hoes." But I need his candor. Even if it hurts, even if it leaves my

Ego wounded, shuffling backwards with his eye black and his nose bloodied, I want him riding herd.

As he exits through the door to the study, I pick up the guitar from its stand in the corner, take a seat at the desk, and begin fiddling poorly with a tune.

Jewel, who sold over a million copies of a book of poems in which she supposedly misused the word "casualty," pops her head in.

"Done?" she asks.

"I guess."

She crosses her arms. "Did it ever occur to you that the actual reason you're a real drag right now has nothing to do with your dumb book? That maybe there are other things you're trying to avoid?"

I stare at her judgmental little blonde face. "Shut up, Jewel."

• • •

I have left the book alone for nearly a month now, and when I sit down to read it, to take a look with fresh eyes, it's not hard to pinpoint where Julie and Steven saw me careening off the rails.

Every writer attacks his or her work differently. Everyone has a different method, a different way to approach the monumental task of dragging a story from the head onto the page. Personally, I have to kick something around in my cranium for a while. It's not just a hat rack; it serves other functions, and I like to let it work something over, usually beginning with a scene or character and growing outward. By the time I jot down the first page, I usually have a pretty good idea where everything is going.

But with this book, I've just been winging it, and it shows. By the fifth chapter I'm off on tangents so wild, so inconsequential to the narrative and the idea, that even I have trouble figuring out what they're doing there. It reads more like a running diary than a fully realized notion, and as I read on, my gut sinks even further.

There is way too much self-pity. I'm a white, middle-class male who has had everything in life more or less handed to him—maybe not on a silver spoon but at least on a plastic tray from Buffalo Wild Wings.

There are way too many thematic non sequiturs. At some point, it seems as if I decided I was writing a psychoanalytic textbook of twentysomethings, which sounds like more fun than it reads (if you can believe that).

There is way too much about my sex life. I mean, in the version you're reading now, there's probably way too much about my sex life, but let's just say no one needs to know exactly what it feels like to have an orgasm while being choked with a belt.[178]

Yes, as I read my book straight from the screen of my laptop, I'm dismayed to see how far afield I've wandered from my original idea, but most of all, I'm disappointed to see how much of this book is about a girl who is no longer in my life. I knew for a while I had not been taking her departure particularly well, and I felt the urge to call her, to hear her voice, almost daily. I fought that urge with more resoluteness than I thought I had in me.

When I did call, it was for her birthday—which I figured was sort of like neutral relationship territory anyway. It was the first time we'd spoken in months, and the conversation was understandably a disaster. I didn't anticipate how much it would sting to hear that she had not folded into a sobbing mess, that she sounded as bright and full of joy as ever. It's a strange contradiction to hear the voice of someone you care about and hear all the things in it that you want to hear, but know that it is likely because of your absence. The follow-up call was worse, though: it came out that she was seeing someone.

And that he was a Red Sox fan.[179]

---

178 But if you really, *really* want to know, the word is: FreakNastyAwesome.

179 Now I don't even particularly like baseball. It's the only athletic endeavor where you absolutely have to be drunk to sit and enjoy a game. Red Sox fans, however, have a special place on my list of team-obsessed douche bags. Yeah, there was no curse, your team just sucked for the better part of a century. And now that they've won a couple of World Series, they still feel compelled to walk around pissing and moaning, the "woe is me" wafting off in pungent drafts. If we could put Boston in a bubble and just

I reacted poorly to this and—not surprisingly—slept with the first girl who had the luck to dial my phone number. She was a friend, and after it was over, lying on the floor mattress in my room, she said, "I'm worried about you."

I stared into the dark, allowing my surprise at this statement to bloom. It seemed I was being surprised all the time these days. Surprised at how soon my Love Interest had moved on; surprised how much this ate at me; surprised by how much I missed her—even now—lying here wishing without spite that this other girl could be her. "I wasn't aware I'd ever done anything to earn someone's concern," I said.

She was all soft brown hair and hot breath on my shoulder. "You're not as bad a person as you like to think," she said. "Not as cool as you think either. So tell me: are you okay?"

"Sure," I replied. "Life just doesn't work out the way you think it will. And it seems that I think if I can just dwell on that notion enough, it will change things."

Silent for a moment, she said, "Sometimes I cry for absolutely no reason."

I wasn't sure if that was meant to make me feel better, but at least it made sense: two extremely lost people looking for that often-mentioned shelter from the storm. I fell asleep that night thinking of that girl in Boston, as I would every night forward from that moment on.

So reading through my book again, I get a sense that I was trying to tell a story of how I wanted to change certain parts of myself— almost a confession or self-therapy in the most self-indulgent way. My hands have been inactive so far because this has just been a reading night, but now I move them to the keyboard. I delete from my hard drive an entire chapter called "Charlottesville," which dealt

---

deliver trophies to their dome every few months, maybe they'd shut up and the rest of us could stop hearing about it.

with my visits to Virginia while my Love Interest lived there. And that's when I hear it.

That's not the chapter you should be looking at.

I look over at my Id, who is lying sprawled out across my mattress. I should have smelled the whiskey.

Go to the chapter you called "Wildheart." He takes a long swig from a handle of Jack that seems to have bacon grease smeared across the label. From his inner pocket, he removes a stick of dried pork and rips off a chunk with his teeth. Chewing loudly, he says, *You'll find a better explanation there.*

"Wildheart" is another chapter I am ready to toss in the trash. It is solely about her, and I can only marvel at how depressing it will be if this book ever finds print. About halfway through the chapter, though, I begin to see what my Id is talking about. I'm obviously not going to reprint the entire thing, but I'll give you the most pertinent point, which is the chapter's namesake.

From the Now Defunct Chapter, "Wildheart"

A lady from a country of indeterminable origin once explained the whole situation to me perfectly.

When I was living in Wyoming and working as a boat wrangler with James, we used to have some long, long days. Despite working on beautiful Jackson Lake in the shadow of the Teton Mountains, we served tourists, who are certainly the dumbest animals you'll find in any national park. We spent most of our time on the docks either annoyed or unbearably bored, coming up with games like "Pretend the Gas Caddy is Your Friend and Take Pictures With It" or "Teach your Turkish Muslim Coworker American Swear Words."

Late one day an Asian family came by with a slip for a motorboat. The father then forgot something in the car and took one of the children with him to retrieve it, leaving me and his tiny wife standing on the end of the dock while a little boy ate the strap of a lifejacket I'd handed him. We had a lot of foreign tourists in Colter Bay, most of whom spoke almost no English, but this woman had a fairly decent grasp. She asked me where I was from, and I told her Ohio.

"Oh? I know Ohio," she said through a heavy accent. "Very good. Very good."

"I tend to think so," I said.

"And you work here for how long?"

"Just the summer."

"Then you go to school."

"No," I said. "Done with school."

"Done with school?" She nodded smiling. "What you do then?"

I shrugged. "I'm going to drive around the country until I run out of money." This was the standard answer I gave whenever chitchat led tourists to ask me this question.

"But where do you go?" she kept on.

"I don't know. Vancouver. Portland. L.A. I don't know. Wherever I can."

"You drive places?"

"Yeah, for as long as I can."

She laughed, a high-pitched, tittering sound made charming by her broad display of teeth. She wore a white visor to protect her eyes from the sun, and the shadow it cast on her face hid her eyes. "Oh," she said, like she finally understood, like I had just let her in on the joke. "You wildheart."

"Sorry?" I asked.

"You wildheart."

At first I thought she was saying "wired-heart" because of the "R"s and the "L"s, but the second time I heard it.

"Wildheart?" I said. "What does that mean?"

She threw up her arms and slapped them back down by her sides, an expression of happy acquiescence. "Wildheart. You go where you go."

I was tired and sweaty and more than a little cranky from a long day of dragging around motor boats and canoes and teaching tourists how to use the throttle and the kill switch and pumping gas and tethering the cruise ship to the dock. I was tired, so it didn't strike me then that this was an important conversation. Thinking back on this petite woman from somewhere on the other side of the world, I wish I had asked her where she got that word, what it actually meant, and most importantly, if "wildheart" is a good thing—a song for those who have the Fire in them—or a kind of curse. Of course, I'd like to think the former but fear the latter.

I sigh at my artfully worded self-aggrandizement.

That's some gooood writin', Tex, says my Ego, who is sitting on the corner of my trunk. He is also clearly drunk, mixing a flask of spiced rum into a cup with root beer before crushing the can and tossing it at me. *I'll tell you what, Spanky, this guy over here's gotta point.* He points to my Id. *He knows his stuff, and I'd listen to him if I was you.*

My Id holds up his drink in a toast.

"What?" I ask. "That I'm an asshole? I didn't need you two to tell me that."

My Id cackles. *You don't get it, do you, Markley, you sorry little prick?* He takes a straight razor from the pocket of his leather jacket and begins to scrape at the thick stubble, leaving a map of bloody nicks on his cheeks and throat. *What if I told you that tomorrow you were gonna meet some nice, pretty little lady, marry her in a year, work at Cars.com for five, and then move over to write columns for the Tribune? And then you'd move out to Schaumburg and commute because you'd want to live in a good school system for your two kids. How would you feel if I told you that?*

"I don't know. Disappointed."

My Id cracks up, looking from my Ego to me while he slaps the blankets and hops up and down on my bed. My Ego, enjoying the spectacle, claps along.

Disappointed! The smarmy motherfucker says disappointed! My friend, do you know how many people there are out there who would fucking kill for a life like that? Who to these cock-charmers, that sounds like a great deal? He takes a long swig from the bottle and passes it to my Ego, who trades him the flask of rum. *The reason that has no appeal for you, buddy-boy, is because—well, it's like you said in the chapter. You're restless.* He hisses the words and snaps his hands into fists. *You've got the Fire, and it makes you good at enjoying life and really, really, really fucking bad at making a woman happy.*

My Ego shakes his head in wonder at the wisdom of my Id. *Man, I fucking love this guy! C'mere, let me kiss you.* He springs on my Id, who attacks him by trying to goose him with the rum bottle.

As they wrestle, I say, "It's funny but I wonder if she—or anyone, for that matter—could ever compete with this itch. I sometimes think that you two are the only beings I'm beholden to."

C'mon, you little bastard! my Id cries. *Take it like a man!* He releases my Ego with his mission left unaccomplished and turns to me. *What you just said? Yeah, that's right. That's the stuff I'm talking about.*

"I don't know," I say. "Sounds like selfishness to me."

Who said it wasn't? retorts my Ego. *We all are what we are.*

"You're wrong," I say. "I love her."

The words are a surprise to me, but as soon as they're out of my mouth, I know they're true.

Of course, this sends both my Ego and Id into an outburst of laughter so violent that for a full minute they can do nothing but roll around on the bed and bray while intermittently taking snout-fuls of crushed-up painkillers from the crease of a pro-abstinence brochure. My Ego recovers first.

Markley, did we say that you didn't love her? Did that opinion ever come from either of these camps?

Fuck no, says my Id as he wipes tears of mirth from his eyes.

Of course you love her. What's not to love? She's hot!

And smart.

And hilarious.

And she gets you. She likes that you're weird and make jokes about fellatio.

And she's hot.

So fucking hot. Oh Christ-in-a-sex-swing, I would hit that so hard, day and night, season-to-season, year-goddamn-round. It'd be like that Dr. Seuss poem: in a car, in a bar, on the beach, with a peach—

Man, you have hit that, my Ego explains. *We're all the same guy.*

Oh, yeah! cries my Id, and the two of them high-five.

Our point, Markley, is that it's easy enough to love someone. But if you wanted her to love you back, then you owe her something. "Something" it turns out, is a steep price.

Oh, nice speech, jeers my Id. *Are all egos gay or just the really poetic ones?*

I ignore their back-and-forth and say, mostly to myself, "She had this wit about her, you know? Underneath this bright, approachable exterior lurked the gallows humor. When she got a sore throat, she'd say something like, 'I haven't been able to swallow anything for two days—so there goes my day job.' That quickness, that easy charm—it drove me wild." I laugh. "The people she hates the most are the ones that make jokes but aren't funny, right? She hates having to fake a laugh—I think because she loves to laugh, and it's a sound that's just so… loud, so joyful. She throws her head back, opens her mouth, and closes her eyes. Her whole body shakes with it."

My Id and Ego—my two most reliable sources of wisdom—eye me suspiciously from the mattress on the floor. Maybe it's all the painkillers they just snorted, but for once they are solemn.

"You know what I'm going to do already, don't you?" I ask them.

My Id shakes his head. *I'm warning you, pal, I'm not exactly stable.* To prove his point he gets up on his knees and begins gyrating on my mattress, whiskey sloshing around in its glass confines. *If you had any sense, you would go find a nice petite blonde chick and ask her if she's ever wondered what it's like to choke a guy with a belt.*

"I've already made up my mind," I say.

My Id and Ego exchange a glance.

Just don't say, says my Ego.

That we didn't warn you, my Id finishes.

• • •

"What if her boyfriend's there?" says Ritesh. "Markley, her boyfriend'll probably be there, you dumbass."

Ritesh and his girlfriend, Roochie, are not being helpful. I'm already halfway to Boston.

That day at work I told my boss I was feeling sick. I took the train home, packed a bag, and got in my car. I took the Dan Ryan down to the turnpike, then it was onward through Indiana to Ohio. In order to split up the sixteen-hour drive, I stopped for the night in Kent, Ohio, where Ritesh goes to school. When I told him why I needed to spend the night at his place and why he needed to take me to Walmart to help me buy flowers, he hit me on the arm. Really hard. "Okay, stupid, why didn't you think of that a year ago? God, Markley, you fucking retard."

It's nice to have friends.

Now we sit on the couch in Ritesh's apartment watching his roommate trash the Boston Celtics with the Cavs in a basketball video game. Ritesh's apartment is like a shrine to LeBron James with different styles of his jerseys hanging on the walls and one enormous poster where the King sits on a throne with lions docile at his heel. The child of Indian immigrants, Ritesh is probably the most American kid I know, from his sensitive palate for fast food to his ever-escalating penchant for driving forty miles over the speed limit. His broad, square face should probably replace Hamilton on the ten dollar bill.

"Her boyfriend won't be there," I tell the two of them.

"Why wouldn't he be?" asks Roochie. "I'm here at Ritesh's place."

"Because," I say definitively, "I told her I wanted to talk to her on the phone at a certain time. She's not gonna have some guy sitting in the living room while she talks to her ex-on-again-off-again guy-dude-lover-friend. Then, instead of calling her, I'll just knock on the door."

"And give her flowers. How come you never get me flowers?" she asks Ritesh.

Ritesh is incredulous. "Do you remember when I bought you that plant! I bought that plant for you, and what happened to it? You left it outside overnight in the cold and it died."

"That's not the point."

"You had the plant for less than a day," he says, laughing. "That counts as flowers. They're both plants, and you let the last plant die!"

"Guys, guys, guys," I interrupt. "You're missing the point of the story, which is not the flowers."

"Then why'd you have me drive your dumb ass to Walmart to buy flowers?" Ritesh asks.

"The point," I continue, "is that once during a fight, she recounted to me this one time from like senior year when I made fun of some kid who bought his girlfriend flowers for her birthday—which is so true! Flowers are such a stupid birthday present. But she remembered this, so during this fight I said to her, 'I didn't even know you liked flowers, and she says to me, 'It's not about the flowers, *Steve.*' Because flowers are inherently stupid, but that's what love is about: being really, really stupid."

I sit back in triumph. "Thus, the flowers."

Roochie looks at Ritesh. "I still don't see why her boyfriend wouldn't be there."

• • •

The next morning Ritesh is already gone when I wake up, and I grab my flowers from the pot filled with water where we dumped them last night, and I take off. The drive takes me ten hours, which unfortunately is too long spent in one's own head.

I try to make some phone calls and corral the remaining friends of Justin's whom I've targeted for giving his kid money, but it's difficult to avoid returning to a question that's been nagging me since I first dreamed up this bizarre idea to drive over a thousand miles to try to get back a girl: am I doing this for the book?

Think about it: what a great way to end a book, right? Arrogant, solipsist writer abandons arrogance and solipsism to win back the girl of his dreams. What a great story! So is this entire trip just my way of trying to cram real life back into the narrative of my book? And in doing so, am I cruelly exploiting a girl I supposedly care about?

Once, before we were dating, I was home for the summer and went up to Cleveland to hang out with her and a few other friends. That night, I volunteered to drop my not-yet Love Interest off at her house before driving back to Mount Vernon. A long-simmering crush had vaulted skyward that day, and I thought forlornly of fall semester, when she would be studying abroad in Luxembourg. Her mom insisted that I stay the night in the guest bedroom, seeing as how it was so late and I had a two-hour trip home. I did not want to do that because I knew I wouldn't sleep—not for a moment. I knew I'd lie awake all night and think of her just down the hall.

Her mom went to bed, and the two of us talked while I sipped at a Coke (using the excuse that I needed some caffeine for the drive). We talked about our mutual friends, about my fitful and brief female relationships, about her boyfriend, about school, about our newly declared majors, about politics, about books we were reading, about her parents' divorce, which shocked me in its messiness. When she told me that story, I saw uncanny strength and bravery in her humor and grace and refusal to offer even a hint of self-pity.

"I just can't believe that," I told her. "You're shockingly well-adjusted considering that story—you know that, right?"

She smiled and looked at the rim of her mug of hot chocolate, her thin lips pulling back to bare teeth and then returning as the smile faded—but faded softly so that when she spoke her face did not seem hard. "Well, if that's the worst thing to happen in my life,

I'll consider myself lucky. I try not to feel sorry for myself unless I have a whole can of vanilla frosting nearby."

"Frosting?"

"Sure. If I'm gonna feel all pitiful and stuff, I might as well get to eat frosting with a spoon."

I drained my Coke and set the dish in the sink. "You sure you don't want to stay?" she asked. "It's really no problem. I'll wake you up however early you need."

I wanted to see genuine hope in her face, hope that I would stay— but because I wanted to see it so badly, I knew I couldn't trust it.

My previous quick wit completely blew apart. "No, I really should get going. I have a lot of—um, stuff—and you know, just things. To do. Tomorrow," I explained.

When I lowered myself into the seat of my car, a shiny new '04 Corolla, I held my hand up in wonder because I couldn't stop it from shaking. Whipping it back and forth gently against the wheel, I laughed at myself. Then I sang Springsteen at the top of my lungs the rest of the way home.

So this memory wasn't far when I finally began to understand: when Julie first called to tell me that she loved the proposal, and she wanted to work with me, when I first saw a light at the end of the tunnel and the possibility that I might actually find a publisher, I told myself I was elated. Yet even as I walked around from day to day trying to enjoy this accomplishment, trying to bask in a little of the reward, I found, when it came down to it, I couldn't care less.

Because I hadn't told her.

There are those people in your life who you want to share your finest moments with. There's no point in drinking an expensive wine or sampling a delicacy by yourself, and the same goes for life's most crucial moments. My Love Interest was always the first person I wanted to get a hold of when I stumbled upon these instances. I wanted to watch her lovely eyes go wide and the pitch of her voice reach upward and the beautiful sound of her laugh when I told her that my book ends with the twist that I'm actually dead and have been a ghost this whole time.

Book or no book, I need this girl's laugh, her eyes, her strength back in my fucking life.

So driving to her with my Walmart flowers in the backseat, I sing Bruce Springsteen for several hundred miles just like after the night she revealed her love of frosting, wailing away about the Promised Land at the top of my lungs, because I am young and dumb and impetuous but one day will not be, so I might as well wring all the joy I can out of it now.

Right now gas costs no less than $3.50 per gallon and tops $4 in most places. Fortunately, my Corolla—faithful since I drove her off a Columbus lot in the summer of 2003—still pumps out over thirty-five miles for each gallon. Over the border through Pennsylvania and on through the Appalachian Mountains, slicing through a tip of New York, then Connecticut, buds on the trees signaling spring, gas stations where cashiers begin to talk in jaunty New England accents, up into Massachusetts, onto the turnpike, stopping at the last rest area before Boston, going into a toilet stall and making violent vomiting-like motions that end up as a series of belches and dry heaves. Then I'm into the city, paying the tolls, following my carefully mapped directions, which slice through sections of Harvard and Cambridge. I creep along, looking for street signs, get lost a couple of times, turn around once or twice, but suddenly I am standing outside a small, junky building on a street called Ivaloo, which sounds like a species of bird in a sci-fi movie. I have the dozen roses in one hand and with the other, I rap on the door.

It is, of course, the wrong apartment.

When I find the right door moments later, I knock on it.

She answers still wearing her workout clothes, including baggy sweatpants, an old, long-sleeved pink shirt, and a sweat-soaked headband. Her hair is a mess, her makeup a bit smeared around her dirty mojito eyes. She looks amazing.

"No waaay," she says slowly, a grin spreading on her face.

"Hey," I say, as she notices the flowers dangling from my hand. "Sorry. I didn't want to talk on the phone anymore." I check the background of her kitchen, but no boyfriend with a Red Sox hat appears present. Of course, I had sixteen hours to plan out what I was going to say, and I did, but that is all gone now, so all I can do is start talking and hope for the best, beginning with an explanation of why I sound a bit insane.

"So I had sixteen hours in the car to try to think of what I would say when I got here, but now that I'm standing here, looking at you, my heart is kind of breaking, so you're just going to have to stand there and bear with me while I babble. But—uh—basically, it's like this: I know I've been a disappointment to you before, and that goes with the territory, and I'm sorry because you're the last person in my life I've ever wanted to let down. I have this fire in me and it makes me really good at some things and really, really shitty at others, but I don't want to be shitty at those things anymore. I don't want to be the guy you can't believe in. I want to be the guy who brings you flowers and says stupid things to make you laugh and generally does all the things that you deserve, and I'm not saying I'm going to be able to change overnight, and I sincerely doubt I'll ever be perfect or even approximating a person who deserves you, but I'm asking for the chance to at least try because you really do make me want to be the best version of myself, and you just look—So. Fucking. Beautiful right now, I feel like this is the part where that U2 song 'One' comes on, and I kiss you."

So I do. I kiss her like some sappy romantic comedy with Hugh Grant or maybe Matthew McConaughey.

Chapters written, chapters erased.

When we pull apart, I leave my hands on her hips and her eyes are a plane with a cargo full of diamonds exploding over a rain forest, and I say, "Oh, and also: I wrote a book and got an agent for it, so there's a good chance it'll get published, and it turns out it's kind of about you."

She's grinning madly but somehow finds the audacity and comic timing that should have stopped surprising me years ago.

"Jeez," she says. "Who would have thought Steve was such a pussy?"

The Footnotes

Remember way back in Chapter 9 when I refused to capitalize the first word of every new paragraph? Well I have an[180]

---

180 even better idea for this one, and I know, you're already freaked out about over-working your eyes, but trust me, I'll find some big thematic reason to tie this technique into the narrative, I'm sure.

For now, though, let's focus on where I find myself, which is best described as intellectually stranded. It's now creeping up on a year since I first began this weird, wicked project, and although I've made phenomenal progress by nabbing an agent, I'm in uncharted territory, which couldn't be more evident from my disaster of a book proposal.

When I send it to Steven, he writes back with appropriate bluntness.

"This is not very good," he says in an email. "You don't sound excited about the book, so why should an editor?"

You know how sometimes you know something without knowing it? That's how I felt about his critique of the proposal. I know something is good when I'm having fun writing it, and putting together that proposal was not fun. It was the opposite of fun. It was Fun's archnemesis, who frequently kidnaps Fun's family, threatens to blow up the city Fun has sworn to protect, and, when it captures Fun, puts Fun through ghastly methods of torture.

Steven sends me his take on the proposal—a brief three pages, sure, but I am almost embarrassed at how good his version is compared to mine. I print it out at work.

The night before I leave for Kdoe's wedding back in Ohio, James tells me to look for how many Obama house signs I spot on the drive. After that initial scare at the end of the summer, we've come to the agreement that Barack is going to wipe the floor with McCain, but it's too early to get cocky. "I just donated another fifty to the campaign," I tell him. "How much influence do you think I've bought in an Obama administration?"

"Oh, dude," he says. "The Steve Markley PAC is going to be running the country. What are you gonna lobby for?"

I tick the goals off on my fingers. "That the Star-Spangled Banner be replaced with 2Pac's 'White Manz World.'"

He follows along on his own fingers. "'Kay, cool."

"Everybody gets a tax cut except for Grover Norquist, who will pay 98 percent of his income directly to welfare recipients."

"Check."

"We bomb Belarus back to the stone age."

"Had it coming."

"And white chicks for everyone!"

"What about Hannity and O'Reilly? Shouldn't they be made to make out in public or something?"

"You're right, man. And Sean Hannity and Bill O'Reilly have to make out in public every Tuesday."

"*And* finger each other's butts."

"And finger each other's butts."

We laugh. "Pretty soon," I tell him, "no one is going to know what we're talking about anymore. It'll just be us cracking up at our own hilarity."

"I think we're there."

Elliott strolls through the living room. "Pane's?" he asks, referring to our favorite sandwich joint.

"Not tonight, man."

"You going to Cleveland tomorrow?"

I tell him only to pick up my Love Interest. "Then we're going to my buddy Kdoe's wedding."

"That's cool. How's it going with her?"

It's been almost two months since I made the drive to Boston. In that time, my Love Interest and I have managed to see each other twice, once in Cleveland at her friend's wedding and once when she visited Chicago. "So far so good," I say.

"What's next? Isn't she in school?"

"Well, she's supposed to start on her master's in Boston, but that's two years. We're trying to figure something out."

Indeed, I am shocked by how little it occurred to me beforehand that once I drove to Boston, all of the same problems would still exist. I was so focused on getting her back, I chose to ignore that we still lived over a thousand miles apart, that she had built a life there and I in Chicago, and that one way or another, one of us was going to have to give that life up.

Bringing me violently out of my lull, Erik suddenly appears, crashing through the front door like Kramer.

"Whoa! Who's this guy?" says James.

He strides into the room, unshaven, hair askew, dirty yellow sweatshirt, suitcases in tow. "Look at these cum-guzzling sluts," he says of us.

"Where've you been?" Liam asks, coming out of his room adjacent to the living room.

"Salt Lake," he says. Political organizing takes Erik randomly across the country, so he will disappear from our house for weeks at a time only to resurface at unpredictable intervals. "Mormon bitches everywhere." He looks at my suitcase. "Where are you off to?"

"Ohio, baby. My buddy's getting married."

"Oh, that shithole, Mount Vernon?"

Whoa, now you're all like: "What are we doing back up here in the non-footnote portion of the text?" Have the footnotes now become the story and the story the footnotes? Am I only doing this to[181]

"Better than fucking Zanesville," I say of Erik's hometown. "Hey, what does a guy from Zanesville say after getting a blowjob?"

"I don't know, what?"

"'Sit, Fido! Sit!'"

Hearty laughter ensues.

We spend the rest of the night drinking beer, watching political coverage, and arguing about women, elections, drugs, and jobs. The five of us haven't hung out as a unit in quite some time, and it feels good just to get the book out of my mind, just to be twenty-four and talk about the problems associated with being that age and trying to cut a niche in the world. Liam wants to ride his bike along the California coast and up to Alaska. Erik wants to be neck-deep in a major political campaign in two years. Elliott wants to dream up the next Google, make a fortune, and retire to play guitar for the rest of his life. James wants to form a band, quit his job, and write songs where he professes his love to *New York Times* columnist Maureen Dowd. We all have it in us, this idea that we can pull the stars down and make them our own. It's good to sit and hear how it plays out in conversation, swirling and melting and reforming. The next day I'm bound for Ohio.

181   "Amuse you," I tell my Love Interest when she asks why I'm telling her about the door that leads into the garage of my parents' house.

We are getting ready for bed, and I'm explaining to her how I snuck in and out of the house when I was younger. The door to the garage was really the only viable option, but it squeaked and rattled like hell, which meant my mom could usually figure out when I was doing something I shouldn't be doing (which was fairly frequently and required a lot of eggs and toilet paper). One time she locked me out and made me knock to avoid sleeping out in the woods.

"Hell was thus raised," I explain to my Love Interest. "And much amusement had by all."

"Oooh, you egged houses? It makes me so hot to think of little Steve egging houses."

"Eggs were unleashed, baby. That's just how the crew rolled. You stepped up or you backed down."

"Oh my," she says. "My loins. What happened if you 'backed down'?"

"We took you out on the playground and beat you with chains."

She throws back her head and laughs. As we sit in my childhood room where posters from *Pulp Fiction*, *A Clockwork Orange*, and a map of global death penalty statistics hint at a very strange kid coming of age, I decide that I can now recategorize things.

"Things," you see, are no longer hit and miss. They have taken a seat decisively in the "doing well" section of the cafeteria. Our calls are frequent. Her voice no longer falters when we speak of an uncomfortable choice coming for one of us on the horizon. "We'll figure it out," she says, and I think she is right because this is a girl selfless enough to work in a nutrition program for underprivileged children and brush it off with a joke about padding her résumé. This one, in other words, is a keeper.

While she's in the bathroom brushing her teeth, I take a moment to drag my proposal and Steven's version from my bag and place them side-by-side. I've already begun to rewrite the most problematic chapters. I feel like I've managed to pare down and refocus the story so that it finally reads like an account of my journey rather than a ride

Are you upset because I'm ignoring the conventional rules of footnote usage, and the regular blocks of text have nothing to do with each other, and the footnotes continue a thought rather than adding a new one? Well, it's like what our esteemed president Jimmy Carter once said:[182]

---

through a twisted hall of mirrors only vaguely resembling an experience. After sending Steven the rewritten third chapter (which is, for the most part, the version you read at the beginning of this book), he wrote back, "This is about a billion times better… This has the voice of chapters 1 & 2, which cracks wise but is still so likeable… This is excellent work. It may have taken you awhile, but not everything out of the gate is going to be a winner. Congratulations." He makes a few other minor comments—gripes and praise—but the sum total is that I finally feel like I'm not insane. That I *do* have something here.

The proposal is still giving me fits, however. Reading through both versions again, the differences between my original and Steven's retake are stark. A sample sentence from the first paragraph of my attempt: "*Publish This Book* would have broad appeal to a number of different reader constituencies."

I can already hear the sound of clinking silverware as editors search for a fork with sharp enough tines to quickly penetrate their eyes.

Excited, I think. *This is my book. This is my shot at a lifelong dream, and right now I sound like I'm selling a used Mercury Mariner. It has to express why a person browsing at a bookstore would pick it up, read a couple pages, and want to spend the money on it. I have to be excited about it before they will.*

I take a moment to jot a few notes on Steven's version. I'm still afraid to sit down at a computer and actually type. My fear is that I'm on the verge of blowing this, and that after having come so close, I might not be able to get back on the horse again. This isn't an agent sending me a couple of interested emails. This is the best chance I've ever had, and I feel all the appropriate pressure to make it work or risk this drive, this purpose I've felt most of my life relegated to some kind of scrap heap of lost passions.

I hear the sink shut off, and my Love Interest returns while I toss the two bundles of paper back into my bag.

"Watcha doing?" she asks.

"Eh. The book. Just… stressing. I don't know."

"When can I read it?" she pleads, folding her arms around me. I've been fielding this question since I told her about the book, but it's not ready yet. Not for her lovely eyes, at least, and this is what I tell her now. "Hmm…just as long as I sound pretty and wonderful," she muses.

"So lie, lie, lie. Got it."

She laughs. "Yes. As many flattering falsehoods as possible, please." She breathes me in. "Now shut up. Less talky, more letting me climb on you like a jungle gym."

I crack up and then lean in to kiss her.

182   "Sweep this shit up, you lazy pussy."

I take the broom from Ian. "You smell like a trash can," I tell him.

"Man, I've slept like four hours in the last two nights. I'm all caffeine right now."

In high school, my friends and I spent a lot of nights at Ian's house out in the country.

A strip of concrete with a lot of blind curves called New Zion Road will take you out there (and be sure to watch for deer unless you really want to have to buy a new car not the color of doe innards). Sitting on the empty outskirts of Knox County, overlooking farmland on three sides and a serene pond on the other, the home couldn't be a better teenage playground unless it had an aboveground swimming pool… which his parents eventually built, followed by an enormous wraparound deck.

Now it is our Fourth of July party, which will precede Kdoe's wedding the next day. As I diligently shuffle leaves off the side of the deck, the guests begin to arrive: Ritesh, Phil, Justin, Loren, Jaxson, a slew of other Mount Vernon High School class of 2002 graduates, and—looking like some weird genetic mishap where each of our gene combinations melted apart—our parents. My Love Interest is immediately inundated by the other parents who want to know who she is. I chat with Justin's mother and Phil's father. My mom and Phil's mom reprise their conversation about growing up in Dayton, which is now a theme every time they see each other.

Kdoe hands the six groomsmen a glass of Guinness as our wedding party gifts. Ian and I flip beef, chicken, and tofu kabobs on the grill. The house is crowded and alive. Everyone wants to hold Jaxson, who by now has grown a bit and become far more aware. His eyes stay open, and he looks at you with a face so bright and bewildered. Like he may be thinking: "Whoa. What the fuck is wrong with this giant? That's not either of the two giants I'm used to. This giant is all weird-looking and smells funny. What are these noises he's making? Oh, those noises are pretty funny. Haha! Wow, great noises, giant! Oh man, priceless! You weird giant bastard, where did they get you? What are—whoa! Where are you taking me? Where am I going? What the—*What the fuck is this? Who is this fourth giant? What the fuck is wrong with this thing, it looks like a monster! Jesus fucking Christ where are the two giants who normally make the noises! Where's the giant that gives me the food? Get one of them! This giant is fucked! Completely fucked, do you hear me? Am I not loud enough right now? Is anybody fucking listening to me? HOLY FUCKING SHIT! Now it's bouncing me around! Now this fucking giant is bouncing me around like a fucking lunatic. FOR THE LOVE OF FUCK SOMEBODY HE—*Oh, hey this giant again! Not the food-giving giant, but this one's okay. All right, not bad. Yeah, I like *that* bouncing. That's some good bouncing right there. You're okay, familiar, non-food-giving giant. Oh, I just shit myself, by the way. Get on that."

Anyway, the party progresses and it is a feeling of being home—not just because we are all home in the literal sense, but because the jokes are the same, the conversation is familiar, the smiles, the laughter all ring true. As my Love Interest puts it to me, "I'm this close with maybe two people I went to high school with. You guys have this weird, extended-family thing going."

"Sorry, does that freak you out?" I ask, pushing a strand of that bright blonde hair behind her small ear.

"No! I think it's great. I just like being around and pretending I'm a part of it."

So the party continues, and I make my rounds, trying to soak in everyone while I can.

I find Justin balancing a plate of food and a beer in the kitchen. I sidle up beside him.

"How's it going?" I ask.

He nods. "Good."

We chew on food. I try another approach. "How're things?"

"Good," he says. "Better."

I nod. "Good."

"How're things with her?" he asks, referring to my Love Interest.

"Good," I say, smiling.

"Good," he says.

"We're making a bonfire tonight after the parents leave. Just like old times. You should stick around."

He shakes his head. "Can't. We gotta take Jaxson home."

"Right," I say, because Justin is *the parents* now. "That makes sense. No point in exposing him yet to his real family."

Justin grins. "Yeah, I told Loren, I have only one rule: No leaving our son alone with Markley. Or Ian or Phil. Or Ritesh. Or Kdoe. In fact, just keep him away from all those guys no matter what."

I laugh. "Good rule. Looking ahead to the problem areas. I like that."

Ian taps both of us on the shoulder. "Present time," he says.

It takes four of us to drag out Kdoe's wedding gift, a 42-inch hi-def TV. His eyes light up the way a child's might if on Christmas morning he got an actual fighter jet instead of a toy. "Something told me you'd like it," says Ritesh.

"I thought it was a joke," says Kdoe. "I was about to punch one of you guys for being a bunch of assholes."

"Ah, Kevin, now I have so many more reasons to hang out with you," says Phil.

"Finally, someone with a really awesome television," says Ian.

"In fact," continues Phil, "I think mostly I wanted to get this TV for you so I could watch it when I come over."

"Thanks, guys," says Kdoe, hugging his gift awkwardly with those bony runner's arms.

"See, you don't even need a wife now," Ritesh says. "This is much better."

We take a picture with all of us and the TV, and I hold Jaxson up there, so he can be in his first group picture with his new uncles. Then Ian tugs at my shirt and beckons me back into his house. We go to the back room where we've stashed the cards and the enormous check Ian's mother has made, just like Publisher's Clearing House. We take it all outside, and on our way, we collect the party guests, ushering them down to the lower deck beside the swimming pool. Justin stands talking to Loren, oblivious. He's explaining something, smacking the back of his hand against his palm, and I can practically hear him explaining baseball statistics or investment strategies or giving some other very Justinesque lecture. He sees us coming down the stairs and stops speaking—not surprised, only curious. Justin's parents look up as well. A few people are still talking, so I make a general announcement.

"Hey! Guys! Everyone! Can we have your attention for a moment?" And we get the hush we're looking for.

Ian takes it. "So," he begins. "Justin, Loren... Basically we all wanted to come up with a gift for you guys that would be better than anything any one of us alone could get you, so what we did is went to our friends—your friends, our friends, all of our parents—and we each put in a hundred bucks." My eyes move from Justin's confused face to Ian's steady one. He is a compact, lean, goofy guy with wide lips and large white teeth. Rarely do I see him say anything too serious, but the honesty now on his face suits him. "When we began," he continues, "we thought it would just be the six or seven of us guys, but once we got going, it turns out you have a lot of people who like you—"

"Much to our surprise," I helpfully add.

Look, this book is hardly about my friend Justin having a kid. That book would be quite a bit more complicated to write and would require an unraveling and examination of so many people's lives, we'd never have time for jokes about cussing babies. In fact, when I began this book, Justin was a footnote. My Love Interest was

---

"So this check is for you guys. Two thousand dollars toward little Jaxson's future college education. Just as long as he doesn't go to Duke or Notre Dame," he says.

This gets a small laugh. It's now my turn. I step beside Justin and Loren. I have a bottle of Rolling Rock in my hand. I look across all these familiar faces. The air is warm, the day shining and soft around the edges.

"I just want to say real quickly that the reason it was so easy to get this money together is because there are a lot of people who are with you on this." I pause. This is one of those moments where I wish I could step out of time, sit alone at a desk, and write what I want to say with a chance to edit and revise before I step back into the real world and let it leave my lips. Everyone waits for me to continue. I feel a tight, joyous smile flit across half my face. "Jaxson's a lucky kid," I say. "He's starting out with a lot of really good people in his corner." I hold up the Rolling Rock in a toast. "So we just want you to know, we love you guys. Cheers."

The applause rattles and glasses and bottles are clinked and digital cameras click and buzz and cheers are shouted into the summer and the rest of the crowd quickly inundates the young couple. I slip away.

I take up beside Ian at the grill. He says, "We did good, Markley."

I nod. "I think I got my one good deed for my life out of the way, at least. It's all hedonism from here on out."

I glance back over my shoulder at Justin and am a little surprised to see him wiping tears from his eyes. It may be the first time I've seen him cry since we went to our last funeral together, which was sophomore year of high school. Quickly, I look away, but not before I feel that little lump with all its jagged edges rise into my throat, pushing past my sinuses and into my face. Ian and I flip kabobs and laugh about that one time... (Which "one" time? Who cares which one time? All of them.)

Justin continues to grip his enormous fake check while Loren holds their child. The two of them exchange a glance, a look that almost serves as an inside joke between them. I am both curious and envious. I will never know the specific kind of emotion and intensity that has passed between these two friends of mine. They have their own epic inside joke going that no one else can ever be in on.

Justin finally walks over to me and Ian. "So I hear you two were the masterminds of this."

"We figured golf clubs wouldn't really do your son any good," I tell him.

"Especially if he's as shitty as you," Ian adds.

Justin puts his arms around us, and we three young men hug as awkwardly as you might imagine. "Thanks, guys," he says. "I truly mean that. Thanks."

"No problem," I tell him. "But when I knock up a chick, I expect payback."

He smiles and starts back to Loren.

"With interest, Justy!" I call after him. "Inflation! Think of the inflation!"

a footnote. Yet as I got out of those first few chapters, I began to see what my problem would be: sometimes the footnotes to your story become the story itself.

That's how I look at that day at Ian's house, when a good chunk of the people I love and care about the most in this world were eating the same chips and dip and kabobs and salad and cookies and cake; when we all arrived from our separate corners of the country—Chicago, New York, L.A., Boston, Ohio, Alaska—and we all brought beer and we all had stories from our new lives, but they weren't really as good as the ones we already knew so well. And later, after[183]

---

183 Justin has left, we sit around the campfire in Ian's backyard, cooking marshmallows, drinking, and looking up at the bazillion stars that cook the dark space above our heads. The next night, we will walk down a grassy outdoor aisle and watch our friend get married. Phil and Ritesh will give a rambling, amusing give-and-take speech as Kdoe's best men before he dances with his bride to the tune of Bob Dylan's "All I Really Wanna Do." Justin will laugh more that day than I've seen in months, and Ian will spill food on himself. We will laugh when Ritesh can't figure out his cufflinks, and my Love Interest will throw her head back and cackle until tears pop out of her eyes when I make a well-timed comment about chocolate sauce and her low-cut dress. We will rehash our old victories just to make sure we won and chalk the old losses up to bad luck. We'll dance madly into the early morning. We'll steal away to furtively make love and laugh about how badly we fail at it later.

But the moment I'm talking about now is under those stars. Living in the city, you forget how they can look, how they can make you forget to breathe. That night and those stars make me think of the scope of things. Scope is an important concept because it is about the endless capacity of life's possibilities. For instance, say you have a young man who begins to measure his life only in its immediacy, who wants everything so fast and so intensely that he begins to look past the footnotes, and all he sees is story story story, forward progress, logical conclusions wrapped up in tight, cohesive packages. He then forgets about the Scope, which is remembering that footnotes will not only pop up with alarming regularity but that occasionally they will be the finest part of the manuscript.

So we sit around the fire and eat charred, gooey marshmallows that won't wipe off our fingers in the grass and drink cheap Natty Light made even cheaper by Ohio's low sales tax and steal glances at the stars and wonder if there's really anything more to it all than this.

TWENTY-ONE

So You Know What Happens with This Book

When I get back to Chicago, I take Steven's version of the proposal, set it next to mine, and meld the two together. Two days later I send it to Julie. Within hours, she writes back with the words: "It sings!" By the end of the week, she is unloading it onto the desks of editors at publishing houses.

Now it is time to dispense with the suspense.

Obviously, this book got published because you're sitting here with your grubby mitts on it. It would be a pretty cool-ass trick if I could somehow end the book with the major revelation that the book never actually made it to print, and somehow what you hold in your hand right now is *not* my book but maybe just a compilation of sunbathing tips or a motel Bible. (Kind of like Edward Norton finding out he's actually Brad Pitt in *Fight Club*.) Alas, that is well outside of my skill as a writer, so we'll have to stick to the facts (as I see them).

Remember how way, way back at the beginning of the second chapter, I wisely declared that in life you go through long periods of stagnation only to have the shit hit the fan all at once?

That was prescient, considering how closely the period of stagnation in the early fall of 2008 mirrors the stagnation that sparked this book in the early fall of 2007.

Julie begins by sending the proposal to editors she thinks will look favorably upon it. She never really explains why this would be, but usually the words "young," "hip," and the phrase "will get it" are involved.[184]

The responses Julie gets back are encouraging in that they do not read, "Mr. Markley has a knack for finding the basest elements of a narcissistic culture of self-reflective memoir and amplifying them to a point that frightens and embarrasses the reader. I don't know where you found this young man, but ask the rehab clinic if they can accommodate him awhile longer or if the plastic on the furniture has been completely spoiled by his ever-escalating amounts of regurgitated bile."

Here are a few of the responses Julie forwards my way.

From: "Jane"[185] of Simon and Schuster
To: J___@aol.com
Subject: RE: Publish This Book by Stephen Markley

Hi Julie,

Thanks so much for sending me PUBLISH THIS BOOK. Stephen is clearly a very talented writer, and I really enjoyed his sharp wit and self-deprecation. I did, however, find it a bit too self-indulgent and circular, and while reading the proposal was great fun, I'm not sure the concept could sustain itself at book length. I regretfully have to pass, but thank you so much for giving me an opportunity to read, and I'm sure you'll find a great home for this project.

Best,
"Jane"

---

184 "Hip" now apparently describes individuals who wear tennis shoes out on Saturday night and think it's fun to discuss infrastructure investment and women's education in developing countries.

185 Obviously the editors of these houses are not weirdos who put their own names in ironic quotations. I have disguised their identities here so they will not know I'm coming for them when I use my millions from this book to run them out of the publishing industry. That's right, I'm coming for you "Jane!"

From: "John" of HarperCollins
To: J____@aol.com
Subject: RE: Publish this Book by Stephen Markley

Hi Julie,

A million apologies for my delinquency! Stephen is super
talented, but as much as I appreciate the Eggers comparison,
I don't necessarily agree that a book about the process of
writing a book (while a clever idea!) will automatically reel in
the Eggers, A.J. Jacobs, and/or Klosterman audiences. The
book isn't an ode to pop culture, and it's not really an armchair
traveler's memoir. The category is curious. I think it will find
readers who work in books, and perhaps some working writers,
but I'm just not seeing the bigger audience. So, I'll defer to
those who are more optimistic about its commercial prospects.

All best,
"John"

From: "Jim" of Perseus Books
To: J____@aol.com
Subject: RE: Publish This Book

Dear Julie,

I've had a chance to review the material, and while I do
find the project to offer some potentially interesting insight
into the desire of today's twentysomethings to be famous/
successful simply by being and expressing themselves, I worry
that a large chunk of the audience for this (young people who
could identify with Stephen) would be too focused on their
own quests to be published to pay to read about the author's.

There's a very good possibility that other publishers will disagree with this assessment, and I wish you and Stephen all the best pitching this particular project to other houses. I also hope that you will stay in touch and that should Stephen find a different subject to write about, you might consider sharing that with us, as well. He writes with a distinct voice and considerable wit, and I'd be interested to see it applied to a subject other than himself. But as is, this project in particular unfortunately isn't for us.

Thanks and best,
"Jim"

This last one I find particularly intriguing. *A subject other than myself?* I think. What the fuck is that guy talking about? Or does he mean like how *I* affect climate change or how *I* eat cheeseburgers or how *I* deal with the co-pay for my health insurance or how *I* feel about investment portfolios or how *I* hate celebrity magazines? Sure, I suppose those could be interesting topics.

In all seriousness, I find a lot of solace in how far the rejections are from dismissive. I can feel myself pushing at a barricade here, chipping the concrete and warping the steel that has held me out before.

• • •

But what becomes even more interesting is that I've somehow ended up trying to publish my first book as the landscape of the publishing industry undergoes major upheaval.

How are books published? Who decides which books are worthy of landing on a printed page and distributed across the country at an enormous cost?

Let's say you are a writer named George Blooney and you have a book about how awesome it is to eat jelly beans. Your agent sends your book to a bunch of big New York publishing houses like Penguin, Knopf, and let's say Candy Media, Inc. Ideally, all three houses would want a fascinating new book that sheds such fine light on America's love of jelly beans. In this case, they would start a bidding war, pushing up the amount of money they want to advance you for the book. Knopf bids $20,000 but then Penguin offers $25,000. Finally, Candy Media—recognizing the kinship— jumps in with a whopping bid of $40,000 and wins.

More likely, however, Candy Media simply offers you, George Blooney, a $20,000 advance, and you take it, ensuring yourself half of that money now and the other half when you deliver your jelly bean memoir. After your book earns back your advance (in other words, your royalties add up to $20,000 from the book), you can start to earn additional royalties on each book sold.

This is the standard model—and one that may no longer be working so well for publishers.[186]

The publishing industry faces declining sales and myriad challenges—challenges that exist even before the economy blows up in mid-September 2008. First of all, people are buying fewer and fewer books, and no one really knows why. Perhaps the expansion of Internet media has given people more options for their reading material. The Internet is free, and the information comes in nice, bite-size nuggets. Perhaps people are simply getting stupider (although I don't like this explanation because any student of history can see that people have pretty much always reveled in being stupid).

Whatever the reason, this leads publishers to a conundrum: how do we sell books? And who are we selling them to? Unfortunately, it turns out there is no decent way to predict which books take off and which books fail miserably. Standard marketing practices

---

186 Lest I be accused of piggy-backing on the ideas of others: Many of my opinions of the publishing world began gestating under Steven's tutelage, but there are a few fascinating articles that provoked much thought on the topic, including: (Kachka, Boris. "The End." *New York Magazine*. September 14, 2008.) and (Rich, Motoko. "Publishing Displays Its Split Personality." *New York Times*. November 25, 2008.)

simply have no bearing on what people read. So publishers find themselves marketing the piss out of a book like *Requiem for Jelly Beans*, jamming ads in magazines and newspapers, pumping it up with a prime review from Michiko Kakutani,[187] flying the author around the country for speaking engagements—and yet still no one buys the book.

This has led publishing houses to the "blockbuster strategy." The blockbuster strategy involves selling a shit-ton of one specific book that essentially earns the house all of its profit while the rest of the publisher's authors must scrape to make money on their respective works. So publish a hit book like *Harry Potter* or *The Da Vinci Code* and then let the stratospheric sales of that book support the house while it prints two dozen other authors who might break even or make a pittance. In publishing, profit margins are small.

This strategy could best be summarized by the following piece of advice I have imagined a corporate publishing house CEO telling his editors:

Okay, people, we have no fucking idea what people like. Publish a little of everything, and as soon as one of these shitkickers hits the jackpot, give him a million fucking dollars to write another one—Oh! And find half a dozen of these other writer fucks to copy it, and then get those books on shelves ASAP. Now where the fuck is my squeezy stress ball? God, you people are miserable pricks.

Thus we readers end up with the shelves of our bookstores lined with volume after volume detailing people who learn lessons from pets or women who get divorced and then find happiness in some exotic locale or thrillers where investigators uncover historical

---

187 "Blooney invokes the very essence of the American ideal in this elegant, perhaps even transformative, undertaking. *Requiem for Jelly Beans* strikes at the heart of a sour age and finds sweetness."
—Michiko Kakutani, *New York Times*

clues to unravel some greater mystery—with danger and intrigue to boot.

The race is always on to find the blockbusters, which in turn leads to publishers doling out massive advances to secure the authors of those blockbusters.

Take our old friend James Frey, for example. Following the smashing success and subsequent scandal of *A Million Little Pieces*, Frey wanted to publish his first novel, *Bright Shiny Morning*. Despite his taint, it's rumored that Harper paid Frey $1.5 million for the book, figuring a controversial author will sell whether he's an asshole or not. After an initial print run of 300,000 copies, Frey's novel sold only 65,000 (according to Bookscan). This left Harper short about $1.06 million, which is the danger of the blockbuster strategy.

A business that began as a bunch of rich, eccentric gentlemen wanting to spread the written word long ago shifted to a familiar corporate structure. The names Knopf or Harper or Straus or Farrar or Giroux—those all were once actual people. Then in the '60s, the houses began to consolidate, and these houses were absorbed into media conglomerates. Now you have approximately five media moguls (like our old friend, Emperor Palpatine) controlling most of the publishing industry while independents and midsized publishers battle at the fringes.

This means safe bets. Candy Media does not want to take on those risky projects because it has to pay for the printing, distribution, and marketing of every book. Why take on something bizarre and intriguing when you can print another five books about a warlock who must come of age at a sorcery training camp or a guy's beagle helping him overcome an eating disorder?

Thus when your average editor gets a manuscript or proposal on his desk that describes a book about its own path to publication and seems to have an obsession with toilet humor, he must do a simple cost-benefit analysis: artistic merits be damned, will this book push paper?

This has led to obscene amounts of money being wasted on fairly awful books and the entire medium dissolving even further as powerhouse booksellers like Amazon.com and Barnes & Noble control more and more of the market share.

This is the publishing environment that I—and countless other unpublished writers—are up against. It's difficult to break in unless you have a "platform" from which to work.[188] The bottom line is that publishing is far from what writers like to think it is, which is some kind of benevolent multi-armed god of literature and culture plucking genius from the Earth and lifting it to the Heavens so its author can be recognized and fawned upon. No, publishing is a business, and the only real questions one has to be ready to answer is, "Who the hell is this guy?" and "Why will people want to buy his book?"

As Steven puts it to me after I forward him a few of the rejections notes, "This basically says, 'This book sounds really exciting and great but I'm too much of a coward to fight for it.'"

Julie likewise seems unperturbed and chalks it all up to editors who are risk-averse. Maybe they didn't see how the concept could sustain a whole book or maybe the editor liked it but the publisher balked.

Personally, I don't blame them. I'm not even sure if the book is sustainable at this point, and I'm almost finished with the son of a bitch.

• • •

The problem is that these replies don't all come the first two weeks. They come slowly, achingly, numbingly over the course of months, each one so far removed from the other that I can't add up what they are saying: they like the idea, they like the writing, but the book sounds unsustainable.

But again, obviously this book did get published, so let's dispense with the drama and cut to the chase.

---

188 A "platform" basically means that you're already famous. For instance, if you're Kevin Federline or Joe the Plumber. That would help a lot.

For this, it will be helpful to utilize the time-honored tradition of the narrative-advancing montage where an incredible amount of emotional or physical progress is accomplished in the space of one song. This montage will cover every montage-worthy thing that occurred in my life over the summer of 2008, right up until fate steps in. So slip on your favorite tune for the following section, but I highly recommend downloading "Airplane/Primitive" by The Slip, which I feel properly encapsulates the excitement, the wonder, the melancholy of the summer of 2008:

A Narrative-Advancing Montage

By Time, Fate, or God
(with Stephen Markley and The Slip)

Gas prices hit record levels, the presidential campaign heats up.

The writer and James sit on a couch toasting John McCain's vice-presidential selection of Sarah Palin. This woman is clearly a desperate stab by a desperate candidate. James and the writer laugh and cheer and crack wise—only to have their smiles fade as Palin quickly explodes into a populist Conservative darling courtesy of her—ahem—"executive experience" and ability to see Russia from a distant island on the tip of Alaska. The two young men exchange looks of horror.

Summer reigns in Chicago.

The parks are lush and beautiful, the beaches of Lake Michigan packed. The heat rises from the pavement but the winds still manage to blow strong and cool. The writer runs along the beach, sweat pouring down his red chest and back. He stops for a drink of water and looks out over the lake. Pretty girls in bikinis walk by in droves. The nightlife takes him and his friends across the city, from the hipster bars of Wicker Park and Bucktown to the hangouts of yuppies and college kids in Lincoln Park and Wrigleyville.

Beers are thrown back, laughs exchanged. The writer stumbles down a street with James, Elliot, Liam, and Erik, shouting and gesticulating wildly.

A plane ticket is purchased.

Elliott, James, and the writer look on in wonder when Elliott discovers a $340 round-trip ticket to London. The three young men exchange momentary glances before purchasing three, jumping and shouting in their living room, until James stops them and says, "We should probably go to Stockholm, too."

A Love Interest visits.

In Chicago, the young couple wanders the quiet streets of Hyde Park. They traverse the University of Chicago campus and eat at one of Barack Obama's favorite restaurants, Calypso. They take in the Lincoln Park Zoo, they watch a rainbow ride a wave over Lake Michigan from the bar at the top of the Hancock building, they listen to Josh Ritter perform at a street festival on the west side of the city.

In Boston, the two ride the T to different colonial destinations. He studies her at her job working with underprivileged kids in East Boston. They watch in a downtown bar as the Cavs narrowly lose to the Celtics in the playoffs, while he just barely avoids getting in a fight with angry Boston fans. They go sailing with friends in Rhode Island and sip coffee on a quiet bay just inland from the Atlantic. They fight, they make up, they wonder where they are and what events or longings drew them to this moment. They retire to different rooms in two great American cities, pulling each other's clothes off, drawing breath from each other's lungs.

A city revels in its prime.

As a young Illinois senator shows unbelievable cool under fantastic pressure, a city rises. The writer and friends take in the street festivals where they drink all day and argue about politics and religion and life at the heart of a moment of ever-escalating importance. They watch in awe as Heath Ledger creates an instant classic, the IMAX screen towering above their joyous, amazed faces, and they patter away happily about the incredible film as they walk from Navy Pier back to the train. They attend the Pitchfork music festival where slices of M. Ward, Animal Collective, Vampire Weekend, Bon Iver, Spoon, and Fleet Foxes splinter their stoned consciousness. The writer passes out on a couch in a cell phone booth, all the music a sweet cacophony in his head.

A plane departs from O'Hare, bound for London.

Elliott, James, and the writer stride through the streets of London, past the Eye, through the Tate, the British Museum, Piccadilly, Notting Hill, and the Imperial War Museum with its cut of the Berlin Wall. They visit pub after pub and sleep in dirty hostels where the bar stays open till four in the morning and clink mugs with foul-mouthed British kids, who call their various countrymen "fuggin' coonts" more often than they use pronouns. The weather is dark and gray and drizzles throughout their visit, but no matter. They walk the entire city, refusing to spend a minute wasted in an underground subway or the backseat of a cab. The writer botches a hostel reservation and they end up spending the night on the far west side of the city, waking up to discover their hostel overlooks a massive graveyard—a city of sleeping slabs of concrete and browning grass.

They hop a Ryan Air flight to Stockholm where the city is cool and crisp and the women so beautiful, none of them dare utter a word in their presence. They marvel at the precision of the city, a network of clean streets and waterways blending into the distinguished architecture of Old Town. They find the bars that don't close, they meet beautiful French people, they dance in 7-11s at 3 a.m., they talk about the U.S. election with Palestinian clerks who profess their hope and admiration for Obama. They marvel at the Vassa, an epic, enormous, fully recovered battleship from the seventeenth century sitting in the middle of an indoor museum.

They refuse to eat at or enter the T.G.I Friday's, which seems to be an oddly popular nightspot for the Swedes. In the hostel, the writer checks his email at a dusty, well-worn Mac and finds a message from his agent telling him to hang in there. The economy sucks, the book market is a dry riverbed in a water-starved African desert, and the big houses aren't looking for risk, but there are still options. The writer puts it out of mind as he and James marvel at a Swedish girl who looks like Aphrodite's hotter younger sister.

The writer returns to Chicago and the economy implodes.

The government rescues begin. Lehman Brothers collapses. The writer changes his Facebook picture to an image of Wall Street with a homemade cardboard sign intruding into the frame. It says, "Jump, You Fuckers." John McCain stutters, starts, coughs, and looks like a man adrift. Barack Obama ascends, cool as a cucumber in a cobalt casket. The writer's head bobs at the growing gap in the polls. He marvels at the panic gripping the country.

The song winds down, the scenes slow, the final shot shows the writer perched on the front stoop of his house in Lakeview, saying good-bye for the night to his Love Interest and snapping the phone shut, looking off quietly as the sun slips behind the proud, aging homes of a hushed Lakeview street.

• • •

"I mean Jesus Christ," I say to James as we listen to the news of major financial institutions toppling like Imperial Walkers wrapped up by steel cables on the ice planet Hoth. "I know these assholes waited until I finally have a chance to sell my first book."

"What are the odds of that, you think?"

"Of a bunch of dipshit finance majors fucking a bunch of smart, meek humanities majors? Pretty good. Reminds me of college."

"You know what I like most about this?" he asks while munching on pasta salad he's brought home from Pane's. "It's left humanities majors across the country scrambling to understand stuff like credit-default swaps and mortgage-backed securities. It's kinda fun."

"Well, all's well that ends well, I guess."

"Even if Barack wins, it's a hell of world he's gonna inherit."

I put my head in my hands, my sandwich momentarily forgotten. "Aw, we're screwed! Everyone's screwed! We're gonna be stuck in pointless jobs forever, because we'll be lucky to even have jobs. Goddamn Bush. Goddamn Phil Gramm. Goddamn predatory lenders and stupid finance fucks making money off a glorified pyramid scheme."

I smack our coffee table, and Elliott shouts, "Fuzzy, man!" from the kitchen when he hears the noise.

James nods his agreement. "Hard to sell a book in the middle of the greatest financial crisis since the Great Depression."

"Even harder when that book is about nonsense. Maybe I should change chapters two through fourteen to tips on how to bludgeon your neighbor to death for the last pack of bologna at the grocery store."

"Or how to melt down the shopping cart for scrap metal," he suggests.

I read Julie's frequent email updates with increasing skepticism as John McCain suspends his campaign and David Letterman ridicules him. As the financial rot spreads to the rest of the world and Iceland goes bankrupt (Who even knew it was possible for an entire country to go bankrupt?). Publishing houses are slashing their book buys and scaling back their advertising. That an editor would want to take a chance on a long-shot like me seems even more improbable than it did when the economy was on its feet.

When I moved to Chicago over a year earlier, it was an adventure. I wanted to see what I could do with my meager resources. Now, however, I feel like a man with something to lose, which I guess is the problem with having anything. Now that I've tasted health insurance and a regular salary and what it might be like to publish something on a national scale, I of course feel entitled to it all. Hard to go back to the farm when you've seen the lights of the city, right?

If the book doesn't work out, I toy with the idea of going back to school, but now it seems like an incredibly poor choice to give up a paying job with benefits just because it bores me a little.

Then there is the x-factor: my Love Interest is about to start school in Boston. Who knows, I think, maybe this is for the best.

I begin to assume that this book is a lost cause, a novel idea that took me to places I never imagined I'd explore (mostly because I didn't know of their existence), but in the end that is all it will be.

• • •

The email from Julie arrives—seven months after I signed with her and three after she began sending out queries—with the subject line "*Sourcebooks hot for you.*" She wants to speak immediately, ASAP, without delay.

"Okay," she says, the excitement in her voice ringing sharply all the way from California, "This editor, Peter Lynch, he loves the book… He wants to talk to you."

"To me?" I ask, as if I'm incredulous that he doesn't want to talk to the real author.[189]

"Yes. I think he wants to get a feel for you, see what kind of ideas you have for marketing. I told him you would be great to just put in front of college students and let you go to work. A true performer."

"Ah," I say, suddenly unable to get out of my head an image of me juggling knives while I read excerpts. "Okay. Give him my number and let him know he can call whenever."

Sure, I say this, but I'm thinking at Julie: *You want me to speak to*

---

189 What if it turned out I was actually Norman Mailer? Or James Frey? Or what if I was J. K. Rowling like after I (J. K., that is) took too much mescaline and had a drug-induced psychosis that left me thinking I was not a British lady, but an overstimulated twentysomething American male, and I sat at my laptop in fuddy old England banging out a new classic of Americanized excess? Holy shit, that would be crazy.

an editor who is interested in the book? Why would you do that? Aren't
you supposed to protect me from making an idiot out of myself in front
of people like this Peter Lynch? Couldn't you just have told him I'm a
tortured artist? A recluse and savant who can't hold a normal conversa-
tion for fear I'll jump up out of my chair and bite someone's cheek off?
Isn't that part of your job description, Julie?

Moments after hanging up with Julie, my phone rings again with
an unfamiliar number. I rush to find a quiet spot in the office to talk.
I want to be nervous, but I don't get nervous when I'm intimidated.
Instead I get dumb. Really, really dumb. And inarticulate.

The moment I pick up the phone, I am agreeing with every word
that comes out of Peter's mouth. I can't recall very well how the
conversation went, but it probably sounded something like:

"Hi, is this Stephen?"

"Yes, it is."

"How are you doing?"

"Yep, pretty good."

"Well, I gotta tell you, I really enjoyed your proposal. I think it's
got a lot of promise."

"Sure, right. Promise. Yes."

"It was really funny and some of the observations were dead on."

"Yeah. Right. Good. Observations. Cool."

"And now I'm thinking to myself, 'Oh, am I gonna be in the book?'"

"Haha! Yes, right. Exactly."

"Do you have any ideas about marketing? I think this book would
be great once you got it into someone's hands, but the question is:
how do you get a reader to pick it up?"

"Exactly. Sure. How to pick it up. Totally agree."

"I think you'd sell a lot of books if we had you perform gastro-
intestinal surgery on a living, cognizant human being—preferably a
homeless man."

"I've had that same thought myself."

We finally hang up, and I have no idea what I've said to this man.

I try to organize my thoughts and feelings about what just went down with this actual editor of an actual company that acquires books so that they may be printed, bound, and sold. I come to two conclusions:

First, I am not a good judge of character, but I am a good judge of people who suck, and from our conversation, I know this Peter Lynch does not suck. I can tell he has what I look for first thing in every human being, which is a sense of humor.

Second, I hope he does not base his opinion of me on the conversation we just had because I'd like to go ahead and not be a big watercooler joke at the offices of Sourcebooks, Inc.

Peter: *So I interviewed this Markley character.*
Watercooler guys: *Oh, yeah? How'd that go?*
Peter: *He agreed to wash my car.*
Watercooler guys: *[Guffaws]*
Peter: *And he said he has the penis of a male daffodil.*
Watercooler guys: *[Guffaws]*
Peter: *I think I'll call him back and see if he wants to hold a Bic lighter to his eyelid for a while.*

Yet Julie emails me to say that Peter "really enjoyed" our chat.

I chalk this up to a white lie and immediately go back to believing I blew it. How could I not have blown it? How could this possibly be the real thing?

"What do we do now?" I ask Julie the next time we speak.

"We wait, kiddo. He's gotta go to his board to get approval, and then he comes back and makes us an offer."

I turn to Sourcebooks's website and to *Jeff Herman's Guide*[190] for more information and discover that Sourcebooks is the leading independent publisher in Chicago and one of the "fastest-growing

---

190 This, you'll recall, is the $40 book Julie had me buy after I signed with her, which I have cracked approximately three times, making each nugget of information worth about $13.33.

companies in America with many bestsellers." After a thorough scan of its titles, I conclude that 1) Sourcebooks has never published anything like this book, does not have the resources of a major New York house, and will likely offer me a fairly meager advance and b) who gives a shit, they put words on paper between covers.

My Ego thrashes, throwing his shoulder against the heavy oak door of the cellar where I have entombed him. I keep my own shoulder lowered and my weight in place. No expectations, I tell myself.

• • •

October is a wild month. The second is my twenty-fifth birthday, and my old friend Allison   my editor from long ago at *The Miami Student*—calls to say she's secured tickets to watch Springsteen play a show for Obama in Columbus. Allison works for Ted Strickland, the governor of Ohio, and her offer of VIP standing space is a birthday present like no other. Five hours after this conversation, I'm in Oxford spending the night at Justin and Loren's place.

They live in a little apartment on the far south side of town, and Loren is nice enough to stay with Jaxson for the night so the boys can go out and play. Before we leave, I bounce Jaxson around in front of my face, and he grabs my nose with decided interest before finding my eyebrow of more immediate importance.

"Yeah, I remember you, giant," he seems to say. "I like your sticking-out thing with the two holes in it; that's kinda funny. But then look what you got up here; I mean what the shit is that? Little furry patches just growing out above the two looky-balls? What *are* these magnificent things, giant? What kind of creature are you? You have the noise machine at the bottom, the thing with two holes, the looky-balls, and the furry patches. It doesn't make a goddamn bit of sense! Don't get me wrong, I'll play with all this funny shit, but I want answers!"

Justin and I head uptown to Mac 'n Joes to watch a Buckeyes game. We talk a little bit about the money, which Justin put in mutual funds and which has already lost over nine hundred dollars in the economic crisis. We share a moment of head-shaking, and I wonder if that day at Ian's house on July 4 will have an ugly asterisk beside it.

Waiting for the bartender to turn the channel from women's Ultimate Fighting to football, I decide now is the time to inform Justin that he is a central character in my book.

Pouring a pitcher of Natural Light into two plastic cups, I say to him, "So you know this book I'm writing?"

"Yeah?"

"You're kinda one of the larger characters."

His face is noncommittal. "What's that mean?"

"You're like the third or fourth largest character."

"Who's the first?"

"Well, me, you jerkoff."

He shakes his head sadly. "So egotistical, Marklcy. What makes you think people want to read a book about you?"

"That's why there's other stuff in it. Like you."

"Do I get royalties?"

"I don't know. Do you wanna get paid in sucking my dick?"

He smirks. Mac 'n Joes is full of college girls, chirping and smiling brightly. An awful Bon Jovi song[191] plays on the jukebox. With the game yet to begin, we sit at the bar watching female Ultimate Fighters pound each other's nose cartilage into jelly.

"I'll change your name, if you want me to," I offer. "I've already changed Loren's."[192]

---

191 Not that there's any other kind.

192 And long after this conversation, when Loren proved a good sport, I changed it back. Unfortunately, to change her name throughout the book, I use Microsoft Word's "Find and Replace" tool. I had previously used the pseudonym "Elle" for Loren, and what I didn't realize was that Bill Gates's goon software would go back and replace every instance of the letter combination "e-l-l-e" with "Loren." Thus, "booksellers" becomes "booksLorenrs" and "intellectually" becomes "intLorenctually." So I had to go back through and fix every single one of those. The result was that for a period of

He shrugs. "Is it truthful?"

"Of course it's truthful. But sometimes the truth kinda sucks, you know?"

He shakes his head. "Whatever. If it's the truth, what do I care?"

I look at him skeptically. "Justin, think about the typical conversation between, say, you and me and Phil. We offer to pay each other royalties in fellatio."

He downs his beer. "Markley, let me tell you something: I got a kid now."

His statement hangs in the air, world-worn and absurd. I throw my head back and bark laughter. A few of the cute college girls look up at the sound. "What the hell does that have to do with anything?" I ask.

We are both laughing now. Justin's cheeks turn round and pink. "I don't know," he says. "It's the truth." I'm cracking up and have to bury my head in the crook of my elbow to stifle the noise.

"I see: now, that's just what you'll say every time you got nothing else. From now on it's, 'Markley, I've got a kid now, I can't buy plain old Crest toothpaste.' 'Markley, I've got a kid now, I can't wear underwear that's not straight from the dryer.'"

Still chortling in his funny little way, Justin sips at his beer. "When's this book come out?" he asks.

"I don't know. I have to get this deal done first."

"Well, let me know. Maybe I'll see if they have it at the library."

• • •

The next day, I am standing twenty feet away from a stage on the Oval at Ohio State. Bruce Springsteen stands alone, backlit by a gorgeous Ohio sun setting gently in the west, throwing a glow up behind him that would be comically religious if it weren't for the

---

fifty-six hours, I hated Loren, hated the letter combination "e-l-l-e," and wanted to torture and murder Microsoft Word's "Find and Replace" tool.

very real religious feeling I get while watching him. Playing the guitar and harmonica, he launches into a rendition of "Promised Land" with its Rattlesnake Speedway, driving all night chasing some mirage, the dogs on Main Street, and all the rest.

Out of all my over-worshipped pop heroes, Springsteen stands alone, mostly because I find it criminal that at times his celebrity has overwhelmed his enormous artistic talents. People always know six or seven of his standard songs, but if you get into the back room of his catalogue, it's hard to argue that he doesn't stand as the Walt Whitman of our time—an all-American poet cataloguing that story in its every incarnation.

Allison is there, as are other old friends I don't see enough. Here in this awesome little moment, it's hard not to feel the possibility and danger and brilliance of one's life.

Once in a Mount Vernon bar called Rookie's, I spotted a small line of graffiti above the toilet much different from the other crude limericks and slurs. It said, "The measure of a man is the good of his passions."

This seemed far too wise for a bathroom wall in a small-town bar, but that won't force me to disqualify it. This day I find myself thankful for my measure, the good of my passions.

This is how I know I'll probably publish the book now: because I don't really care if I do or not. Obviously, I *want* to publish this book, but there's always the Scope. What seemed all-important today will feel like an afterthought tomorrow. I know I'll publish this book. It's like having your hand caught in the pickle jar: once you let go of the pickles it comes sliding right out.

Bruce strums his guitar madly, howling across the crowd of thousands, and I sing along, if I could only take one moment into my hands.

• • •

Peter makes an offer for a $3,000 advance. My initial reaction is to say, "Yes! Ohyesohyesohyesthankyouthankyouthankyou!"

Which is why writers have agents, I gather.

Julie says that she'll go back to Sourcebooks and try to get the advance money up a bit. There are also other considerations, other details to smooth out, standard things like foreign rights, first serial rights, author's copies—and of course, there is always the 5 percent chance that this entire thing will blow up—but for the most part the deal is in place.[193]

"Congratulations," Julie tells me over the phone. "You're going to have a book in seven thousand bookstores."

Walking back to my desk in the Cars.com office, my Ego follows by my side, panicking.

Are you out of your fucking mind, Markley? he asks, his eyes desperate, his breath reeking of stale cigarettes and peanut butter. *You can't let them actually publish this nonsense! It's crap! It's garbage! It's the inane ramblings of a disturbed mind! Call Peter. Go over Julie's head! Tell him to back out while he still has a chance!*

"It's cool," I say calmly. "It'll be fine. I know how to finish it now."

Oh! Well then! Happy day! Excuse me while I go screaming through the streets in cele-fucking-bration! You know "how to finish it." Little Steve Markley knows how to end his special little precious bookie-book—Shut up! Shut the fuck up! Delete it right now! Say you lost it! You can't let this thing see the light of day! Oh my Christ, I'm freaking out. You're talentless. You're a hack. I was wrong about everything. Ohgodohgodohgod.

My Ego looks around the Cars.com office desperately. Finally, he goes sprinting at a window, screaming, *Mary, I'm coming hooooome!* and crashes through the plane of glass, shrieking in agony and horror as he plummets eight stories to the ground below.

I return to my desk to write about the new four-cylinder engine option for the Pontiac G6.

---

193 Whatever, I'm rich! Republican Party, looks like I'm joining you! Now show me the secret handshake, you fair and decent men!

TWENTY-TWO

Autobiographical Digression #3: Why We Write

There's nothing like actual work to make you appreciate the value of an education.

One summer when we were all home from college, Phil and I worked construction, while Ian worked at a golf course and Justin as a clerk at a Sunoco gas station. After work, we often met up at Phil's house to drink beer and play pool. One day Justin came in, and you could tell something was up: his face had an indignant menace to it. "You're not gonna believe this," he said and told us this story:

He's standing around the gas station on a slow day, selling lottery tickets and packs of cigarettes and gallons of gas (back when no one had heard of a three-dollar gallon). He's bored out of his mind, fiddling with the cash machine, when the bell tinkles above the door and a very tall, very ugly old white guy strides in.

Funny: it's NBA superstar, icon, legend Larry Bird.

Out of all the places in the world, this is about the last one he'd expect to meet Larry Bird, who walks straight for the cashier, which, Justin thinks in amazement, just happens to be him. Justin tears a scrap of paper from the line of receipt tape to ask for an autograph.

Larry Bird has grabbed a twelve of Miller Lite and asks for a pack of smokes. Justin—still holding the scrap of receipt tape and trying to figure out how to broach the delicate topic—tells him they don't carry that particular brand, and Larry Bird gets pissed, muttering under his breath. He asks for another brand.

Bird is already in his wallet. Justin knows he may not have another chance. "Um, excuse me," says Justin, reaching for the pack of cigarettes. "I don't mean to bother you, but... Are you Mr. Bird?"

As well-mannered a young man as exists on this planet, Justin nevertheless sees that Larry Bird looks annoyed.

"No," he says flatly.

Justin knows this is Larry Bird. There's no mistaking him. He presses on. "Really, I don't mean to bother you, but I know it's you, and it would just really make my day if you signed your autograph for me." He pushes the torn piece of receipt tape forward.

"Would you hurry up so I can get the hell out of here?" the guy says.

It's like a bomb went off in his face. Justin stands with the pack of cigarettes in his hand, confused, hurt, even devastated that he will not have a memento to mark this unbelievable once-in-a-lifetime moment. Justin rings up his order, but Larry Bird doesn't wait for his receipt. He snatches up the beer and cigarettes and in two strides is out of the gas station.

"What an asshole," said Justin, plucking a pool stick from the wall. "Can you believe that?"

This is hard to understand if you did not grow up worshipping athletes. Basically, this is like if Pat Robertson were mowing his lawn and Jesus Christ showed up to gather his clippings. Obviously, Phil, Ian, and I did not believe him. We didn't believe that Larry Bird stopped to buy beer and cigarettes in a little podunk gas station in the middle of Nowhere, Ohio.

"Sure, Justin," I said. "It's just like that time Phil and I saw Magic Johnson at the bowling alley."

Phil's sharp eyes sparkled when he heard me say this. We spent a long summer standing in the ninety-five-degree sun with nothing to do but dick around. Our arms and faces were pink and we could create tapestries of ridicule like Miles Davis jamming with Clarence Clemmons. We could develop these self-perpetuating structures of inside jokes that built on top of each other for hours at a time. We constructed these towers of humor around things that were only funny to us, but as far as we were concerned, man, did they ever spiral to the sky. Phil sensed one of these in the making. "No, Markley," he said, scornful of my poor, quixotic memory. "You're thinking of when Tiger Woods was waiting at the Star Bright to get his oil changed."

"I mean, he's Larry-fucking-Bird," said Ian, attempting to sympathize. "He's worth more money than we'll all see combined. He doesn't need to walk into a gas station to buy beer and cigarettes. He has groupies doing that for him or something."

"No, no," I said, trying to be the voice of reason. "Phil, you're thinking of when Michael Jordan came into Hunan Garden and got the sweet and sour chicken."

We are cracking ourselves up.

"You can all go fuck yourselves," said Justin, smacking the cue ball so hard that the balls exploded across the table like the beginning of the universe. "I swear on my mother's life it was Larry Bird. I've been watching his ugly ass since I was a kid. You can't exactly mistake just anyone for Larry Bird."

"Justin, I'm sure the guy looked like Larry Bird," I said. "I'm sure you thought he was Larry Bird. But Larry Bird has no reason to be in the middle of bum-fuck, Ohio. It doesn't make sense."

"Don't worry, man," Phil told him as he sipped Natty Light and lined up his shot. "One time I thought I saw Anna Kournikova at the movie store."

Justin shook his head. "Fuck you guys."

The next day I was eating breakfast before work when I spotted a copy of the local paper, *The Mount Vernon News*. With nothing better to do, I began riffling through the pages, if for no better reason than to read the nutty letters to the editor that come in from rural Ohio's greatest men and women of letters.[194]

The first page I flipped to, I saw a picture of none other than Larry Bird. The caption beneath said that Bird was indeed in the area that week participating in a charity golf tournament.

I met Phil at his house before we drove over to the build site together. When I walked into his dining room, he held up a copy of the newspaper.

"Looks like we owe Justin an apology," I said.

"Yeah, can you believe that?" he said, grinning so widely he exposed his crooked back molars. "Kid was right! Who would've thought?"

"Sure, but it was worth not believing him. I think we got some real priceless shots in there."

"Oh," said Phil, frowning gravely. "No doubt. I thought it was some of our finest work."

The next time we hung out, Justin was apoplectic. "I told you guys!" he ranted. "I told you it was Larry Bird, you dumb assholes."

"All right, Justin, don't get your little knickers all twisted," said Phil.

"Wow," said Ian. "Turns out Larry Bird's a dick."

Justin immediately forgets to rub it in that he was right, his singular focus now on what a douche bag Larry Bird is. "I swear if I ever see that guy again…" he said, as if this was a possibility he would have to prepare for. From that point in our lives forward, none of us has ever been able to even mention Larry Bird in passing without

---

194 Typical letter-to-the-editor: "It is distressing to me that people in our own town could support a communist sympathizer and traitor like John Kerry. John Kerry clearly faked his injuries during Vietnam and then made a deal to aid the Viet Cong through an elaborate series of antiwar protests that undermined our war effort there. He also supports the murder of babies. John Kerry is the most liberal person to ever run for the presidency and wants to take money from everyone who works and distribute it to welfare recipients. He doesn't think Osama bin Laden is all that bad. John Kerry is also a cross-dresser."
—Mike T. Tucker, Mount Vernon

Justin shaking his head and looking like he's about to punch the face off the first person he sees, those words—*Would you hurry up so I can get the hell out of here?*—burned into his mind forever.

"Yeah," I agreed. "Same goes if I ever see Magic Johnson with my bowling shoes."

• • •

What's the lesson of this story?

Aha! Trick question. There is no lesson. It's just some funny, funny shit that happened to my friend and then became even funnier when we didn't believe him. Of course, we haven't met a whole lot of people who find it as funny as we do. Perhaps that contingent now includes the audience of this book.

None of us knows why we find this story so endlessly amusing. We just do. We retell it to every new person we meet. Every new girlfriend, every new guy we hang out with, every parent or cousin or convenient stranger—one of us will repeat this story of how Larry Bird went into a gas station to buy cigarettes and beer and treated Justin like shit. Then we go on to explain how we didn't believe him and made up great jokes about Magic Johnson taking us bowling. It doesn't matter how many times we tell it, the story never gets old. The weather of time and distance never fade it even the least.

"I think my favorite part," Phil once said, "is not even that it was Larry Bird, but just how sure we were that it couldn't possibly be Larry Bird."

"My favorite part," said Ian, "is that he called him 'Mr. Bird.' Such a well-mannered young man."

See, the story is more than just a story to us. At some point, it took on the trappings of a legend. It is a story that has power for us because it reminds us of those essential parts of ourselves: that we were boys who worshipped the athletic heroes of our youth, that as kids we held crummy jobs, that our small-town Ohio upbringings made epic even the slightest news or the smallest deviation from the norm, that an NBA legend walking into a gas station could be one of the defining moments of our lives if only that legend would not be an asshole.

The story reminds us of those essential truths, yes, but it also reminds us of our friendship, hard-won over years of upheavals and distance. This story belongs to us. No one else can ever have it or ever tell it correctly. Even if it does not obey the standard dramatic arc, even if it really isn't all that funny to anyone who didn't live it, this story is ours.

And yet this is also a small example of how stories create identity. We lose millions upon millions of memories every day. We have no way of cataloguing all of the things we don't want to forget, but some moments—certain strings of events—manage to stay with us and live in us and occasionally even define us. Everyone has these stories, even if they are unaware of them. They lurk behind our prejudices and our fears. They are the force behind our love and hope, behind the terrible, the wonderful, and even the mediocre. They are the moments that inspire us to write the rest of the story eventually.

• • •

Every once in a while you'll hear one of these stories from someone else—usually in a time and place you would never expect it. Suddenly you recognize what is happening, and you just listen.

Right before spring break my sophomore year of college, my friend JR had invited a group of us down to Sarasota, Florida, for the week to stay in his great-aunt's beach house.

After what became an immensely complicated trip[195] we arrived,

---

195 The same weekend, Phil and Justin wanted me to go with them to Pittsburgh to visit Ian (where he went to school) for St. Patrick's Day. This also sounded like fun. Being the bright, confident young man that I am, I decided I could easily do both. I would drive straight from Oxford to Pittsburgh on Friday morning (five to six hours), stay until Sunday, and then get up at 7 a.m. to drive to Columbus (three hours) to pick up two members of our traveling squad, Josh and Jeremy, and then all the way down to Sarasota that day (seventeen hours).

a motley collection of twenty-year-old kids without much of a clue about anything, set loose on a pristine beach with our own house where we could play all kinds of wonderful games.

The night that sticks with me, however, is when a group of girls we knew from school drove over from Orlando, and the ten of us found ourselves out on the beach on a cool March night, sipping beers and playing a simple game where we recounted the best and worst moments of our short lives.

The ebullient mood faded, became mellow. The emotional proximity shrunk. Suddenly everyone was revealing things about themselves that they may never have told anyone, moments that might not even have occurred to them before they were forced to think about it. Missed opportunities, family members falling ill, first dates, nights out with friends—everyone had a story that somehow explained where they came from or defined what they wanted from this life.

It is now approximately four and a half years later, and I cannot recall most of those stories—save this one. Sitting in a rough circle on the beach, listening to those Gulf waves surge and fall back, the

---

The plan seemed foolproof, but—and you may find this hard to believe—complications arose. A few of the complications: Ian passing out while a group of us (including Justin, Phil, and Ritesh) covered his entire body with images and slurs from a Sharpie marker; Ian peeing on himself in the middle of the night and then attacking Phil with his urine-soaked hands, rubbing them in his face while Phil sleepily tried to stave him off; me driving twenty-one hours to Florida on four hours of sleep; the girls on the highway in another car not responding to Josh and Jeremy's handmade sign "Florida Private Beach House Give Us Your Number"; running into the freezing waters of the Gulf of Mexico at four in the morning; sunburns galore; meeting two attractive young women from Dayton, of all places; playing drinking games with said girls while seven guys vied for attention; police being called because of noise complaints (no one in the private beach house being over twenty-one); police being nice and not asking us for ID; making out with one of said girls under the stars on the beach; watching both girls run into the water in their underwear while shrieking drunk before collapsing messily into the sand; Dave and I walking girls home; Dave and I returning to private beach house to tell Josh, "Man, you will not believe what just happened. We just totally had sex on the beach"; Josh's face framed by an expression of unbearable wonder and jealousy; Dave following with punch line, "Yeah, if you don't believe us, you can ask those girls. They watched."

foam bubbling arhythmically, my friend Jeremy told us how he met his high school girlfriend.

Jeremy went to an all-boys Catholic high school in Cleveland. As Jeremy once said to me about this experience: "My penis hated me, and it hated Catholicism." He was tall and skinny and very, very smart, which everyone knows is a complete liability in high school. "Perhaps I lacked self-confidence, is the charitable way to put it," he told us.

His senior year, he was driving to a party on the east side of Cleveland when his car broke down. He called the police, who helped him push it to the side of the road and then gave him a ride to the party. Imagine showing up in the back of a cop car at a party where underage drinking is the point—it was an instant conversation starter. And of course, there was a girl whom he couldn't stop looking at. She had short black hair and a brilliant smile, and he had his perfect opening. "Jesus Christ," said Jeremy on the beach. "Suddenly I was talking to her, and I couldn't remember how, except I was thinking to myself, 'Oh my God, she's laughing at what you're saying! Quick, shut up before she realizes you're an idiot! No, keep talking, she's laughing!'"

This girl's name was Mel, and after the party he needed a ride back to his broken-down car. A friend drove both of them back to Jeremy's abandoned vehicle where they waited with him for the tow truck. Jeremy had his guitar in the trunk, so he pulled it out and began playing. He hammered away at chords and made up nonsense words. He sang about their situation, ad-libbing stupidly, creating bizarre chord changes to accompany his songwriting blather. And Mel loved it. She laughed joyfully and sang along when he repeated his nonsense choruses. Jeremy could do no wrong, and thank God, he thought, the tow truck driver took over an hour to get there. When the two girls finally dropped him off that night, Mel gave Jeremy her number and not long after they were dating.

It's not particularly impressive as far as the best moments of one's life go, but what did strike me about this story was that when Jeremy told it to us on that beach, he and Mel had been broken up for over a year. Jeremy and I were freshman roommates, and I was there the night they called it quits. I walked into our room and saw him on the phone, a hand over his face, and his voice shaky as his first real relationship came crashing down. Over a year later, though, he still had the ability to recognize the night the car broke down for its importance. He could separate that from whatever came after.

Everywhere we hear these stories that are too good to let fade into the ether. Some of us write to retain those stories, even if it's only in fragments, even if it's dressed up as someone else's life, or even if it's just one moment, one slice of emotion or humor or dialogue or truth that blossoms into a wider piece of fiction. We tell stories because whether they involve a long-ago love interest, a random encounter with an asshole basketball star, a space station swirling around the rim of a black hole, a record store owner trying to salvage his love life, a drug addict struggling to piece his humanity back together, a masked vigilante trying to defeat corruption and chaos in his beloved city, a biracial law student in search of a legacy from a father he barely knew, or a young, impetuous writer with a wild idea for a book, these stories are somehow common to our collective humanity.

When we were driving home from the trip a few days later, Jeremy rode shotgun in my Corolla while Josh and Dave slept in the backseat. "You never went," said Jeremy out of the blue. "I think everyone told their best and worst moment except for you."

I looked at him over the rim of my sunglasses. It hurt my sunburned face just to move my eyes. "Man, that was like three days ago. How do you even remember that?"

"I'm just curious is all. I wondered why you never said anything."

"I don't know," I said. Gray highway rushed beneath the wheels of the little Toyota. We were somewhere in Georgia, a long and merciless state that consists mostly of Waffle Houses. "I just liked listening to what everyone had to say."

"I suppose I can guess your worst," he said.

I nodded. This vacation was the first time any of these guys had seen the tattoo on my ankle: three letters written at about the height of a short pair of socks. Of course, I'd had to give them the bare-bones version of the story.

"Yeah, you probably can."

"I just can't believe I never knew that about you," he said.

We were quiet for a few minutes because I didn't know what to say and neither did he. *This is why I rarely share the story*, I thought. Jeremy stared out the window, brownish Georgian foliage looking dim and lonely in the long, flat stretch of land before us.

Finally, Jeremy said, "Jesus Christ on a pogo stick, I can see three different Waffle Houses right now. Three fucking Waffle Houses all close enough that people can go outside and talk about which one has the best grits."

This allowed us to laugh, which allowed me to get away from the story the way I always try to get away from it, diverting and laughing. But stories, it seems, have their own life force. Even after you spend so much time dodging them, they just ask to be told. No matter how long ago or how much distance you've put between yourself and that time and place, you can't reach the end of your book, your song, your tale without telling this one last little piece.

• • •

When I was fifteen, I developed a crush on a girl my age named Sarah Pressler.

Kids determine their friends by who they spend the bulk of their time around. Thus, Justin and I, with almost nothing in common, found ourselves bound together first by basketball, then by our academic achievements. But if you don't share any classes or sports or clubs with someone, it's unlikely that you'll develop any kind of friendship. Thus, despite having gone to middle school with Sarah for three years, I had never said word one to her until our freshman year at Mount Vernon High School.

In the ninth grade, we sat next to each other in first period—Algebra 2 (which I understood almost none of). It would have been impossible for me not to grow fond of her in such close quarters. She was one of those people who just seemed flawless in pretty much every way. Thin, with long brunette hair and a small, sharp nose, she would obviously have intrigued any fifteen-year-old boy. Add to that a personality so magnetic that it almost had its own gravitational pull, and I'm not sure how I ever could have avoided falling for her.

We had dances in our cafeteria after basketball games. For me, a freshman who weighed all of 130 pounds, these were always terrifying propositions. Fully metastasized seniors the size of Buicks would crowd the center of the dance floor while the other grades would orbit around them in expanding circles. You couldn't *not* go to the dances because socially speaking in Mount Vernon, this was pretty much the only game in town. At the same time, you did everything you could to get through them unnoticed.[196]

Only once that year did I find the opportunity to ask Sarah to dance. We were just friends. Friends danced with each other all the time at these shindigs. I didn't give it a second thought. So I tapped her on the shoulder and said something purposefully goofy like, "Hey, we haven't done *this* before."

I don't remember the song. All I can recall is that she wore something yellow and we talked the whole time. When we pulled apart, I felt the urge to ask her to dance again… And again and again and again and for the rest of the night, if she wouldn't mind.

In the days and weeks after, I began to think about this dance a little too much: the way it felt to hold her waist, the way her hips

---

196 One time Ian made the mistake of wearing a wife-beater to a dance (I forget why; maybe as a joke). A hulking football player promptly dragged him to the bathroom and made him trade shirts. The football player got the wife-beater, which exposed his thick layers of muscle, while Ian got a sweat-drenched T-shirt two sizes too big.

felt pressed against mine, the pressure of her arms draped across my shoulders. To look her in the eye from less than a foot away, long brown hair streaked with blonde; her bright, clear face with a small, smooth forehead, this tiny imperfection on her tooth—a little blip of white on one of her canines. Dancing in the near dark amid all the other horny teenagers.

By March of that year, I had it bad—a palpable, gut-wrenching boyhood crush on all fronts.

She threw a party that month during which eight of us got in her hot tub and then sprinted across the lawn to sit on her trampoline for the ever-popular game of Truth or Dare. The night was cold and we slight, bony adolescents all wore bathing suits, so the eight of us sat in a tight little circle, warming each other with our body heat, hugging our knees to our chests, and confessing whatever meager secrets we had at that age.

Sitting by her on the trampoline, squeezed against her shoulder and thigh, marveling at how impossibly soft her skin felt, I pretty much figured I could die happy.

Eventually, the line of questioning came around to who everybody "liked." Two of the other three guys present confessed to liking Sarah. Seeing how uncomfortable this made her, I kept my mouth shut when it was my turn. (Oh, yeah: I was all about subtlety then.)

When it was her turn to confess, I knew she wouldn't say the name of anyone there if only to avoid embarrassment and spare hurt feelings. Instead, the name that came from her mouth was "Drew."

Drew was a junior (two years older than us), who played on the basketball team. He was also probably the nicest guy I'd ever met, with a grin that stretched impossibly wide to reveal impossibly perfect teeth. I could see how Sarah would dig him.

And dig him she did.

Maybe a month after that party, on her fifteenth birthday, Sarah told me that Drew had said that he "thought he liked her."

And the history of our lives began to take shape.

I pretty much ceded that I had lost. I wanted to be mad, and I tried my best—I really did. In the weeks that followed, however, I could see how happy his affection made her. And Drew was as hard to dislike as any person I've ever met. Besides, what was one shattered boyhood crush? I'd had dozens of them come and go. So has everybody.

Then came sophomore year. Tenth grade. A year older and infinitely wiser. And guess who was in all but one of my classes?

And so my naïve little crush began growing into something much greater and much more mature. Over the next half-year, Sarah and I got to know each other about as well as either of us had ever known anyone—and we said as much. We talked about everything because we had the time to talk about everything. From class to class, my locker to her locker, lunch hour to the inevitable afternoon crash, we spent almost every minute of the school day together. She became more than a crush. She became my best friend.

The solidifying of that friendship began on the second day of classes, after we'd realized our situation. I told her that she was lucky to have the smartest, funniest, best-looking guy in the school with her in every class of the day. I thought I was being so clever.

She responded instantly, "Don't forget the most modest." My panic was only momentary (*Oh no! She's cleverer than me!*) before I burst into laughter.

The year tumbled into a steady stream of inside jokes, anecdotes, quips, and shared, knowing looks. You see, the difference between your average high school kid who develops a crush on a girl and me is that I have a writer's mind. Your average high school kid looks at a girl and says to himself, "She is sooo hot." Whereas I would look over and see Sarah stretch during class—watch her sweater rise to reveal a flat, tan stomach and the divot of a navel, and I'd think of blowing the fine, nearly invisible hairs on her flesh until they stood on end.

Yes, we all have those moments with the loves of our youths—I just happened to have catalogued mine in absurd detail. These were the scraps that seemed mundane and even inconsequential at the time but that added up to more as the year went on. You build friendships a joke at a time, a secret at a time. They seem to mean nothing at the moment of their conception, though, which in a way is the best part. These were the jokes, the secrets between us:

• • •

Sarah and I built a relationship out of mocking each other's oddities. For instance, she was a girly girl—almost absurdly fashionable. She came to school with new, creative outfits every day and frequently teased me about my complete lack of fashion sense. Once in chemistry class, I noticed that her brown leather belt matched her shoes flawlessly, down to the small golden buckles. Offhandedly, I remarked, "Nice job with the shoes and belt."

"Huh?" she asked, looking up from some last-minute homework she was racing to finish.

"They match."

She looked at me like I might have had my parietal lobe removed. "Are you serious? They're supposed to match."

"What? Belts and shoes?"

"Yeah. You don't know that?"

"Is that like a thing?"

She looked at me carefully, her face finally spreading into a grin. "Wow. Maybe it's a good idea you don't try to wear real clothes."

Up until that point, I had never worn a belt, relying on my bony hips to hold my pants up. Not long after that conversation, I bought two belts and two pairs of shoes and made sure to always match them correctly.

It's embarrassing to say, but in high school all I ever wore was a rotating combination of white T-shirts and jeans or khakis. The only time I ever broke away from my slacker's uniform was for basketball games when we had to dress up in a shirt and tie during school. On one particular game day, I was sitting in English class feeling a little hot and decided to roll up my sleeves. I unbuttoned the little buttons on the sleeves of my shirt and crammed them up past my elbows in two fell swoops, securing the mess by tucking the material into itself.

Sarah, who had been watching me, gripped her face with both hands in dismay. "What," she asked, "are you doing?"

"What?" I said. "Rolling my sleeves up."

She just shook her head.

"You don't like the way I roll up my sleeves? This isn't good enough for you?"

"Just…" She clenched her hands into fists in mocking frustration. "Come here."

I leaned into her desk, and she took my arm. After undoing my method of sleeve-rolling, she showed me how to fold the cuff back in a crease and then continue to fold the sleeve so it would stay. She did the first, and after allowing me all of ten seconds in a failed attempt at the second, snatched my arm back and rolled that one up, too.

"Isn't that better?" she asked. "Aren't you glad someone's around to teach you all the simple stuff like how to roll up the sleeves of your shirt?"

"Yeah, if you wanna show off," I told her, pretending that her hands working meticulously on each of my arms had not left me a little dizzy.

To this day, I still remember her folding back the cuff every time I roll up the sleeves on a shirt.

• • •

One of the classes we shared was Introduction to News Writing. Sarah wanted to be a journalist; I wanted an easy credit. Together we learned about the history of American journalism, laws applying to the profession, such as libel and slander, and then spent the rest of our time writing news stories to prepare us for the staff of the school newspaper, *The Jacket Journal.* Quickly we discovered how

God-awful boring it was to gather quotes from our peers about the student mediation program or the new sign in the football stadium. Mostly we walked around the building during our study halls jabbering to each other and questioning the importance of getting our friends to say, "It's a good thing for the school. I think that sign makes it easier to see the score during the game."

Eventually we realized that all students sound the same on paper, so we just started making up our quotes and attributing them to random people—sometimes people we didn't even know. We were little Jayson Blairs. Sarah dared me to just make up a name and then attribute an age and quote to this fake student. I didn't quite have the balls to take it that far.

Between news stories and fake quotes we had to kill the time somehow. Writing haikus became a favorite pastime. She would tap her pen on my desk during class and point my attention to her notebook:

Fuzzy fleece in sweats
Looks like sleep and winter warmth
Could you please hug me?

Mine usually took a darker tone:

We all fear dying
No one can live forever
But we all will try

"Maybe something cheerier next time?" Sarah suggested.

• • •

She could surprise me.

The summer before our sophomore year, I'd hosted a party at my house (unbeknownst to my altogether too trusting parents), and perhaps this party included trace amounts of alcohol. Well, word gets around quickly in a small town, especially among high school kids. Yet I had a lot of friends who looked down upon this sort of thing. I always thought of Sarah as one of those people. I didn't want her to know about any of the bad stuff I did.[197] Sarah went to church. She belonged to the Fellowship of Christian Athletes. She believed in abstinence before marriage.[198]

So imagine how awkward I felt when, out of the blue, she asked me about my party.

We had spotted each other walking into the high school early one morning. I laughed nervously and tried to play it off.

"Not a big deal," I mumbled.

She didn't seem upset or disappointed. She just gave me a knowing smile, so radiant I had to look away, just barely catching that spot on her tooth that glowed a brighter, sturdier white than the rest.

"You better invite me next time," she said.

"Uh-ha! Heh! Ehm, ah-huh," I said, blushing furiously, not realizing at the time that there might be layers to her that I didn't give her credit for and that perhaps I was not the only sixteen-year-old who had figured out where his or her folks kept the booze. "You bet," I finished, and we walked together into the high school—laughing at me.

• • •

The school assigned us usernames for the computers. It was just your first initial tacked on to your last name. One day we were writing up stories for News Writing class in the computer lab. Sarah watched me sign on and then broke into a loud fit of laughter.

"What?" I asked.

---

197 Although I hardly think four shots of vodka followed by an hour of stumbling around pretending to be way more intoxicated than I really was marks me as a rebel without a cause. At the time, though, I liked to think of myself as one bad motherfucker.

198 As did I, but not by choice. It was actually the girls of Mount Vernon High School who decided this for me.

"Smarkley," she giggled.

"Why is that funny? Yours is Spressler."

"Okay. Whatever, Smarkley."

• • •

All the cheerleaders were assigned members of the basketball team for whom they made locker signs and baked cookies for away games.[199] Sarah had chosen me and Justin as her players.

Sarah was already absurdly smart (she scored in the ninety-ninth percentile on her practice SAT—I mean, Jesus) but was also outrageously meticulous. This not only translated to straight A's on her report card but also to my insanely detailed locker signs. The cheerleaders got photocopied pictures of our mascot, the Yellow Jacket, which most of them just colored in. Sarah's included glitter, colored glue, and little stuffed bumblebees. My name and number were outlined to the point where I felt like I was starring in a Broadway musical.

People would write all sorts of things on locker signs, most of them sarcastic and unflattering. One day we stopped at my locker and saw that someone had written "Hot Studly!" in a corner.

Sarah, unsatisfied with this, removed her trademark blue pen (she only used this one specific kind of blue pen, and she used it for every homework assignment, test, or note) and added beside the word studly, "+modest."

"Satisfied?" I asked her.

"I put a lot of work into that," she told me. "We can't have you libeled."

"You mean slandered."

"I mean libeled. Pay attention in News Writing."

---

199 This was a terrible idea because long bus rides to Columbus usually led to nibbles, which turned into devouring ten cookies or brownies before we arrived. I played many a basketball game with what felt like a bowling ball in my stomach.

• • •

When I took choir my freshman year, I got a C on the exam. The choir teacher told me that I was one of the least talented students she had seen in her career (and she was on the verge of retiring after like forty years or something). This grade dogged me for the rest of high school, and, I think, unfairly. I was no better or worse than your average fifteen-year-old male vocalist, but I tanked the exam tape because I didn't think there was any way the teacher would take the time to listen to a hundred-plus kids sing that stupid Neil Diamond song about America. Obviously, she did.[200]

After Sarah found out about this, she mocked me pretty mercilessly, and I responded by frequently bursting into song as if we were on the set of a musical. Because I was mostly listening to 2Pac in those days, I only had a four-song repertoire, which included Nine Inch Nails' "We're In This Together," "Hanging Around" by Counting Crows (a song about being in a depressing nowhere town that Sarah always said reminded her of Mount Vernon), and Kid Rock's "Only God Knows Why."[201] Finally, there was this Robbie Williams tune called "Angels" that I'd heard on the radio a few times. Sarah caught me humming it under my breath during Spanish.

"Is that that 'Angels' song?" she asked.

"No," I said.

"I love that song."

"It wasn't," I said.

"How do you know it?"

"I don't."

"Whatever, you were just singing it."

---

200 And now I'm completely freaked out that she kept the tape, and someday I'm going to show up on YouTube, 130 pounds and bad acne, creakily singing, "On the boats and on the planes/ They're coming to America!"

201 I was sixteen. Do not let this serve as an endorsement of either Kid Rock or his "music."

Begrudgingly, I admitted to liking it—sort of, kind of, a little—too. So I began singing it all the time. She would walk into class and I'd start belting it out in my best ballad voice. It cracked her up. I remember catching her at her desk, focused on trying to decode a Spanish sentence, and basically shouting the words into her ear. She jumped and pulled back from her desk, and then I was dancing beside her, raising my hands to the sky in uplift, as the other students filtered in and found their seats. Her head fell back and she laughed at the ceiling, her dark brown eyes brimming with tears.

• • •

The strange thing was that as I grew closer to Sarah, my friendship simultaneously deepened with Drew. He had an all-American innocence to him, an appeal that blended a goofy sense of humor with outright earnestness. We collided physically during basketball practice when the jayvee scrimmaged the varsity. I drove him home after practices. We talked about Coach Stahl. We talked about college, where he would be in a year. We talked about Sarah. He mused about how utterly remarkable she was, how she leveled the way he thought about things and built them back up from scratch. I could only agree.

Even as I recognized that I had bypassed my crush on this girl—that I had fallen in love with her in a way that shocked me with how mature it felt—I grew to like Drew more and more. He was funny and talkative and kind, and that year—1999 and stretching into the new Millennium—he somehow became one of my closest friends.

So I had these competing loyalties inside of me because I still envisioned him going away to school in a year. I still saw myself as having the chance to tell Sarah how I felt about her—maybe in a year, maybe sooner—and that was all I needed for the moment.

The notion of how I would reconcile this sticky situation was still vague and fuzzy in my head.

• • •

A while later we were studying medieval literature in English, so for our project, Sarah, Justin, and I made a video of our own medieval romance. The video included another friend of ours, Sarah's little brother, Nate, and—in some stock footage between scenes—her mother. It took us a whole day to shoot and consisted of me wearing a blanket and a crown, wielding a fake plastic sword, and Justin in sweatpants and a gray T-shirt (it was supposed to be armor) slashing at me with a piece of cardboard as we vied for the princess's love.

Obviously, we laughed a lot. Mostly, I recall, because Justin was such a pathetic actor.

I remember we rushed through the end of the video because Drew was coming to pick up Sarah. They were going to a movie. It was the only moment I ever felt anything about the two of them. Not jealousy exactly, just a twinge of regret that as close as I was to her, my best hope was a distant second.

When Drew pulled into her driveway in his ancient white Jeep, we shook hands. With Drew it was always a handshake or a hug. Before climbing into my minivan, I stood and watched them drive away.

• • •

Sarah and I went to see a movie with a group of our friends. The film was *The Bone Collector* with Denzel Washington and Angelina Jolie. At some point I leaned over to whisper to her, "I bet you the killer is Leland Orser."

"Who's Leland Orser?" she whispered back.

"The guy who was in *Seven*."

"I don't know what you're talking about."

After it was revealed that the killer was indeed Leland Orser, I hit her lightly on the arm. "I told you it was that guy!"

"What? No, you didn't. You mumbled something about *Seven*."

"Yeah! Leland Ors—"

We got shushed from a row behind us.

I offered her a ride home after the movie—those days I was driving my mom's Toyota minivan and was one of the few among us with a license. On the drive home, she asked me about a girl, whom she happened to know liked me. "What do you think about that?" she asked playfully.

I shrugged. "She's nice. I just don't think of her that way."

"Well, I have it on good information that she likes you."

"I know."

"Oh, you know? So modest."

"What? I can tell she likes me! I don't mean it like a cocky thing. I can just tell."

She leaned against the window, and looked at me, assessing, grinning, her head propped on her fist. "Shut up, Smarkley."

"Spressler," I muttered, smiling underneath a fake snarl.

I admit: that night I took the long way home.

• • •

She handed me a Christmas card during chemistry. I watched her give out another one and joked, "Hell, I don't feel special now."

"No," she protested, "you should, Stephen. I only give these to girls. You're one of three guys that I made one for, and one of them's Drew, so that doesn't count."

I narrowed my eyes into slits, "So who's the third guy, Sarah?"

She rolled her eyes.

"Don't you turn away from me! I know what's going on here!"

Written in her efficient cursive and trademark blue pen, this is what the card said:

Stephen,

Wow, it's been a busy year. Between writing haikus, making up quotes for news stories, and getting detentions I just don't understand

*how you can be so intelligent, good-looking, and modest!? I'm glad
that someone as nice as you is someone I can call my friend. I'm
sure I'll be seeing you over break for our English video, basketball,
and whatever else. Hope you have a happy holiday season!!!!!!!!!!*

-love ya-
Sarah

• • •

During the winter, Sarah and I were at our friend Jenna's house for
a party. These were not the binge-drinking, puking, pissing, pie-
humping parties that teen movies always depict. This was a clean-cut
watch a movie, listen to music, eat chips, drink pop type of ordeal.
Everyone was there, but still you can only stretch that type of entertainment so far. Sarah suggested that we take a walk around the
block, and I agreed.

We left. I know it was winter, but I don't remember wearing a coat.
We talked. I kept her laughing with my usual approach of saying as
much as I could as fast as I could (this was my method with her; find
the button and then just push it till the damn thing sticks).

After a while, the block became two, then three. And slowly the
conversation developed the way it sometimes did with us. What we
wanted to do after high school, who we secretly disliked amongst
our enormous group of friends, where we saw ourselves once we
broke out of this shell of a town. Sarah talked about her family.
Her father was my dentist, so I knew the Presslers somewhat, but
Sarah told me things I never would have guessed at, surprising, sad,
touching—all of that. She explained her relationship with Drew, her
distant, absent worry about what would happen when he left for
college in a few months. I know I told her things, too, I'm sure, but
they are all long forgotten.

There are moments in your life that you never want to forget, that you feel you must cling to above the rest. Now I can only vaguely recall the way her nose crinkled when she smiled, how in the street-lamps of Gambier Street, the little spot of polished white in her tooth shone more brightly than usual.

It's strange how it all happened. She elbowed her way into my life. She took up residence in all the corners you reserve for the most important people. Her breath put flesh on my bones.

• • •

The point being that you never really know anyone, but I knew Sarah as well as I had ever known another person—this high school crush of mine, this pleasant, lovely notch on my path through adolescence. I knew what kind of pen she used, what beverage she preferred, the grades she received in each class.

And these are the stories of her that I've retained. They have no connection except to themselves, yet obviously they add up to more—the more being the hardest part, because there is more. And this is where I completely suspend the snarky footnotes. This is where the glib-but-knowingly-glib voice becomes entirely useless.

• • •

Maybe two weeks after we took that walk at Jenna's party, I was watching a TV movie with my mom and sister, a reunion of the show *Homicide: Life on the Streets*, where Yaphet Kotto's character is shot and the old detectives all team up to find his would-be killer. The phone rang, and it was for me.

I grabbed the portable phone from my mom and walked outside of the living room to take the call.

"Markley?"

It was Ian. When you've been calling each other since third grade, you don't need more than a word to recognize the voice.

"Hey," I said. "What's up?"

"How are you?" he asked.

I paused. *Odd question*, I thought. He sounded hesitant. I immediately picked up that something had happened, something big. It felt like it had the year before when one of our classmates had committed suicide with his dad's handgun.

"I'm fine. Why?"

The other end of the line hung in silence for a moment. "You haven't heard?"

"Heard what?" Interestingly, I was more curious than scared, more excited than worried. Maybe Coach Stahl had a kidney stone that required surgery and he was out for the rest of the season. *Oh woe would be me!* I thought with perverse giddiness.

"Um…" he began, and I heard his throat click. "At six o'clock tonight, Sarah Pressler and her mom were killed in a car accident."

I'll never forget the way he said that. *Why say the time, Ian?* I thought at that moment. *What the fuck does it matter what fucking time?*

"Hello?" he said. "Markley? You there?"

So many thoughts to process, but the one that sticks out is the calm: *Okay, but not really, right?* It wasn't real. I knew that. It couldn't be real. They were just words out of Ian's mouth, but their meaning started to sink in, layer by textured layer. I left the stairs, past the piano to the dining room, no direction to my movement.

"Markley?"

I'd been silent for a while. Now I spoke, but I didn't recognize the voice, the way it quavered—like a flag beaten by the wind. "Ian," I said. "I swear to God, if this isn't true… This is the sickest fucking joke I've ever heard."

"No," he exclaimed immediately. "It's true."

There was no light anywhere. Just pinpoints of stars in my vision.

"Markley?"

"I've got to go," I said and hung up. It was February 13, 2000, a day before Valentine's Day.

• • •

Basically, the time following that moment is a carefully laid-out blur that I can recall with near-perfect clarity. I say blur because none of it made any sense. I wept uncontrollably all night. Friends called me. My grandpa called, unaware of what had happened, and I had no idea what to say to him. There was basketball practice. There were calling hours. There was Sarah's dad hugging me, looking so much more composed than I could manage, and he even rescheduled the wake so it didn't interfere with an upcoming basketball game that pitted us against our divisional rivals. There was a party—a goddamn party—after the funeral where the host's mother made omelets. There was the family member of Sarah's at the funeral who said that people of the Christian faith could take particular comfort knowing that they had a leg up when it came to being with Sarah in the afterlife, and I've never thought the words *fuck you* harder at a person without them actually leaving my lips. There was the state patrolman who explained what had happened: Sarah driving home with her mother from a shopping trip in Mansfield, veering off the side of the road for some reason, overcorrecting, and sending the car head-on into a van coming the other direction. There was disbelief that this could be happening, that everyone's life could be changed so abruptly, so permanently. There was a 2Pac song that I listened to incessantly. There was Robbie Williams's "Angels." There was my family tiptoeing around me, unable to help because I couldn't go to them for this; this was mine, and I didn't want them near it. There was every class skipped. There were school psychologists making rounds. There was an awful, dreadful song written by our class, including, I'm ashamed to say, me, which I'm sure Sarah would have winced at if she had not laughed in our faces outright. There were people crying and laughing and sometimes I couldn't tell the difference. One moment I would feel like collapsing and the next, an older kid named Purse would crack a joke about the relative ineffectiveness of a one-day postponement of basketball practice ("Oh, good," he dead-panned. "I was afraid all of this was going to get in the way of doing the three-man weave"), and I was cracking up, giggling despite myself. There was a string of notes written to Sarah on a piece of butcher paper spread out across a table in the library. There was—and forever will be—before February 13, 2000, and after.

And there was Drew walking into the library on Valentine's Day.

That was where we had all congregated. Where parents and school shrinks patrolled and the butcher paper was laid out and no one knew quite how to stand or what to do with their hands. When Drew walked in, he was immediately surrounded. The guys from his class—Purse and all the rest—enveloped him. I leaned against a table, staring at the ground, numb and desperate and catatonic and bleeding out.

I knew I had to go over and say something to him, although for the first time in my life I had nothing to say about anything. I waited until the crowd had opened a little and sidled into the group. I waited with my arms crossed and my chin on my chest as my eyes continued to leak their seemingly endless parade.

It was Drew who finally turned to me. His eyes were swollen and red, his face streaked from hours and hours of this.

"Hey," I said, unable to meet his eyes.

He put his hand on my shoulder and almost shook me until I looked at him. "Stephen—"

My entire face wet, breath sucking in and out of my tired throat, I managed to raise my head and look at him. I shook my head. "Drew, I don't know what to s—"

"You should know," he interrupted, his tears on hold for the briefest moment, "you should know that Sarah always considered you one of her very best friends… and she always talked about you like you were her best friend."

Those words crippled me. Even if they pulled me through some of the darkest times of my life over the next year, they crippled me. "Jesus, Drew, I'm so sorry." My voice cracked and failed.

And then I collapsed into his arms, my head on his shoulder, just sobbing in front of everyone I knew and not caring at all. He hugged me so fiercely my ribs hurt. It was the moment I would have shared on that Florida beach if I'd had to—the best moment of my life.

• • •

So here's the question: now that I've told you this—this story that I hold sacred, that I've built every moment of my life around in one way or another—how do we go back to laughing through the graveyard?

There is much more to this, of course, but it has no climax, no conclusion—just a long, drawn-out period of recovery. The way I cried at first felt like a test, like if I could only hit a peak—if I could hit that ceiling of anguish, then I could come down the other side. Unfortunately, that's not the way it works. It never goes away—it only fades over time. In the months that followed Sarah's death, I didn't sleep. I spent a lot of nights at Drew's house. The two of us would sit on his bed and go through pictures of her and take turns muttering stories while we wept.

After Drew left for school, it got harder. I never really felt close enough to talk to anyone about her, so I just internalized what I felt and let myself turn mean and angry more often. I had moments when I treated people cruelly for no real reason. I spent too much time by myself.

Two or three times a month I would tell my friends I couldn't hang out because I had to do something with my family, while I would tell my parents that I was off to a friend's house. Then I would drive out into the country.

One thing Knox County, Ohio, is great for is deserted little pockets of nowhere. Farms and forest and trickling rivers for miles. So I would go out to those hidden corners on the outskirts of town and climb up onto the hood of the Toyota Sienna I was using and sit and watch the grass get knocked around by the wind. In the summer, there was the smell of corn and manure, and at night when the stars came out, I acted like a child and talked to them, as if they were her and she could hear me.

And suddenly she was in my writing—all over it, in fact. She invaded this longstanding hobby and gave it a new awful thrill. I'd never in my life felt anything so visceral, so real: this darkness with a physical form that at the worst moments I could almost glimpse from the corner of my eye. So I'd go out to those vacant county roads and try to stare it down, try to catch it in its fleeting, billowing entrails of black, but of course that's a lost cause. So I'd sit on the hood of the minivan and watch the wind ripple that grass or look out over winter's ruined corn fields and watch those empty little patches of the world, thinking of her, thinking of the stories trapped in my head, suffocating, wanting to get out.

Of course, I made it back from those days, and now they seem strange and foreign and maybe even a little melodramatic. I lost my virginity. I fell for my first girlfriend. I quit basketball. I wrote two novels. I went to college. I got Sarah's initials tattooed on my ankle.

Drew went to school, graduated, worked for a while, didn't like it, joined the military. He went to Iraq, and even though we had both done a poor job of staying in touch (especially once we were both out of school and I was knocking around out west), when he told me he was going over there, I got sick to my stomach.

It was right in the middle of the falling-out with my Love Interest, of nabbing Julie as my agent, of Justin preparing to have a child, and I already felt like my head was being pulled in eighty different directions. When we spoke on the phone, I felt like such a coward. I probably should have told him that even though we'd lost contact a bit, he was the one person who was there for me during the hardest time of my life, that I owed him in a way I could never repay. For some reason, all that came into my head was a petulant, childish whine: *Don't go.*

This all sounds very heavy, I know, but that's where I find a strange comfort: that life can contain such multitudes, that I could laugh on the day my best friend died, that Drew and I could sit in his room and he would remind me that Sarah always told him he needed to get new shoes.

"And I always said, 'What's the matter with my shoes?'" said Drew. "'Why are you always so down on my shoes? They work. They protect my feet. They keep the gravel out. They're fine shoes.'"

And that we could find this so very, very funny.

• • •

Maybe I wanted to be a writer before February 13, 2000—before I even met Sarah. It's likely I would've become a writer all the same. Still, when I sit at my desk (wherever that desk has been over the years) and glance at the picture of her I keep there… Let's just say the stories are all about her, even when they're not. Because some stories are too good to keep to yourself, too important not to tell, and so they stick around and begin to grow, and soon they branch out and then those branches grow vines and the vines grow moss and soon this one story—this one little piece of yourself that you thought lived inside you like a stone—has taken over everything.

I still dream of her, but not in the desperate, cinematic I-just-want-to-touch-your-cheek kind of way. I wish they were, but instead we are usually talking about something trivial. Often we sit in space—literally a field of stars, or along a stretch of rainbow highway that leads from the front door of her house and off into oblivion (I'd like to say this has some kind of deep significance, but even in the dream I recognize it clearly as a level from "Mario Kart" for Nintendo64).

We try to talk about Drew, about her father and brother, about all the myriad directions life has knocked me. Still, it's hard to stay serious; it's difficult to keep our voices solemn when there's so much debate to be had about issues of importance.

"Heath definitely should get the Oscar," she says. "That part where he makes Batman choose between Rachel and Dent, then tells him the wrong locations? So creepy."

"What? That's not right," I say. "Batman went after Harvey Dent."

"Wrong. He meant to go after Rachel," she explains. "The Joker tricked him."

"No, no, no," I say. "He went after Dent because he was more important. He mattered to Gotham more."

"Did you even watch the movie?" she asks, smiling as that little flaw on her tooth catches starlight. "He tells Gordon he's going for Rachel."

"Oh yeah, that makes a lot of sense," I say, rolling my eyes.

She shakes her head, "Whatever, Smarkley. Don't you have a book to write or something?"

"I'm taking a break!" I protest.

"Okay, but when you put me in there, don't make up a bunch of quotes for me," she says. "This isn't Introduction to News Writing."

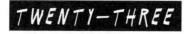

This Book, Published

Even after I write the last word in this book, there will be other stories, other obstacles, other travails, other noteworthy moments. For instance, there will be contract negotiations between Julie, Peter Lynch, and some amorphous "board" that Peter reports to. I'll picture this so-called "board" as a consortium of old white men who look either like Texas oil barons or high-powered investment bankers. Peter will stand before them in a dark corporate office backlit by evil green desk lamps and report Julie's request of a 10 percent larger cut of the translation rights. One of the old, white oil barons will look to a well-coiffed investment banker with a handkerchief neatly protruding from his breast pocket, and this investment banker-looking guy will give a slight, nearly imperceptible nod, and Peter will return to his email to report the good news.

There will be all sorts of details to work out in the contract—things a writer should probably know something about, but in which I can't dredge up much more than the most passing interest. First periodical rights at 90 percent? Sure, sounds great. Publisher's reserve against returns? Yeah, whatever. Permissions and indemnities? Jesus Christ, I nodded off in the bathtub and almost drowned! Be careful.

After she gets the advance up to $5,000, Julie will want to negotiate for higher rates on most of the different rights, which is great, and I guess that's why writers have agents because if Peter had put boldfaced print into the contract that said:

Author will cede all proceeds of any kind to publisher, who will dispense them to author if and only if author can defeat five prison inmates from the Illinois State Penitentiary for Violent Offenders in hand-to-hand combat in Battle Royals unsupervised and unregulated by the State and witnessed solely by a coterie of mysterious businessmen known only as the "board" for their gambling opportunities and general amusement.

...I'm sure I would have quickly and happily agreed to such language.

The only part of the contract that will concern me at all is the word count, which Peter has set at 75,000. This will dismay me because when I check, this book is clocking in at around 148,000, nearly double Peter's estimate. I will have a one-day panic attack that Sourcebooks will not accept a manuscript of this length, and I will be forced to make massive cuts.[202] Luckily, this will turn out to be a paranoid fantasy.

There will be subsequent conversations with the people who appear in this book. Justin will still claim he'll only read it if it's at the library. Phil will senselessly worry about his professional career. Bruce Springsteen will not return my calls to see if I can use his real name.

And there will be a long conversation by telephone with Steven.

• • •

No exotic imaginary locales this time, just me in my room sitting cross-legged on my floor-mattress with my cell phone and he in his

---

202 In such an event, I fully planned to rename my tome *Publish Half This Book, You Dicks.*

house in Indiana, just across the Ohio border. The call is part update, part congratulations. Steven has not seen the rest of the book but tells me he can't wait to read it.

"I look forward to it," I tell him. "Partly with excitement and partly with terror."

Out of all the writers I've had conversations with over the years, the tops—in quality and quantity—have been with Steven. I first wandered into his office as a sophomore to confront his suspicion that I'd plagiarized my story, and after that I unloaded so many manuscripts onto him, I've lost count. I also probably owe this book to him.

I had learned about the mechanics of publishing in a class he taught called The Literary Marketplace. One day in class he spoke of his own career, which he calls "totally scattershot with no plan at all."

He capped off a long description of his published work by showing us a copy of his last contract for a children's book. He read through it a bit until he came to a line describing why he had not yet begun to earn royalties on the book. He pointed to it, cocked his head at the class, and said, "I have no idea what this means."

Here was one of the smartest people I knew, a writer who had the keys to the castle, so to speak, whose sheer depth of intellect intimidated the hell out of me, so that I stammered and false-started and trailed off whenever I spoke to him, and even he found this whole publishing thing overwhelming and at times mysterious.

Now that I have my very own book deal, I am eager to hear his thoughts.

"This is the reason writers have agents," he tells me over the phone. "They're really a firewall. Some writers have this idea that a publisher is a conduit for bringing genius into the world and it will treat your manuscript lovingly—well, horseshit. It's a business and they're out to make money. So when I left my agent and sold the children's book, I remember how powerless I felt talking to the editor. She offered me a small amount of money, and I thought, 'Well, no. I want more money,' but I felt so slavishly indebted to her, I probably would have gone and worked the printing press myself if they'd asked."

I ask Steven about his "scattershot" career again because more than anyone I know or have met, I feel like it is an honest depiction of what this life is like. Even those writers who find success rarely have the success they had imagined. Early in his career, Steven encountered the writer John Gardner, who wrote *Grendel, October Light,* and *The Sunlight Dialogues,* among others. After hearing Gardner speak at the Bread Loaf Writer's Conference, Steven was inspired to write his first novel, *Satyrday.* He sold it to a New York house based on the first seventy pages, a method of selling a book that was and remains unheard of. It was well-received, published in England, Germany, and the Netherlands, and was listed as one of the American Library Association's best young adult novels.

"I didn't know it was a young adult novel," Steven tells me, "but I thought, 'Okay. Now it's got that attached to it.'"

Steven went on to write the novelization of a Sissy Spacek and Mel Gibson movie called *The River,* and Universal Pictures liked it enough to offer him a job creating short stories out of television scripts for Steven Spielberg's *Amazing Stories.*

"There's another story behind this," he tells me. "I was working on a second novel of my own, and I harbored these fantasies of putting out a great novel, and—you know—the young lions and I would all be having drinks in New York and so forth. Gardner really liked the second book—he had been the instigator for the first, and I worked closely with him on the second, which at first I called *The Night We Danced with the Rednecks' Wives,* but which I eventually renamed *Good Fortune.* Anyway, he was who I went to for advice— he was my mentor—and I always had John in the back of my mind when I was writing.

"It was around 1980 that I began working on the second book. I started teaching at Miami in the fall of 1982, and in early September John was killed in a motorcycle accident. I had a complete crisis of confidence and stopped writing."

Our conversation hangs for a moment on the telephone. My left hand finds a loose thread on the sleeve of my T-shirt, and I begin to absently tug at it. Not long after I took my first creative writing class with Steven, he gave me a book by Gardner called *On Becoming a Novelist*, which had one of the most brilliant, beautiful metaphors for writing a novel that I've ever heard. "It's like driving a car at night with the headlights on," Gardner wrote. "You can't see all the way home but you can see enough of the road ahead to get there eventually." I've wondered about the man ever since.

Now as I tug at the T-shirt thread, I imagine Steven sitting at a desk in Indiana and wonder how he found out about his friend. I wonder about the tortured moment when he got a phone call that changed his life. I wonder if someone told him what time it had happened and he thought, *What the hell does it matter what time it happened?*

"So what happened to the book?" I ask.

"It never got published. My agent took it to twenty New York houses and it was rejected by every one. I put it in a drawer and turned my back on it."

"Jesus." I cannot believe that somewhere in a drawer sits this novel, untouched.

"That really took the wind out of my sails," he says.

In the years that followed, Steven placed a book of poems that he'd been working on for a decade and published two children's books. The first, a picture book, he wrote when an editor suggested he try the form. "I thought, 'Holy shit: three to five pages of text? Why am I wasting my time on six-hundred-page novels?'"

I laugh. "So not what you were expecting?"

"Steve, I thought I was going to be a mainstream novelist. That's what I thought my future was when I started out, that's where I thought I was headed. So I'm in kind of wounded retreat from a career I did not expect."

"How much of that would you say has to do with teaching?"

"Well, that's another choice I made. I get a great deal of pleasure from teaching, and I've invested a lot in certain students over the years. Some of my colleagues treat it like a fellowship, like they're mostly getting paid to write, and I envy that in some respects, how they can put writing before teaching. I, on the other hand, feel like I have to leak blood from my ears."

I laugh again. Steven speaks like a scalpel, slicing the English language into its finest components.

"But I've always felt I had an obligation: if I saw a young writer come along who I thought was special—like you—I always took it seriously. It has had a negative effect on my writing, but that's okay. I'm happy with my life."

The thread pulls free, unraveling from the cloth with all resistance removed. I'm trying to tell Steven something of myself here and doing a very poor job of it. "I feel like—I've always felt like…" As always, I feel as if intelligent phrases and well-articulated ideas completely evaporate when I try to talk to this man. "I get more out of your story, like I learn more about what I want out of life, than with anyone else."

"My story is anomalous," he warns. "If you want to be a writer, don't follow my example."

I feel our conversation winding down. Glancing up at the clock beside my bed, I see that we've been talking for over an hour. There are things to do in Indiana: dogs that need to be walked and errands run. Here in Chicago, I have a mother lode of editing waiting for me on my laptop.

We wrap up by talking about a trip I will make to Miami in the spring to speak in his class. I tell him I'll send the book when I have it as finished as I can manage.

"And does this include all the nasty emails I wrote you in the early stages?" he asks with wry, self-deprecating pleasure.

"Oh, of course," I tell him. "How could it not? And when you get the whole thing you can offer your thoughts or eviscerate it completely."

"Oh my God, are you kidding? I can't wait!"

I search for words that can describe my appreciation for his help, his wisdom, his friendship, but of course I am stymied. Clunky thoughts trip and tumble down flights of stairs in my head, and I'm almost forlorn with the realization that I'll never be able to properly thank this man, that all the things I've left unsaid over the years will live on as marks against me in the end. "Thanks again," I say, hoping that maybe Steven just already knows. "For everything."

"You're very welcome. We'll talk again soon."

• • •

There will be a conversation with my Love Interest.

Right before I turn in the book to Sourcebooks, I will send the nearly completed manuscript to her. This will happen nearly three months after I (mostly) finish this book, nearly nine months after I drove to Boston.

I am nervous to hear what she thinks about so many things, but she's only complimentary. She loves it, she says, yet this answer doesn't satisfy me. "Just tell me what struck you," I ask her.

"I don't know. Everything. I loved it, Steve… I felt bad when I read the part about Sarah. It was so sad, and I felt terrible that I was learning most of that for the first time… That we've never really talked about any of it."

I remain silent. It's not exactly a subject I want to broach through thousands of miles of cellular signals.

She goes on. "Yeah. But I think I said to you once, I can't stand it when people read anything I've written, let alone something like this where you put yourself so out there."

I press her. "Do you think your mom will be horrified?"

What follows is the longest pause ever. "Uh…" she says.

"Oh my God, she will," I wail, and my Love Interest cracks up.

"That pause was worse than a 'yes'—it was a full-on admission of just how horrified she's going to be."

She laughs brightly through the phone. "Don't worry. I'll prepare her."

"Well, what else?"

"What else do you want me to say?"

"What about all the scenes with other girls? I basically admit I have a raging hormonal imbalance when it comes to women."

"That stuff certainly wasn't fun for me to read," she says, pausing. "I won't lie, if you asked me right after I read certain parts—if you'd caught me in the moment—I'd be upset, and I certainly cried a few times, but it's not like those moments don't belong in the book." I stand and move away from my mattress, where I've been lying. Just the thought of bringing tears to her eyes fills me with dread and guilt. This is another one of those *What have I done?* moments that have arisen nearly every day since I sold the book. "But you know," she says, her voice turning sunny again. "Then you go and talk about how great I am!"

"Well, you are kinda great."

"You're *wel-cooome*," she says in singsong.

"What did you think of how I portrayed you?" I ask. Throughout the book I have tried to keep her opaque, as anonymous as possible while still retaining those attributes that make her so *her*.

"First, you were far too generous. Second, I'm very afraid people are going to think I'm a weirdo."

"Why?"

She sighs. "Steve, the average person doesn't hear me say stuff like, 'Oh, I want to sit on your face.'"

"I know, but do you understand that's what I like about you? I like that you're funny and startling and clever and kind of filthy?"

"I know, and it's fine, but whenever I advertise for you and tell people, 'Hey, you should read Steve's book,' they're going to know that I like to climb on you like a jungle gym."

I smile. "Sorry. Had to be honest."

"No, I like it," she says. "And it's always fun reading about how much someone likes you! All the different ways you describe my eyes…" she muses, maybe kidding, maybe not.

"And that brings up a good point, babe: this book—even if it tanks and even if it's out of print in a year—it will still exist forever. You and I—no matter what happens to us—we'll have to live with this around our necks, over our heads. This little love letter I wrote. It will always cast a shadow over our lives. You know, plenty of people have lost loves from their youth, plenty of people have failed relationships, but not everyone has those relationships documented."

"Yeah," she says slowly. "But I'm not sure that's a bad thing." I hear her hesitate. "To have the love of your youth written down somewhere."

Hallowed stories, I think to myself. *Those chapters written and chapters erased.*

The problem is that hanging over this conversation about my book is another, larger conversation that as of late has choked us, stifled us, left us lost. I need to know if she can live with this book because our future has sailed right onto a shallow bed of rocks. It actually boils down so very simply that it's practically a math equation.

This book has tethered me to Chicago for the foreseeable future +
She has at least a year and a half left in Boston / We can't sustain the
distance much longer = One of us must make a sacrifice.

Now I have a competition again: it pits my love for her (and my knowledge that when you find something in life as important as I have found in her, it's pretty stupid to let it go) versus that wildheart. And maybe I've already begun to feel its first creeping tentacles.

I don't know where it came from or how it grew in me without my noticing, but I know what I feel now so well: this restlessness, this feeling that whatever it is I'm doing, wherever I am, that's not where I'm supposed to be, this fierce compulsion to be everywhere and everything to everyone all at once that leaves me tired and ragged yet still always searching. So I find myself stranded in places having forgotten why I'm there, what I'm supposed to be doing, trying to lose myself and in the process getting disoriented and messy and chasing the fireflies until I've jumped from dream to dream and light to light and shooting star to shooting star so many times I can't even remember what it was I set out to find in the first place.

You see, I know there's some kind of adventure out there still waiting for me. Another book to be written. Another story to be told. And doesn't she deserve better than that? To at least be warned that such a choice may be a rather large mistake? Or can I cling to her for as long as possible—stuff down that feeling and just pretend it's no longer there? Occasionally, I become sick with the thought that she would be better off if she'd never met me; if I had never seen her at that party in college, if somehow our eyes had crossed paths without stopping, and all we'd ever know of each other in life was a glance.

We hang up and once again leave the questions unsettled as we have been doing for months, for years. I stand alone in my room.

All those chapters written and so many of them erased.

• • •

There will be my physical signing of the contract, which I will print off at work before lunch.[203] I will sign all four copies with a slightly trembling hand, and as I slide them into the 9 x 11 manila envelope, I will think of all the hundreds and hundreds of stories and queries I've loaded in the exact same way. I will think of all the rejection letters and non-responses and dashed hopes that have begun in this same exact fashion. It is a moment of utter unreality. That this is actually happening will not yet have sunk in, and I'll wonder in all

---

203   Four copies total, which means another sixty pages of paper and ink stolen from Cars.com. Bless office printers. Bless them hard.

honesty if it ever will, and if it does, *how* it will do so. I will drop in a note to Peter that reads:

Peter,

Thanks again for giving me this opportunity. I'm looking forward to working with you. And yes, this note will be in the book.

—Steve

P.S. This is freaking surreal.

There will be hard work finishing this book.

There will be nights where I will stay up until three and four in the morning, reading, editing, and rewriting. There will be hasty editing suggestions by members of my writing groups. There will be attempts to save my meager advance from Sourcebooks, but $5,000 doesn't buy a lot of good investments in the midst of an epic financial crisis, while it does buy booze, books, and plane tickets. I will take to thinking of myself as a one-man economic stimulus.

There will be moments of panic, of extreme anxiety when I think, *Holy ass-loving grannyfucker, every person I know and everyone I ever meet will be able to read this thing. Every thought and action and dirty secret and sexual escapade and bit of foul language will be available for their perusal, examination, and out-loud discussion. Jesus Christ, people are going to know that I have thoughts that begin with "holy ass-loving grannyfucker." Oh my God, what have I done?*

There will be no way to assuage fears like this. All I can say is that the Truth is fickle and not always clear, but usually it involves uncomfortable phrases like "holy ass-loving grannyfucker." I will only be able to look at something I wrote in the first chapter, and take some solace in that: "This book won't be boring, and it won't be full of shit."

"Okay, swell," I will say. "All's well that ends well, I guess."

• • •

Of course, none of that is the end of this book.

It's a story from before all of this. It's the story of the day I find out—beyond any reasonable shadow of a doubt—that I am going to be a published author. Strangely, it happens to be the same day that Barack Obama wins the presidency of the United States.

Obviously, I have my ticket to Grant Park that night. We crowd in, as Barack is fond of saying, White, Black, Latino, Asian, Native American. The atmosphere is giddy, electric. I've never seen so many people this joyful without the aid of alcohol. The night is warm, the sky clear. CNN plays on a screen so large that Wolf Blitzer's head makes me think of a child's image of God. Liam, Elliott, Scott, and I spend our time among friends (Erik being in Ohio, trying to turn out that youth vote). We are a part of this anxious, rapt crowd, and we cheer as one when they call Pennsylvania for Obama.

Helicopters buzz overhead. Chicago's skyscrapers glow, one building in particular with the letters "USA" spelled out by the lights of the windows. We scream in excitement when Obama wins Ohio. James and I exchange an extra-special hand-bruising high five at this, our various Republican family members for once feeling the other end of the stick.

I've not told anyone yet, but that afternoon Julie emailed me to say that yes, Peter had agreed to the terms of the advance. We had a deal. It took me most of my mental reserves to not tell someone, anyone—just for a hint of celebration, but I staunchly refuse, feeling the possibility of a jinx damning the country to four more years of Republican incompetence.

Still, it's remarkable beyond my ability to comprehend. After all, I am not only selling my first book, but selling it in the midst of the worst economic crisis since the Great Depression. I almost want to call Peter Lynch up and bark at him, "Is this for real, man? Do you guys have any idea what you're doing over there? The economy has imploded! And publishing? Publishing's fucking dead, dude! Dead to the point where the major book publishing houses are shedding jobs, cutting back book buys, cowering in fear—hell, Houghton-Mifflin announced it plans not to *buy* any more books. That's like a car company saying it's just not going to make any new cars—it doesn't even make logical sense! Damnit, Peter, let me help you guys out and tear up this contract right now!"

The dread does not linger for long tonight, though. Worrying about the manuscript he just bought is Peter's job. My job is to watch this huge-ass CNN screen.

My friends and I play games while we wait for the returns. We shift our feet to redistribute weight. We tuck our hands in our pockets. We smile at the people who stand beside us. The crowd screams for a guy to lower his massive American flag so we can see the screen. The crowd laughs together scornfully when CNN interviews will.i.am via hologram.

The West Coast polls close and CNN calls it. President-elect Barack Obama.

A roar goes up like I've never heard. People are screaming and weeping and high-fiving. I find myself embracing a burly black guy in a brown leather jacket. I'm hugging everyone I can find. The roar won't die down.

I know the country is in a hole so deep we can barely see the sky anymore. I know on his first day in office, Obama will face one of the most shocking, dire situations a president has seen since FDR. I know we're still stuck in two wars, the economy is imploding, and those are only the most immediate troubles—forget about health care, energy, immigration, entitlements, civil rights, or just undoing the general catastrofuck that was the every move of the Bush administration.[204]

---

204 Incidentally, the "Bush administration," as of this night, can now be used as the ultimate pejorative term, as in, "The Los Angeles Clippers are the Bush administration of the NBA" or "*Publish This Book* is the Bush administration of memoirs."

For just this moment, though, we can bask in the glow. We can set our troubles to the side and realize that as of November 4, 2008, the world has changed in a profound way. Everyone is calling me: Ian, Phil, Dave, Justin, Jeremy, Jill, Alberto, Allison—most are drunk or jubilant or both. I listen to them and laugh into the night.

Barack comes onstage, and I stand on my toes so I can see him: this skinny, nerdy black guy who has not only beaten the odds but exploded what we as a people once thought possible. His speech is sober, thoughtful. The crowd of a quarter million hangs on his every word. For a moment, he pauses, a rhetorical device that has probably found its way into thousands and thousands of his speeches, but now when he does it, the hush that falls over the crowd is so deep, so perfect you can almost hear the waves chop on the shore of Lake Michigan.

Then he is out onstage with Michelle, his girls, and the Bidens, and everyone is again screaming. They wave and smile, and our adoration is palpable. Sure, it's possible that this guy will be a colossal fuck-up as president. Maybe he'll be caught in an embarrassing scandal that makes Bill Clinton's cigar blush, and al-Qaeda will have free reign on the country's monuments. Maybe he'll roll over and let Putin have Alaska and raise everyone's taxes until the economy collapses into a system of feudal exchange. But somehow I doubt it.

Obviously, it's incredibly difficult for me *not* to compare my journey with Barack's. This is not to say that publishing a book about publishing a book is in any way comparable to the first black man becoming the president of the United States, but as he fought for that job, over the same period of time, I fought for my book. And then we both go and realize our dreams *on exactly the same day*? Are you kidding me?[205]

As Grant Park empties, Springsteen is playing on the

---

205 "Is it really fair?" I will ask James later. "That the two best things to ever happen to America in its history—Obama becoming president and me publishing a book—happened on the same day? I mean, shouldn't we save something for another generation to feel good about?"

speakers—everyone coming on up for the Rising, that post 9/11 anthem now the perfect song to describe the awakening from our long national nightmare. My Love Interest calls and she too is wild with glee and possibility. The past few months have been hard on both of us, and I wish she were here now. I wish I could write her into this moment. But one thing I've learned is that you can't cram life into an easy narrative, and we still have our problems: the distance, the time, the slowing momentum, the youth that makes us stupid and naïve and unhindered in our belief that we can keep all these balls in the air and never drop one and never stumble. Tonight, however, we have a break.

"Barack Obama just became president," I tell her. "Bruce Springsteen's playing on the loudspeakers." *I'm going to publish my first book*, I finish in my thoughts.

She laughs. "Steve—uh—I think this is probably as good as you're ever going to get it."

"I'm in for something bad, aren't I? I'm going to lose an arm in a thresher or something."

"*Wooorth* it," she says in singsong.

"I love you," I tell her, and no matter what happens afterward, no matter what life brings to our respective doorsteps, this is the truth.

Then we are walking down Michigan Avenue as thousands upon thousands of people stream home. Merchants hawking buttons, young people dancing on the divider that separates the north and southbound lanes, people climbing street signs, chanting, shouting, waving flags and banners and screaming up at the sky. Hundreds of cameras flash, and we all must be part of a hundred thousand pictures that people will proudly show to their grandchildren. I feel like sprinting as fast as I can, shouting as loud as my lungs allow, riding the top of the El like a surfboard, making love with an angel, driving a flying car through a plate-glass window from the ninety-sixth floor of the Hancock Building and soaring off over the lake.

"Aren't you glad I made you move to Chicago?" I ask James as we meander along through the crisp fall night, glowing orange from the street lamps, marveling at the way a thousand faces and voices blend into the most mesmerizing cacophony. "I totally knew Barack Obama would win a historic election and we could go celebrate in the streets."

He shakes his head. "Man, it's a good thing you plan ahead. That's what I always tell people when they ask 'What's Steve Markley like?' I say, 'Steve Markley? Oh, he's a great guy: a planner! Always thinking ahead! Nicest registered sex offender you'll ever meet—that's Steve Markley.'"

We look out over the rush of bodies dancing down Michigan Avenue in the orange-rocket glow of the streetlights.

"Not bad," I tell James.

He nods. "Pretty good."

It is late, but we are not tired.

The Wrap-Up

Okay, so that's it! That's the book. Not bad, right?

Well, taste is subjective, I guess.

Now that we're done with this book, and everyone can get back to their lives, I feel like I have to hang on to your attention for just a few pages longer while we take care of a few extraneous but important details. Here following is the wrap-up:

Truth vs. Narrative

Of course when reading a book that purports to be completely true, one has to wonder just how accurately the author has hewn to actual events. Memory, after all, is fickle, and people can interpret the same events very differently.[206]

So let me get it all out of the way here:

- Except for where I have made it obvious that I'm making shit up (i.e., Justin and I battling with sword-scythes), this all happened and is entirely true. That includes the part about Ian peeing on himself and rubbing his pee-hands on Phil's face.

---

206 For instance, where my family remembers opening presents on Christmas Day in 1993, I remember the first time I saw a naked lady in a movie, which involved Jean-Claude Van Damme groping a woman's boobs in *Timecop* (it happened months earlier, but I had yet to move on).

- I *have* moved events around chronologically to present a more fluent, coherent story. As I have discovered again and again, and as I keep saying, life stubbornly refuses to conform to my book-writing schedule; therefore, to quote that all-American hero, Joe the Plumber, I've had to tap-dance like Sammy Davis Jr. to make it all fit.

- Dialogue has been invented. I said this at the beginning of the book, but look: I don't remember every fucking word and conversation of my life. I remember the gist. So what you read is as accurate a representation of how these people speak as I can manage without walking around with a tape recorder every single day. Most of the choicest phrases are apparent because I absolutely could not make them up (see Phil about SoCal women: "It's like shooting retarded fish in a barrel"). If you are in this book and don't like that I've used our private conversations as grist for my plot, well, tough titty said the kitty to the committee.

- I am not nearly as much of an asshole as I portray in these pages. Basically, I'm like anyone else: sometimes I buy homeless guys food and sometimes I steal milk from my roommates.

- I *never ever ever* plan to write another book about myself. To put it mildly, reflecting on one's own life for a sustained period of time (longer than a year in this case) is unbelievably unfun. This was an exercise in armchair psychology that borders on insanity. I can only think back to three words Steven said to me: "There lies madness." He ain't fucking kidding.

- Certainly there were concerns voiced by the real people who appear in my book. As James put it to me, "Are my parents going to read this, and just—I don't know—not respect me at all again ever?" In his case, yes. Or as another friend asked me, "Is this something that's going to make me completely mortified?" To which I thoughtfully responded, "What is your definition of mortified?"

- How much of this book did I plan and how much was dreamed up on the fly? Isn't this the cathartic question? For the reader to understand how much attention they should pay to the man behind the curtain? It's funny because this book is more or less exactly what I thought it would look like from the get-go, yet the actual content is nothing I could ever have anticipated. The easy answer is, I knew that these chapters would exist almost from the start: 1, 2, 13, 21, 23.

Career Timeline

In case you want to keep track of my movements or know when to expect each new masterwork, I have helpfully plotted out the rest of my career.

- 2010—*Publish This Book* published to critical acclaim and mass sales. Michiko Kakutani calls it "a hyperkinetic masterpiece that rivals the work of any author who's ever attempted a postmodern screed. Markley and I need to get a beer."

- 2011—First novel *Dreams from My Father-in-Law* published to mixed reviews.

- 2012—Marry sweet, respectable girl in extravagant wedding that costs most of the advance for the next book.

- 2013—Film version of *Publish This Book* hits theaters. Nominated for Best Adapted Screenplay. Move to Los Angeles, begin cocaine habit.

- 2014—After receiving obscene advance bordering on reckless, deliver incomprehensible book that somehow is about God, Tajikistan, and global warming. Reviewers have difficult time panning it because they can't figure out what's going on. Michiko Kakutani rescinds offer of beer.

- 2015—Enter rehab for cocaine addiction.

- 2016—Divorce sweet, respectable girl, marry supermodel. Develop prescription medication habit.

- 2018—Have threesome with supermodel wife. Video leaked on Internet.

- 2020—Divorce supermodel wife. Enter rehab for prescription medication addiction.

- 2022—Publish book so cynical, so depraved, so scathing, vicious, mean-spirited, and generally wallowing in the cruelest shadows of human behavior that riots erupt in the Middle East, South Asia, and Ann Arbor, Michigan. Reviewers declare: "Markley is back!"

- 2023—Re-marry original sweet, respectable girl. Divorce two months later after incident the press dubs the "Tijuana meth-smuggling cavity search" scandal.

- 2024—Publish memoir about various addictions and recovery. Win coveted spot in Oprah's Book Club.

- 2024—One of Mitt Romney's kids elected president on values issues. Contemplate leaving country.

- 2025—Move to Stockholm, date ever-escalating herds of young, slender Swedish women.

- 2032—Sasha Obama elected President. Return to country with younger Swedish model in tow.

- 2033–2037—Enter period of general stability and happiness. Publish middling novels to tepid acclaim. Have two children, Svenna (named for her maternal grandmother) and Jackson (to rival Justin's kid, so they can push each other to win our respect in the marketplace of parental love).

- 2038—Enter rehab for alcoholism, which, apparently has been the actual problem all along.

- 2040—Divorce Swedish model. Date up-and-coming pop singer thirty years my junior. Not bad.

- 2041—Discover up-and-coming pop singer is a self-destructive nymphomaniac who likes to mildly electrocute herself and partner during coitus. Not bad at all.

- 2042—Embarrassing lovemaking mistake with pop singer leads to hospitalization. Cucumber no longer suitable for eating. Relationship becomes strained.

- 2049—Jackson reveals to me that he is gay. I tell him I love him no matter what and respect whatever he does with his life.

- 2050—Jackson moves in with his older partner, Jaxson. "Hey," I tell Justin. "Tell your kid to stop boning my kid."

- 2053—Justin and I pay for Jackson and Jaxson's wedding, just legalized in Ohio. Bill for the band is outrageous.

- 2056—Re-marry that one sweet, respectable girl.

- 2060—Die from heart attack.

- 2062—Resurface in Belize after faked death. Live out twilight years as fish-boner operating in small shack on the beach. Giggle frequently at term "fish-boner."

Tips for Movie Adaptation of *Publish This Book*

Every book gets made into a movie these days, and I'd really prefer that Michael Bay does not get a hold of mine and fuck it like a cheap hooker. So here are some tips that any director who chooses to tackle *Publish This Book* should heed before proceeding with his or her interpretation.

- The following actors may *not* portray me: the kid who plays Harry Potter, the main guy from *That 70's Show*, or Shia LaBeouf. Especially Shia LaBeouf. Under no circumstances will Shia LaBeouf be allowed to portray me.

- Absolutely no clichéd music. If I get to the scene where I reunite with my Love Interest in Boston and U2's "One" is actually playing, I'll file a lawsuit. Also, no Bon Jovi. Likewise, any of the songs that I hate most in this world, which is a pretty long list. In fact, maybe I should just provide you with a list of acceptable songs, so you can't fuck it up.

- Here is a preapproved list of songs that influenced me at key junctures: The Decemberists, "Engine Driver"; Dead Prez, "Propoganda"; Old Crow Medicine Show, "Wagon Wheel,"

"James River Blues"; Pearl Jam, "Marker in the Sand," "Inside Job"; 2Pac, "Against All Odds," "Krazy," "Still Ballin'," "God Bless the Dead"; Warren Zevon, "Lawyers, Guns, and Money," "My Shit's Fucked Up," "Mutineer"; Radiohead, "Nude," "A Punchup at a Wedding"; Guster, "Parachute"; Rolling Stones, "Beast of Burden"; Wu-Tang Clan, "Gravel Pit"; The Beatles, "I've Got a Feeling"; Red Hot Chili Peppers, "Snow"; Talib Kweli, "Drugs, Basketball & Rap"; Bob Dylan, "It Takes a Lot to Laugh, It Takes a Train to Cry," "Don't Think Twice, It's All Right," "Mississippi," "Most of the Time" (bootleg version, please); Mos Def, "The Easy Spell"; Conor Oberst, "Moab,"; Outkast, "Chonkyfire"; Mike Doughty, "No Peace, Los Angeles"; The Band, "When You Awake"; Jurassic 5, "Sum of Us," "Quality Control," "Freedom"; Band of Horses, "Weed Party"; Bright Eyes, "Travelin' Song," "Classic Cars"; Immortal Technique, "The Cause of Death," "The 4th Branch"; Sufjan Stevens, "Chicago (Adult Contemporary Easy Listening Version)"; The Wallflowers, "Three Marlenas"; Ryan Adams, "To Be Young," "Dear Chicago," "Gonna' Make You Love Me"; Arcade Fire, "Wake Up"; Dr. Dre (featuring Xzibit, Eminem, and Phish), "What's the Difference"; Josh Ritter, "Role On," "Good Man"; Fort Minor (featuring Common and Styles of Beyond), "Back Home"; Atmosphere, "Smart Went Crazy"; Bon Iver, "Skinny Love"; Alexi Murdoch, "All of My Days"; Tom Petty, "Between Two Worlds," "Down South"; 2Pac+Outlawz, "Y'all Don't Know Us"; Bob Seger, "Night Moves"; Common, "Chi City"; and anything by Bruce Springsteen except for "Pink Cadillac." Got it?

- There should be exactly three dance sequences: the first will involve me and the roommates at one of our generic house parties, dancing madly to Outkast's "Rosa Parks" (for this scene it will be necessary that the actor portraying me wear a wife-beater, an open button-down shirt, and a brown mesh baseball cap carefully cocked to the right). The second dance scene will involve just me and my Love Interest dancing languidly to Wilco's "Jesus, Etc.," which is one of the best love songs ever written.[207] Finally, the credits will roll to an all-out, full-fledged zoot suit dance number featuring the version of Bruce Springsteen's "Open All Night" from his *Live From Dublin* album. The song lasts like fifteen minutes, so the dance number will inexplicably feature every character from the book, even those that could not possibly have met. Therefore, Coach Miller will dance with the girl I met in Portland and Kevin from the Navajo reservation will partner up with my friend Luisa, while Julie, my agent, twirls away with Phil, and finally, my Love Interest and I will dance madly, only to switch places to partner up in a dance-off with Barack and Michelle Obama. Michelle and I will win.

- Feel free to idealize. This book is not the truth. Like any piece of nonfiction, it is truth rendered through a prism. In other words, idealized. So when adapting for a film that has to come in at or under two hours, feel free to simplify and whittle further. For instance, feel free to cut extraneous asides that contribute little or nothing to the story.[208] Also, composite characters may be a useful tool. Do we really need an Ian *and* a Phil? Why not just mash these two characters into one loud, loutish, drunken, long-distance friend? Actually, this may be a strategy these two should pursue in real life. It would cut down on the number of people I have to text every time the Browns play like shit. So go ahead and make me look cooler than I am or cast a real good-looking dude to play me or make me seem like a better person. That's all fine. However...

---

207   As Elliott puts it: "I can't imagine a world in which the song 'Jesus, Etc.' does not exist."

208   But not the tale of Josh's penis ring. That's just too ridiculous. The people have to know.

- Do not make the scene where I reunite with my Love Interest in Boston the centerpiece of the movie. The worst, most derivative genre of movie is the so-called romantic comedy. It presents life as a simple question: "Why can't these two get together?" Oh, and then they do. End of movie. Yeah, thanks for that stroke of genius, Hollywood. Now every young person in the Western world has grown up believing that being in love is as easy as kicking Owen Wilson out of your house because he's so craaazy. The hard part isn't driving to Julia Roberts's apartment in a limo to tell her you love her. It isn't standing outside of a girl's window with a blasting boom box held over your head. It isn't driving to Boston to tell someone how you feel. That stuff's easy and ham-handed. The hard part is having the courage and faith to see it through. It's the weeks and months and years that follow the stunt that will always be the ones that count. Was it a mistake to include this young woman in my story? Yes, undoubtedly. Part of the insanity of this book is that I more or less wrote it in real time.[209] I was and am writing about this relationship knowing that anything can happen to it in the future. We make mistakes. We question ourselves, each other. So even if I write that we reunited and fell back in love, it's certainly possible that this will not be the case when this book hits shelves, right? If I'm to be honest about how tricky a situation this is, I have to concede that and examine the implications should things not work out: despite what she says, will my Love Interest find herself hiding the existence of this book from every guy she ever meets? And as for me, forget about it. What girl will ever want to date me? To have to live in

---

209   Kinda like the worst episode of 24 ever:
       "Jack, it's Steve! I just got another rejection letter!"
       "Damnit! I'll try cutting off Grubechev's finger!"
       "Wait! Why? What good will that do?"
       "Damnit, Steve, it's the right play! Let me do my job!"

the gargantuan shadow cast by someone I wrote an entire book about? I'll say it one last time: life will never conform to your narrative. Life is messy and human relationships even more so. There are stories that can never be told and others that must be invented because the full truth can't be explained so easily—not just about me or my Love Interest, but Justin and Loren and Steven and Phil and Ian and Dave and Jeremy and everyone else who has appeared in these pages or, for that matter, has ever drawn breath into his or her lungs. We live our failures and inconsistencies, our bleak moments and periods of conflict and confusion. For the greater good of the story, I have omitted some of these, or at least buffed them down. The film version can certainly buff further, but let's at least agree on the basic premise: figuring your life out is sloppy, difficult work. Figuring it out while documenting the entire thing so you can share it with every Jesus-Christing person you've ever met is more of a challenge than you can appreciate until you try it. Don't lose the complications inherent in this (or any) relationship with the temptation of a clichéd scene where my Love Interest and I appear to solve all of our problems while kissing on the back stoop of her apartment building in Cambridge.[210]

• Speaking of my Love Interest, cast a really hot actress to play her. No, not just because I want to flatter her for being beautiful (although she is) or myself for having bagged her (except I do rule for getting into her pants in the first place), but because in order to tell the story right, she has to be *that* kind of girl. You know what I mean: the kind of girl who you watch on the screen and just cannot peel your eyes away from. The kind of girl that every guy leaving the theater sorrowfully wishes he

---

210   Although it was pretty awesome. You've never kissed someone until you've driven sixteen hours to do it.

had a chance at. The kind of girl you just can't wait to see in a backless dress or hear her next thought on the moral hazard of Tom Cruise films. That's what it's going to take to play this chick, trust me.

- No pulling punches. Not only does the film version of this book deserve an R rating, it practically requires it. In fact, why are people even making PG-13 movies anymore? What the fuck sense does that make? And what system is the MPAA actually using to make their decisions? It must be a Magic 8 ball or an imaginary dog they think is talking to them. The film version of this book would probably get an R rating based on its consistent and hilarious use of the words "fuck," "motherfucker," and "cock-engulfing fuckfist."[211] Meanwhile, I saw that movie *Hostel 2*, which has a scene where a guy gets his dick cut off. That, apparently, is just as bad for our children as the word "shit." Yeah, good job, MPAA. That makes perfect sense. Say whatever you want, but at least no one in this book gets his dick cut off.[212]

- No low-budget indie, art house bullshit. Look, I'm a big fan of independent film and as the recounting of my time with Todd Sklar should make you well aware, I dig movies that rely on their own ingenuity instead of a budget. As far as the movie from my book goes, though, pony up the cash, you cheap studio scumbags. We need involved special effects for the various fantasy scenes. We need to license all of that good music I mentioned previously. We need to hire name actors like Jared Padalecki and Tony from *24*.

---

211 Admittedly, this is the first use of that term, but now that I've discovered it, I feel like it has many applications, including but not limited to: My old House representative John Boehner, this one guy who honked at me on the highway once, and professional hockey.

212 Gotta save something for the sequel!

- Somehow, someway let me meet Jennifer Aniston. I've been all about Jennifer Aniston since I was nine. I don't care if she's in the movie (too old to play my Love Interest, too young to play Julie or my mom), but just put it in the contract that she has to get lunch with me or something.[213]

---

213 Holy shit: I just thought, *What if Jennifer Aniston did play my mom?* That would be the most sexually confusing situation of my life.

Acknowledgments

Obviously, I have many people to thank, many people who helped me on the journey of pulling this book together. However, I've decided that due to my gangbuster success as a published author, I don't really need any of you leeches and hangers-on dragging me down. So to all of my friends—the guys who have been like brothers to me for these last unpredictable, unbelievable years—Phil, Ian, Ritesh, Kdoe, Jeremy, Dave, JR, Alberto, Josh, Scott, Jack—I no longer need you idiots. Shia LaBeouf, the guy from *That 70's Show,* and I are going to a party in Beverly Hills. I'll let you know how it goes.

To my extended friends (and here is a list of names that will mean nothing to you if you're not one of them, so feel free to skim) Lee, Mark, Ross, Trev, Drew, Megan, Ashley, Luisa, the Barones, the Costas, the Andorfers, Anna, Loren, Allison N., Allison C., Allison K., Cat, Sohn, Marie, Smallz, Geordie, D'Amico, Emily, Bain, Syd, Amanda, Pat, Geoff, Jen, Chris, Alex, Leah, Graham, JD, Ryan, Roger, Margo, Kate, Michelle, Dan P., Nancy, Nino, Sumukh, Julie, Lisa, Amy, Lindsay B., Amita, Adam Hockey, Shannon, Tony, Chrissy, Rachel, Robert, Ben O., Kaitlin O., Emily G., Swati, Silas, Todd, Stacey, Elizabeth, Thompson, Purse, Sara, Adam, Jenna, Feasel, Andrea, Sam, Kelsey, Brian, Bojo blahblahblah—all of you people who've meant so much to me in your support and friendship for all of these years can now go take a flying fuck at the moon. I've

PUBLISH THIS BOOK

hit the jackpot. I'm big-time. Any and all communication in the form of congratulatory phone calls, texts, emails, or wall postings on Facebook will either be disregarded or returned by form response via my publicist.

To my roommates, Liam, Erik, and Elliott: guys, I never thought we'd end up growing so close and becoming such good friends, and I was totally right. Erik, if you ever run for public office, I will move to your precinct, district, state, or country to vote against you. Liam, I drank more of your milk in the time we lived together than you will ever know. Elliott, maybe being in a book won't help your weak stomach but it might at least get you laid (although probably not).

To James, traveling companion, fellow mediocre Renaissance man, general sexual deviant who if it were not for blind luck would have warrants out for his arrest in five states with eleven very pissed-off pig farmers hot on his trail: our partnership is hereby terminated. Without me prodding you to do things with your life, you may now feel free to move back to New Philly and work at Damon's like you always wanted to.

To my parents, Bob and Laurie, you guys are horrendous role models. Your unconditional love and support over the years, your willingness to indulge my wanderings and gently nudge me when I strayed from the path, your recognition that I had to figure things out for myself, that I had to fall down and pick myself up, your good humor and love have virtually ensured that I will someday seek out a psychologist who will let me blame all of my problems on you. You call that parenting? In retaliation for your years of love and pride, I'm going to stick you in one of those old people homes where the nurses pinch you viciously when you don't behave and take your goddamn pills.

To my sister, Hannah, who is not only smarter than me but probably on her way to doing something of great intellectual import that will make this book look like a vapid collection of aggressively unfunny psychobabble:[214] Consider the sibling rivalry arms race begun, my friend. I will crush you!

To my grandparents Henry, Nikki, Rock, and Carol, those members of the Greatest Generation who overcame a depression and won the war against fascism—nice job coming home and producing George W. Bush in the Baby Boom. And a special note to Henry Markley: Grandpa, I will readily admit that I was terrified of what you'd think of this book, but now I only wish I still had the chance to hear you critique it.

To all of my massive extended family, weaving from Dayton to Connecticut to the Carolinas, and a hundred spots in between. I'm not lending any of you money.

To Jon Stewart, who helped me through eight of the most discouraging, dehumanizing, darkest years. You are a legend, sir: the premiere source of political commentary and potty humor on television, the Jonathan Swift of our age. Now have me on your show, you slimy bastard!

To Miami University. I am now the most famous person to come out of your esteemed institution behind Pittsburgh Steelers' quarterback Ben Roethlisberger and that twenty-year-old Billy Joel is fucking. As soon as I put some money together, I'm going to make the biggest goddamn donation that school has seen this side of Richard T. Farmer—but only under the stipulation that it be called The Stephen Markley School of Journalism. That, or the Stephen Markley Institute for Study Abroad. Either one works.

To Mac 'n Joes. I will still drink at you.

To my intrepid agent, Julie, who took a chance on an imprudent little shit of a writer and in return for her hard work got almost no money and a client who will likely sink her reputation in the publishing world as he explodes into a one-man cocaine-fueled insurgency. Tough break.

---

214 You better believe that phrase is going on the back of the book jacket.

To Peter Lynch and all the good people at Sourcebooks. I have made your company! I have made your careers! You all work for me now! You hear me? I said, *do you hear me, you pathetic oozing scum?* I will buy and sell your souls before lunch! And then after lunch I will buy them back and use them to wipe my ass!

To the writers of Thousand Fibers, Katie, Suzanne, Mary, Bridget, Rebecca, Josh, Jayne, and for a while there Margaret; and also to the writers of Literary Writer's Network, Anne, Chad, Denis, Bobby, Caela, Alex, Ian, and April. To say that I could not have written this book without you guys is not an understatement. In fact, it is a complete lie. While writing this book, I found myself continuously awed by your insight, suggestions, and comments, not to mention your talent as writers. Now that I've finished it and published, however, I will be immediately relinquishing your services. Richard Russo, Cormac McCarthy, Alice Sebold, and I have formed our own writing group.

To all my buddies at Cars.com, Patrick, Dave, Eamonn, Lindsay, Amanda, Merritt, Kelsey, Gersh, both Joes, Eric, Mike, Colin, Bill, Beth, Jenni, and Matt. Like it's a Monday morning and I have my headphones on, I have nothing to say to any of you people.

To Bruce Springsteen, who every so often seems to be writing about me in his music. Get out of my head, you maniac!

To the staff at *RedEye*, especially Tran, Curt, Leo, and Steph. Thanks for letting me hitch my apple wagon to your star. Now I will leave you to hold the sinking ship that is print journalism by your damn selves while I hop onto the sinking ship that is the publishing industry.

To all the writers whose conversations I stole for this book. Jared, Katie, Chad, Josh, Phil Margolin, Denis, Margaret, Nick Hornby—I wish all of you the best in your careers, unless of course some of that luck belongs to me, in which case I want it back. Now.

To all the teachers whose lessons and wisdom have influenced me over the years, from elementary school through college. Coach Miller, Coach Savage, Bell, Alrutz, La Botz, Shriver, Jones, Cunningham

(Mr. and Mrs.), Hanson, Freshwater, Graham, Geiger. Truly yours is the most important profession in America, and I hope that is reward enough, so please no bitching about long hours and a slim salary. You all have no one to blame but yourselves.

To Barack Obama. Maybe it's a bad thing to consider your president a major influence and personal source of pride, faith, and hope, but I do. As a politician, as a civil servant, as a writer, and as a man, you've reconstituted my belief in the possibility of the individual and the state. Now don't fuck it up.

To my Love Interest: you are a shocking and amazing person. Your beauty, your grace, your kindness, your brilliance, and most of all your humor continue to astonish me every moment we spend with each other. I certainly don't deserve you, but that you've been willing to let me into your life not only as a sometimes-lover but also as, truly, a best friend has been the honor and privilege of my life. I can't promise that happy ending because no one can, and it would be foolish to attempt to do so. I can promise you that no matter what, you have carved a deep and permanent groove in my heart, and that should I fall behind, as Bruce says, you will be the pain I will drink away shot by shitty shot of tequila in a cantina somewhere in Guadalajara while I sing boisterously about better days and surely—surely!—it will be your face I see on the prostitute I lead back to my motel, who—I will not be aware until well after the fact—is actually a man.

To Steven. Your advice and friendship have been invaluable, not only to this book but in harnessing my wild, sometimes reckless talent into coherence and thoughtfulness. Your life and intellect continue to fascinate and challenge me. While this may not have been the book you expected from me or the one you wanted to see, rest assured I am never satisfied with anything and will promptly get to work on something better, which, I'm sure, you will be just as candid in critiquing and just as important in shaping into a worthy piece of writing. Oh, also, I'm now going to pretend like I did all of this by myself and that your contributions were highly exaggerated for dramatic effect at the insistence of my publisher.

To Justin. Thanks for getting Loren pregnant so I could put it in the book. I was really having trouble thinking of stuff for a while. Also, just keep in mind the Scope. We're all a little thrown off sometimes, but you have the advantage of being a pretty bright guy and having some pretty good people behind you (by this I mean your parents, Loren, and anyone else who is not me). I also plan to thoroughly ruin your son's image of you as quickly as I can in the coming years.

Thanks to everyone who was reading my stuff when no one was reading my stuff. I would like to say that I will remember this in the future and that I will return your gracious support with gracious indulgence of your time and opinion, but this is not the case, and if you approach me in an airport or bar, I will have my bodyguard, "Crisp," mace you.

Okay, For Real, That's It

That's it. That's the book. Done. Finished. Over. After an entire book spent flouting the rules of writing a book, I can't very well just put "The End" but I'm not really into any of the other ideas I came up with, like:

BOOK CONCLUDED

Or:

READING EXPERIENCE TERMINATED

And then this one:

CONCLUSION REACHED FOLLOWING CLIMAX AND DOWNWARD TREND OF ACTION

Let's just say, I hope you enjoyed reading this as much as I enjoyed writing it (which is to say I hope you had frequent panic attacks, crises of confidence, cold sweats, unbridled ulcer-inducing anxiety, loosened bowels, dry heaves, intellectual malaise, erectile dysfunction, and a sinking sense of dread-drenched despair so bleak and powerful it left you weeping at the sight of a bird crushed under the tire of a car). If you liked it, tell your friends, so maybe some day soon I can write another. If you didn't, well, just keep it to yourself. Either way, we'll leave it at this: I'll see you when I see you.

About the Author

Ian Merritt, IDM Photography

Stephen Markley is now the author of *Publish This Book*. Markley is one of the featured columnists for the Tribune Company's *RedEye* newspaper and maintains his own website, www.stephen markley.com. In addition to his pursuits as a writer, Markley is a Rhodes Scholar, the esteemed representative from Ohio's 11th district, and a member of the irreconcilable Taliban. He lives in Chicago where he has multiple paternity suits pending.